MW00582097

Philip Johnson & Texas

FOREWORD BY PHILIP JOHNSON

DRAWINGS BY BRIAN FITZSIMMONS AND LANDRY RAY

Philip Johnson & Texas

Frank D. Welch

Photographs by Paul Hester

University of Texas Press, Austin

Publication of this book was aided by generous subsidies from an anonymous donor and from the Amon G. Carter Foundation.

Printed in Hong Kong

First edition, 2000

∞ The paper used in this book meets the minimum requirements of ANSI/NISO Z39.48-1992 (R1997) (Permanence of Paper).

LIBRARY OF CONGRESS CATALOGING-IN-PUBLICATION DATA

Welch, Frank D., 1927–
Philip Johnson & Texas / Frank D. Welch ; foreword by Philip Johnson ; principal photography by Paul Hester ; drawings by Brian Fitzsimmons and Landry Ray.—Ist ed.
p. cm.
Includes index.
ISBN 0-292-79134-8 (cl : alk. paper)
1. Johnson, Philip, 1906—Criticism and interpretation. 2. Architecture—United States—Texas. 3. Architecture, Modern—20th century—United States. I. Title.
NA737.J6 W44 2000
720′.92—dc21 99-053829

This book is dedicated to all my children and grandchildren

Contents

Foreword

Texas is my favorite country. In Texas there is more interest in carrying out the American dream than anywhere else in the United States—and this leads to wonderful things for architecture.

Maybe it is the Texan lack of connection to the East Coast "motherland." All I know is that there is a more progressive approach to modern design in Texas. All my important work is there, from the Menil House in Houston to the upcoming Cathedral of Hope in Dallas. Texas has been, for obvious reasons, my favorite part of the world.

The people there make the difference. Their attitude toward creating a new America makes them, quite naturally, greater patrons than the rest of us. My personal history in Texas is framed by people I know and love—people like Gerry Hines, Ruth Carter Stevenson (daughter of Amon Carter), and a transplanted French lady, Dominique de Menil. It is Texas that has been responsible for my professional development. As I often say, if I had been a little younger in 1950, when I first worked in Houston, I would have moved to Texas myself.

Frank Welch is a wonderful architect who understands the Texas scene. That he should choose to write a book such as this is typical of the Texas picture to me. Frank Welch is inseparably part of Texas—as am I.

Philip Johnson
New York, June 1999

Preface

Philip Johnson, America's most famous architect, waited inside the glass walls of his house for yet another group of visitors to his estate in New Canaan, Connecticut. It was a brilliant fall day in 1974. His eyes twinkled with anticipation; he never tired of showing the place off. The sixty-six-year-old world celebrity had received hundreds of groups curious to see his parklike estate dotted with its rich assortment of small structures. But this particular group had a special meaning to him.

A bus carrying an elite group from the Dallas Museum of Art, high-paying affiliates in something called The Associates, had passed through the picturesque colonial village of New Canaan and slowly climbed up a rolling road through a forest of maple, oak, and chestnut toward Ponus Ridge Road. Johnson's place was the last stop and the climax of a four-day tour of private art

A "farmer's wall" and The Glass House, New Canaan, Connecticut; Philip Johnson, architect. Photo by Paul Hester, 1994.

collections in New York. Carefully entering the gate in an old stone "farmer's wall" the bus moved slowly down a curving drive past a grove of white pines to a level parking area by another aged stone wall. Speaking to each other softly and self-consciously, the casually well-dressed group slowly disembarked, passed around one end of the wall, and filed, singly and in pairs, down a trim diagonal path of crushed rock across a perfect emerald lawn to the entrance of the most famous modern dwelling in the United States, known to the world as The Glass House.

Reflected in its transparent wall, the owner and architect of the house stood smiling expectantly on the white stone stoop, his hands clasped behind him. Philip Cortelyou Johnson, nattily dressed for the country, slender and column-straight, with eyes sparkling behind his familiar, heavy black horn-rims, thrust his hand out and greeted the first guest with: "Welcome! I'm the greatest architect in the world!"[1] The eyeglasses, the self-mocking crack, and the sassy verve of the Ohio-born booster that he is, are all signatures of this most celebrated man, a free-ranging, vocal proponent of the avant-garde in architecture for over forty years.

The cheek and charm of this cultural squire, standing at the door of his extraordinary, glass-and-steel box of a house, framed today in brilliant color, quickly captured everyone's attention; it was something he was exceptionally good at. The man and the rolling forty-acre setting for the carefully placed structures he had erected there over a twenty-five-year period—"playhouses," one visitor in the 1990s observed—represented a lifetime of scholarship, connoisseurship, showmanship, and controversy in architecture. Though incontestably, and by his insistent admission, *not* the world's greatest architect, nor near-greatest, he is unarguably the most influential and best-known American architect working in the final part of the twentieth century.

There was some added meaning for the host on this splendid day: the visitors were from Texas, and the large part of Philip Johnson's fame and accomplishment derived from friendly connections with important Texans. This began in Houston in the 1940s and continues throughout the state to the present. The fact that it was Dallasites on this bus added extra zest to Johnson's greeting: word was out that planning was under way to build a large, new museum in that city, and Johnson knew museums. Though by nature generous and enthusiastic with anyone interested in art and architecture, the practical, practicing architect in him always had an eye out for a new building. He loved to tell students what H. H. Richardson, the famous nineteenth-century American architect, called the cardinal requirement for the successful architect: "Get the job!"

And no one needed to remind him that his extraordinarily successful career as an architect not only began in Texas but flourished there. Not counting the carefully composed and critically praised group of small buildings he has designed around his Glass House, the most distinguished buildings in Johnson's long career have been built in Texas cities for Texas clients. Many important buildings were built in New York and elsewhere, but something about Texas inspired him to outdo himself. His best—but also some of his worst—buildings stand as his testament in the Lone Star State.

In the late 1940s, after he had opened a New York office as an unlicensed architect[2] and word was getting around about the radical steel-and-glass house he was constructing in Connecticut, Johnson met his first Texas clients, and the worlds of art, architecture, and scholarship coalesced for him in Texas, forming the foundation of a career marked with celebrity, controversy, and the highest honors his profession could bestow. It's doubtful that many of the Dallas visitors realized the key role that his Texas clients and patrons had played in Johnson's life as an architect. With many highly publicized buildings in Houston, Dallas, Fort Worth, and Corpus Christi, he had become the rich state's favorite "out-of-town architect." When this was pointed out to him in the early 1990s during a slow time in his New York office, he snapped: "I should have moved there, it's the only place I have any work!"[3]

Why was Johnson, the sophisticated, quintessential big-city architect with both feet planted firmly in New York's cultural world, called to the state more often than any other architect-for-import when influential Texans sought nameworthy talent? The answer lies in the intersection of personality, intellect, energy, and creativity and the context of elevated social culture that Johnson embodies. Initially he had a way of attracting clients blessed with money, imagination, and courage. That formed the foundation of his Texas career. Later he attracted commissions from members of the hard-headed corporate world for his ability to produce commercial buildings with specialness of character which proved attractive to the marketplace and made everyone rich. "Philip Johnson" became a high-style designer label.

There was no little luck of circumstance in this brew, and there is no doubt that Johnson zestfully and instinctively willed the public and media perception that made him the late twentieth century's noble celebrity of art and architecture. But from the beginning, and as with every selection of an architect, the choice lay with the client-patron, not the architect-creator. When the fit of client aspiration and architect inspiration was good a successful symbiosis was forged among money, mind, and passion to create a special chapter in architectural history, uniquely American and specifically Texan. Philip Johnson was a leading character in the state's architectural story during the munificent half-century which followed World War II.

Acknowledgments

A number of people, architects and nonarchitects, have asked why I was writing a book about Philip Johnson. As an architect my identity is with things Texan, wasn't it? There was, I imagined, some slight accusatory puzzlement in the queries. It prompts me to attempt to analyze why I did undertake to write the story of Philip Johnson and his role in the architectural history of Texas.

There is another architect, a native-born Texan, who has played a far greater part in my life as a professional: O'Neil Ford of Pink Hill, Sherman, Denton, Dallas, and San Antonio. Through friends in Houston, two artist sisters, I was lucky to meet Ford as a young architect in my twenties, and be drawn into the orbit of his personality and dedication as an architect. I worked for him briefly, but better, he became my friend, mentor, and promoter. While I was practicing in Midland in far West Texas, he would, when I was around, declare with mock seriousness, "Welch is the best architect between San Antonio and El Paso!" (a vast arid stretch).

As I have concluded from my research, Johnson and Ford shared certain characteristics, though Ford considered Johnson a lightweight and a carpetbagger. Both were voracious readers with encyclopedic visual and mental memory. They shared an impish, bad-boy stance toward the architectural establishment, with a notable penchant for hyperbole. Johnson and Ford were uncertain about their abilities, yet were eager for approval, and each was a paterfamilias to several generations of younger architects. Further, Ford and Johnson were forever ready to leap into any bully pulpit to skewer the boorish and promote the excellent in architecture, as each very differently viewed the scene.

Contrasts between the two—one a wealthy, influential, and urbane New Yorker in pinstripes, the other a venerated regional folk artist in khaki—were obvious and striking. Ford was born in the hamlet of Pink Hill in North Texas, son of a railroad fireman; Johnson was born into upper-class wealth seven months later in Cleveland, Ohio. Ford, the populist, never got a college degree, while Johnson, the patrician, was Harvard-educated. But each enjoyed a distinguished career and the patronage of wealthy clients grounded in the force of his personality and the passion of his feelings about architecture. I believe I was drawn to Philip Johnson and his Texas story because I had been affected by my rich experience with O'Neil Ford, another maverick. In any case, Ford's impact on twentieth-century Texas, seminal and lasting, has been well documented by Mary Carolyn Hollers George's *O'Neil Ford, Architect* (Texas A&M University Press, 1992) and David Dillon's *The Architecture of O'Neil Ford: Celebrating Place* (University of Texas Press, 1999).

As a student and later as an architect, I gained knowledge and a quasi-experience of far-flung architecture through photographs in the architectural journals, in much the same way that I experienced life in the wider world through the films that came to the movie theaters in my small Texas hometown. From my professional beginning, photographs of Philip Johnson's work, like his Glass House and his other modern houses in and around New Canaan, Connecticut, struck my developing modernist sensibility as strong, emphatic *images,* clear and understandable, maybe something I could do!

The word *images* should be emphasized, for when I was taken by an employee of Johnson's to see the rather recently completed Glass House in 1953, on an overcast June day, I was not bowled over with the sight. It looked *better* in the photographs! However, the first house that I designed, a moonlight job in Houston, had as its model a recently published shoe box of a house, with a long trellised gallery, by Johnson in Connecticut. Through the years, his published buildings always caught my attention, and hearing his eloquent extemporaneous acceptance of the American Institute of Architects (AIA) Gold Medal before a big crowd in Dallas in 1978 was, for me, a riveting event.

In the early 1990s, I undertook a piece in two parts for *Texas Architect* focusing on the large number of buildings in Texas that Johnson had designed. When finished with the articles, I felt the need to delve deeper. I didn't think of this dissatisfaction consciously, but the research and interviews involved in writing this book satisfied my earlier curiosity about what made Johnson tick and how that ticking resonated for so long with a Texas patronage. What *was* it that caused influential Texans to call him back time and time again after the construction of a house in 1950 for Dominique and John de Menil in Houston? Did the cultures of the various cities contribute to his being chosen over local architects for important buildings? Philip Johnson is as slippery a subject as the state is multifaceted; I doubt I have succeeded fully in answering my questions.

To tell his story properly, I felt I should begin with Johnson's background, before moving on to the buildings, clients, and social-cultural terrain he found here in 1948. I felt that the story must, to some extent, flow beyond the borders of Texas to include aspects of Johnson's career and buildings that affected *and* were affected by what was built here. I like pictures, so I determined that the book would have excellent contemporary photographs of the Texas buildings, plus sufficient casual and archival photos to visually score the story.

I hope the account contains some intimation of the basic and vulnerable humanity of the man: the flaws and virtues, passions and detachments, his witty high spirits and periodic bogs of depression, and, particularly, the pride and self-doubt that characterize most creative people. My hope is that, in certain ways, the story delineates how and why Philip Johnson has had such a huge influence, for seventy years, on the architectural culture of our time and shows that the pivot of that influence was here in Texas.

First, I salute Louisa Stude Sarofim of Houston. Without her help this book would not have been published by the University of Texas Press; I am forever indebted to her. Louisa's grace, generosity, and intelligence cut a deep swath in the cultural life of Houston and Texas.

Stephen Fox of Houston's Anchorage Foundation is Texas's foremost architectural historian, and his important suggestions with the manuscript helped and encouraged me immeasurably. Steven served as mentor and muse. Architect and professor Burdette Keeland Jr., a longtime Johnson protégé, was in on the project from the beginning and forever patiently helpful. Paul Hester enthusiastically started his wonderful photography of the buildings long before there were funds for his work. Joanna Hitchcock, Director of the University of Texas Press, was an early champion of the book, and Jim Burr, the Press's Humanities Editor, guided the project most professionally. Heidi Haeuser's design of the book is very beautiful, and copyeditor Paul Spragens's careful work has, I'm sure, given me some "cover," as did the staff at UT Press.

The following people and institutions furnished valuable information:

Jeannette Johnson Dempsey of Cleveland was always eager to share her memories of her brother and family.

In Houston: Dominique de Menil was gracious with her time, as were Gerald D. Hines, J. Hugh Liedtke, Jane Blaffer Owen, and Anderson Todd. Other Houstonians who helped were: Cameron Armstrong, Marguerite and Charles Barnes, Gertrude Levy Barnstone, Preston H. Bolton, Raymond Brochstein, John J. Casbarian, Elsian Cozens, Sissie Farenthold, Ann Holmes, Ben Hurst, Terrell James, Karl Kilian, Lars Lerup, Jim Love, Edward Mayo, William Merriman, J. Victor Neuhaus III, Danny Samuels, Martha Seng, William F. Stern, Cynthia Rowan Taylor, Herbert Wells, and Peter J. Zweig. The Houston Public Library, the Menil Collection, The Museum of Fine Arts, Houston, and the Gerald D. Hines College of Architecture Library furnished valuable information and material. In Fayetteville, Texas: Lisa Hardaway.

In Fort Worth: Ruth Carter Stevenson spent generous time with me, as did Cynthia Brants, Mrs. Edward (Josephine) Hudson, and Gwen Weiner. Others of that city who contributed information are Hunter Barrett, James Blake, Jane Brown, Sandra Cantey, Georgeanne Carter, Mark Gunderson, Edward Hudson Jr., Don Kirk, Patricia Loud, Tom Seymour, Frank Sherwood, George Wright, and Katherine Votaw; also the Amon Carter Museum, the Burnett Foundation, the *Fort Worth Star-Telegram,* the University of Texas at Arlington's Architecture Library, and the University of Texas at Arlington Library's Special Collections provided important material.

In Dallas: Edward Baum, Gene Bishop, Betty Blake, Duncan Boeckman, Eugene Bonelli, Nancy O'Boyle, Richard Brettell, George Charlton, William B. Croft, David Dillon, Jo Cleaver Doremus, Raymond Entenmann, Yolette Garcia, Reagan George, Anne Cleaver Grabowski, Jerry Henderson, Dwight Hunter, Ferne and Arthur Koch, Janet Kutner, Max Levy, Stanley Marcus, Margaret McDermott, Tyree Miller, Dan Nelson, Michael Piazza, Joanne and James Pratt, Steven Sands, Phillip Shepherd, John Schoelkopf, Ellis Shamoon, Randy Spraberry, Peter Stewart, and Jeff West of The Sixth Floor. The Dallas Public Library, *The Dallas Morning News,* the Dallas Museum of Art Mayer Library, and the Hamon Art Library and Fondren Library at Southern Methodist University provided welcome sources.

In Corpus Christi: Blissie Blair, James Bright, Mack Colley, John Dykema Jr., Edward Harte, Alan Lessof, William Otten, and Edwin Singer. Marilyn Smith and the staff of the Art Museum of South Texas provided valuable help. The Library at Texas A&M University, Corpus Christi, furnished important information.

In College Station: Julius Gribou, Ward Wells, and Dean Thomas Regan of the College of Architecture at Texas A&M University. In Presidio, Texas: Simone Swan; in Austin, Texas: Joel Barna, Hal Box, the Lyndon Baines Johnson Library, and Jean and John Works; in Santa Monica, California: Frank Gehry; in Columbus, Ohio: Jeffrey Kipnis; in Oberlin, Ohio: Geoffrey Blodgett and Gordon Craig; in Orlando, Florida: Eugene Aubry.

In New York and Connecticut: Jay Presson Allen, Rosamond Bernier, Peter Blake, Nina Bremer, Peter Eisenman, Gigi Fernandez, Richard Foster, James Inigo Freed, John Johansen, Maureen Knorr, Cathleen McGuigan, John Manley, Alan Ritchie, Theodate Johnson Severns, Robert A. M. Stern, and David Whitney. The Avery Library of Columbia University and the New York Public Library furnished valuable documentation, as did the Museum of

Modern Art's Archives Department and its Department of Photographic Services and Permissions. The office of Philip Johnson/Alan Ritchie was always helpful in expeditious ways.

Foremost, I am indebted to Philip Johnson for his encouragement, good humor, and endlessly informative and stimulating observations. When I was finished writing and he had the manuscript in hand at The Glass House, I spoke with him on the phone and he enthused, "Frank, I have been reading your book and I am absolutely *riveted!*" That gave me a good feeling.

Several weeks later I was in New Canaan, seated with him at the marble dining table where he was signing papers in front of a wall of glass. The subject of the book came up and, looking up, he solemnly observed, "You know, Frank, it's not very well written." Somehow it didn't faze me.

The photographer would like to acknowledge the support of the Rice Design Alliance, Farish Gallery of the Rice University School of Architecture, the Rothko Chapel Foundation, Adelaide de Menil, and the Texas Historical Foundation for some of the earlier photographs; and the pleasure of looking at buildings with the author.

Philip Johnson & Texas

Prologue

Philip Johnson was born in Cleveland, Ohio, in 1906 to Homer H. Johnson, a gregarious, successful lawyer, and Louise Pope Johnson, thirty-two, a reserved and well-born intellectual with a deep interest in art who was six years younger than her twice-widowed husband. Philip was the third of four Johnson children, the others being: Jeannette, the elder sister; a brother, Alfred, who died young; and a sister, Theodate, one year younger. The parents doted on two-year-old Philip with special zeal after the loss of their first boy at the age of five. Philip and his sisters were raised quietly in an upper-middle-class area of Cleveland Heights and at Townsend Farms near New London, some sixty miles to the southwest, where Homer Johnson had been raised as a "farm boy." Jeannette, Philip, and Theodate led close and carefree young lives, spending time together at home with a German governess—who taught them her language—and at the farm and on the travels away from Ohio with their parents. Numerous crossings were made to Europe, and the Johnsons escaped the harsh Ohio winters in Pinehurst, North Carolina, where Homer played golf and Louise founded a small school for her children to attend and gave art lectures to the community. In the 1920s she hired the prominent New York designer Donald Desky to decorate rooms in their house there in a deco style.

Germany was the cultural capital of Europe at the time, and its music, art, and literature were admired and extolled at length by Homer Johnson. This admiration of Teutonic culture was not unusual in upper-class Midwestern families. The family spent vacations in Germany and lengthy times in Paris; all three children attended schools in Switzerland. Louise Johnson, a Wellesley graduate, represented the Victorian ideal of cultural self-improvement. She was avid about the children's intellectual and artistic development, which her husband pretty much left to her. Not remembered by the children for her warmth, the emotionally reserved "club woman" mother ensured that the minds of her three children received exposure to literature and the fine arts. Architecture, i.e., European architecture, was very much a part of the mother's cultural agenda for her children. Louise's first cousin, Theodate Pope Riddle, grew up in Cleveland and was, along with Julia Morgan of California, one of the country's first renowned female architects, designing country houses and private schools in the East.

Jeannette Johnson Dempsey recalls:

> On Sundays in Cleveland, Mother would conduct slide-illustrated "seminars" on art and architecture, including the "modern" stuff, for Philip, Theodate, and me in the living room. Philip just soaked it up. His aptitude for the arts was pretty clear to Mother very early.
>
> She and Father adored Philip and spoiled him; he was the replacement for the boy they had lost to mastoiditis, and when Philip developed ear trouble later it caused great anxiety. He was sick a great deal of the time, and with our moving around all the time he never developed any friends.[1]

Before Jeannette was born, Homer and Louise talked about building a new house. The fact that her choice of architect would have been a maverick thirty-four-year-old Chicagoan named Frank Lloyd Wright indicates her questing, vanguard taste. The baby's arrival was too imminent, so they remained in the Tudoresque house that Homer had purchased when they married. But soon Louise chose J. Milton Dyer, Cleveland's best architect and its first graduate of Paris's Ecole des Beaux Arts, to do something in the Art Nouveau style for a new master bedroom. Philip Johnson recalled that "It was an extraordinary thing for those times in Cleveland. She was always way out, in that sense."[2]

The Johnson children were, from their earliest years, at home in Cleveland's art museum and symphony hall. This immersion in the city's fine arts culture, directed with determination by their mother, had a telling effect: Jeannette became a lifelong, prominent supporter of all the arts in Cleveland; Theodate, only a year younger than her brother and often taken to be Philip's twin, studied in Europe to be an opera singer, had recitals there and in New York's Town Hall, and for years, with Philip's support, published the authoritative journal *Musical America.*

Philip's life as critic, architect, and art collector can be traced to his mother's exaltation of the creative, intellectual life. At one point, before discovering architecture at Harvard, he planned to be a concert pianist. While Philip Johnson would later assert that his mother was distant and cold compared to his warm, outgoing father, she was the key factor in his development into one of the major figures in the twentieth century's world of art and architecture. On a tour of Europe with his mother and sisters, the thirteen-year-old boy burst into tears when he entered Chartres Cathedral, overwhelmed by the soaring space of the thirteenth-century Gothic church. "There was a funeral taking place, and it was years before I realized that everyone didn't have the same reaction as mine when they entered Chartres,"[3] he remembers.

Jeannette says her sociable father "belonged to all the country clubs in Cleveland, where he liked to claim that he got more new legal business in the locker rooms than he ever could sitting in his office downtown."[4] The extroverted attorney was well known both nationally and internationally, accepting an assignment from President Woodrow Wilson on a government commission in post–World War I Europe which dealt with reparations to Jews. With her husband in Washington and Europe a lot, Louise Johnson steadily accepted the prime responsibility for raising the children until she wearied of that and took the children and joined him overseas in Paris. There was little entertaining in the Johnson home. Though an active member of clubs dealing with the arts and civic improvement, Louise Johnson was a "loner" socially according to her son, caring more about the hearth and home than society. Homer more often than not contented himself with a social life at his clubs.

The children spent their happiest days during summers at Townsend Farms outside New London, which Johnson today calls his "hometown." The three-thousand-acre farm property had come down to Homer Johnson through his mother's family. There the self-sufficient band of three led a lazy, idyllic life of horseback riding and fishing while Mrs. Johnson devoted herself to flowers and landscaping. Philip recalls her obsession with developing an apple orchard, which his father had to halt because of the cost. Her love of horticulture transferred to her son, who often liked to say, when he was shaping the landscape of the grounds of his place in Connecticut, that he was a "better landscape architect than architect."

His father, with an energy that came down to Philip, commuted the sixty miles back and forth to Cleveland once a week. Though owned by others today, the farm's headquarters is unchanged and still a loose but orderly compound of large and small gabled white buildings beneath towering elm trees. Scattered neatly on several acres around a simple, one-story 1845 Greek Revival house, it is a composed picture of genteel Midwestern rural life, a precursor to what the adult Philip Johnson created in exquisite avant-garde terms on his own spread in New Canaan.

Jeannette asserts that "Philip got the intellectual part from Mother and the gregarious charm from Father."[5] Both parents supported music and helped found Cleveland's art museum. Though he was a joiner, Homer was very independent politically, often drawn to reformist causes. Conservative Cleveland nearly ostracized him after he voted for Democratic reformer Woodrow Wilson, and in his declining years he remained an ardent, outspoken pacifist.

Townsend Farms, New London, Ohio.
Photos by the author, 1995.

In 1924, when the children were young adults, Homer Johnson bequeathed them an early inheritance. To his daughters he gave important downtown-Cleveland real estate, and to Philip he presented a large block of stock in a Pittsburgh metals firm that Johnson had helped an Oberlin College classmate form. In 1886, while they were both undergraduates, Homer's friend Charles Martin Hall had developed a process which led to the commercial production of aluminum. For his later legal help in setting up Hall's production company, Johnson received shares in the Aluminum Company of America, the company that bought Hall's patented process. The stock wasn't worth much at the time young Philip received it, but in a few years, during the 1920s, its value increased dramatically, so that when Johnson graduated from Harvard in 1930 he was a millionaire and richer than his father.

Homer and Louise Johnson shared a strong belief in the value of the best possible educations for their children. Homer, born in a rural community in 1862, was raised in New London at Townsend Farms but attended college in nearby Oberlin and at Amherst in Massachusetts. Deciding on a career in law, he applied and was accepted at Harvard Law School, where he graduated summa cum laude. Louise Pope came from a well-to-do Cleveland family superior to that of her future husband's. The Pope family's money came from shipping instead of farming, and she was grounded in a privileged urban life with its attendant cultural amenities. She, too, was drawn to the New England educational establishment, graduating from Wellesley in 1891 and staying on to receive a Master of Fine Arts in art history. After study in Italy for a year, she returned to Ohio and taught school until in 1901 she married Homer Johnson.

The pattern of leaving Ohio for education in the East would be repeated with all of the Johnson children. The perception among many of the educated parents in the nation's hinterlands was that the best schooling was found along the East Coast in the oldest universities. For Philip Johnson, his later scholastic sojourn in the Ivy League world would prove seminal and, like that of many other Midwesterners, develop from a temporary leave from home to a permanent relocation in the cultural and financial capital, New York.

Young Johnson attended private schools in Cleveland, New York, and Switzerland. Never spending enough time in any to put down roots, he never established friendships. Bright, spoiled, and inept at sports, his only companions were his sisters. The impression is clear that he was favored by his mother, who recognized the brilliance and quickness of his mind. Hackley School near New York was chosen as his prep school, where he came into his own with fellow students and, even more, with his teachers. The outsider became the insider by dint of the ardor and avidity of his high-strung disposition. His conspicuous personality and the brightness of his mind made him a standout, sometimes a show-off, among the other well-scrubbed scions of the rich. His lifelong course of being a pacesetter was more or less set at Hackley. Throughout his life he has always needed a group—students, architects, or a lecture audience—to stand before and lead. Graduating second in his class assured him entry into his college of choice, Harvard.

Cambridge's Harvard, on the Charles River near Boston, with its concentration of scholars, intellects, and bright undergraduates, was an eye-opener for Johnson. Its myriad attractions for the mind were a watershed in Johnson's development, and his restless, varied interests led him down many paths there. Besides considering a career as a concert pianist, he also excelled in Greek literature and mathematical physics. In his third year, however, he settled on philosophy as his major interest. Alfred North Whitehead, the great Harvard philosopher, was Johnson's professor and with his wife became friends with the bright nineteen-year-old. Johnson remembers being inspired by Raphael Demos, a tutor whose work on Plato was required reading.

Philosophy offered a sort of absolute moral ordering that appealed to Johnson and would later characterize his initial architectural tendencies. He lost interest in philosophy before leaving Harvard and turned to modern art and architecture, writing criticism pieces for *Hound and Horn,* the student avant-garde art publication. Johnson felt the influence of art historian Paul Sachs, who "bred a generation of future stewards of high culture at the pivotal moment when modernism became respectable in institutions."[6] Sachs's students Lincoln Kirstein (who founded, funded, and edited *Hound and Horn),* Edward M. M. Warburg, and John Walker started the Harvard Society for Contemporary Art and opened the country's first modern art gallery in second-floor space on Harvard Square. It was a forerunner of New York's Museum of Modern Art. Warburg and Kirstein would be Johnson's lifelong friends and influential figures in his future as an architect.

All through his time at Harvard—it took seven years for him to get through—Johnson was wrenched with conflicts and spent many months and whole semesters at home in Cleveland, away from Cambridge. Harvard's intense academic world, with its heightened social distractions, exacerbated the incipient homosexual leanings that Johnson had harbored for years. This stress of confusion and concealment led him, in the spring of 1925, to a Boston doctor who counseled him to return home for rest and reconciliation with his sexuality.

Johnson says he spent months alternately crying and devouring mystery novels, but the doctor's prescription worked finally and his severe depression lifted. To the relief of his parents, particularly Homer Johnson, he returned to

Harvard the following term. At one point, according to Jeannette Dempsey, he was in love with a beautiful classmate of Theodate's, and he and Jeannette determined that he was heterosexual. But there were slip-backs away from convention, and he eventually made peace with his sexual inclination and went on with life. Despite the parental anxiety about his son's turn away from the norm, Homer Johnson gave Philip a father's support throughout his long life. When his son was beginning his years as director of the Museum of Modern Art's Department of Architecture, Homer Johnson helped underwrite an exhibition being mounted by Philip. As a longtime trustee at Oberlin College and also executor of the estate of his client Charles Hall, Homer Johnson had a position to influence the award of architectural commissions at the college, particularly those funded by Hall money. Though Philip was only beginning as an architect in the 1940s, Homer Johnson tried for several years to get him the commission for the 1950 Sophronia Brooks Hall Memorial Auditorium, a memorial to Charles Hall's mother. Arthur Vining Davis, another Oberlin trustee and president of Alcoa Corporation, was influential in getting the job for Wallace Harrison, whose New York firm, Harrison & Abramovitz, had designed Alcoa's Pittsburgh headquarters.

In 1928 Johnson saw a copy of *Arts* magazine at Harvard and was struck by the illustrations of the work of the Dutch architect J. J. P. Oud and an accompanying article by Henry-Russell Hitchcock. He was as taken by the sharp writing of Hitchcock as he was by the crisp, unadorned white buildings of Oud, the best-known Dutch architect designing in the new mode of stripped esthetic purity devoid of ornamentation.

Alfred H. Barr Jr. © 1999 the Museum of Modern Art, New York.

During the Harvard years, Johnson had continued the pattern of summer vacations in Europe begun with his family, but now he traveled alone, or with a friend, and with an increasing interest in buildings, both the old and the very new. In the summer of 1928, a visit to the Parthenon in Athens affected him so deeply that once again he was moved to tears by a monument of architecture. He later asserted that the experience on the Acropolis, along with Chartres and the photographs of Oud's modernist work, was the transforming experience which led to his conversion to architecture. Before his graduation in 1930, Johnson made two friends who were to become pivotal to his cultural and professional life: Henry-Russell Hitchcock and Alfred H. Barr Jr.

Referring to his own development as critic, curator, architectural scholar, and architect, Johnson in later years would say, "It all began with Alfred Barr." Born in Detroit in 1902, Barr came from a line of Presbyterian ministers and educators and like Johnson left the Midwest at a young age for education in the East. After a Maryland prep school and a Master's degree in art history at

Henry-Russell Hitchcock. Courtesy of Smith College Archives, Smith College.

Princeton, he taught at Vassar College and at Harvard, where he impressed Paul Sachs. In 1926 he went to Wellesley College, where he developed the first course in America devoted to the study of modern art. Like Johnson, Barr had traveled in Europe, but with a more studied attention to the new architecture than Johnson, whose main interest was with historic monuments. Barr had visited architect Walter Gropius's revolutionary Bauhaus school at Dessau, where he was impressed with its comprehensive approach to arts education. Painting, sculpture, photography, industrial design, cinema, and architecture were taught together under one philosophical umbrella. To Barr, it represented an exciting Machine Age extension of ideas for arts integration practiced in the late-nineteenth-century Arts and Crafts Movement by John Ruskin and William Morris.

In the spring of 1929 Johnson met Barr at his sister Theodate's graduation from Wellesley. Louise Johnson, always alert to new trends and a trustee of her alma mater, had written Philip about Barr, whom she described as the Wellesley teacher who knew all about modern architecture. The two were introduced during the commencement weekend and immediately took a liking to each other. Barr's quiet, scholarly enthusiasm for modern art and architecture struck a nerve with Johnson, himself vigilant to the vanguard in art. The undergraduate's enthusiasm and eagle eye for what was happening at culture's leading edge, coupled with Barr's knowledge of what was going on, made them a complementary pair immediately. After talking with Johnson for many hours that weekend, Barr offhandedly asked him, "Do you want to help start a modern art museum?" After Barr's explanation of what he was up to, Johnson's reply was an emphatic "yes," and he excitedly wrote his mother that Barr wanted him to form an architecture department in a new modern museum in New York and that he had "much to learn and quickly!" When he returned to Europe that summer, Johnson planned to concentrate on seeing the new buildings that Barr had described, and he would see them from the driver's seat of a new green Cord convertible, purchased in New York before sailing and stowed in the ship's hold.

Earlier in 1929 three wealthy New York matrons had an idea for a new museum devoted solely to contemporary art and were looking for someone to run it. Mrs. John D. Rockefeller Jr., Mrs. Cornelius P. Sullivan, and Miss Lillie P. Bliss consulted with Paul Sachs, who told them that they should contact Alfred Barr. When the twenty-seven-year-old was chosen to head the new Museum of Modern Art, he set about creating a unique institution intended to be a symbiosis of all the modern arts behind one intellectual banner of advanced and renewing avant-garde artistic activity. It was to be an institution located in the middle of Manhattan and dedicated, in Barr's words, to "the art of now." No establishment with such a mission existed. Three generations of the immensely wealthy Rockefeller family have been the key philanthropic element in the museum's development. (John D. Rockefeller, the patriarch, made his enormous oil fortune in Cleveland.)

When twenty-three-year-old Johnson started his drive through Europe in the summer of 1929, he went first to Stuttgart, Germany, to see the Weissenhof housing exhibition, a "group show" of European modernist architects exhibiting their designs in a master-planned community of white, flat-roofed housing on a hillside site overlooking the city. He wrote his mother that Weissenhof was the perfect spot for him to begin, "my first view of things by Le Corbusier, Gropius and Oud, the three greatest living architects." Barr had called them the "finest masters among the moderns."[7]

He then traveled to Dessau, where the Bauhaus school was located in buildings designed by Walter Gropius. Marcel Breuer, Josef Albers, Paul Klee, and Ludwig Mies van der Rohe, who was director for three years after Gropius resigned in 1930, were part of the roster of artists and architects with progressive social ideas, teaching a new esthetic inspired by machine technology. But it was the *style,* the appearance of the buildings at Dessau and Stuttgart, that appealed to Johnson, not their sociological "intentions." He was grounded in the visual result of a building, not the how and why of its realization. His appreciation of architecture would always have this basis.

From Paul Klee he purchased his first modern painting before proceeding to Berlin to seek out Mies and Walter Gropius. Gropius was chilly to the dapper, well-heeled Johnson, but Mies, the dour self-educated idealist, was happy to share schnapps and dinner with the spiffy, keen American who spoke German. Carefully following Barr's prescribed itinerary, the high-strung Johnson experienced intellectual and sensory highs throughout the summer, meeting the architects and seeing the buildings on Barr's list. In Holland he saw the lyrically pure geometry of Oud's smooth, pale buildings and became friends with the "charming, outgoing, sensible" architect, the first modernist to have caught his eye back at Cambridge.

The new architecture that was so compelling to Johnson is a reductive, abstract language of spare, clear structure with economy and purity in its material expression, fitted to a program of intensively analyzed function. In a building's ideal realization there was a taut "weightlessness" in the sensitive, yet logical, assembly of light, functional building parts. Walls of glass or plaster were referred to as "skins," structure was "skeletal." In terms of form it was to traditional architecture what cubism represented in the context of academic painting. The old and familiar rules of architectural image and composition were jettisoned.

Le Corbusier called the house "a machine for living," and the ambience and details of his strikingly lean buildings with their open decks and steel railings were compared to ocean liners. A sort of consensus of design principles emerged among the Europeans and flowered in the mid-1920s in Germany, France, and Holland in reaction to the dense, eclectic architecture that served officialdom throughout the Western world. Though manifestations of the new esthetic had been appearing on both sides of the Atlantic since 1910—Irving Gill was doing anomalous "modern" work in Southern California before the war and in the same period Frank Lloyd Wright's early prewar work in Oak Park got the attention of Europeans like Walter Gropius—the tenets of the new style coalesced following World War I.

The new philosophy of design encompassed both esthetics and sociology, offering a rational agenda for building configuration to replace the prevailing academic discipline of pictorialism, which for a century had emerged from the ateliers of Paris's Ecole des Beaux Arts. The emerging European modernists felt strongly that the new architecture should represent, in constructed terms, the ideals of an improved way of living for humankind: build economical, functional buildings, standardized where possible, and spend the savings in money to enhance living standards. But to a young patrician connoisseur like Johnson it was the bold, dramatic *style* of what he was seeing, via Alfred Barr's guidance, that transformed his appreciation of the building art. A building's objective quality was what appealed to the youthful Johnson, not its social underpinnings. This personal response of his—exalting the esthetic, the artistic, and eschewing the sociological—would distinguish and make controversial his future career in architecture. The reformer in him was directed at the physiognomy of buildings, not their social and political relations. He would remain an architectural visualist forever.

Throughout his long career, Johnson has been criticized and derided for the seemingly unprincipled ease of his philosophical shifts of sensibility regarding architecture. Some of the criticism results from his bent for contrary, impetuous change and challenge. But from the beginning he had a nervous, earnest desire to always be ahead culturally, to be *au courant,* up with the head of the pack, not left in the wake of the zeitgeist. This instinct of his for the artistic high ground irritates some people. They expect him to possess an enduring "faith," accusing him of being an arts dabbler, a dilettante. But as the world has changed through wars and social and cultural turmoil, and rapid turnovers of critical judgment regarding the desired character of the built world have occurred, Johnson has invariably had his ear to the ground and his nose in the wind, divining and interpreting the changing artistic tempers. Paul Goldberger, architecture critic of *The New York Times,* once called him a "bloodhound" for the way he could anticipate revisionist trends in taste and architectural thought. Johnson puts it like this: "It's like spoor! You can feel it in the air."[8]

Thus, in his early twenties, with one more year at Harvard to complete before graduation, Johnson returned to America, fired up after a summer of fast-paced exposure to the cutting edge. He immediately got in touch with Alfred Barr in New York and soon met Hitchcock. Before long, Johnson was traveling regularly from Cambridge down to Manhattan, where the new museum was being created by Barr and a small, youthful group. Margaret Scolari, who was to marry Barr, was a graduate student at New York University and recalls that Johnson would join her and Alfred and the coterie of young acolytes for Chinese food in the Heckscher Building on West Fifty-seventh Street, at Fifth Avenue, where the infant museum was first located on an upper floor.

In the late 1970s Marga Barr remembered that the conversation around her future husband was "incredibly exciting and youthful. The ideas came thick and fast and Philip was in the middle of it from the beginning. He was handsome, always cheerful, and pulsating with new ideas and hopes. Wildly impatient, he could not sit down! His rapid way of speaking, that quickness and vibration have not changed at all."[9] Johnson was awed by Hitchcock at the meetings in New York and during his last year at Harvard developed a close friendship with the rumpled, bearish intellectual with such a vast knowledge of architecture, both ancient and modern. The core of the progressive New York cultural establishment, in which young Hitchcock held bona fides, was well formed by the early 1930s after passing through Harvard's intellectual "boot camp" of the 1920s with its radical ideas for an improved world. Only three years older than Johnson, Boston-born Hitchcock was teaching at Wesleyan University and was the recent author of *Modern Architecture: Romanticism and Reintegration,* which traced the origins of the modern movement in architecture from the nineteenth century. While the book was well received in academia, it was considered by Barr a little too dry in style for the broad audience that the young museum director was seeking. He was already thinking about a large modern architecture exhibition that would stake out the new museum's turf of inclusion for all the arts. Barr asked Johnson and Hitchcock to tour Europe and gather material for the exhibition.

The two new friends sailed separately for Europe in the spring of 1930 to meet in Paris, where Margaret Scolari and Alfred Barr were married in May. Soon after the wedding, and with Barr's coaching, the pair began a detailed tour of the continent's new architecture in Johnson's convertible. With Johnson's money and elegant car and Hitchcock's knowledge of where to go, they crisscrossed the continent. As they carefully inspected and discussed the buildings and met their architects, the two started an amplified rewriting of Hitchcock's book. The new volume was to be titled *The International Style: Architecture since 1922,* employing a term coined by Barr as a designation for

Philip Johnson and Henry-Russell Hitchcock, 1985. Courtesy of Philip Johnson.

the new style. The book was intended to have a broader appeal than Hitchcock's earlier volume, with many more photographs and a more "popular" writing style.

Though Johnson was knowledgeable for his age, not unfamiliar with the new architecture, the deliberate, scholarly Hitchcock was the pair's leader. He was older, had his Master's from Harvard, and already had written an important book featuring modern architecture. In 1993, Johnson remembered that for the new book he did "all the dirty work. I was the 'advance man.' Russell was nice enough to list my name, but it wasn't an equal collaboration by any means. I was learning so much and did the work gladly and wrote to all the architects making arrangements for meetings. It was hard to collect photographs because these architects, besides being poor, weren't publicity-minded, so I sometimes had to go there and take the pictures."[10] When Hitchcock died in 1987 Johnson would say of his longtime friend: "Of our generation, he was the leader of us all. He set a new standard of architectural scholarship and accuracy of judgement which has yet to be equaled."[11] Over twenty books on architectural history bear Hitchcock's name and form the armature around which subsequent scholars of many periods work.

Johnson, attracted to the raw and radical *newness* of the European buildings, and Hitchcock, though the more settled and methodical historian, came to a similar conclusion that summer that the new architecture's value was its style. Johnson's verve and Hitchcock's scholarship made them a complementary pair to document the modern Europeans, and Johnson's fluency in German and French was no small asset; it gave them an access to the architects whose personal stories fleshed out the book.

They worked as a team. As Hitchcock directed the tour, Johnson drove and did the legwork, lugging a large German view-camera and lining up drawings and interviews with Mies, Oud, Gropius, Breuer, and Le Corbusier. The architects, some down-at-heel, were happy to receive the young, open-handed explorers speeding around the continent examining architecture of the future from Johnson's sleek, open-top car. Oud was warmly hospitable, Le Corbusier was self-absorbed and detached, and Mies van der Rohe, in Johnson's hyperbole, was "starving in a Berlin attic," but the phlegmatic German made the most profound impression. The elder architect liked conversing with Johnson after several schnapps. Of all the buildings he saw that summer, Mies's rigorously abstract designs appealed to Johnson the most. Mies had designed two hypothetical glass-sheathed towers which stunned Johnson with their audacity. In Johnson's eyes there was about Mies's buildings an objective sureness, an authority of pure rational form rendered with elegant materials, that made Johnson a disciple of Mies's for almost three decades. His sharp eye and intellect recognized the greatness and intuitive artistry of the withdrawn German, twenty years his senior, who possessed an almost spiritual philosophy of reductionist, structure-generated forms. A significant anecdote about Mies concerned his first visit to Italy. "He found that he did not like the endless Mediterranean sun and he openly longed for the 'grey heavens' of Germany."[12]

Before the summer ended, Johnson had visited Mies's newly completed Tugendhat house in Brno, Czechoslovakia, and was so enraptured by the spacious, flowing, luxuriously appointed residence that in a letter to Hitchcock he compared it to the Parthenon and called it "unquestionably the best looking house in the world."[13] Before Johnson returned to New York, Mies agreed to design the interiors of the New York apartment Johnson had just rented.

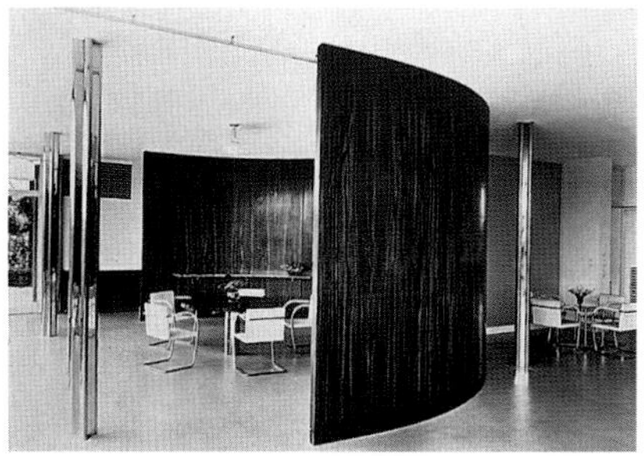

Interior, Tugendhat House, Brno, Czechoslovakia, 1930; Mies van der Rohe, architect. Courtesy of Archivision Inc. © Scott Gilchrist.

When Hitchcock and Johnson returned home in the fall of 1930 the two had visited France, Belgium, Holland, Germany, Sweden, Denmark, and Switzerland, with Hitchcock visiting England and Johnson going to Austria and Czechoslovakia. The manuscript for *The International Style: Architecture since 1922* was finished in a rough form. Alfred Barr was anxious to put together an exhibition to accompany the book's publication. It would be a unique and comprehensive survey of the best recently designed modern American and European buildings.

Johnson was now officially director of the museum's nascent Department of Architecture, using his apartment as office and paying a secretary out of his pocket, a practice he would continue during all his years with the museum. When arrangements for Mies to design the exhibition fell through, Johnson designed and organized it, with help from Barr and Hitchcock. It opened at the Museum of Modern Art's temporary space in the Heckscher Building in early 1932 and featured the Americans Frank Lloyd Wright, Raymond Hood, Howe and Lescaze, Richard Neutra, and the Bowman Brothers.[14] The Europeans included were Le Corbusier, Mies van der Rohe, J. J. P. Oud, and Walter Gropius. Models, plans, and large photographs of several different building types, primarily single-family housing and schools, were shown. It was the American public's first exposure to such landmark European buildings as Le Corbusier's Villa Savoye, Mies's Barcelona Pavilion, and Gropius's Bauhaus.

Philip Johnson, curator, preparing for installation of "Machine Art" exhibition, the Museum of Modern Art, 1934. Photo by Paul Parker; courtesy of the Museum of Modern Art, New York.

The exhibition, *Modern Architecture—International Exhibition,* stirred the New York architectural scene. It began modestly as a *succes d'estime,* with a meager amount of lukewarm comment from the media and only some thirty-three thousand people attending the exhibition during its six-week run. But the ultimate impact on the United States was broad. While a few buildings embodying the imported esthetic had been built in the United States—buildings such as Howe and Lescaze's high-rise Philadelphia Savings Fund Society Building (1930) and Richard Neutra's Lovell House (1929)—International Style modernism's appeal to the American architectural profession really began with the museum's epochal exhibition and endured for forty years.

For several years following the book and the exhibition, Johnson was busy mounting other exhibitions, writing catalogues, and delivering lectures while maintaining a colorful, fast-paced social life in Manhattan's elite, Upper East Side salons as well as in the offbeat world of poets, artists, dancers, and musicians. When he wasn't adventuring downtown he developed a lifelong relationship with beautiful Eliza Bliss, niece of one of the museum founders. It was a nimble duality of social and cultural positioning for which he was to display an enduring knack. The Rockefellers, Goodyears, and Blisses were museum confidants and solicitors of his artistic opinions. The creative denizens of Harlem and Greenwich Village were beneficiaries of his openhanded largesse and cultural adventuring. But always paramount in his life alongside his protean wanderings in New York's Bohemia was the lasting friendship with Marga and Alfred Barr.

Abruptly, on Christmas Day in 1934, Johnson began a five-year odyssey

Philip Johnson with Margaret and Alfred Barr Jr. in Cortuna, Italy, 1932.
Courtesy of the Museum of Modern Art, New York.

away from the special niche he enjoyed at the Museum of Modern Art among New York's cultural cognoscenti. The Great Depression that began with the stock market crash in 1929 was devastating the country, and Johnson and his intellectual friends were casting about in idealistic ferment for radical solutions to what they saw as their country's flawed political system. Johnson remembers that most of his intellectual and artist friends were leaning toward communism, while Johnson was listening to a right-wing writer and fellow Harvardian named Lawrence Dennis, whose *Is Capitalism Doomed?* espoused a populist fascism for the United States' ills.

Johnson was no stranger to Populism, the political philosophy supporting the rights of the people in their struggle against the privileged elite, which had a history in the United States, particularly the Midwest. Anti-Semitism was definitely an element in Populism, focusing on the financial power of "international Jewry and the Rothschilds." Economic Populism was the issue with Johnson, not the racism that was a certain factor in Populism. Anti-Semitic prejudice, outside Populism, certainly existed throughout the country, even among the Jews themselves: "Some of my best friends are Jews" and "He's a great guy even though he's Jewish," and "We are German Jews, *they* are Polish."

So it wasn't such a stretch, under the circumstances of economic strife, for Johnson to literally and figuratively buy into Dennis's ideas, spending money and time with the authoritative figure. He was not naïve about the fascistic system of a centralized political dictatorship merging government and capitalism. He was aware of what was going on in Germany and was impressed by its turnaround from postwar chaos through the National Socialist German Worker (Nazi) Party and its charismatic demagogue, Adolf Hitler. During his summer vacation in Europe in 1932, Johnson was invited by Helen Appleton Read, a New York art critic for the *Brooklyn Eagle,* to go with her to a Nazi rally where Hitler spoke to a large crowd in a field in Potsdam, a suburb of Berlin. Johnson was magnetized by the drama of the event.

His emotions were engulfed by the feverish theater of the scene: the martial songs, the flags, the marching phalanxes of handsome young troops, the precise Teutonic orchestration, climaxed by the appearance of Hitler with his riveting harangue. This was something totally new: fear-and-paranoia politics rendered in a grandly scaled form of visual power that, in the hands of the Germans, was overwhelming and operatic in effect. Johnson's critics, as well as Johnson himself, are still assessing the effect of this mesmerizing political pageant on him.

When Johnson left the Museum of Modern Art in late 1934, he was joined by Alan Blackburn, a friend from prep school and Harvard whom Johnson had brought into the museum administration. Blackburn was a practical-minded organizer who served a purpose that others would fulfill throughout Johnson's life: the dedicated, methodical backup for his interests of the moment. Before the sudden departure from the museum, Johnson had begun independent design work, including Miesian apartment interiors in a Beekman Place building for his adventurous friend Edward Warburg, one of several Jewish friends who remained loyal following Johnson's fling with Nazi politics. Warburg felt that Johnson's "wires got crossed" in Germany through acquaintances he made there.

Warburg grew up in a Gothic mansion on upper Fifth Avenue but since college had been identified with modernist causes. With chagrin, one of his brothers described Eddie's chaste new Beekman Place apartment this way: "The whole place was so antiseptic that you have the feeling you're in a dairy. When you go into the bathroom, you don't expect the usual fixtures, you expect to find a *separator.*"[15]

The Warburg apartment brought Johnson his first notice as a designer in a 1935 *House and Garden* article, a modest beginning of publicity for one who was to be the most written-about architect of his time. Later, he and Warburg secured a U.S. visa for Josef Albers and his Jewish wife Anni, the Bauhaus artists and teachers desperate to escape Germany after the school was closed by the Nazis in 1933. Through Johnson's letters and influence, the Alberses located at a new, experimental school in a former religious retreat in the mountains near Ashville, North Carolina. Speaking little English, Anni and Josef Albers joined the small faculty of intellectuals at Black Mountain College in its first year, he as head of the art department and she as instructor in weaving. Josef Albers pumped energy into the avant-garde school with his Bauhaus teaching principles; Texan Robert Rauschenberg studied under Albers after the war and considered the time at Black Mountain as the defining experience in his beginnings as an artist. Before closing in 1956, the school's tiny, loosely structured art department, with students like Robert Motherwell, Jacob Lawrence, and Cy Twombly, served as lodestar for the postwar New York School in painting.

Johnson's attempt to find a teaching job in the United States for his first architectural hero J. J. P. Oud was unsuccessful. His second and most lasting design *meister,* Mies van der Rohe, soon came to the United States, through his and Alfred Barr's efforts, and settled in Chicago. Meanwhile, in bizarre juxtaposition, Johnson was being coached in fascist dogma. This duality, Johnson's need to be a leader *and* a follower, was manifest early and became an enduring aspect of his long life.

It was ironic that as Johnson was receiving the first public recognition of his talent as a designer, the contrarian in him spun him in the opposite direction to pursue a perverse political grail devoid of art. Johnson and Blackburn's abandonment of the Museum of Modern Art, the flagship of culture on which they served, to organize a right-wing political party was front-page news in New York and Cleveland. Jeannette Dempsey says that it caused embarrassment to the family and her husband turned his back on her brother. Johnson and Blackburn impetuously headed down to Louisiana in Johnson's big Packard to meet Governor Huey P. Long, described by some as the nation's "down-home fascist."

The backwoods Populist was an odd choice for veneration by Johnson. Long, nicknamed "The Kingfish," gave fist-pounding "share the wealth" speeches, taunting the nation's big names and demanding they use their riches to feed the hungry: "What's Morgan and Baruch and Rockefeller going to do with all that grub? We got to call Mr. Rockefeller and say, come back *he-ah!*"[16] With Johnson's refined, privileged background, it was a peculiar juxtaposition indeed. More puzzling was his sudden espousal of radical social causes after shunning them in the European modern architecture movement.

Johnson recalls that "It was the depths of the Depression and the country was going to pot and no one could do anything about it. FDR seemed powerless. People were hungry on the streets of the richest country in the world. It was absurd."[17] But Long's shirt-sleeved staff turned the eager Ivy Leaguers back—they never saw Long—and Johnson and Blackburn later drove across the country's highways in a futile quest for support for their hazy cause. Johnson returned with Blackburn to Ohio and tried running the family farm from the two-story white frame Johnson home on New London's Main Street. He put a modernist mark on the old house by knocking out two facing walls in the living room and installing large, floor-length plate glass. Restless in the rural village, Johnson involved himself in the politics of the fifteen-hundred-citizen town, getting on its park board, trying to organize a milk strike by dairy farmers, and signing up, then backing out from, running for the Ohio legislature. Huey Long was assassinated in Baton Rouge in 1935, and Johnson and Blackburn's Young Nationalist Party sputtered out in a few months. Blackburn married a local girl and returned to New York.

The contrast of this series of failed ventures with Johnson's achievements in New York as curator, scholar, and man-about-the-arts was striking, baffling, and depressing to those close to him. Apart from the egregious moral aspect, Johnson's stray wanderings constituted a record of failure and misjudgment in realms outside the reach of the high-strung esthete that Johnson so clearly was. But oddly enough he returned once more to Germany in 1939 as war enveloped Europe. Curious to see the political spectacle again, he finally "saw" and returned to America shaken by the appalling implications of the Nazi "new world order."

Today Johnson is hard put to rationalize this still agonizing and strange interlude. He offers: "There was this strong desire to change the world. Most of my friends wanted to do the same thing but through communism or socialism. I went the other way and I cannot explain it or atone for the fact."[18] From advocating changing the world artistically through architecture, he had inexplicably shifted to a course of radically addressing the nation's domestic problems politically. In both spheres he was drawn to foreign ideas and leadership that were revolutionary and absolutist. The pull of these disparate magnets of art and politics was conditioned by a pervasive steeping in German culture at home and abroad during his youth, and by a weakness for authoritative certitude of the broad-stroke variety. Friendships in Germany played a part.

The Museum of Modern Art, West 53rd Street, New York City, 1939; Philip L. Goodwin and Edward D. Stone, architects. Courtesy of the Museum of Modern Art, New York.

Sensing finally the enormity of where Hitler's Germany was going, and chastened by the pursuit of a poisonous political quarry, he came back to New York and soon applied to Harvard's Graduate School of Design (GSD) to study architecture. In his absence a striking Museum of Modern Art building had been completed at 11 West Fifty-third Street, designed by Philip Goodwin and Edward Durell Stone, and he could have regained his position there. But his life as critic and neophyte designer had been on hold during his political maladventures, and he yearned to regain his bearings and return to his original passion, architecture. He wanted to be a *creator* of modern buildings, not just their connoisseur. He still enjoyed friendship and counsel from Alfred Barr, who urged him on to become a *real* architect. Referring to Johnson's conflicting roles as designer and critic, the grand old architect Frank Lloyd Wright said, "Philip, you can't carry water on both shoulders!"[19] So in the fall of 1940, at age thirty-four, he nervously returned to Harvard, putting the recent past behind him, and started a new life. But his abject failure at politics and the accumulating darkness in Europe would haunt him forever. It's doubtful that he knew what Theodore Roosevelt had once written to the poet Edward Arlington Robinson, that a "devil masters each of us," but that "it is not having been in the Dark House, but having left it, that counts."[20]

Johnson recalls that the train trip from New York to Boston was nerve-wracking. Here he was, feeling that he was approaching middle age, having left the lofty position of Museum of Modern Art curator for a disastrous exploit, the implications of which would magnify and cling to him. He was still an intellectual of repute and a self-styled scholar on matters of modernism, but with a paltry résumé in the matter of design, presumptuously enrolling in the nation's leading school of architecture with a group of college kids. And there was the problem of drawing ability: he had none. "I never could *draw.*

It has always been a terrible handicap!" he recalled fifty years later. But Marcel Breuer, a Gropius colleague and Bauhaus émigré, who now taught architecture at Harvard under Gropius, respected Johnson's reputation as a champion of modern architecture, International Style; it preceded him quite handsomely. The Harvard carpet was out for "our friend," Mr. Philip Johnson, and his acceptance as a graduate student in architecture was engineered smoothly without the requisite test. No one mentioned the recent political aberration, and when Johnson confessed to Breuer that he couldn't draw a line, the Hungarian architect asked Johnson to move his hands and fingers, then observed, "They work all right, I don't see any problem."[21]

Johnson immediately rented a two-story house on Cambridge's Memorial Drive and before long was entertaining lavishly by penny-wise Harvardian terms. Carter H. Manny Jr. was an architecture undergraduate much taken with Johnson and wrote home about lunch at Johnson's, "Has a maid and the whole works . . . beautiful china, silverware, etc. . . . but he is too much an aristocrat architect, caring nothing for practicality or cost" and "This guy must be made of money, for he spends it like a drunken sailor."[22] There were doubtless others there with Johnson's wealth, but no one else showed or shared it with his panache: everything was first-class for the younger students that gravitated to the gregarious champion of modern architecture. I. M. Pei, Edward Larrabee Barnes, and Paul Rudolph were Gropius's students at the time who came to know Johnson in Cambridge and later developed celebrated practices in New York, often competing with him for prestigious design commissions. Also enrolled were future architecture notables Ulrich Franzen, Eliot Noyes, John Johansen, and fellow Ohioan Landes Gores, whom Johnson later drew into his first architectural office as a partner. A young patrician Houstonian, Hugo V. Neuhaus Jr., a Yale graduate, was among this group, as was Thomas M. Price, who would later be Galveston's foremost modernist architect.

With characteristic brio, Johnson charged into academic life, adapting his seniority smoothly into the student fabric. In 1992, John Johansen recalled:

> He was an unusual character as a student—there was his age and his experience at the Museum of Modern Art—he was certainly more of a scholar of the modern movement than any of the rest of us. He fitted in very well however, didn't stand above or to the side of us in the studios, though the wealth showed through in the off-campus entertaining that he loved to do. We didn't see him as having much talent and didn't take him seriously as a designer. Dealing with ideas and esthetics and getting a degree—and having fun doing it—seemed to be his main objective.[23]

Interior, Ash Street House, Cambridge, Massachusetts, 1942; Philip Johnson, designer. Photo by Ezra Stoller © Esto.

Johnson soon started an unusual project: for his graduate thesis, he got permission from Breuer and Gropius to design and build a house for himself there in the middle of Cambridge. The many hours of tedious drafting required for a studio thesis were circumvented with the extraordinary idea. With no shortage of confidence or money, Johnson hired draftsmen to prepare construction drawings, and the house on a corner of Ash Street was completed in 1942.

Houston architect Anderson Todd, a professor of architecture at Rice University, recounts that while a Princeton undergraduate he was a visitor to Cambridge one weekend for a date with a Barnard student. While wandering through the Graduate School of Design studio on a Saturday afternoon he paused to study an unusual drawing on one of the drafting tables. A voice behind him said, "What do you think of it?" Without turning Todd asked, "I think it's great but what is it?" Philip Johnson replied, "It's my house. Do you want to come see it? I'm moving in today." Todd declined, explaining that he had a date that afternoon. Johnson asked, "Is she rich?" Todd nodded. "Is she pretty?" Another nod. "Then bring her along!" Johnson declared. Later in the afternoon Todd and his date went to the sparkling little house on Ash Street, and while Todd helped Johnson's manservant unpack boxes, Johnson served cocktails to the charmed Barnard woman.[24]

Johnson's house soon became a social focus of the architecture faculty and young students who were lucky enough to be included in its soirees. According to Johansen, the house made Philip Johnson Harvard's most popular "salon-keeper." Drinks and hot hors d'oeuvres, served by the servant, were as plentiful and tasty as the gossipy chitchat. Johnson's role as munificent elder among equals has stayed with him all of his life, possibly filling something missing from his friendless youth. Ulrich Franzen remembers how the small, spare dwelling, modeled after one of Mies's courtyard houses, had a big impact on the Harvard intellectuals. "It was very simple and very beautiful," he recalls. The structure, a flat, wood-framed rectangular box with a wall of glass along one side facing a high-fenced, street-side courtyard, was an exciting thing for the tradition-bound area of Cambridge around Harvard Square, or, for that matter, anywhere in urban America. The anonymity of the blank wall of striated plywood on the street was a polemical statement in a city with a heritage of colonial boxes of brick and clapboard set in a greensward. Franzen goes on, "It was the first time that I saw someone walk into a glass wall. The person fell to the floor more or less unconscious and I remember Philip looking very annoyed and saying something like 'damn fool!'"[25]

When Johnson graduated in 1943 he sold the house for $24,000, close to what it cost him to build. Many people, including Gropius, did not much like the house, either through pique over the "splash" caused by a rich, bright graduate student or, in Gropius's case, because of personal differences with Mies, Johnson's hero, or even abhorrence of Johnson's political past. Johansen added, "The house was stunning, it shocked us that he had that kind of money! I remember someone saying, 'What good luck! He'll never do it that well again!'"[26] Yet even today, a half-century later, Johnson bemoans the shallow roof overhang on the house's sides and rear: designers' regrets die hard.

After Harvard and before joining the wartime army, Johnson designed a modest, modern equipment barn for his family at Townsend Farms. He is rueful that it was the only building that he was asked to do in his hometown area. "For years Cleveland never asked me back. I had been politically naughty," he recalls.[27] Most of his time in the service was spent doing menial jobs like "peeling potatoes and the other things that army privates do," Johnson says, but he looks back on the experience with an appreciation of the broadening effect that lower-echelon military life had on his outlook. He believes his prewar political activity, which caused the FBI to start a file on him, prevented his being promoted above the rank of private.

After doing the required army time, Johnson returned to New York and set himself up as an "independent designer," first as a one-man office in a

Lexington Avenue apartment, later in larger quarters on East Forty-second Street. At Alfred Barr's insistence, he resumed his job at the Museum of Modern Art directing the Department of Architecture. Also at the museum was returned war veteran Eliot Noyes, a bright, attractive Harvard acquaintance of Johnson's, who was to be the museum's first Director of Industrial Design. In 1940, with the help of Johnson and architect Wallace Harrison, Barr had lured Noyes away from Gropius and Breuer's Cambridge office to work in New York at the museum. During the war, Noyes became a glider pilot stationed in Washington and occupied a Pentagon office next to Thomas Watson Jr. Watson would become head of IBM and Noyes's leading client when Noyes left the museum and started his practice in Connecticut.

All of Johnson's acquaintances at Harvard were soon established in New York, beginning or furthering their careers in architecture. Looking back, it was a hopeful time in America's cultural and financial capital as the nation shook off its wartime attitudes, and plans for resumption, renewal, and expansion of prewar ideas found life in the art and architecture world. The public, with a lingering postwar energy, was primed for the Now. Critic Robert Hughes observes that postwar America "fell in love with modernism." After the army, Johnson reconnected in New York with his old network of prim, monied culture, along with the offbeat Bohemia of Manhattan creative life. As before, Alfred Barr remained the articulate, eagle-eyed bridge between the two.

Johnson made new friends among the advancing postwar cultural elite, both up- and downtown. One was the sculptor Mary Callery, whom he met at an East Hampton cocktail party in 1947. Callery had left a studio overlooking the Seine in wartime Paris as the Germans advanced and returned to New York. With her was an important collection of paintings: "more Picassos than anyone in America" was the word at the Museum of Modern Art. Callery was also acquainted with New York architects, meeting Wallace Harrison, who was in Paris in 1927 with his wife Ellen Milton Harrison, a Long Island childhood friend of Callery's. Wally and Ellen Harrison were introduced to her Paris artist friends Henri Matisse, Alexander Calder, Fernand Lèger, and Aristide Maillol; Wally Harrison became a lifelong friend of Calder and Lèger's and a robust advocate of the best art for the big buildings he would later design. Harrison recalled that Mary Callery was "the most elegant and beautiful woman he had ever met." He remembered the vision of her "in a green dress, wearing an emerald the size of your fist."[28]

Tall, blonde, and striking, Callery was born in New York in 1904 and raised by wealthy parents in Pittsburgh and Manhattan. Besides being worldly, smart, and talented, she was fun and had money. When she and Johnson met, her elongated, figurative bronzes were being exhibited and receiving critical acclaim at the best New York galleries like Curt Valentin and Sidney Janis. She embodied both of the social poles that Johnson was drawn to: cultured old money and avant-garde creativity. Johnson had already heard about her trove of paintings through the alert Alfred Barr, and she and Philip immediately became very close friends, enjoying each other's company as often as possible over drinks and dinner. Twice married and divorced, and with a strong, independent, slightly Bohemian streak, Mary was one of a number of bright, attractive women that Johnson has held in close affection throughout his life. Of no small significance in her appeal to Johnson was the fact that after Johnson introduced them, she carried on a casual, romantic affair with Mies van der Rohe, his hero of the time. Mies designed a studio for her in Huntington, Long Island.

Mary Callery, New York City, mid-1940s.
Courtesy of Madeleine Callery Hussey.

Certainly Mary Callery had a way with artists and architects, particularly men. Rumors of her liaisons with Lèger and Pablo Picasso followed her to New York. In the early 1940s, when Callery returned from Paris, architect Wallace Harrison had become a major player in the city's corporate architectural world. He was a Rockefeller intimate through his wife Ellen, whose brother was married to Abby Rockefeller, the oldest child of John D. Rockefeller Jr. Harrison was the Rockefeller "court architect" and would, with a number of partners, undertake many large projects for various members of the family, beginning with Rockefeller Center in the 1930s, continuing with the United Nations Headquarters in the 1950s and Lincoln Center in the 1960s, and ending with Governor Nelson Rockefeller's enormous South Mall complex in Albany in the 1970s. Harrison would include the work of Lèger and Calder and other leading artists in his buildings and commissioned Mary Callery for a sculpture above the proscenium of the new Metropolitan Opera in Lincoln Center. In the late 1940s, Johnson's social chum became the cohesive figure responsible for Johnson's introduction to a Texas patronage that would be crucial to his fame and the architectural history of that state.

With his Harvard classmate Landes Gores now in his office to translate design sketches into working drawings, Johnson began getting a few commissions to design houses near New York City, the first for some people named Booth, who, Johnson remembers, "just walked into the museum one day and asked me to design a house for them in Westchester County. We talked about how much money it would cost, they said they couldn't afford it and they were right."[29] Its construction was not completed as drawn.

Another was for Mr. and Mrs. Eugene Farney, who were introduced to Johnson by his sister Theodate. Their 1947 house is located on a dune facing eastward to the Atlantic in Sagaponack, Long Island. Crisp, boxy, and wood-sheathed, the symmetrical H-shaped house is raised on wooden log piers above the sand and reflects aspects of Miesian design ideas and Breuer's Harvard teaching. Like many of Johnson's early houses, it has been altered.

While he was being asked to design a few residences, Johnson was also writing the first book about Mies van der Rohe, who was teaching and living in Chicago. In the late 1930s Johnson and Barr were instrumental in getting Mies out of Germany and into the United States. He was Barr's choice, and failed candidate, to design the new museum building on West Fifty-third Street. Then, through Barr, he was considered for a chair in Design at Harvard, something Mies quashed because Walter Gropius also wanted the job. Loyalty to the former Bauhaus head wasn't the issue; Mies felt the school should simply hire *him.* Soon Barr scored for Mies by convincing Mrs. Stanley Resor, a museum trustee, to hire Mies to design a summer house in Jackson Hole, Wyoming. That got him to America. It was 1937 and the German master of *Sachlichkeit,*[30] little known in the United States, sailed away from Nazi Germany to reconnoiter and sink roots in America's huge, varied world. In only a few weeks, he traveled west to see the Resors' site facing the Tetons and started a design for them. Mies was received warmly by the formidable, "anti-European" Frank Lloyd Wright at Taliesin in Wisconsin, and also accepted the director's post at the School of Architecture of the Armour Institute in Chicago (later the Illinois Institute of Technology [IIT]), all without being able to speak a full sentence of English.

Meanwhile in New York, drawings were signed "Philip Johnson, Designer," and Johnson had run afoul of New York State's building authorities since he did not have a license to practice architecture in the state. Legally he was not a real *architect.* He was told that he could no longer operate an architectural office without accreditation, so in late 1950 Johnson and Landes Gores packed up and moved his small office to a two-story red-brick building on the main street of the quiet, colonial-era Connecticut village of New Canaan. Gores already lived there. (After moving, Johnson failed the New York licensing exam repeatedly until, with tutoring, he passed it some years later.) The idyllic little town, an hour's drive north from the city, was already home to a handful of young Harvard-educated architects beginning their way as artist/professionals.

Eliot Noyes had moved his family out of New York and started an architectural office in New Canaan in 1947 with an IBM contract. He had discovered the charms of bucolic New Canaan from the air while looking for land to purchase for his family's house. He landed his rented plane and picked out some property from one of the numerous plots of rolling, open land around the village and soon started construction on a simple flat-roofed house, whose design was derived from the Harvard-Bauhaus teachings of Breuer and Gropius. Years later Noyes would recall that he was afraid to show the model of the house to his New Canaan neighbors: "There were no modern houses here then."[31]

Boston-born and personable, Noyes set up a small office as architect and industrial designer and, according to Johnson, became the "lodestar" that drew the Harvard group of architects one by one out of New York.[32] In Johnson's case it was a favor returned: Noyes's interest in modern architecture began many years before in the early 1930s at Harvard before the German émigrés arrived and made their mark. Johnson, an articulate and well-traveled fellow undergraduate and still a philosophy major, impressed Noyes back then as he expounded on the merits of the European modern architecture he had seen and the lack of important, relevant design at Harvard.

Following Noyes to the Connecticut countryside was his and Johnson's former teacher Marcel Breuer, who continued to commute to a New York office. In 1947, Breuer built a small frame hillside house marked with a dramatic cantilever. It was publicized widely with stunning photographs by Ezra Stoller. Next came Johnson's partner Landes Gores and John Johansen, both of whom joined Breuer and Noyes in building modern houses that conceded nothing to the semirural colonial fabric of shuttered, two-story white clapboard. "Packing boxes" was the natives' term for the flat-roofed intruders. The last to come was Johnson, who was drawn to New Canaan because Breuer, his erstwhile Harvard mentor, was there. Soon all would have client houses to design in the area.

The reunited college modernists, separated by the war after Harvard, shared a belief in the future of modern architecture. They were cordial competitors and came together with their wives for evenings of talk, food, and drink, with accordion music often provided by Noyes, the congenial catalyst for the gathering of talent. New Canaan clients joined the high-spirited get-togethers, which were often dominated by Johnson's witty intellect and brittle repartee. He was the peripatetic ringleader of the quiet, leafy New Canaan scene of ambitious young architects and their brave wives and adventurous clients. Though the architects and their clients felt they were "in front" with modern design, none knew they were unwitting players in a broad popular revolution. The war's upheaval of old ways—social, political, and cultural—affected the timeworn conventions of all architectural design, houses as well as high rises. The insular little town of New Canaan was soon to become, quite ingenuously, the cusp and reference point for modern design for much of the United States.

Prior to moving his office to New Canaan, Johnson was busy performing

Philip Johnson and Mies van der Rohe in the galleries of the exhibition "Mies van der Rohe," the Museum of Modern Art, 1947.
Courtesy of the Museum of Modern Art, New York.

the juggling act at which he thrived: mornings in his small office on East Forty-second Street, then uptown ten blocks in the afternoon to the museum, where he headed its Department of Architecture as a "noble obligation," and finally evenings out on the town. Johnson wrote the Mies book with the master's cooperation, traveling often to Chicago to interview him, studying his buildings in progress on the IIT campus and looking at the plans for unbuilt projects, particularly a steel-framed glass-walled house to be built near the Fox River outside of Chicago for a lady named Edith Farnsworth.

Johnson's book was published by the Museum of Modern Art in 1947 to coincide with a major retrospective exhibition there of the German-American's work. After completing the book Johnson spent a year preparing this major exhibition of the German master's work, which Mies himself designed. The personal wealth Johnson enjoyed afforded him a freedom none of his peers in the creative world had, though he never for a moment chose a life of leisure: working, creating, instructing, and planning filled his time and would always. His after-hour social life was varied and active as ever, seeing Mary Callery several times a week for cocktails and art-world gossip. Soon after he introduced Mies to Callery, she was on Mies's arm at the opening of his big exhibition at the Museum of Modern Art.

After Johnson's move to New Canaan Noyes soon talked him into looking for sites for a house and arranged for a realtor to show him around. "It was the first piece of property that was shown to me," Johnson recalls, "five acres of tall, dense scrub and large trees sloping down from an old stone wall on the road. There was an open, flat area on a bluff looking west with a grand view of the broad Rippowam Valley. I liked it immediately and didn't look any further."[33] He bought it an hour later.

Landes Gores recalled visiting the site on Thanksgiving Day with Philip, his sister Theodate, and Pam Gores:

> Philip's excitement was easily understood once we passed through the opening in the tumbled down old farmer's wall along Ponus Street and the indifferent woods, doubtless third growth and principally of ash. At once we were struck by the distant prospect of what we would later recognize as High Ridge in North Stamford.
>
> But we had seen nothing yet, Philip avowed, the place for his house was definitely not near the road, though this was the highest point. Down a long slope, the land flattened out, and, beyond another farmer's wall with a central gap, a virtually flat promontory stretched well over a hundred feet in each axis. For panorama the view yielded nothing to the prospect from higher up, but the topographical setting had gained a hundredfold. All three projecting faces consisted of gigantic rock chunks. The prow was virtually treeless, curiously so against the dense, spindly thicket all along the downslope. Beyond the rock ramparts rose a profusion of mature hardwoods below the dropoff to the Rippowam River valley that was so sharp and commanding, we gasped, inwardly at least: Philip had surely hit the jackpot this time.[34]

For several years Johnson had been making rude little sketches of a plethora of schemes for a country house, briefly considering New Jersey for its location. The designs derived from the European court-house designs of Mies van der Rohe. For two years Landes Gores worked from time to time on almost eighty schemes, most of them under Johnson's direction. Out of twenty-some clearly distinguishable approaches emerged the final scheme, an indication of the thoroughness of Johnson's search for the correct solution for his own house, and the uncertainty of a forty-year-old novice with more creative knowledge than creative means. But he had time and money to burn devising his personal statement.

According to Gores the idea of a house with glass exterior walls had intrigued Johnson since 1945, when he bought the property, but its technical feasibility eluded him until he saw Mies's all-glass scheme in early 1946. Most of the earliest sketches for his house beginning in 1945 employed glass walls with masonry, either as enclosures or dividers, in compositions of dual elements. Masonry arches, a modernist anomaly, appear in several sketches. In 1946, after his hard look at Mies's steel-and-glass design for Miss Farnsworth, Johnson focused on an all-glass design and spent several weeks with Gores on plan and siting considerations before a final resolution was reached. Construction began in early 1948 with New Canaan's best contractor.

Professor Eugene George, a native of Wichita Falls, Texas, and a graduate of the University of Texas at Austin, was a Harvard GSD student in 1949. He recalls that his heroes in architecture were Alvar Aalto, Mies van der Rohe, and especially Marcel Breuer, his favorite professor in the GSD. He went down to New Canaan with three others to see Breuer's and Noyes's houses. "We called up Johnson and asked if we could see his house," George recalls.

> *The New Yorker* and other magazines were already running glass-house cartoons and we were interested in seeing it. Johnson said, "Come on over!" The place was not finished; site work and landscaping and the little brick guest house were not complete but Johnson was living in the glass house and very cordial to us. It was a wet and bitter-cold day—he cautioned us to not track mud on the stone steps—and it was my first experience with radiant floor heating, which warmed the brick herringbone floor. The impression I had inside was being protected in the midst of a forest. It was sort of a "fireplace in the woods"; the brick cylinder dominated the transparent box. All the Mies furniture was in place and Johnson immediately credited the German master as inspiration for everything that we saw.
>
> He confided in us, "After the steel framework for the house was erected, I got up on the roof and shifted my weight back and forth, which caused the steel columns and beams to rack and move back and forth with my weight. I thought I had made a big mistake until the glass was installed and everything stiffened up."[35]

Finished, it was two structures: one a transparent, rectilinear cage near the bluff's edge, framed in steel, raised slightly on a brick stylobate, with glass doors centered on its four facades. The other piece was an opaque, all-brick linear block, off-axis with its vitreous companion thirty yards away. A centered slab door and three large round windows marked its west and east facades, respectively. It served as a guest house and housed mechanical equipment, a not unfitting adjunct role for the mute, menial structure. Before the glass house was finished, Johnson asked Mary Callery up to New Canaan on New Year's Eve 1948, the day he moved in. "We had a martini or two or five and toasted the new year and my new place and Mary ended up spending the night, sharing my platonic bed. She was my first and favorite guest," he recalled many years later.[36]

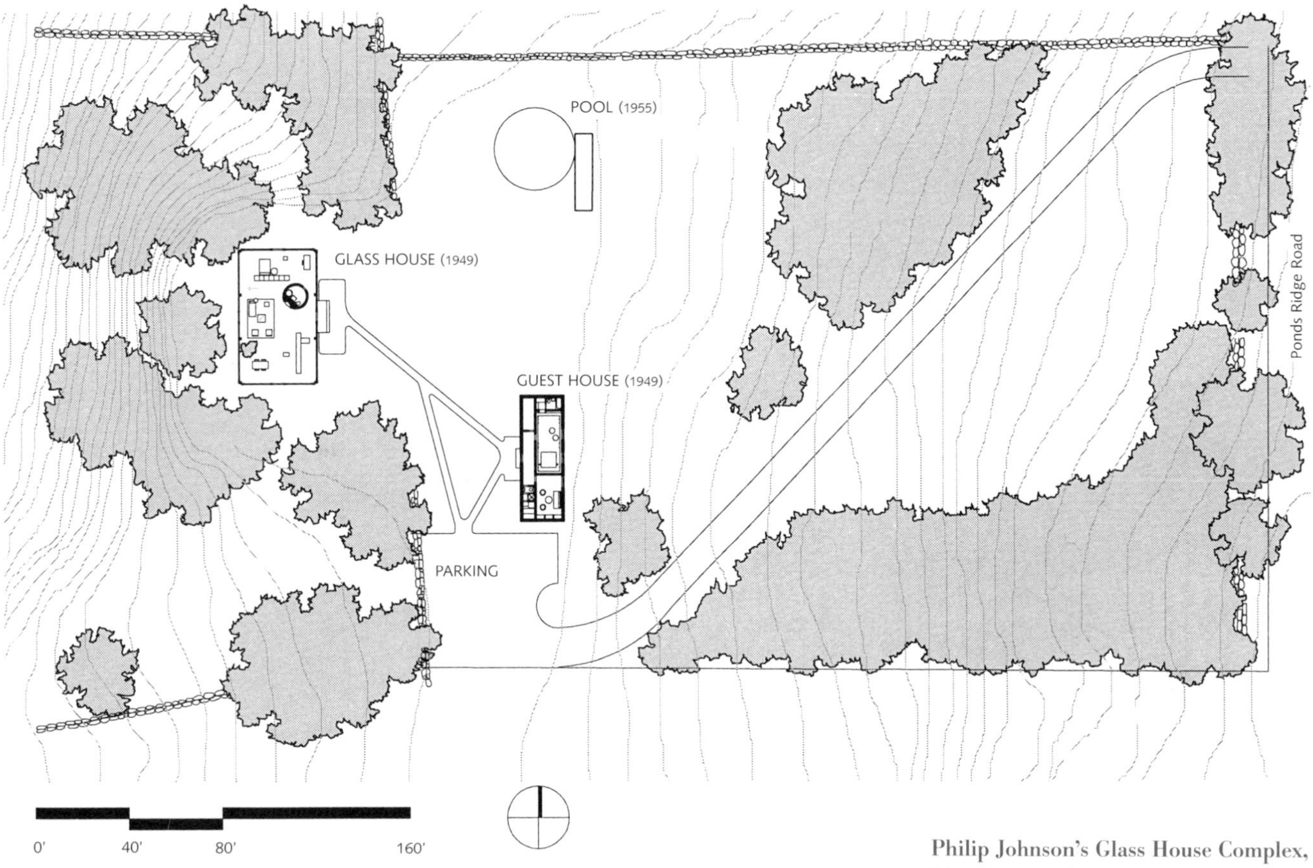

POOL (1955)
GLASS HOUSE (1949)
GUEST HOUSE (1949)
PARKING
Ponds Ridge Road
0' 40' 80' 160'

Philip Johnson's Glass House Complex, New Canaan, Connecticut, 1949; original 5-acre site plan, with Glass House and Guest House.

Glass House and Guest House, 1949; Philip Johnson, architect.
Photo by Ezra Stoller © Esto.

Photographic reproduction, *Suprematist Painting. Rectangle and Circle,* Kazimir Malevich, 1915. Courtesy of Busch-Resinger Museum, Harvard University.

When people saw the two completed buildings, the all-glass dwelling created a sensation in both the popular and professional press: it was simultaneously icon and iconoclast. While the derivation from Mies van der Rohe was obvious, it was too simple a conclusion to describe Johnson's glass house as a knockoff. The design for both Johnson structures was static and centered in a classical way, unlike the asymmetry Mies employed in his residential designs. What was dynamic in Johnson's composition was the arrangement of parts on the site: the glass house, guest house, a sculpture podium, the diagonal connecting paths, and the entry drive. A brick cylinder containing the fireplace and a bathroom was located off-center in the glass-walled 56' x 32' x 10'-6" space as counterpoint to the taut orthogonality of the bold, matter-of-fact one-room house. Freestanding cabinets of walnut articulated the bedroom and kitchen parts of the completely unfettered plan.

In 1950, the British journal *Architectural Review* published an eight-page article simply entitled "House in New Canaan, Connecticut" and generously illustrated it with plans and photographs. Johnson wrote the commentary for the piece and referenced no less than nine sources for the design. This was the age of the heroic, authoritarian creator exemplified by the architect Howard Roark in Ayn Rand's *The Fountainhead. No* architect credited his design's antecedents. It was an attractive and unique trait of Johnson's to credit his sources, now a common practice among critics and many architects. For the article he summoned up names as varied as nineteenth-century German Neo-Classicist Karl Friedrich Schinkel, Le Corbusier, Russian abstract painter Kasimir Malevich, and the classical historian Choisy, in addition to Mies van der Rohe. It could be read as a designer's full disclosure or scholarly name-dropping. When Howard Roark's model, the venerable old individualist Frank Lloyd Wright, who kept a covert, squinted eye on European design developments, was asked if the motifs in the paintings of Austrian artist Gustav Klimt were not the source of Wright's geometric glass designs, he replied that "the exposure to Klimt had 'refreshed' his work."[37]

In October 1949, *House and Garden* gave Johnson's house a ten-page spread. It was the second article about Johnson in a national periodical but the first of the hundreds of major pieces that would be written about him during the next fifty years. After noting how the house "of timeless elegance and classic simplicity" astonished the residents of Connecticut's Fairfield County, it made the first reference in print to Johnson's personality and unique view of modern architecture: "Philip Johnson is a man who combines warmth and sensitivity with a restless intellect, impatient of bromides." It went on prophetically, "His interest in architecture being scholarly as well as creative, he feels no compunction about looking backward for inspiration."[38]

The neighbors did not appreciate the numbers of sightseers who began to invade their village. They came every weekend to stretch a look over the high stone wall on Ponus Ridge Road at the extraordinary transparent dwelling standing in lonely splendor with its masonry partner on the bluff facing the valley and wooded hills. Modern house tours became an annual, money-raising event beginning in the spring of 1949 when seven houses by Noyes, Breuer, Gores, and others were shown to over a thousand visitors. Four years later the seven original houses had quadrupled, and New Canaan became "the place to see" among the architecturally literate. A joke made the rounds about a lonely Texas rancher who went to New York's Time Square one Sunday to meet people and found the streets empty. He asked a policeman where everyone was and the officer replied, "The Catholics are in church, the Protestants are on the golf course, and the Jews are up in New Canaan looking at modern houses."[39] While Jewish clients have been leading patrons of vanguard architecture, there is an acrid irony here: New Canaan at the time still had restrictions against non-Anglo-Saxons. The tight, tucked-back hamlet reluctantly received media coverage and the subsequent sightseers, with the center-stage Glass House receiving most of the attention. Critics recognized it early as a classic, a modern landmark.

Johnson enjoyed entertaining at his house. Nancy Millar O'Boyle of Dallas recalls that in the early 1950s, while she was still at Smith College, the young Dallas architect Enslie Oglesby was in New York and suggested that the two drive up to New Canaan to see Philip Johnson's house. It was summer and they put the top down on Nancy's convertible for the trip up the Merritt Parkway. Oglesby used a pay phone on New Canaan's Main Street to call Johnson. "Hello Mr. Johnson, I'm an architect from Texas and I would love to see your house." Johnson replied, "Of course, come on out. It's very kind of you to call, most people just drive in and gawk!" Oglesby and O'Boyle went out to Ponus Ridge and were received with great hospitality by Johnson and invited to join the group there enjoying a poetry reading.[40]

Nina Bremer, a longtime New Canaan resident and owner of one of Eliot Noyes's first houses, recalls being with Johnson and George Howe at an informal party at the Breuers one evening in the early 1950s. Howe was the esteemed Philadelphia architect who, with William Lescaze, designed the landmark modernist PSFS Building there and was then chairman of Yale's Department of Architecture. When Johnson and Howe left the Breuers to have dinner at Johnson's house, they took Nina Bremer with them. She recounts that Philip had made the place magical with dozens of votive lights placed next to the glass walls, had classical music on the phonograph, and had a dinner of perfection served by two waiters. Johnson, in his forties, and

Howe, in his sixties, spent a good deal of time at dinner talking about their psychiatrists.[41]

Johnson continued his curatorship at the Museum of Modern Art by commuting to and from Connecticut. He was "hot" now, proving himself to the public, if maybe not completely to himself, as a serious, possibly important, architect, a *builder* of buildings, not just a theorist. There was a lot of talk about the exceptional place he had built for himself in New Canaan, and because of this and the social contacts at the museum, he gained important commissions in the 1950s from MoMA and the Rockefellers. For this, he received criticism. There was truth enough that he obtained the museum commissions via his connections there, but with his intellect and enthusiasm Johnson has had a lifelong affinity for connecting up with wealthy people of taste and ambition. The museum affiliation was secondary.

As the publicity mounted around his exceptional dwelling, Johnson began to entertain there, conducting what has been described as America's only architectural salon. Students, architects, and critics like Yale's Vincent Scully visited there often for food, drink, and chat, continuing Johnson's familiar penchant for hosting.

Dallasite James Reece Pratt, a student at Harvard's GSD in the 1950s, was a part of several groups who traveled frequently down to New Canaan from Cambridge and New Haven. "There was a wonderful richness in the Glass House," Pratt recalls.

> I remember first going there in 1952 with the Master's Class on a crisp fall day at the height of the leaves and being enthralled with the reflections of red, wine, orange, green and yellow leaves bouncing around in the glass, contrasting against that black frame with the real leaves beyond.
>
> Another time, a warm summer night, I remember eating crème brûlée at a party for the historian Nikolaus Pevsner and watching the sky turn red from inside that transparency until the light faded and the flickering images of the guests grew stronger in the darkening glass. Philip of course had lighted the surrounding green podium to prevent the glass walls from going completely black. I went outside, and as I stood looking back in at the tableau vivant, fireflies looped around me.

On that trip to New Canaan, Pratt visited Johnson's second-story offices on Main Street. "I was impressed by [their] absolute order. There was nothing out, everything was in drawers, behind doors, and put away. Not a scrap of a sketch do I remember, only an impression of space as a light minimalist abstraction with many cupboards and drawers. There were only two people there."[42]

The Abby Aldrich Rockefeller Sculpture Garden, the Museum of Modern Art, fall 1953; Philip Johnson, architect. Courtesy of the Museum of Modern Art, New York.

Soon Johnson was at work on a 1950 addition to the museum, a seven-story black-steel and glass Miesian infill north of the West Fifty-third Street facade; it was demolished in 1981 for museum expansion. The outdoor space for sculpture between the original building and West Fifty-fourth Street was replaced by Johnson in 1953 by the highly praised Abby Aldrich Rockefeller Sculpture Garden. He designed a serene urban space, or rather a series of spaces, subtly defined by groups of trees (European weeping beeches and birches, and Japanese andromedas), linear pools of water, and a fourteen-foot-high brick wall on West Fifty-fourth Street. The composition of the parts harks back to the sliding planes of Mies van der Rohe's Barcelona Pavilion. The floor of the 80' x 200' space is paved with large slabs of a boldly marked grey-and-white marble ("It was cheap,"Johnson says) and articulated by level changes which make the space seem larger than it is. Being three feet lower than the museum's lobby floor gives the visitor a subtly orienting overview of the richness of the design. When Johnson is reminded of his claim to being a better landscape architect than architect, he says, "It is all the same art."

Philip Johnson in the Sculpture Garden on the occasion of his nomination to the Board of Trustees of the Museum of Modern Art, 1957. Courtesy of the Museum of Modern Art, New York.

One day in the late 1940s on the museum elevator, Mrs. John D. Rockefeller III asked Johnson to recommend an architect for her proposed town house, to be built for guests across midtown on East Fifty-second Street. When Johnson began listing names, Blanchette Rockefeller interrupted, saying,

"Philip, you are an architect, why don't *you* design the house?" And he did.[43]

Later, in 1957, he designed a private art gallery for Nelson Rockefeller. There were other jobs for the museum down the line, the most notable being the 1964 East Wing and extension of the Sculpture Garden.

Two exceptional Texans who often visited New York in the late 1940s were Dominique and Jean de Menil of Houston, recent French-American émigrés of impeccable social and cultural pedigree. She was a Schlumberger and a meditative intellectual, whose father and uncle pioneered and developed the world's most sophisticated system for subsurface oil discovery. Jean, also an intellectual, was a passionate and charming outgoing Parisian who, with his wife, shared an enthusiasm for modern art. Artist friends of the de Menils in New York and Paris were numerous. One was Johnson's friend Mary Callery, who was closely connected to the Paris and New York art worlds. In 1948, Callery was asked by Jean de Menil to recommend an architect for a modern house he planned to build for his growing family in Houston.

Mary Callery lived and worked in a converted garage in Manhattan in the East Thirties below Murray Hill, and it was there that Philip Johnson and Jean de Menil met and were charmed by each other. The architect, competent in French, had an exceptional background in the European culture of art and architecture but had no résumé as an architect. What he had was a bright,

John D. Rockefeller III Guest House, 242 East 52nd Street, New York City, 1950; Philip Johnson, architect. Photo by the author.

engaging, and confident personality and a grounded position in New York's contemporary art world, of which the Museum of Modern Art was the center. Being a trustee at the museum was a goal of Jean de Menil's. In addition, word of Johnson's revolutionary new house was creating a stir in the New York circles to which de Menil gravitated. Both men had magnetic, enthusiastic, and outspoken personalities; each had something the other wanted. Mary Callery's art-filled studio was a perfect setting for the meeting.

Johnson recalls, "Mary had wonderful taste, the place was immaculately laid out, and the living part where we had cocktails was lovely. Her bedroom was upstairs but the lower level was like the converted lofts you see today, but with all these wonderful paintings she had brought back from Europe. I recall many Picassos and a number of Lègers and a Matisse. Her tidy studio was in the rear and it was all attractive and neat. She was very beautiful, you know."[44]

Soon plans were made for Johnson to visit Houston to meet Dominique. When asked later if he had been excited about doing something so far away from New York, he replied without hesitation: "You bet I was excited—my first important house and in *Texas* to boot!"[45] The trip to the Southwest and the growing relationship with Dominique and Jean de Menil would lead to a half-century saga of architectural triumph and controversy for Johnson in Texas, the state which epitomized brash independence and bold ventures, a myth and state of mind far removed from the refined East Coast world of art and academia that had sustained and nurtured the forty-one-year-old transplanted Midwesterner.

John de Menil, 1968. Courtesy of the Menil Collection.

Chapter 1

With his intellect, personality, and cultural footing in New York, Philip Johnson would have been successful as an architect without ever leaving the East Coast. Yet the casual meeting with Jean de Menil in Mary Callery's Manhattan studio was the opening page in a story of lucky circumstances and connections among Texans that would lead to success for Johnson undreamed of by any of the participants. He was keen to design another house, other than for himself, even if it was in the large, faraway, provincial state. But he was adventurous and curious by nature, and as his long career would prove, enduringly eager for more work; the invitation down to remote and unknown Texas energized him with enthusiasm.

Johnson's acquaintance with the state was meager; he had only been there briefly, driving across its panhandle edge in the 1930s during his fascist digression. With barely more than stereotyped notions of cowboys and loud, garrulous millionaires in a desert landscape, he was unprepared for the Houston of the late 1940s. It was a verdant, semitropical inland port city—New Orleans plus Western expansiveness—possessing an informal atmosphere, a population smaller than 350,000, and an economic base in cotton and lumbering. There was no spring or fall season to speak of, barely a discernible winter, and the humid summers, breeze-softened by the Gulf of Mexico forty-five miles to the south, were often compared to those of Bombay. For years it was seen as "small-town" compared to the more "citified" Dallas. A burgeoning petrochemical industry was beginning to create great wealth which would ultimately build great buildings. But it never occurred to Johnson when his plane touched down in the unremittingly flat place that he would spend so much time and energy there for the next fifty years. It only took a quick look around for him to conclude, wrongly as time proved, that it was an unlikely place for anything remarkable to occur in the field of his passions: fine art and architecture. "There wasn't much there" was his offhand way of putting it. He would, however, spend important years helping create a "there" for the city, which became a twentieth-century landmark of influential architecture.

The easy city, laced by meandering bayous, had two universities: the sedate and conservative Rice Institute (Rice University in 1960), housed in its 1912 Ralph Adams Cram buildings of inspired Neo-Byzantine eclecticism, and the newer, more democratic University of Houston, with a shell-limestone-faced, modernistic main building under construction on its raw campus near the Ship Channel which led to Galveston Bay. The city's Southern persona was symbolized by exclusive and genteel River Oaks, a large upper-income enclave west of downtown, laid out on winding, tree-shaded streets with an amalgam of stately houses, many distinguished: Georgian and Tudor, New England Colonial, Spanish Colonial, and most appropriately, Southern Colonial. Since the 1930s a few modernistic houses had appeared in River Oaks.

The Western, "frontier" aspect of the city was embodied in the annual, ceremonial cattle drive and rodeo, held in the city's Coliseum (1939), a bulky multipurpose Art Deco building downtown, which also housed the town's performance space, the Music Hall. The touring dancer Paul Draper once left the auditorium concert stage in a fury over the rising and falling roar of a deafening roller derby taking place in the cavernous, adjoining sports arena.

The city's streets, only sporadically developed with buildings, were laid out in large, flat gridiron patterns that stretched boundlessly across the coastal plain, north-south and east-west, with many empty, grassy blocks. Several miles straight south of the downtown district—a concentration of offices, ho-

Aerial view, downtown Houston, 1952. Photo by Jack F. Laws; courtesy of Stephen Fox.

tels, stores, and theaters arranged along a broad Main Street—was Hermann Park, with Rice Institute and the Museum of Fine Arts (1924) located nearby. These were part of a district planned in the early twentieth century on the open edge of town on principles of the then-popular City Beautiful movement. This area, near the ranking residential districts of the time, and later distinguished by its mature *allées* of live-oak trees, is today the city's most beautiful planned urban-design element.

As in most American cities, some of the business leadership of Houston took responsibility for encouraging cultural well-being. In most cases, this well-meant obligation was not attuned to an appreciation of contemporary art. It was in the manner of dutiful stewardship that cultural decisions affecting public institutions were usually determined by a wealthy, conservative elite. Houston was no different from other Southern cities in this respect, but the period following the war, the middle 1940s, brought a heightened sense of cultural awareness coinciding with a construction boom that swept the country. Everywhere there was a burst of pent-up energy to remake the familiar, prewar world. Downtown Houston's blocks were a checkerboard of construction sites for large office buildings, while in suburban living rooms to the west, Jean de Menil was encouraging a core of art-hungry newcomers to form a contemporary arts group as an antidote to the stodgy local arts establishment.

The Blaffers, Cullinans, and Wiesses were oil families already in their second generations, with an active interest in art. They held control at the handsome but understaffed Museum of Fine Arts near Hermann Park. The museum's director, architect and historian James Chillman Jr., divided his time there with teaching at the nearby Rice Institute. Though the museum was the first building in Texas built specifically as an art museum, its collection was typical of such institutions in the country's hinterlands: a smattering of second-rank European paintings and sculpture with temporary shows of work by American-born academic artists. Though the winds of cultural change were building up nationwide, in Houston the surface was undisturbed. It was an innocent and uninspiring scene to Johnson, the New York sophisticate.

The fluid population movement across the country that began in the postwar 1940s was bringing new blood and "worldlier" viewpoints to booming Texas communities as varied in character and size as Houston, Dallas, and Midland. This mostly male infusion into the state's business and professional structure included ambitious Big Ten graduates from the Midwest as well as tweeded Ivy Leaguers who moved in "as if they had been sent for," as a long-time Houston native observed about some new arrivals from the University of Virginia. The newcomers, possessing feelings of superiority but eager to take

Dominique de Menil in Venezuela, mid-1940s.
Courtesy of the estate of Dominique de Menil.

part, began to redefine civic decision making in large and small Texas cities. Their ideas were fresh and often brash: an out-of-stater caused an uproar in Midland when he recommended that the school board give numbers to the growing number of elementary schools and drop the traditional Texas Hero designations. The state absorbed the new blood, however, though sometimes reluctantly, and slowly began to lose some, but only some, of the rough edges of its "frontier-colony" persona.

The postwar emigration to Texas included Dominique Schlumberger and Jean de Menil, who brought their young family to Houston from France. Jean came to head the Texas operations of the international Schlumberger oil well logging company founded by Dominique's uncle and father. Earlier, while Dominique remained in wartime Paris with their two small children, Jean worked secretly in the French Resistance traveling through Europe on "business trips," conducting cloak-and-dagger missions for the underground. Though he held and scorned the title of baron, changing his name to John when he and Dominique became citizens in 1961, de Menil went out of his way to avoid pretentious trappings; Marguerite Johnston Barnes of Houston recalls that "John just loved things American and *Texan!*"[1] From the beginning of their life in Houston, he and Dominique identified with progressive, egalitarian causes, and as time went on, their political positions were controversial in "frontier" Houston. Though of aristocratic lineage, with an outgoing and enthusiastic personality, John de Menil grew up without the comfort that his heiress wife enjoyed as a Schlumberger and member of a wealthy

French Huguenot family. Though imbued with continental charm, John de Menil would always push a little harder.

In their twenties, they met at a Versailles ball to which neither wanted to go, and soon after a late evening of conversation, fell in love. The proud, but impecunious, baron and the willowy intellectual married in 1931. Dominique, who had studied physics and mathematics at the Sorbonne, and John, who earned a night school law degree while working in a Paris bank, shared intellectual and cultural interests from the beginning. John, who left his bank job and joined the Schlumberger company, was the more ambitious and socially outgoing of the two, certainly at first. Dominique, who would never lose her reserve, and whose sense of "mission" would develop later, was the more thoughtful and introspective. Marguerite Barnes, a journalist and longtime friend, described them as "the perfect pair, a true partnership in the best sense of the word."[2]

Before leaving France ahead of the Nazis, and through a chance meeting, the couple happily fell under the influence of a Dominican priest, Father Marie-Alain Couturier, an avid authority on contemporary art whose main interest lay in bringing modern art and the Catholic Church together (being responsible for the chapels in France designed by Matisse, Lèger, and Le Corbusier). The priest took the young couple to see Picasso and Georges Braque in the galleries and urged them to begin buying modern art.

Through Couturier, their lives changed slowly but dramatically as they began collecting a few small, mainly Surrealist, paintings. Dominique's conservative parents were bewildered and concerned the young pair would run out of money to live on when they asked the Surrealist Max Ernst to paint Dominique's portrait. Neither cared for Ernst's rendering, and they stored the picture away, wrapped in brown paper, on top of an armoire. When they recovered the painting, untouched, after the German occupation of Paris, their maturing sensibilities saw the beauty of what Ernst had done. Dominique and John honored Ernst twenty years later in Houston with the first U.S. exhibition of his work. By then they were collecting art on a large scale, which would further increase in magnitude in the 1970s and 1980s. As humanitarian patrons of all the arts, including architecture, the Menil family would have no peers.

When Dominique and John decided to build a modern house for their large, young family, which now included five children, they sought advice. Mary Callery was the "link," according to Dominique de Menil: "Mary was well known in New York as a sculptor and owner of European paintings. She was a great friend of the architect Mies van der Rohe, who had opened her eyes to the beauty of Cycladic art, so she had a couple of Cycladic statues and also a couple of Schwitters."

Mies was her sometime lover and Philip was her chum, so Callery replied by giving the couple the names of the architects she knew best: "If you want to spend $100,000 get Mies, but if you only want to spend $75,000 get Philip Johnson."[3] The lower figure appealed to John—the Schlumberger wealth had not begun to flow yet—and though Johnson was a neophyte, he was building that house in Connecticut that everyone in New York was talking about, and he was an important fixture at the Museum of Modern Art. John de Menil met Johnson in Mary Callery's art-filled studio and, charmed by his wit and worldly ways, asked him to come to Houston to meet Dominique.

Before Johnson flew to Houston the de Menils had concluded a search for land by purchasing several acres of undergrowth and trees on San Felipe Road, a straight, east-west thoroughfare which passed through secluded River Oaks. The three-acre Menil property, once part of a pig farm, was in a small entity called Briarwood, which is surrounded by the exclusive River Oaks development, put together in the 1920s by the Hogg brothers. Though San Felipe ("San-FILepee") was basically a service street serving the back doors and garages of the posh River Oaks denizens, John Blaffer, of the Humble Oil family, and his wife, Camilla, had recently built a large, two-story contemporary-style house on adjoining property. The de Menils wanted a totally different kind of house. They wanted it to be unpretentious, modern, and functional, in the spirit of the times as they saw them. Marguerite Barnes recalls that the Menil zeal to improve Houston culture was early evidenced in their selection of Johnson: "John and Dominique wanted to set an example."[4]

While there were several good architects practicing in Houston, there were no designers of International Style houses there, or in any other Texas city for that matter. Karl Kamrath was a very capable disciple of Frank Lloyd Wright, and John F. Staub and Birdsall P. Briscoe were distinguished River Oaks architects of eclectic styles, but these were local architects without the prestige associated with "out-of-town" professionals, who would always have great influence in Texas. While he loved being a "Texan" and wanted his new house to set a design standard, John de Menil's emotional and intellectual strings were tethered tightly to New York and beyond, where the bright lights of the avant-garde flourished and to which he wanted entree. Suave and articulate Johnson, though inexperienced as an architect, enjoyed the reflected glory and snob appeal of his metropolitan associations, and while sophisticated and worldly, the de Menils, particularly John, were not immune to big-city glamour. Johnson's flippant remark "Any New York architect with a briefcase is very persuasive" could perhaps have come only from a transplanted Midwesterner, himself fervently "starstruck."

"There just wasn't much to Houston" is the way Johnson described it in later years; "I couldn't understand how anyone lived there, but that was before the personality of the place came through to me: I found out those people weren't afraid to try *anything!* There was a yearning there for a new start."[5] Johnson was let down when he saw the house that the de Menils lived in at the time, later recalling it as "a tract house." It was a simple two-story, gabled box located on the smaller-scale western edge of River Oaks, near undeveloped forested land to the west. John de Menil liked the house for the large side yard and the attic bedrooms for his growing family. There was no eye-catching art yet on the Menil walls, though the living room had a small Surrealist painting by Yves Tanguy, the dining room held a handsome Joan Miró, and in the entry was a painting, *Red Man,* by the Mexican painter Rufino Tamayo. Not quite enough to turn Johnson's head.

"They were so *poor!* They had this big piece of property but wanted to build the house far enough back so that the front part could be sold off; definitely uncertain about the future."[6] Johnson's growing reputation as a designer with expensive construction tastes might have preceded him to Houston; clients often "talk poor" to their architects, particularly ones with Johnson's wealthy ways. Several years later, in the early 1950s, he told Do-

First Menil house in Houston, Chevy Chase Drive, River Oaks.
Photo by the author, 1998.

minique's sister Sylvie Boissonnas that a million dollars was the very least she could expect to spend on the house he was designing for her.

The truth was that Dominique and John de Menil always lived modestly, without ostentation, though the later flood of Schlumberger money allowed them to gather and share great riches of art philanthropy. Their manner of living in Houston through the years could not have been more at odds with those Texans with new wealth and the flamboyance that went with it. Their familiarity with the trappings and protocol of affluence and social position was an ingrained European one: a reserved, conservative low-profile manner coupled with a liberal sense of social responsibility. Their private life was always quiet, their public life in the arts would always be one of grand-scale largesse. Acquisition and sharing and education would be the equally passionate and ruling trinity of their lives.

They had never built, or seen built, a house, much less an uncompromisingly modern one by a barely proved New York architect, though Johnson was bursting with the enthusiasm and confidence of the beginner. "We were so new at this: we sought advice every step of the way,"[7] Dominique de Menil recalled many years later. There was something of a gamble in the de Menils' selection of the unproved Johnson, but not an awesome one. If he didn't work out they could get someone else. What was clear was their conscious, deliberate resolution to set an example to the community. Said Marguerite Barnes: "They really had the thought that if they brought someone like Philip Johnson to Houston and he designed a nice house, it would lead to better architecture in the city. They definitely wanted to improve the climate even then."[8] It might also give John de Menil the cachet he sought with the New York culturati.

Until the de Menils' interest in art and civic culture heightened, Dominique was a conscientious mother raising five small children and would undoubtedly have been content in a dwelling less prepossessing than what was promised from the charming, knowing disciple of Mies van der Rohe. While she said, "Philip gave me exactly what I wanted," it's doubtful that she knew with much precision exactly what she was seeking, at least in terms of image. In those days, before the flood of "house magazines," few clients, particularly those new at the game, came with arbitrary design specifics for their architects to follow. Dominique agreed with John about the general goal of a functional, durable house, expressive in modern, "democratic" terms: no hierarchy of better and lesser spaces and finishes, one easy to maintain without servants. Johnson listened to Dominique and in response led them to expect generous walls of glass in the Mies manner and an open, fluid floor plan of spaces devoid of "archaic" rooms like a formal entry or dining room, almost a "one-room house," as Dominique de Menil later described it. Johnson's initial 1/8"-scale floor plan for the de Menils remained, without significant revisions, the diagram that evolved into the house that was built.

Dominique de Menil's first meeting with Johnson left her impressed with his energy, enthusiasm, and intelligence. "As you know he's quite a charmer," she recalls with a soft French accent, "and he is so intelligent and he tried to understand what I wanted—just vaguely—and came up with a brilliant solution immediately which we were extremely pleased with. I was so innocent, I had never built a house before."[9]

Johnson was in turn impressed with her refinement and reserved intellect. He noted the contrast between the smooth, forceful, outgoing character of John, not typical for a Frenchman, and the more retiring, ruminative Dominique, though architect Anderson Todd recalls her, in her forties at the time, as "sexy." Johnson was to later describe her as the "powerhouse" and the idea person of the team, while John was, in Johnson's words, the expeditor and "mover" of their evolving, ambitious schemes of cultural betterment for Houston. Once when they visited The Glass House, Philip's sister Jeannette recalls that after lunch John washed the dishes while Dominique and Johnson talked philosophy.

As the French newcomers' mission to improve Houston's cultural life picked up speed in the 1950s and 1960s, feathers were often ruffled among the old Houston caste that controlled the Museum of Fine Arts. There was resentment among some of the old guard about the opinionated, seemingly high-handed ways of the French arrivistes. The Blaffer family, considered Houston's ranking art and culture mavens, had recently built a new wing for the museum in 1954 and was angered when its offer of one of its old-world paintings to the museum was turned down. James Johnson Sweeney was the MFA director at the time. John de Menil had brought Sweeney to Houston from New York's Guggenheim, and the flamboyant Irishman claimed the painting was not authentic. The Blaffers were furious and blamed John de Menil. He and Dominique and Jane Blaffer Owen became close eventually, Jane developing a great admiration for them both, particularly the spirited, charismatic John. In 1979, when the tragic midnight news of the death of their daughter Carol reached Kenneth and Jane Owen, word spread and Dominique de Menil was at the Owens' door early the next morning.[10]

Dominique de Menil and Alfred Barr Jr. at museum exhibition, University of St. Thomas, Houston, 1967. Courtesy of the Menil Collection.

As he would throughout his life, Johnson enjoyed being the loquacious big-city architect in Houston, receiving the curious admiration of the locals, who were eager to rub shoulders with one with such metropolitan allure. He obliged them by spinning gossipy tales of Manhattan's art world and charming, self-deprecating anecdotes of his beginnings as an architect but soon was bored, making him anxious to get back to the intellectual and emotional stimulation of New York and MoMA and New Canaan, where his house was being built. He was already thinking about a scheme for the de Menils.

There was no pressing design business in his office, run by Landes Gores, but projects, mainly houses, were beginning to develop as news spread of his remarkable dwelling in Connecticut. The Rockefeller Manhattan guest house was coming up, as was the first black-steel and glass street-side addition of the Museum of Modern Art, both astute renderings of Miesian, International Style formula. And he was in charge of preparations to construct a house by Marcel Breuer in the museum's garden to demonstrate to the public the design potentials of "low-cost" modernism; the handsome little house proved to be more high-style than low-cost, though. He continued dividing his time between New Canaan and New York.

The design he presented to the de Menils was for a straightforward flat-roofed house, respectful of existing large pine trees, with all rooms oriented either to open courts or the large, tree-covered backyard on the south. One entered a very wide entry hall, skirting a brick-walled courtyard on the left, whose all-glass interior walls connected entry and living room. The living room, centered in the house, also faced a terrace and the deep, green yard on the south through another wall of floor-to-ceiling glass. The master bedroom and guest room flanked the living room on the east, while the children's bedrooms, with the only corridor in the house, were "zoned" in a wing to the south behind a playroom. The kitchen, close to the playroom and carport, was commodious, with room for a large table and chairs, not unlike the kind of space found in American as well as French farmhouses. (This was a period in America, following the war, when the continued use of domestic servants was considered passé, though not in Texas or the South.)

As built, the 5,600 sq. ft. wood-frame house is set back from the street, and has a facing of salmon-colored brick forming a long, solid wall, topped by a wide white fascia. The wall is broken only by a flush glass entry and a series of horizontal kitchen windows set low to the right, which Dominique added to the plans "so that the cook would have something to look at besides blank walls." The glossy black floor, an inexpensive Mexican cement tile that Dominique had discovered, became an elegant foil for the exuberant furnishings and fine art that came to enhance the spaces flowing beneath ten-and-a-half-foot ceilings, which Dominique had asked Johnson to raise from nine feet. It was the first International Style house built in Texas; a puzzled River Oaks matron dubbed the low-slung structure "ranch-house modern."

Neither of the de Menils felt comfortable with the severe, Miesian interiors that Johnson wanted ("We wanted something more *voluptuous*"), so they called on America's preeminent couturier, Charles James, to help with colors and furniture. Born in Surrey, England, in 1906,[11] James was educated for a while at Harrow, where he became friends with classmate Cecil Beaton and Beaton's pal Gertrude Lawrence. His stern, military father pulled him out of Harrow after some of his high jinks with Beaton. Following his study of music in France he was a "fine pianist," according to Dominique de Menil's description.

James eventually began his career designing hats in Chicago, his heiress mother's home. He would later have sumptuous salons in New York and London which were patronized by the European *haute chic* and the likes of Marlene Dietrich and wealthy women like Mrs. William Randolph Hearst Jr. and Mrs. William Paley. Elfin, dark, and flamboyant, noted for the meticulous, "architectural" construction of his costly, dramatic ball gowns, Charles James had been making clothes for Dominique de Menil on the recommendation of a Paris friend, the Duchesse de Gramont. Actually, John de Menil had the audacious idea of getting James, a dress designer, to help them as consultant on the interiors of the house.

James made a theatrical sweep into Houston during the house's construction and charmed and amused the de Menils' friends with his loquacious, attention-getting manner, not unlike Johnson's. "He talked as much as Philip," one friend remembered. "Charlie called from the airport and said that he needed a truck, that he had brought a present for the house," Dominique de Menil recalled in the 1990s in her soft accent. "He had a great opaline vase that wouldn't fit in a taxi, and after he arrived at the new house carrying the huge apple-green vessel in his arms, he put it down in the unfinished living room and ordered some white lilac from somewhere which he placed in the vase, over there where the two chairs are. He said that it would give him inspiration."[12] Responding to their wish for a piano in the living room, James had a full-scale mock-up of a grand piano constructed of orange crates and pasteboard for the appointed space to get, as he put it, "the *weight* of the room."

Noted for his unorthodox combinations of color and texture, James's schemes for Dominique and John's house ran to cerise and chartreuse velvet for the doors and walls of one of the house's hallways, ornately carved chairs by the Victorian cabinetmaker John Belter, and James's own custom-designed, sensuously curvacious seating, which caused one Houston matron to observe: "Charles James designs furniture that looks like ball gowns and ball gowns that look like furniture."

James only sold a limited number of his fastidiously constructed ready-to-wear dresses. In the 1950s and 1960s Dallas's Stanley Marcus bought his dresses for Neiman-Marcus and, while referring to him as "crazy Charlie James," also described him as a "real genius" whose costly creations were hard to sell in

Dallas. In the 1950s Marcus paid James $1,250 for each of the few dresses he purchased. When Charles James received the coveted Neiman-Marcus fashion award in Dallas in 1954, he appeared in tuxedo jacket, blue jeans, and red socks. After an extravagant life of acclaim, being described by one critic as the first American designer to treat fashion as *art,* he was, at the end, unable to control his life and died impoverished in New York's Chelsea Hotel in 1978.[13]

Johnson, gripped in modernist rectitude, more or less turned his back on the Menil house because of the free style of the interiors. To publish photographs of the "heretical" interiors was, for him, out of the question. Much later, in the 1970s, after the cultural revolution in design taste led by the likes of Robert Venturi and Charles Moore, who made personal, eclectic style a respectable component of the vanguard, Johnson, with revised feelings about modernism, spoke with admiration of the way his first, most important Texas clients lived in his Miesian house, surrounded by books, unique possessions, and world-class art.

Dominique de Menil's very personal mise-en-scène there—and according to Johnson and others it was hers, not Charles James's—is today the triumphant aspect of Johnson's first project in Texas. Until her death in 1997, she continued to honor Johnson's original architectural concept, making only minor changes to the house's design. The large custom wood-framed sliding glass doors for the house proved heavy and unwieldy and were a cause of regret to Johnson, but Dominique remonstrated: "Oh, but Philip, your proportions are there and that's what counts!" She also never changed anything that Charles James did in fabrics and colors—though they became tattered and faded—and wore, with great chic, James's classic, vintage clothing. In her late eighties, standing in the glass doorway of her art-filled house, Dominique de Menil mused about Johnson, "I think of him very, very often. There are several kinds of genius in the world and Philip is one of them."[14]

Before the house's construction, on the advice of others, and to Dominique de Menil's regret, she and John signed a contract with the lowest, and, as it turned out, less than competent, bidder, whose inexperience caused structural problems later. Word soon got around, however, that a house by Philip Johnson, modernist scholar of the Museum of Modern Art, was going up on San Felipe Road in the middle of River Oaks. Houston architect Hugo V. Neuhaus Jr., an acquaintance of the de Menils and a classmate of Johnson's at Harvard, was brought in by John de Menil to coordinate the house's construction with Johnson's office. Neuhaus, member of a prominent family and married to a Chicago heiress, became distracted by the itch to start up his own practice and soon designed two Miesian/Johnsonian houses: an exquisite one for Nina J. Cullinan on a wooded bayou site and a larger, very refined

Menil House

San Felipe Road, Houston, 1950

View of house from San Felipe Road; translucent courtyard roof canopy by Barnstone & Aubry, 1965.

PHILIP JOHNSON, ARCHITECT. PHOTOS BY PAUL HESTER, 1994–1998.

Entrance door from driveway; courtyard canopy on left.

Terrace on the south outside of the living room.

View toward living room from foyer past courtyard: Italian settee, mid-18th century; painting on right, *People Begin to Fly*, Yves Klein, oil, 1961; sculpture on floor, *Espace Interieur*, Takis, bronze, 1963; sculpture on wall, *The Death Bird Builds a Nest*, Jim Love, welded iron, 1958; sculpture next to folding screen, *Personage With Upraised Arms*, Dogon people, wood, 17th or 18th century.

Passage between living room and bedroom hallway; works on paper by Juan Gris, Max Ernst, Fernand Leger, Roberto Matta, and others; paintings by Georgio de Chirico, Paul Klee, Rene Magritte, Leger, and Ernst.

Living room, northeast corner; Henry Belter-style side chair, rosewood and black leather, mid-19th century; painting, *La Clef de Verre*, Rene Magritte, oil, 1925.

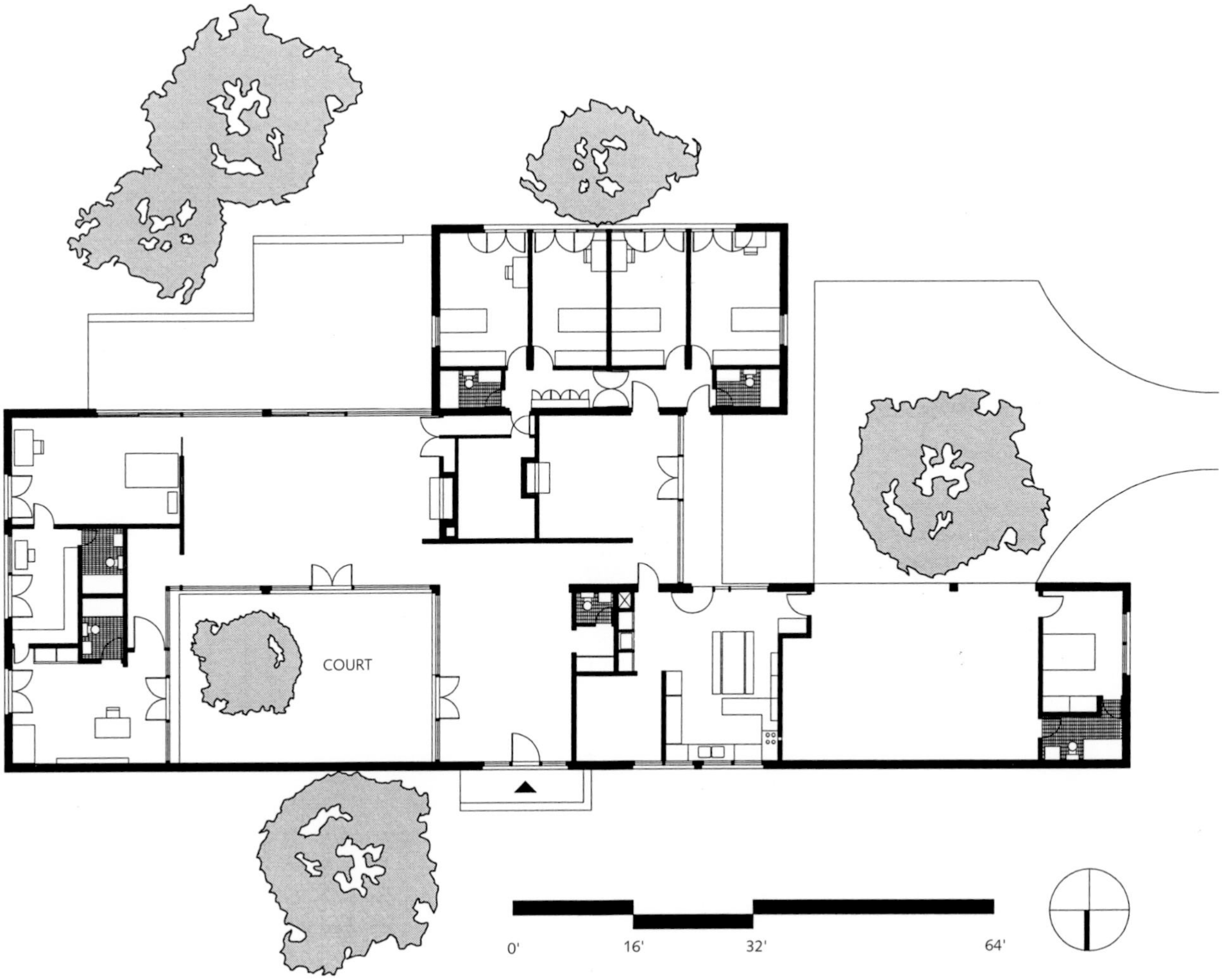

Menil house drawing; floor plan.

one for his family on a prominent River Oaks site. Neuhaus remained, like most old Houstonians, in awe, if not bemusement, of the de Menils' democratic-cum-cosmopolitan style and liked to recall a delicious candlelight dinner he and his wife had with Dominique and John in the very functional kitchen of their new house, beneath a large, primitive, wall-hung wooden cross from Mexico and near casually hung small paintings by Braque and Picasso.

Howard Barnstone with Buckminster Fuller at museum exhibition, University of St. Thomas, Houston, 1968. Courtesy of the Menil Collection.

Howard Barnstone, a young, sophisticated Yale architecture graduate and newly arrived teacher at the University of Houston, took an avid interest in the Menil house. He brought his classes over to see the construction and soon met John de Menil. Barnstone was one of the few people in Houston who knew who Philip Johnson was and what he represented in the big picture of art and architectural culture outside of Texas. The cultivated and well-traveled young Easterner also knew, with admiring interest, that the de Menils were promoting appreciation of contemporary art in Houston. If Johnson was Mies's number one "groupie," Barnstone became Johnson's number one Houston "groupie" and advocate. Thus began mutual and fruitful relationships for Barnstone with John de Menil and Johnson, both of whom he idolized until Barnstone's death in 1985. Barnstone often referred to de Menil as "father."

Barnstone became and remained the de Menils' "house architect" in both senses of the term. When the house developed problems during and after construction, Barnstone was the one John de Menil called in the middle of the night when the roof leaked. An observer at the time remembers, "Howard was the 'maintenance man' over there for years."[15] In the mid-1960s when Dominique de Menil wanted an enclosure for her tropical plants in the house's courtyard, she turned to Barnstone and his partner Eugene Aubry. Aubry devised a translucent "bonnet" of stretch fabric on a light steel frame formed in high vaults.

Howard became almost a member of the Menil family and went on to design a number of important Schlumberger projects throughout the country and abroad while maintaining two successive partnerships with Houston architects (Preston H. Bolton Jr., Eugene E. Aubry) and continuing an influential tenure at the University of Houston. He wrote two distinguished books, one on John Staub, the Houston establishment's favorite architect, and another on Galveston's architectural heritage, with photographs by Ezra Stoller and Henri Cartier-Bresson. Cartier-Bresson's participation was secured through John de Menil, then head of Magnum, the international photography agency. Both books are considered definitive of their subjects.[16]

Barnstone's inclusion in and pursuit of the Menil/Johnson scene assured him a firm place in the city's well-born cultural world. Through his youth, talent, and intellect, his association with Johnson developed into a close, acolyte-priest relationship. It proved provident for the aging New Yorker thirty-five years later when Johnson was selected to design the new architecture building at the University of Houston, where Barnstone was a longtime professor. In addition to securing the Schlumberger commissions through John de Menil, Barnstone remained close, at-the-elbow, in every future Menil cultural or architectural activity. His wife, actress and sculptor Gertrude Levy, describes her husband's life as one fulfilled by Menil patronage and friendship. John de Menil's death from cancer in 1973 was a devastating blow to Barnstone, who by then was suffering severe bouts of depression. His enduring legacy was the standards of excellence in architecture which he held and transmitted to hundreds of students at the University of Houston for forty years.

In 1943, Houston high school graduate Burdette Keeland Jr. went up to Texas A&M College in College Station, with his father urging him into mechanical engineering. That didn't work out. Keeland wanted to be an architect and after wartime service transferred to the University of Houston, where architect Donald Barthelme was getting attention with his unorthodox methods of teaching modern architecture. Keeland found his way to one of newcomer Howard Barnstone's classes, where the two developed a strong friendship—there was only a four-year age difference—which keyed into an equally valuable one for Keeland with Barnstone's future mentor, Philip Johnson. Keeland says that "Howard would do anything for a young designer, and he must have thought I had some talent." Their teacher-student relationship bloomed as, according to Keeland, "Barnstone crammed Hitchcock and Johnson's *International Style* book down our throats."[17]

Burdette Keeland Jr., 1950. Photo by Fred Winchell; courtesy of Burdette Keeland Jr.

"Barnstone represented everything that I *wasn't.* He grew up in the East, went to Yale, and traveled to Europe with his mother twice a year, while I hadn't gotten any farther than the Texas Centennial in Dallas. He had a deeper knowledge of architecture and art than anyone I had ever known," Keeland recalls.[18] On the other hand, in Barnstone's eyes, Philip Johnson had more knowledge than anyone *he* had ever known and became Barnstone's heroic mentor as, in the early 1950s, Johnson developed into Houston's articulate spokesman for modernism. Keeland fell under the spell of both Barnstone and Johnson and became a close friend and collaborator of the former and a professional confidant and "advance man" for the latter, twenty years his senior. After Keeland had become one of Houston's leading designers of modern buildings in the 1950s, Barnstone and Johnson arranged for him to attend the Yale graduate architecture school, where Johnson taught regularly and his protégé Paul Rudolph was dean. Keeland became a lifelong, devoted friend to Johnson in Houston, and many years later, the elder architect's example would cause Keeland to say, "Philip has added ten years to my life!"

In 1948, when John de Menil could not interest the staid Museum of Fine Arts in showing more modern art, he joined some new acquaintances in organizing a Contemporary Arts Association, the CAA (later the Contemporary Arts Museum, CAM), for showing and sharing modern art. It was the first of a number of art institutions in the city that Dominique and John patronized and, in tandem, controlled; their standards of excellence were challenged in venue after venue. "Houstonians thought nothing about spending thousands on a prize bull but drew the line at buying art,"[19] Dominique recalled of the early 1950s period when she and John were gearing their energies and persuasive powers to make Houston a home for contemporary culture.

The CAA became their initial platform for launching community exposure to the best in modern art, and here one must emphasize the word *best,* as in first-class, in defining the Menil approach: their high standards of art exhibition and scholarship would prove a curse and a blessing to all the local institutions they came to favor. Finally, after benefiting one organization after another, until their welcomes were worn out, they established, in the early 1970s, their very own, the Institute for the Arts. As Philip Johnson would say about his collection of buildings in New Canaan, "The only way to get it *right* is to do it for yourself!"[20]

John de Menil was elected to the Contemporary Arts Association's first board of directors—along with Nina Cullinan—and in the early 1950s, with Dominique, proceeded to develop and personally finance a series of exhibitions remarkable for any museum but particularly for such a small, young one staffed only by volunteers. Van Gogh, Ernst, Calder, Miró, Tamayo, Roualt, and Picasso were given their first important Texas showings in the stunning little 2,500 sq. ft. gallery space, designed by Karl Kamrath in 1949 and built with donations of cash and materials for "five thousand dollars." Its unique triangular building section harked back to the drafting studios at Frank Lloyd Wright's Taliesin West. For the extraordinary Van Gogh show that the de Menils mounted there in 1951—the first in-depth showing of the painter's work outside New York and Chicago—John de Menil sent two stalwart museum volunteers, an architect and a designer, to New York to hand-carry the *Portrait of Dr. Gachet* back to Houston in a Pullman car bedroom. Also in 1951, Dominique, who later became an accomplished designer of museum exhibitions, pitched in by putting together a show of modern furniture, *Interiors 1952: Beauty within Reach of Hand and Budget.* Howard Barnstone provided the exhibition's plan layout.

Meanwhile, across town, modern architecture was getting a big pitch from young Barnstone in the University of Houston's loftlike architecture studios located in a sprawling metal temporary building. It was a far less likely

Anderson Todd with Mies van der Rohe at opening of Cullinan Hall, Houston, 1958. Courtesy of Anderson Todd.

turf for the avant-garde than the intellectually elite Rice campus. But Rice's School of Architecture was conservative, with one foot still in the Beaux Arts teaching methods, though it had its own modernist advocate in the person of Anderson Todd of Philadelphia and Princeton, who, while attending Princeton, met Philip Johnson at Harvard and later became a lifelong devotee of the doctrines of Mies van der Rohe.

One of the smooth postwar arrivals from the East, Andy brought an exceptionally distinguished mind to the Houston scene. Sharply confident and outspoken, he deftly stepped into Houston's well-to-do social orbit and soon married Lucie Wray, whose mother was a Cullinan, a daughter of the founder of Texaco. Todd would soon play a key role in bringing Mies to Houston in 1954 to design Cullinan Hall, a major addition to the Museum of Fine Arts. This followed closely on the heels of a conventional addition memorializing

Humble Oil founder Robert Lee Blaffer. Nina Cullinan, Lucie Todd's aunt, gave money to the museum in 1953 to be used, in her words, "for an addition to be designed by an architect of outstanding reputation and wide experience." Indicating that contemporary art now had a champion from the city's conservative elite, Miss Cullinan further specified that the new addition should be shared for exhibitions with the Contemporary Arts Association. She also saw to it that Anderson Todd became a member of the committee set up to select an architect. Through Andy Todd's influence with his wife's aunt and with the museum board, and with modernist backing from fellow selection committee members Hugo Neuhaus and Preston Bolton, the German-American master was hired. It would be Mies's only museum in this country and his first major building outside of Chicago.

Cullinan Hall, the Museum of Fine Arts, Houston, 1958; Mies van der Rohe and Staub, Rather & Howze, architects. Photo © Wayne Andrews/Esto.

Howard Barnstone began asking Johnson to come back to Houston to speak, first to his classes in the metal "barn" at the University of Houston and later for publicized appearances before larger audiences in the university's auditorium. Johnson was, to say the least, an entertaining and erudite speaker. He had what he later called his father's "gift of gab." This was coupled with his mother's sense of cultural mission and his own need to be important and admired, to count for something. He was dashing and cut quite a figure: slender, handsome, and patrician in London-tailored suits. (Burdette Keeland says that in all the years he has known Johnson, in and out of studio or office, he has never seen him take off his coat.) He possessed, with his intense, high-pitched voice, the ability to charm and enthrall, lacing ardent appeals for "more art in our lives" with laughter-rousing self-mocking anecdotes involving himself and god-figures like Frank Lloyd Wright. The impression left was of his serious commitment to art but not to *himself.* The missionary zeal, coupled with his suave self-deprecation, proved a tasty dish. It converted some young minds to believing in the International Style at a time when the philosophical argument was between chaste, man-made modernism and the nature-rooted organic modernism of Frank Lloyd Wright.

One of Johnson's appearances before a large audience at the University of Houston was taped. Following are excerpts from the 1952 speech, which embodies the essence of Johnson before a crowd:

> I'm going to talk about the eternal struggle between idealism and materialism, the eternal struggle that every architect faces, and I'm going to talk to the architects in the audience tonight, the ladies are welcome but I was intending to talk to students and I want to talk to them; they are the people that are going to have to do our buildings, and they are the most important people, saving your graces, in the room.

Philip Johnson on the rostrum, mid-1960s. Courtesy of Philip Johnson.

> What I noticed today showed a kind of art for which Texas is not famous . . . in the East. We have a strange attitude toward Texas, almost as strange as the attitude that Texas has toward *us!* I think every good architect would like to come to Texas to live. . . . we still believe there's gold on the streets. It isn't until we get here that we find that it isn't!
>
> Art is not sourced here we think. Well, one art is and it is a very specific and civic and Texas one, and that is your highway bridges! Now you may call it a minor art, but the fact that it is here and is so widespread makes it *not* a minor art. I don't care where one *finds* art! Those bridges should be universalized all over the country so we can have art in bridgework everywhere!
>
> I want to talk about the great battle that I find in my own work, and I'm sorry that I was introduced as a great architect because I'm not! I know and I think we all must know when we get to be my age [forty-six] where they stand. I know that I'm doing my best, but there is no illusion about greatness! I'm going to talk about some great architects later but leave the hyperboles off! I want to talk about that thing that we have all had to face: the terrible battle that faces the American architect. We in this country have been overwhelmed with the opposition of materialism, the nonartistic approach, even within our ranks. There are those that care less for *art* than they do for *money!* Unfortunately the mental, the cultural, climate in this country is such that your success is measured by how much money you have. I hope and plead that some of us will join in and be the artists among the architects.
>
> A man as great as Frank Lloyd Wright can't hurt *me* by jumping on *me* about my thinking. On the big issues Mr. Wright and I are side by side in spite of his charge that we make sterile, inhuman buildings; we, and I mean the people that I follow: Mies van der Rohe, Le Corbusier, Walter Gropius. If Mr. Wright at his age, eighty-five, wants to stand up and call me names, how can I answer back? *There* is a man that has given me more, and everyone in this room, too, than any other architect living or dead in the world. On the one hand he's the *father* of all the design we do today, no matter how far the forms we use seem to differ. And secondly, he is the greatest artist—this I don't get from my own judgment as an architect but from all the art critics I know—the greatest artist that America has ever produced, so how can he at the age of eighty-five hurt my feelings? He calls my house—you may have heard of my house, without any walls, all glass, no interior partitions, no exterior walls—a *monkey* cage, *built* by a monkey, *for* a monkey! . . . I'm not so sure you should laugh so *heartily*, but . . .[21]

Johnson's repeated visits to the University of Houston—and he loved being asked back—struck a hungry nerve with students, many of whom were ripe to hear a passionate message about modern architecture as a necessary revolt against the status quo. With Barnstone as Johnson's on-the-spot advocate in the UH architecture studios and Anderson Todd's parallel, ardent advocacy of Miesian design at Rice, the combined messages on the two campuses had a cumulative effect on a generation of Houston architects, who were to make that provincial city a broad-based home for International Style buildings of differing scales. Barnstone, Keeland, Neuhaus, and Todd were not the only architects influenced by Mies and his apostle Johnson; architects Preston Bolton, Eugene Aubry, Kenneth Bentsen, Harwood Taylor, William Jenkins, and Magruder Wingfield were the most prominent interpreters of Miesian/Johnsonian design precepts. Johnson's Menil house ushered in an era for Houston, and his frequent presence in the city helped coalesce an evolving sensibility. One can only speculate in hindsight on how Houston's postwar architectural landscape might have developed without the Menil patronage of Johnson.

Soon after their house was finished, the de Menils took an interest in the University of St. Thomas, a Catholic liberal arts university run by a Basilian order of priests. The school operated out of an opulent 1912 mansion on Montrose Boulevard that had been built by J. W. Link, developer of the area. The Link House was acquired in 1946 after the Basilians received federal money to start a university for returning veterans.

Shortly after the Menil house was completed, Jane Blaffer Owen suggested to John de Menil that he should hire Philip Johnson to design a new parish complex for St. Michael's Catholic Church, where he and Dominique worshiped. Jane had heard about Johnson and had seen the Menil house and, though an Episcopalian, knew that St. Michael's was seeking help for a new building. The tiny church was located next to a pine forest on unpaved Sage Road in far west Houston. With John de Menil's backing, Johnson prepared a schematic design for a new church in 1953 that was ultimately vetoed by the Catholic Bishop of Galveston. Johnson's concept for a church complex featured a gable-roofed Romanesque-like church with a bold, arched entry and large-scale, curved masonry walls. It was a heretical—and prophetic—departure for an acolyte of Mies's.

When their architect's design was turned down, the de Menils' philanthropic attention turned toward the University of St. Thomas and its goal of a permanent campus. Some Basilian fathers who were friends of Dominique's heard of her husband's generosity to St. Michael's and went to see him. In a short time John de Menil, with Dominique's backing, agreed to pay for a Philip Johnson–designed master plan for a new campus on the school's newly acquired blocks in the Montrose area.

The de Menils entertained often in their new house, and the people they invited were as heterogeneous a mix as one could imagine in Houston. To Dominique and John there was nothing odd about having local artists and architects, a visiting filmmaker, Catholic priests, university professors, the odd River Oaks millionaire, and just plain friends to rub shoulders in their elegant and spare house, set in its three-acre green park on San Felipe Road. Anderson Todd recalls that it was at the de Menils' that he saw the first African American being entertained socially by whites in Houston, "and in the midst of rich River Oaks, too."[22]

Karl Kilian, owner of a Houston bookstore near Rice University with Texas's finest selection of arts and architecture books, shared a carpool in the 1950s with one of the Menil children and remembers being surprised when he was first in the house:

> It was the stage of my life when I associated rich people with large houses containing large rooms and these de Menil children's bedrooms were *small!* I was amazed and puzzled, but that was the beginning, I guess, of my education about certain stereotyped values. Much later, after Dominique and John de Menil had brought Jermayne MacAgy to Houston from San Francisco's Palace of the Legion of Honor and paid her director's salary, first at the Contemporary Arts Association, then at the University of St. Thomas. I was an entering sophomore English major and met Jerry and was swept away by her charismatic knowledge of art. It sort of changed the direction of my life and I added art history to my major in English.
>
> Along with other St. Thomas students, I was often asked to the Menil house and we were entertained like adults. Fred Hughes, who later became Andy Warhol's business manager, was a St. Thomas friend and another frequent visitor at the de Menils'. When they would have New York visitors that they wanted to impress, we were sort of shown off as exhibits "A" through "J" to persuade the Easterners of the education quality coming out of St. Thomas. I think at one point John de Menil saw the school's potential as another Black Mountain College.
>
> At lunch one day at the de Menils', James Johnson Sweeney, another recruit of Dominique and John's who was briefly the director of the Museum of Fine Arts until he became too controversial, came in while we were all seated in the kitchen. He told Dominique that a fine Pollock was available for $100,000 and would she and John stand for half of it. She replied "yes" and asked Sweeney to settle the terms for payment as she continued eating.[23]

Another Menil social occasion a few years later involved Kilian and illustrates something about the de Menils, their interests, and the Houston milieu they dealt with in achieving their objectives. The Italian film director Michelangelo Antonioni was their guest, and he requested to see a rodeo and some big, rich Texans. Dominique and John organized a diverse group to accompany Antonioni to the rodeo before an alfresco dinner at their house. During the meal a boisterous oilman guest became upset at an adjoining table conversation about race. Kilian was at the table. The oilman began berating young Kilian about his views, which were defended by Gertrude Barnstone. In a few seconds the brawny guest managed, with racial and religious slurs, to offend the servants, Howard Barnstone's wife, and all guests within earshot. This prompted the young, slightly built Kilian to ask the offensive older man to leave, declaring that he was spoiling the party. Later, as Kilian was leaving, the oilman came up to Kilian, who was with John de Menil and turned to see the man take a swing at him, which he ducked as John was blindsided by his guest. Dominique and John dealt with all types in their money-raising efforts to benefit Houston's cultural life.

Dominique and John de Menil with a Dogon figure at a University of St. Thomas exhibition, 1967. Courtesy of the Menil Collection.

The cross section of guests at the many social occasions at the house on San Felipe foretold an ultimate, fifty-year Menil task as shapers of the history of their adopted city: the creativity of artists and architects would be tightly woven into all of their activities of museum patronage, art acquisition, and building construction; Basilian priests would play an immediate and important part in their adoption of and later withdrawal from the University of St. Thomas; close involvement in the academic worlds of St. Thomas and later, briefly, Rice University would consume almost twenty years; and they would integrate Houston's oil and industrial rich into their many plans for expanded museum programs of acquisition and construction, even with the many millions the Menil Foundation would give to the city. The couple's early Houston friends, and there were only a few outside the realms of art and culture, would remain close through the decades of expanding wealth and civic involvement.

The casual presence of African Americans in the Menil social life was a precursor to Dominique de Menil's intensified human rights activities beginning in the early 1970s after John's death from cancer in 1973. With the completion of the ecumenical Rothko Chapel in 1971 near the St. Thomas campus, the de Menils launched a well-funded, worldwide human rights crusade which had its genesis in the repugnance they had felt when they arrived in Texas in the early 1940s and came face-to-face with Southern racial segregation and abuse. The Black Arts Center began during John's lifetime, and he was instrumental in Mickey Leeland's rise to prominence as Texas's first African American congressman. In 1986, Dominique de Menil, with former president Jimmy Carter, established the Carter-Menil Foundation, which gives biannual awards to individuals or institutions that are distinguished in the fight against human oppression.

For the University of St. Thomas, Johnson prepared a master plan based on Thomas Jefferson's "academical village" at the University of Virginia. He proposed an elongated scheme stretching north-south over three city blocks, with buildings arranged along the length of a mall-like "lawn," a la Charlottesville. All the buildings would be connected by a continuous colonnade on each side, terminating in the school's chapel at one end of the lengthy quadrangle, like the University of Virginia's Rotunda. During the planning, the chapel's location shifted from the south to the north end of the quadrangle and changed shapes from a square to a cruciform footprint.

Johnson's master plan was a straightforward, comprehensible scheme that could be completed incrementally by adding buildings and colonnade as funds allowed. It would have a monumentality, albeit horizontal, that was an essential element of Johnson's sensibility, a result of those years, from childhood, of *looking* at historic European buildings. The "add-a-pearl" feature of expansion at St. Thomas would assure the concept's integrity.

Architecture's history and precedents were an ingrained part of Johnson's creative judgment. This was natural for one who began as a scholar and historian of the modern movement. And from his Sunday afternoons at home with his sisters seeing Europe's great art and architecture in his mother's illus-

Dominique de Menil and Philip Johnson planning the University of St. Thomas at the Menil house, San Felipe Road, Houston, mid-1950s. Photo by Henri Cartier-Bresson; courtesy of the estate of Dominique de Menil.

Memorial Hall, Illinois Institute of Technology, Chicago, 1946; Mies van der Rohe, architect. Photo © Wayne Andrews/Esto.

trated "lectures," Johnson found the artistic past to be intensely compelling. For him history, whether shallow or deep, existed as an archive for inspiration and formed the rationale for his building designs. He was never uncomfortable with sharing his design sources, a unique thing for a midcentury architect who presumed a creative life in architecture as art. But in the 1940s and 1950s, the period he later called his "pupil-architecture," his mentor Mies van der Rohe guided everything that Johnson undertook, and no one ever "did" Mies as *stylishly* as Johnson. Anderson Todd built a house for his family, a few years after the first St. Thomas buildings, in a Miesian mode so faithful that Philip Johnson, after seeing it, remarked to Andy, "It's more Mies than Mies!" though critic Stephen Fox thought it had its Johnsonian aspects.

The Basilian Fathers at St. Thomas interviewed several nationally known architects whose names, along with Johnson's, were suggested by John de Menil. The selection committee chose Johnson to design the new campus, a choice as much influenced by his intellectual energy as by the de Menils' patronage of him. When he was tapped, Johnson was ready to propose buildings hewing closely to the language of Mies van der Rohe's buildings for Chicago's Illinois Institute of Technology, begun in 1942. The IIT buildings, of brick, glass, and exposed steel structure, were "industrial" in their boiled-down structural technology and an arresting sight to American eyes accustomed to the popular ideal of Collegiate Gothic and Georgian. Creating an entire campus of buildings of this character on 110 acres on Chicago's poor Southside was remarkable and maybe only possible in a city like Chicago, with its strong protomodernist tradition. (It was only ten years after the International Style exhibition and four years since Mies's arrival in Chicago.) The Chicago campus was developed in a consistent architectural style over time with buildings arranged in shifting, orthogonal relationships, not unlike the way the interior spaces and massing of Mies's early European houses eschewed axial symmetry, achieving architectural "weight" via intuitive, abstract composition.

Johnson's proposal for St. Thomas had a strongly axial, Jeffersonian scheme of two-story blocky buildings tied lightly to parallel, steel-framed double galleries. The buildings, and there were only three built with their attached colonnade in the first phase in 1958, are IIT-like in appearance: an exposed steel column-and-beam structure, painted black, with infill of glass and grey-pink, wood-mould brick, the same one used at Rice Institute. Howard Barnstone and Preston Bolton looked after the construction and coordinated with Johnson, who did not visit Houston often, sending Richard Foster, the tall, lanky new member of his staff, for inspection visits. During this time, Johnson was busy teaching at Pratt Institute and later at Yale, maintaining offices in New York and New Canaan plus the pro bono one at the Museum of Modern Art.

Johnson's designs until the late 1950s were all Miesian in appearance but with a subliminal fillip that was Johnson's own, usually achieved at the expense of the structural design "integrity" that Mies van der Rohe considered essential. The appearance, the style, the *aura* of a building were what Johnson responded to. During the 1950s he produced the precise and exquisite Rockefeller guest house in Manhattan and three of his best and most dramatically picturesque suburban houses: the Wiley, Leonhardt, and Boissonnas. The chef d'oeuvre of the period, however, was the Abby Aldrich Rockefeller Sculpture Garden at the Museum of Modern Art, an enduring twentieth-century urban landmark.

Houston's fire protection code required that the interior steel structure of the St. Thomas buildings be covered with fireproofing. Later buildings at the university, in the interest of economy, had structures of reinforced concrete, with steel facings applied to the exterior as symbolic continuity with the original Miesian design language. It made for visual harmony but was nothing more than mock "half-timbering" in steel. As the campus grew and new buildings were added to the extended double gallery on each side, Johnson's conception of a Jeffersonian "academical village" around a linear quadrangle reached final form.

The buildings were brittle and light by comparison with Mies's Chicago campus complex. Cumulatively, they ultimately took on the aspect of a surrealist cell block girdling a lush greensward with huge trees beneath a cloud-chased Gulf Coast sky. The University of St. Thomas definitely raised Houston's architectural profile in terms of international modernism, and while "tastefully" ordered in the Miesian vein, the design had far less *weight* than the original in Chicago, being almost capricious in manner when set beside

University of St. Thomas

Houston, 1958

Welder Hall, upper gallery, looking south.

PHILIP JOHNSON, ARCHITECT; BOLTON & BARNSTONE, ASSOCIATE ARCHITECTS.
PHOTOS BY PAUL HESTER, 1995–1999.

Strake Hall, east and north elevations, above; view of the campus mall looking south, below.

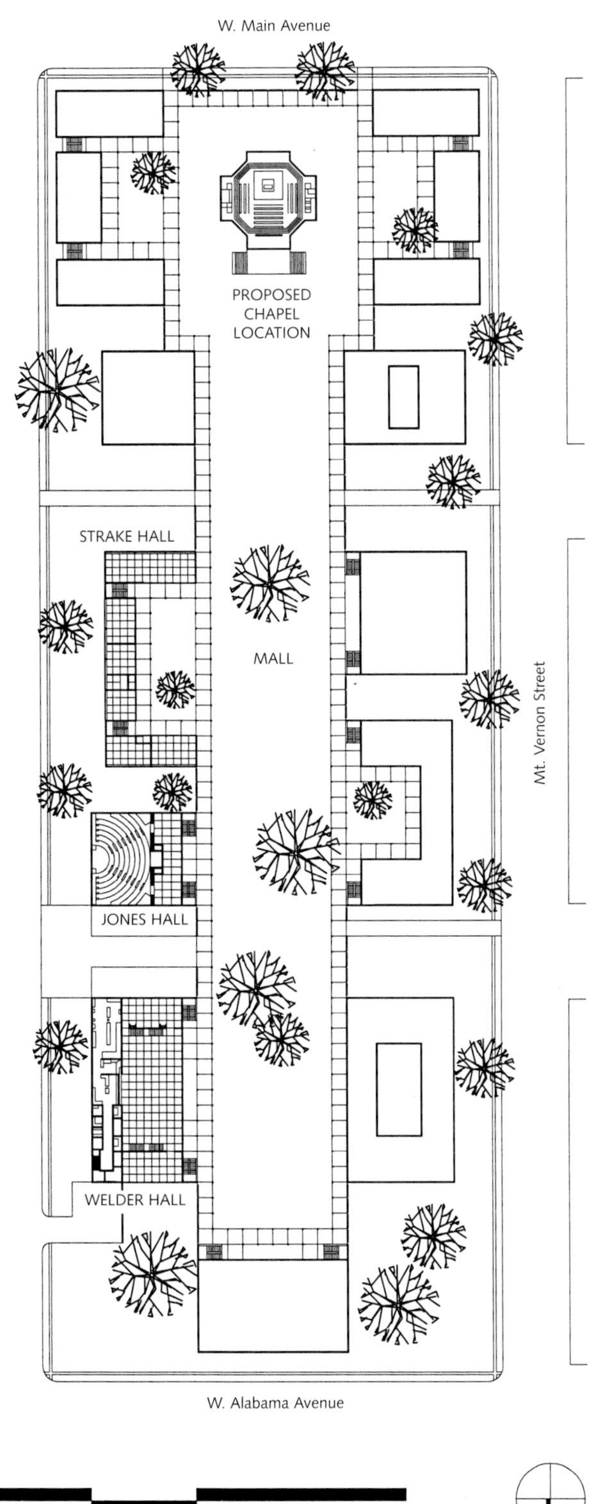

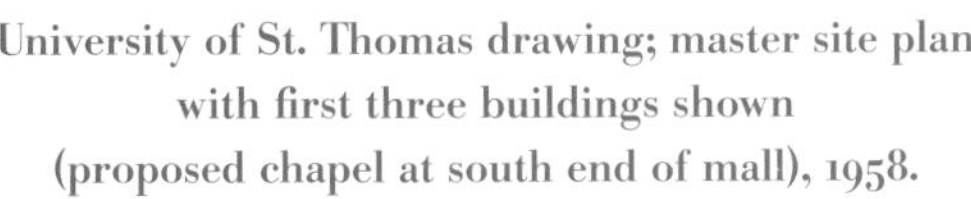

University of St. Thomas drawing; master site plan with first three buildings shown (proposed chapel at south end of mall), 1958.

Jones Hall, lower gallery stairway.

the Museum of Fine Art's Cullinan Hall, completed in 1958. Mies van der Rohe could never and would never employ architectural allusion as a design armature.

John de Menil was instrumental in getting Johnson the job of designing new dormitories at Sarah Lawrence College in Bronxville, New York, where a Menil daughter was a student. There he designed a pair of two-story wings with repetitive, narrow structural bays of concrete, with brick infills, topped with shallow vaults. The buildings weren't distinguished, but Sarah Lawrence College would later prove a catalyst for Johnson's next step into Texas.

When the first buildings at the University of St. Thomas were dedicated in 1958, Dominique and John de Menil were more important "players" at St. Thomas than in 1956, when they brought Johnson into the picture. They had since shifted their allegiance and financial support to the school's art department from the Contemporary Arts Association after policy disagreements with the board there over how and what kind of art should be shown. The de Menils had personally "adopted" and funded the CAA's vibrant new museum director, Jermayne MacAgy, whom they hired in 1955. She was a scholarly and brilliant designer of thematic art exhibitions who put Houston on the national stage with theatrical shows like *Totems Not Taboo* and *The Trojan Horse: The Art of the Machine.* With Dominique and John's urging, she exhibited works by the African American faculty of Texas Southern University, nine years before the Museum of Fine Arts dropped restrictions limiting African American attendance to once a week on Negro Day. In 1959 they brought her to St. Thomas with them from the CAA when her contract there was not renewed amidst controversy over the Menil grip and MacAgy's radical ideas.

Earlier MacAgy had guest-curated a major exhibition of modern art for the St. Thomas buildings' dedication in 1958, when the de Menils lavishly entertained, for several days, visitors from the culture capitals of the United States and Europe, including visitors from Dallas, San Antonio, and Fort Worth who had come at their invitation to honor the little university's first buildings. A chapel, though the centerpiece of Johnson's master plan, was not included in the first construction phase for the Catholic school, and it would be forty years before one was built. MacAgy's gifted tenure at St. Thomas was cut short with her sudden death in 1964; Dominique de Menil took over her job as curator and became an exhibition designer of great distinction.

Johnson could not get the chapel design right for all the clients: the university fathers, the de Menils, and finally for Mark Rothko, the New York artist whose heroic paintings had been commissioned by Dominique and John for the building; his opinions of the building became integral to the building's design resolution. Johnson's initial scheme for the chapel was similar in structural language to the Kneses Tifereth Israel Synagogue he was completing at Port Chester, New York. It was a Miesian steel-and-masonry near-cube (66' x 66' x 46'), which in subsequent design schemes evolved into a symmetrically four-square, cruciform-cum-octagon plan, centered beneath a skylight in a tall, tapering conelike tower. John de Menil objected to the "authoritative" tower, which suggested to him an exaggerated symbol of clerical primacy out of step with the democratic values that he prized. After years of wrangling among architect, patron, and priests about the design and its accommodation of the large, brooding paintings by Rothko, Johnson stepped aside in 1967, causing Dominique de Menil to observe, "Philip has sacrificed for the sake of art." Johnson's past experience with Rothko had not been pleasant: the architect wanted large Rothko paintings to decorate certain walls of his Four Seasons Restaurant, but after he commissioned Rothko and paid him for his work, the artist backed out and kept the paintings.

Howard Barnstone and his partner Eugene Aubry took over for the de Menils and in 1971 finished what became the ecumenical Rothko Chapel on cleared Menil land several blocks from the St. Thomas campus. A gift of Barnett Newman's tall steel sculpture *Broken Obelisk* was made by Dominique and John to the City of Houston. It was to stand in front of the new city hall addition, but their gift was refused when John de Menil surprised and chagrined the city council at the dedication by announcing, at the end of his remarks, that the sculpture would be inscribed as a memorial to Martin Luther King Jr. When the city council refused the sculpture with de Menil's inscription, he suggested another: "Forgive them for they know not what they do." It stands today in a reflection pool in front of the Rothko Chapel.

The Rothko Chapel, built of the same buff St. Thomas brick, has a base

Rothko Chapel, Houston, 1971; foreground, *Broken Obelisk*, Barnett Newman, 1970; Barnstone & Aubry, architects. Photo by Paul Hester, 1997.

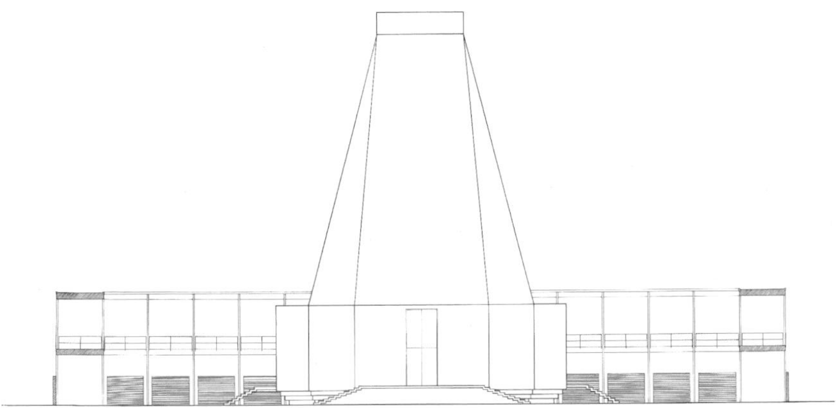

Elevation of University of St. Thomas chapel, 1957; Philip Johnson, architect. Courtesy of Philip Johnson.

plan largely matching Johnson's, but a huge skylight—inveterately troublesome as natural lighting for the dark Rothko paintings—replaced the tower that was key to Johnson's concept. The chapel was the first building in the multiblock Menil-owned district west of the university, nicknamed "Do-ville," which came to include three museums, an exhibition space in a converted retail building, and an art-book store—all this amidst ranges of 1920s bungalows, painted a uniform grey, gathered around the grand, cypress-clad Menil Collection building, by Renzo Piano, completed in 1987. After the University of St. Thomas opened its new steel-and-brick buildings without its chapel, Johnson's creative ability was soon stretched in remarkable ways with the design of another place of worship, very ambitious and unique, in Indiana. It would become his "breakout" structure, freeing him with expressive originality from his devotion to the style of Mies van der Rohe.

Jane Blaffer Owen is a daughter of Robert Lee Blaffer, a New Orleanian and one of the founders of the Humble Oil and Refining Company. Her mother, Sarah Campbell Blaffer, who grew up in the small Central Texas ranching town of Lampasas, developed a taste for European "old masters" and instilled in her children, particularly Jane, a sense of the dramatic. Like her mother, Jane has an ethereal, romantic personality, a soft, mellifluous voice accented with broad *a*'s, and a bent for the spiritual. In the Blaffer house in Houston where Jane grew up, "Sadie" Blaffer, according to local observers, had little use for electric lights, entertaining guests by candlelight and insisting that the children speak French at home. Described as fey by her friends, the understatedly stylish Jane combines her mother's quest for old-world allusion with a no-nonsense attitude derived from her father. In 1941 she married Kenneth Dale Owen at the palatial Blaffer retreat in Canada in a ceremony with "forty-one bagpipers and a fly-over by the Norwegian Royal Air Force."

Kenneth Owen's British ancestor, Robert Owen, built a nineteenth-century utopian socialist community in Indiana, and soon after their marriage, Jane saw tiny New Harmony, Indiana, for the first time. She immediately had the idea of restoring the picturesque farm community as a memorial to the Owen family. Long before the nation took up preservation of its architectural heritage as a cultural cause, the Blaffer Trust became a source of funds in bringing the village on the Wabash River back to a semblance of its original self.

"I saw it only briefly after Kenneth and I married. . . . the very *stones* were crying out for rescue," Jane Owen recalled in New Harmony in 1994. "Over there where our church stands, they were making *oil tanks* . . . loud and clear . . . to where a *bird* wouldn't come anymore! It was *devastation*, a paradise lost. But I found people here, lovely women, educated women who didn't have any money: they were like embers of fire, like vestal virgins, keeping the memory of New Harmony alive!"[24] As restoration proceeded slowly through the 1950s Jane Owen developed a feeling that a special place for the town would focus its spirituality. Jane worshiped in St. Stephen's, a tiny Episcopal church— "sheer Jane Austen!" in her words—but she had developed strong notions about a unifying, universal shrine for all faiths in the heart of Indiana farmland.

Preston Bolton, Howard Barnstone's partner, was a friend of Jane Owen's since his days on the debutante circuit. Knowing of her interest in meeting Philip Johnson, who was her friends Dominique and John's admired architect, Preston asked Jane to come along once when he picked up Philip at the airport. It was the middle 1950s. Johnson was coming to Houston to present his first St. Thomas architectural designs to a group organized by the de Menils and the Basilian Fathers to solicit support. Duly impressed in the car ride by Johnson's suave energy, Jane Owen was even more impressed by the New York architect when he spoke to the assembled group with such passion about architecture as art and transcendent expression. "I immediately felt that Philip was the one with the kind of poetry in his soul for realizing for me what was only a dream at the time," Jane Owen remembers. "I asked him if he would be interested in helping me and of course he was very enthusiastic and soon came to New Harmony and suggested I should get more land than the corner lot that I had secured. It took two years to clear those oil tanks out, but all the time the plans were germinating."[25]

The beginnings of the dialogue between client and architect over the design for the shrine were not auspicious. Jane Owen rejected Johnson's first design. "It was all sharp *angles* like that nuclear reactor he had done in Israel! Indiana has a 'bosom' and Israel doesn't't! I told him to send that design to the desert where it belonged and come back to Indiana and absorb the *softness* of our countryside." Johnson returned, took another look, and developed a design of great originality and expressiveness that sensuously reflected his client's desires. "Philip wrote me and thanked me for introducing him to the *round* in architecture," Jane Owen fondly recalled, though Johnson had been toying with curving architectural forms for some time.[26]

As he redesigned the central feature for the shrine, he retained or paraphrased the basic formal language of the Israeli reactor compound, which is that of a gated, high-walled enclosure with an open "cloister," a four-sided peristyle of oddly tapered columns, framing a tall, dominating shallow-domed reactor structure of folded wall planes. The faceted concrete Israeli reactor building had its restatement in New Harmony as a high, lobed dome facing a walled, paved courtyard. The Shrine for the Blaffer Trust, as it was titled on the plans, was dedicated in 1961 and soon became known as the Roofless

Philip Johnson, with Jane Blaffer Owen on his left, at the groundbreaking for the Roofless Church, New Harmony, Indiana, 1959. Courtesy of Blaffer Foundation.

Church. When asked about the origin of the "roofless" concept—was it Johnson's idea?—Jane Owen states: "Oh, that was always my *desire!* Call it a vision, call it a dream, this ecumenical idea. Only one roof is wide enough, broad enough, for all worshiping humanity: there has to be the *sky* as our roof!"[27]

"I had been searching in my heart for this place," Jane recalled as she stood in the church's courtyard in 1994. "New Harmony needed resurrection and without sounding pious I knew I had to call on the Lord to help me because it was such a formidable task. This is not a memorial to anyone or any group; it's a *cry:* 'Dear Lord, please come down and help us in our chaos!' There are no strangers here, we are all children of God." In a way the church evolved from the need of a home for a Jacques Lipchitz bronze Madonna, *Our Lady Queen of Peace,* which Jane Owen had commissioned to present to the National Trust for placement in the capital's National Cathedral. "They didn't *want* her! They had no great contemporary sculpture there but that year they chose a George Washington on *horseback* instead! They were preparing for *Korea!"* she remembered. "As Philip and I were working out the design of the church my intuition told me that the Madonna and the church had to work there together and so she did find a home finally under the canopy."[28]

With a mind steeped in history, Johnson says, "The church in New Harmony is a *temenos,* which is a Greek word for a sacred enclosure surrounding a holy spot."[29] The Roofless Church's formal idea is a very strong and simple one: high masonry walls, of a plum-colored brick, forming a long, rectangular 9,800 sq. ft. *cortile.* A landscaped "narthex" at the east end forms a transitional space between monumental, gilded gates by Lipchitz and the "sanctuary" proper. The courtyard, with the exception of the narthex, was paved in Indiana limestone, with planting areas formed by "eroded," geometric edges similar to those in the Museum of Modern Art garden. A secondary gate serves the west side and a narrow loggia overlook above the cornfields is located on the east wall. It was, symbolically, an architectural scheme of protection and removal as venerable as a medieval church's cloister or an Islamic mosque's courtyard.

The shingled canopy, the baldachin, is axially positioned, hovering above the altar and Madonna on rib supports anchored delicately to six husky, ovoid limestone footings. The "draped" dome shape was achieved through sophisticated geometries explored and developed between Johnson and his brilliant collaborator, structural engineer Lev Zetlin. The dome's plan outline is generated by the intersections of a ring of six circles, the inner faces of which form points on the circumference of the altar. Laminated-wood ribs on steel "toes" support the roof and terminate at an open circular skylight. The fluid folds of the shingle-covered canopy are those of a scarf-draped lamp, the bottom edge rising and falling gracefully between the supports. Many remarked on its evocation of an Indiana haystack, but in Johnson's long career of form-making, the New Harmony "church" was a watershed design within his particular canon of modernism. The original paving was replaced in 1992 with large panels of lawn flanking a central "aisle" leading from the main entry gates to the altar, for, as Jane Owen had observed, "Indiana summers are *hot;* the poor geraniums couldn't grow with all that stone!"

Jane used the church as a gathering spot for various religious leaders. German-American theologian Paul Tillich was a frequent visitor, and Thomas Merton came to participate in theological seminars relating Christianity to modern culture that Jane Owen organized. In front of the Roofless Church is a small, bosky park which Jane had created and called the Tillich Grove after Tillich's death in 1965. She commissioned a heroic bronze bust of her spiritual mentor which stands amidst the dense trees. Following the construction of the Roofless Church, Jane Owen asked Johnson to design a new building for St. Stephen's Episcopal Church in New Harmony. His striking design for a clustered group of skylit steeples marking the sanctuary was never built; Jane Owen and Philip Johnson's warm relationship ran aground.

Model, St. Stephen's Episcopal Church project, New Harmony, Indiana, early 1960s; Philip Johnson, architect. Photo by Paul Hester, 1994.

Roofless Church

New Harmony, Indiana, 1960

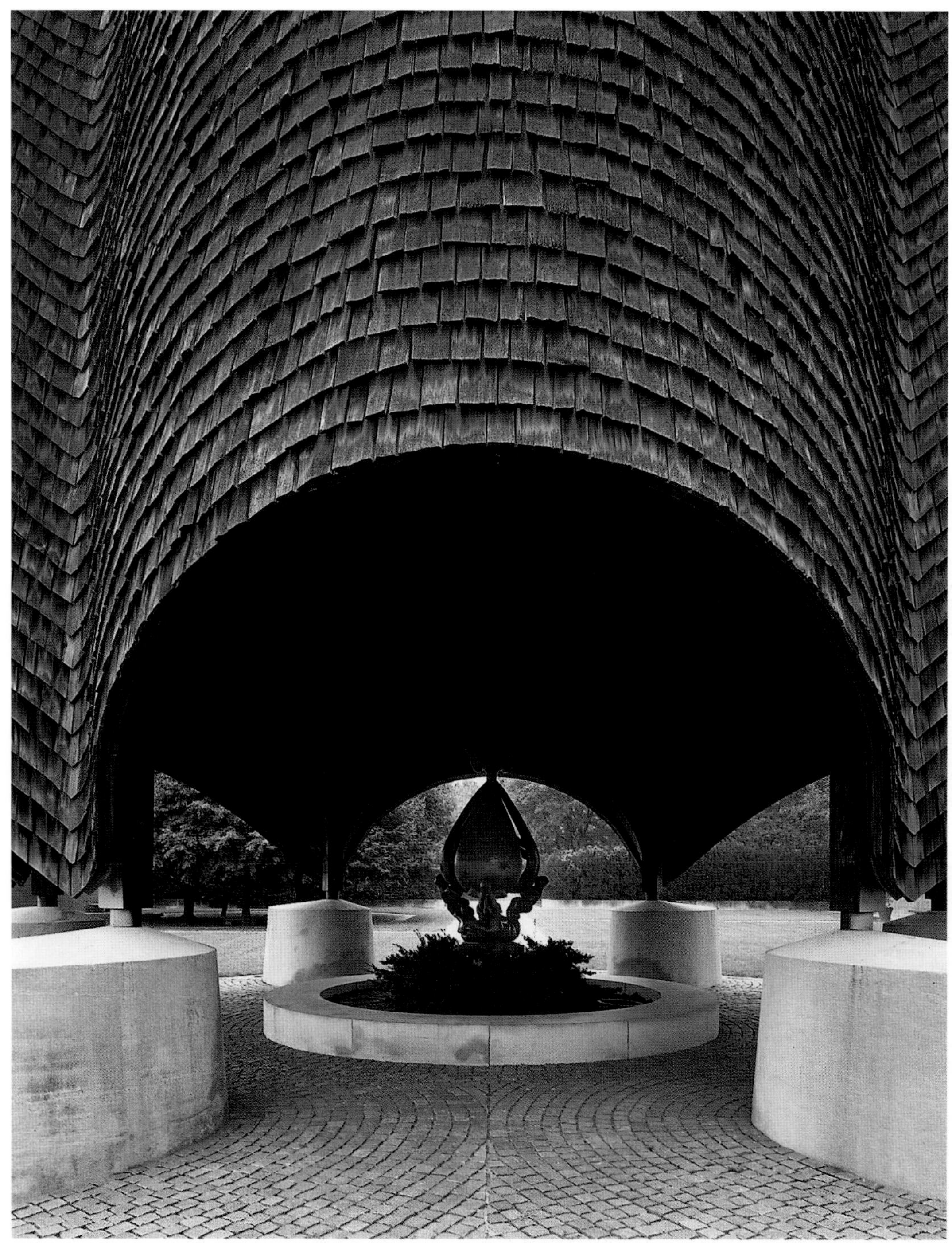

Interior; sculpture: *Our Lady Queen of Peace*, Jacques Lipchitz, bronze, 1961.

PHILIP JOHNSON, ARCHITECT. PHOTOS BY PAUL HESTER, 1994.

View from entrance;
courtyard remodeled in 1994.

Jane Blaffer Owen at the entrance; gilded steel gates by Jacques Lipchitz, 1962.

View of courtyard and overlook from beneath the canopy.

Limestone loggia overlook.

Limestone footing eroded by rainwater from roof.

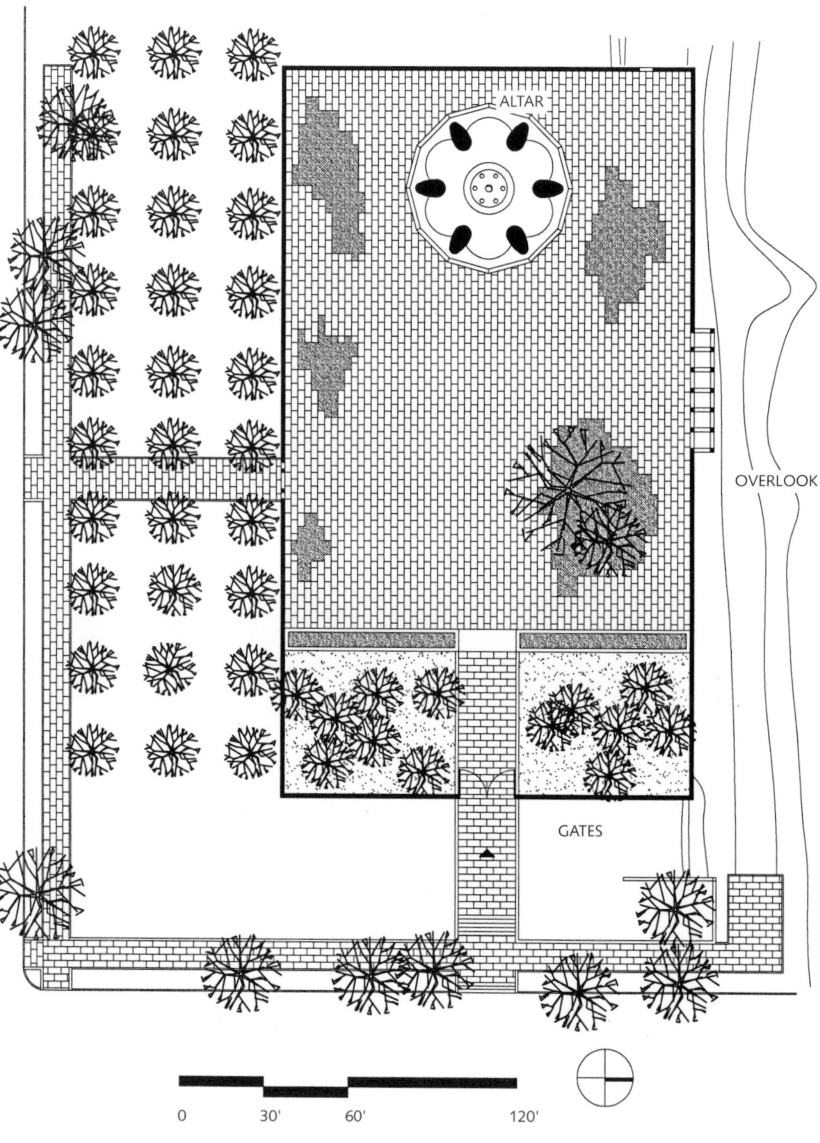

Roofless Church drawing; site plan, 1961.

As successful as the Roofless Church was from the client's philosophical standpoint, it encountered serious technical problems years later which created a bitter split between Johnson and Jane Owen and destroyed their close relationship. Before the problems, they continued to see each other regularly in New York, and when Homer Johnson died at ninety-eight and was buried without ritual in Cleveland, Philip, though indifferent to religion, asked Jane to have a small service for his father in the Roofless Church. "I brought white geraniums from my greenhouse for the memorial and arranged them at the altar beneath the Lipchitz," Jane Owen recalls.[30]

The brick cavity-walls surrounding the open-air church had no waterproofing cap at their tops. The plans called only for "caulking" of the mortar joints on the upper, flat edges: a minimalist's detail. The walls were soon absorbing rainwater, which froze, expanded, and loosened the upper brick courses. Serious deterioration of the walls continued, and a painful, acrimonious exchange developed between Jane and Philip and raged for years before Johnson made a cash settlement to rebuild the walls, with a protective shield at the top. Things were never the same again between them, though Jane Owen speaks today with admiration of his talent and "flawless eye and sense of proportion."

In 1979, with her backing, a large, sparkling white-paneled visitor and community center, The Atheneum, designed by New York's Richard Meier, was completed on a floodplain near the bridge across the Wabash River. The restoration and enhancement of New Harmony continues to this day under her patronage.

Jane Blaffer Owen, Indian Mound Farm, New Harmony, Indiana, 1998. Courtesy of Jane Blaffer Owen.

Chapter 2

Ruth Carter Stevenson's pivotal role in the architectural and cultural history of Texas began with her connection to Sarah Lawrence College in Bronxville, New York. Ruth Carter grew up in Fort Worth, a favorite child of Amon Carter, that city's larger-than-life leading citizen, known throughout the Southwest as "Mr. Fort Worth." Born the son of a blacksmith in Crafton, Texas, Carter started out washing dishes in a boardinghouse at age twelve and rose to become owner of the South's largest newspaper, the *Fort Worth Star-Telegram,* which he and a partner created in 1909 from two local dailies. He was a multimillionaire oilman and property owner who used his wealth and the force of his personality to make his town a better city, indeed make it a *city.* A born salesman, he practically invented modern Fort Worth, and when he died in 1955, half of the population worked for companies that Carter had lured to the city. He was a magnetic, bigger-than-life man.

Carter had many friends in Washington and was an early supporter of John Nance Garner and Franklin D. Roosevelt; the New Deal administration proved helpful to Carter and Fort Worth. To describe Amon Carter as colorful would be a feeble understatement; many stories and myths attached to him throughout his life, and his only biography is a compendium of anecdotal

Fort Worth skyline from northwest; Tarrant County Courthouse on the left, 1940. Photo by Byrd Williams III.

tales, both rich and apocryphal.[1] Though amusing reading, it is an incomplete record of someone who did such vast good for his city. It is doubtful that any American city ever had a more vivid and generous booster.

Amon Carter's newspaper was important for printing business and oil industry news not covered by smaller newspapers in the vast area west of Fort Worth, but some even credit the paper with the romantic idea of "the Cowboy," particularly the cowboy in West Texas, an enormous arid sea of land that lapped at Fort Worth's western edge. It was considered a *Star-Telegram* constituency, bigger than New York, Massachusetts, Pennsylvania, and Maryland combined. This area's huge readership made Carter's *Star-Telegram* the largest-selling newspaper in Texas. "Where the West Begins" was the paper's slogan, and Carter, who was in no way a cowboy, sometimes wore Western regalia at his Shady Oak Farm near Fort Worth, where he entertained celebrities like Charles Lindbergh and Gary Cooper. In the period between the wars, the cowboy was the surviving American folk hero, exalted in print and film and song, and his primary habitat was West Texas.

A handsome and imposing figure in well-cut suits, Carter wore a standard Stetson hat most of his life (he gave hundreds away as gifts), but his feet were uncomfortable in heeled boots, the de rigueur footwear of cowboy culture. The cowboy became such a vaunted part of American folk culture that by the end of the century, jeans, boots, and ten-gallon hats were a common after-hours costume for young urbanites who thronged Texas dance halls like Billy Bob's in Fort Worth in the 1970s or dressed up in pseudo-Western style for fancy, hugely successful charity galas like the Beef Baron's Ball in Dallas and Houston. Beginning in the 1970s, millionaire male country-music stars never appeared on the national stage without a large, high-crowned "cowboy hat." (The myth endures: in 1999, at Fort Worth's Van Cliburn International Competition for Outstanding Amateurs, the player voted most popular received a pair of cowboy boots.)

Carter's newspaper's slogan, "Where the West Begins," meant exactly that; Fort Worth was indeed located on the western border of the rich farmlands of North Central Texas, and from this edge the great areas of open, dry rolling prairie began and stretched away westward for seven hundred miles of mesquite and sand to El Paso and the Rio Grande. Fort Worth was nicknamed "Cowtown" for the herds of cattle that passed through its stockyards, more than anywhere but Chicago. Forty miles to the east was Dallas, which acquired the nickname "Big D." It was the metropolis of the Southwest, the "capital of 'couth'" as one Fort Worth old-timer derisively put it.

When Dallas snagged the big Texas Centennial celebration of 1936 for its fairgrounds, Amon Carter went to work and, with federal funding expedited

Will Rogers and Amon Carter. Courtesy of *Fort Worth Star-Telegram* Photograph Collection, Special Collections Division, University of Texas at Arlington.

by Roosevelt, erected the Art Deco Will Rogers Memorial Coliseum, Auditorium and Pioneer Tower, named after his show-business cowboy pal and dear friend who had died in a plane crash the year before. (A bronze statue of Rogers on horseback stands in front.) It was also *his* way of celebrating the state's centenary, and he further planned his *own* show, the Texas Frontier Centennial, a crowd-pleaser with a Western theme, near the Coliseum. This entire complex of buildings was located on a part of the parcel, one hundred acres of open land west of the Trinity River, that Carter, in the early 1930s, had convinced Fort Worth's city council to buy and reserve for public use. The price was $100,000, and the purchase was dubbed "Carter's Folly" by critics. Today the property is home to Fort Worth's Cultural District of world-class museums and theaters.

Carter's Frontier Centennial, next to the Will Rogers complex, was a group of entertainment buildings with, as its centerpiece, New York showman Billy Rose's Casa Manana. The Casa Manana was an open-air cabaret theater for 4,500 diners with a huge revolving stage and celebrity performers like Paul Whiteman and Eddie Cantor, *plus* a dancer from Chicago named Sally Rand. Miss Rand performed nude, under pale lighting, with huge white ostrich fans or enormous rubber balloons. Her Fan Dance and Bubble Dance on the Casa

Manana stage and her sideshow of equally bare young women, Sally Rand's Nude Ranch, were what most people remembered of Fort Worth's answer to Dallas. Carter erected the world's second-largest sign opposite the Texas Centennial entrance in Dallas, which blinked its 130-foot message day and night: "FORTY FIVE MINUTES WEST TO WHOOPEE!" with "FORT WORTH" spelled out in tall neon letters.

Fort Worth was brawny and blue-collar, while Dallas was formal, corporate, and a little stiff. Neiman-Marcus, the celebrated specialty clothing store, was founded in Dallas in the early part of the century and had much to do with the character of Dallas's demeanor and reputation. It could be argued that the city's well-developed preoccupation with style, with appearances and the surface of things, emanated from the reach for perfection in attire that the store epitomized. Rivalry and Fort Worth's envy of its tony neighbor to the east were the Minneapolis–St. Paul, Midland-Odessa, Sherman-Denison thing.

Amon Carter once met Stanley Marcus, the president of Neiman-Marcus, at a Fort Worth party and in the course of some small talk complained that ad linage was down at the *Star-Telegram,* prompting Marcus to suggest that it

Will Rogers Memorial Coliseum, Auditorium, and Pioneer Memorial Tower, 1937; Wyatt C. Hedrick and Elmer G. Withers, associate architects. Photo by Byrd Williams IV in *Fort Worth's Legendary Landmarks*, Texas Christian University Press, Fort Worth, 1995.

would help if Carter would let him take ads in the paper. "Not until you have a store here!" was Carter's retort. The rivalry was probably helpful in one way: Carter used it when he was raising money for a pet project in Fort Worth. He would flaunt Dallas's successful record on a similar project, and soon his friends would cough up and exceed what the rival city had done.

Josephine Hudson, widow of oilman Edward Hudson and granddaughter of John Peter Smith, an early settler who gave land to what is now downtown Fort Worth, is a ninety-odd-year-old doyenne of Fort Worth society and has seen it all. Taking a larger view, she explains the "chip" this way: "It was just jealousy, pure jealousy; Dallas was richer and bigger! But *remember* that the culture, the appreciation of art and music, was *always* in Fort Worth from the beginning. Dallas was just interested in *money!*"[2] Until recently, art and architecture achievements in Fort Worth through three postwar decades have in many ways exceeded those of Dallas, and other Texas cities for that matter, but intercity sniping between the two towns still pops up. Civic paranoia dies hard.

Ruth Carter first attended the Madeira School in Virginia with her childhood friend Cynthia Brants, and after boarding school the two went on to Sarah Lawrence College, where Ruth majored in chemistry and Cynthia studied art. Brants says, "She is and always has been the most organized person I have ever known and one who is forever loyal to her friends and the people she works with. She gives her all to whatever she undertakes and expects the same from others. She doesn't suffer fools or shoddy behavior *ever!*"[3]

Ruth once came to a University of Texas Board of Regents meeting with a needlepoint rug and spread it out and sat through the entire meeting with her head down on her needles and stitching, looking up occasionally over her glasses, until near the end of the meeting, when the men had worn themselves out arguing over some minute point. She put down the needlepoint, stood up, and with a few words, cut right to the *bone* of the issue.[4]

Sarah Lawrence was exceptionally progressive in its teaching methods: courses were led by nonacademic professionals in their fields; writing was taught by writers, chemistry was taught by chemists, and art was taught by artists. Ruth's aptitude for analysis and thoroughness made her a star chemistry student. The school's proximity to New York City, where Ruth's mother lived at the time, also made it a convenient location. For Cynthia Brants, the nearby New York painters made Sarah Lawrence a watershed experience. She later returned and taught painting at the school.

Back in Fort Worth, while Cynthia produced paintings in a flat-roofed, glass-walled studio, Ruth married J. Lee Johnson III in 1945, joined the Junior League, and had five children. Amon Carter "wheeled and dealed," and boosted Fort Worth, and continued gathering a large collection of the Old West art of Frederic Remington and Charles Russell, which he began in 1928. His first art pieces were installment-plan purchases of some Russell paintings from a New York dealer.

Heiress Anne Burnett Windfohr Tandy was a dynamic Fort Worth figure and, though a generation older than Ruth, became her mentor and role model. "Anne was tremendously important to me," Ruth Stevenson recalled in 1999. "She told me that no one had to settle for mediocrity, that there were plenty of good architects in the country, and that we should not be limited in our choices."[5] Through John Entenza's California magazine *Arts and Architecture,* which her husband brought home, she learned about California modern architect Harwell Hamilton Harris, who was a gifted Frank Lloyd Wright scholar with a special talent for residential design. In 1955 she and her husband hired him to design a house for their family on a large, sloping site below the old Amon Carter house where she grew up.

Harris was Dean of the School of Architecture at the University of Texas at Austin and, though noted for his California work, had gained only a small foothold in the state as an architect, designing a house in Austin and a Dallas model home for *House Beautiful.* The commission in Fort Worth was the sort of thing a struggling architect dreams of, and when the crisply rambling, one-story house was finished in 1957, Ruth had been happily indoctrinated by Harris into the modern in architecture. With her discipline and decisiveness she readily absorbed what interested her and, as with the other things that she would undertake, became enthusiastic about modern architecture. The house Harris designed for her was a California-Organic style of modern, a homage to Wright's 1917 Hollyhock House in Los Angeles.[6]

When Dominique and John de Menil's daughter Adelaide enrolled in Sarah Lawrence in the 1950s, they became supporters of the school and came to Fort Worth one year to hear the school's president at a fund-raising dinner. Cynthia Brants, an active Sarah Lawrence supporter, knew the de Menils through the school and the art world and during this, their first visit to North Texas, introduced them to her good friend Ruth Carter Johnson. Ruth, Cynthia, Dominique, and John sat in front of the fire at the Ridglea Country Club, and Ruth enjoyed the elegance and intelligence of the unassuming French couple with their enthusiasm for Texas: "*Good lord!* Jean de Menil was the most charming man ever put on this *earth!* He was just terrific and later became my friend and defender as a founding member of the board when I was getting the Amon Carter Museum started."[7]

At the time of Ruth's meeting with the de Menils there was no discussion of the memorial museum for Amon Carter that had been specified for funding in his will; talk of architecture centered on the campus which was under way in Houston for the University of St. Thomas. Dominique and John were always drawn to personalities with drive and directness, qualities that Amon Carter's daughter held in abundance. She in turn was impressed by the French couple's attractiveness and knowledge, and when the two new St. Thomas buildings, one an art building, were dedicated, Dominique and John invited Ruth to come as one of their guests for what Ruth describes as a "three-day *do.*"

"George Anne, Amon Jr.'s wife, and I went down to Houston and stayed at the Warwick in this huge suite as big as three of these rooms," Ruth Stevenson recalled at her house in 1997.

> They had it stocked with every kind of cocktail and champagne that you could imagine: it was first-class and the *essence* of hospitality. The de Menils did everything to gracious perfection! Parties were held all over Houston, and at a luncheon at the de Menils' I met Philip. He was an absolutely enchanting man!
>
> Philip came up to our suite later in the afternoon, and we had martinis and a grand time talking about all sorts of things. He was like some dinner partners that I have been lucky to have: he was so *full* of any kind of information that you might want to talk about, just a terribly charming man, alive and caring and concerned and obviously aware of my lack of knowledge about a lot of things.
>
> I had no deep knowledge of art; I never went to a museum in the whole four years that I was at Sarah Lawrence, but later when my husband and I were living in South Bend, Indiana, I made trips to Chicago's Art Institute and it was there that an interest began. Philip was very sympathetic about my shortcomings in the fields that he knew so much about. Through all these years I have learned *so much* from him.
>
> The impression that I got from everyone there that weekend was this huge admiration everyone had for Dominique and John, who were of course Philip's great friends. I was able to use my schoolroom French some in the bilingual bantering going on at the parties, and this seemed to impress John de Menil: "Philip, what do you think of that? She speaks French!" Philip's French was flawless, of course, and it was all great fun. There was a warm, immediate rapport, and we just got along famously. We talked about everything from gardening to art collecting. Before the weekend was over, I asked him if he would come to Fort Worth and talk to us about designing Dad's memorial. He said indeed he would and was soon back in Texas.[8]

Johnson made his first visit to Fort Worth shortly afterward and was hired by the Amon Carter Foundation to design the Carter museum.

Fort Worth was never the cultural backwater that many on the outside, particularly in Dallas, perceived. Betty Blake, born and raised in Philadelphia and educated there and in Paris, opened the Southwest's first contemporary art gallery in a Dallas shopping center storefront in 1950. Assisted by the initiative of Betty and Edward Marcus of the merchandising clan, her Betty McLean Gallery became the area's beachhead of interest in modern art and sculpture.

"The real interest in what I was trying to do came primarily from Fort Worth, not Dallas," she recalls.

> Sam Cantey was sort of the linchpin over there; he was the cohesive figure with the most passionate interest in modern art, whipping up collecting among his pals. He and Ted Weiner were the leaders. And Anne Windfohr was the zestful buyer with the great *eye!* I was crazy about her style and enthusiasm. She was very *strong*. She would come in the gallery and, looking around, would say, "I want that and that and that! Send them over." One time she saw a little Kelly Fearing of a yellow butterfly that she liked; I told her there was a reserve on it but she said, "I want it!" and threw a check on the table. I said I couldn't accept it and she sort of stormed out. Sam Cantey called immediately from Fort Worth and said I had made a horrible mistake with Anne. I called her when the reserve was released and she said, "Send it over," just like that.
>
> Though Anne bought art from all over, the New York dealers would sort of go to pieces when she walked in. To them she was Texas oil-rich, and it was right after the war and sales weren't too good. Once she was in Knoedler's when they were having a Tamayo show, and she wanted two in the gallery and the one in the window. It turned out that Stanley Marcus had already bought the one in the window. I can't *imagine* how they settled that!
>
> Dallas people were sort of into modern art in a hop-skip fashion, while the Fort Worth crowd were dead serious about it. The Fort Worth Art Center openings were still held in a room of the old library and were packed affairs. The reputation that accrued to Fort Worth later with its outstanding museums was based early in the active and real interest in modern art by a few leaders.[9]

The state's first public art gallery, located in the city's library, received its charter in 1892 and in 1904 purchased a George Inness with money it had raised by public subscription to begin a permanent collection. Fort Worth's population was around 26,000, and membership in the museum association could be purchased for $2.00 a year. The museum remained in the city's Carnegie-endowed library until 1954, when it moved out of downtown to a new building near the Will Rogers Coliseum in the "Carter's Folly" area of city-owned land destined to hold a collection of other cultural buildings. The museum's modern building, named the Fort Worth Art Center, included the Scott Theater and was built with city bond money. It was designed by Bauhaus alumnus Herbert Bayer of Aspen, Colorado, in association with Fort Worth architect Wiley Clarkson and received backing by local collectors of modern art like Anne and Robert Windfohr, Sam Cantey, and oilman Ted Weiner.

Like Ruth Carter, Anne Burnett had grown up in Fort Worth, and she was the granddaughter of another legendary Fort Worth figure, the cattle tycoon and oilman Burk Burnett. Born on a ranch in the early part of the century and raised in Fort Worth, Anne and her Baltimore-born husband, Robert Windfohr, were early financial supporters of the Fort Worth Art Center, now titled the Modern Art Museum of Fort Worth. The museum's vastly expanded program is today overseen by Anne Burnett's daughter and the Burnett Foundation.

Anne Burnett met her third husband, oilman Robert Windfohr, in Santa Fe. Robert later brought Raymond Entenmann from Philadelphia's Pennsylvania Academy of Fine Arts, where he was dean, to be the Art Center's director. Entenmann, a landscape architect, remained at the museum until 1966, when he moved to Dallas. Before his contract with the museum was terminated, he pinch-hit for Ruth Johnson briefly before she hired Mitchell Wilder as the first director of the Amon Carter Museum. Ten years later when another Fort Worth museum, the Kimbell, was being organized, Ruth Johnson recommended, as director, Richard Fargo Brown, formerly with New York's Frick Museum and the Los Angeles County Art Museum and one of the Carter Museum original board members. She recalls that Ric Brown was one of the names Philip Johnson suggested in late 1960 as a board member of the newly formed Amon Carter Museum of Western Art.[10] After the Kimbell Museum directors hired Brown as the first director, he spent a year deliberating about an architect for a new building—at one time he thought Mies was the best choice—but, in 1967, hired Philadelphia's Louis Kahn to design what became an internationally celebrated structure.

Ray Entenmann recalls that Anne Windfohr disliked the popular perception of her hometown as a "cowtown," but loved art and with her uncanny "good eye" began gathering an extraordinary collection of modern paintings and sculpture in the 1930s. Betty Blake says that Anne bought what she liked, not what she was supposed to like. Not anywhere in the private world of Texas at that time had anyone gathered the likes of the premier Modigliani, Gauguin, Picasso, Nolde, Ensor, and Manzu pieces that Anne placed with great style in her home in the suburb of Westover Hills, designed before the war by Houston's John F. Staub. One young Fort Worth visitor to the Windfohr house recalls the small Picassos hung expertly on a powder room wall. Tall, dynamic, and striking, Anne and her husband Bob, along with banker Sam Cantey and his wife Betsey, led a small Fort Worth group in the 1940s, 1950s, and 1960s that was interested in modern art.

In the early 1950s Anne, looking westward, hired Frank Lloyd Wright to design a residence for her and her husband on a hillside site in the Ridglea Country Club area, then eventually fired him because, among other reasons, Wright didn't want air-conditioning in the house with a gilded dome roof that he wanted to build. He had named it "Crownfield." Sensing his clients' resistance on the cooling issue, the eighty-year-old architect suggested that they pipe cold water through the floor slab and open the doors and windows. Before Wright was dismissed, the contractor Thomas Byrne went out to Wright's Taliesin West studio in Arizona with the Windfohrs to discuss the design; he soon called his office and asked an estimator how much gold leaf was. The estimator asked if he wanted square-inch or square-foot prices and Byrne answered, "Hell, I want it by the square acre!"[11] Wright had trouble getting a foothold in Texas. In the 1930s, Stanley Marcus, the young adventurous merchant, asked Wright to design a house for his family in Dallas. The imperious architect paid his first visit to Marcus during some balmy January weather and later proposed a design without bedrooms; he wanted the Marcus family to sleep year-round on open porches. A Dallas architect ended up designing Stanley Marcus's modern house.

Oilman Ted Weiner was also born in Fort Worth but raised in the far, arid reaches of West Texas. He traveled often to New York after the war to meet with investors in his oil company and through them—seeing where and how they lived—became interested in modern art, particularly sculpture. (He once ran a used metal parts business for his father in the little oil-patch town of Wink.) Weiner met art dealer Curt Valentin and in the 1940s began gathering the first large collection of modern sculpture in the Southwest. Pieces by Mary Callery, Jean Arp, Lipchitz, Picasso, Henri Laurens, Henry Moore, and Modigliani, plus the best work of Fort Worth sculptors, were acquired by Weiner. Fort Worth artist James Blake recalls that the first Francis Bacon painting he ever saw hung over the Weiner fireplace; Sam Cantey's niece Sandra says that her uncle considered Weiner the undisputed, number one expert on modern art in Fort Worth. The collection made Ted Weiner a pacesetting collector of modern sculpture whose example predated the direction that Patsy and Raymond Nasher of Dallas began so comprehensively in the late 1960s.

In 1949, through the suggestion of one of his Wall Street friends, Ted Weiner met and hired thirty-three-year-old Edward Larrabee Barnes of New York to design a house and garden for the sculpture on several acres adjoining

Ridglea Country Club. Barnes had been a member of the yeasty postwar group of students at Walter Gropius's Harvard, which included Philip Johnson, Eliot Noyes, John Johansen, Paul Rudolph, Ulrich Franzen, and I. M. Pei.

Barnes located the large, strongly horizontal, and crisply articulated Weiner house behind a tall, street-side stucco wall and oriented the open plan to landscaped terraces leading down to the golf course. It was only the second house Barnes had designed and was marked by screen-walls of grey ledgestone and expanses of glass beneath deep overhangs with oak-sheathed ceilings. The house overlooked several acres of a lushly landscaped sculpture garden and pond that Ruth Stevenson, an avid gardener, recalls was "just perfection!" The Weiner house was the first modern house in the International Style in North Texas.

Ted, one of three sons of a self-made Jewish father who left home at twelve, was charming, handsome, and good-humored, but never an "insider" in Fort Worth's tight social establishment of cultural movers and shakers: the Carters, Moncriefs, Windfohrs, and later the Basses. Yet Ted was a generous contributor to many civic causes and institutions, including the All Saints Episcopal Church that his wife Lucille and daughter Gwen attended. Like other Fort Worth oilmen, Weiner enjoyed entertaining Hollywood people like Bob Hope and Hal Wallis who came to Fort Worth to invest in the oil business and play golf with Ted, who was seldom without a putter in his hand.

In 1960 Ted moved his wife and daughter to Palm Springs, California, but kept and maintained the house and sculpture garden. Through Sam Cantey, the city's unofficial culture-guide and an unabashed Weiner admirer, numerous arts groups from across the country were directed to Weiner's stunning house and garden. Local civic groups often used the house for fund-raising, and it became a place-to-see for citizens and out-of-towners alike. In 1965 Ted offered to donate the large sculpture collection plus the house and garden to the Fort Worth Art Center, where he was a key supporter and longtime board member. His offer was turned down by the board of trustees, who cited a lack of endowment as part of the package. Ted's daughter Gwen recalls that "Ruth Carter was the community 'head-honcho' whose argument against acceptance of Dad's offer was based on economics."[12] Robert Windfohr notified Ted of the board's decision.

The rebuff stung, and soon afterward Ted sold the house and garden, calling the rejection "dumb." He moved the sculpture collection to Palm Springs, where today it enhances that city's art museum. When Dallas's Meyerson Symphony Center, designed by I. M. Pei, was completed in the late 1980s, Gwen Weiner presented bronzes by Lipchitz and Laurens from the collection for the Center's

Betty Marcus Garden; there are no Weiner sculptures in any Fort Worth public space. Edward Barnes returned to Fort Worth in the 1960s to design Neiman-Marcus's first suburban store outside of Dallas and in 1982 was hired by the Dallas Museum of Art to design its large new building in downtown Dallas.

Philip Johnson came to Fort Worth soon after the Menil *fete* for the University of St. Thomas; he met with Ruth and with Amon Carter Jr. and Katrine Deakins (Carter's secretary for forty years), the two other members of the Amon Carter Foundation, which was set up by Carter before he died. Carter stipulated in his will that the foundation, with board members Ruth, Amon Jr., and Katrine Deakins, would control the funding body for the construction of a memorial museum to hold his collection of paintings and bronzes by Charles Russell and Frederic Remington. After Carter's estate was settled and the inheritance taxes paid, the government, according to Ruth Carter Stevenson, said in 1997 that:

> something like $11,000,000 more was still owed because of some claim on an oil production company out in West Texas that Dad had set up for the foundation. We paid it and then went to court and got the money back with 6 percent interest. We knew immediately that this sort of "cookie-jar" windfall would go toward Dad's monument. When he died people wanted to put up a statue in the square and all sorts of things but Amon and I said, "no, it's going to be a *museum*."[13]

Earlier, years before she met Philip Johnson, Ruth had had to do some convincing with her father about the museum architect. Amon Carter was Fort Worth *loyal:* "I made my money here and I want to spend it here!" Czechoslovakia-born Joseph Pelich was the prominent local architect who did all the architectural work for Carter, including the 1936 outdoor theater for the Casa Manana and the Amon Carter Airport terminal east of town. Pelich was his natural choice for the memorial, but Ruth felt that she should have the freedom to select the best-qualified architect for the job, regardless of where he lived. Anne Windfohr had told her that there were plenty of good architects and she never had to settle for second-best. Ruth Carter Stevenson recalls, "Anne was wonderful! She took me under her wing and influenced me in so many ways; she certainly raised my sights about architecture. That was even before I asked Harwell Harris to design my house."[14]

Ruth, described by many as her father's daughter, was no slouch as a salesman herself. She posed it this way:

> "Dad, look, no one in Fort Worth has ever designed a museum that would be the kind of museum that I think you want. Remember when you added on to

> the *Star-Telegram* and the new Goss presses had to go in there, you got someone that the press people recommended, a special architect to design that part of the building. So all I'm asking you to do is to give me the leverage to bring a consultant in or someone that knows about art museums." He agreed to let me find the right architect for the job. I told my brother, I said, "Look, you run the newspaper and you do the Boy Scouts and the YMCA, but this I'm going to do because I know more about it than you and Katrine Deakins do. You just give me the money and let me take care of it." And he said, "That's fine."
>
> Later, after Dad died, for a while we worked with the architect from Aspen who came down, Herbert Bayer. Katrine, Dad's secretary, took over. She was going to replicate Dad's office and was calling Bayer every fifteen minutes to tell him something else she wanted in there; he and I barely got a word in edgewise. He finally threw up his hands and backed out. So there we *were*, and right at that time I met Philip at the de Menils' in Houston.[15]

Philip Johnson found Fort Worth a refreshing contrast to Houston. Its terrain rolled up above each side of a Trinity River plain that separated the downtown business section from the residential, suburban districts to the west. Sycamore street-trees informed the grid of brick-paved residential streets that diagonally crossed broad Camp Bowie Boulevard, the primary artery from the river plain to the prairie and ranch land beginning on the city's western edge. Ruth toured Johnson around, and his historian's eye noted quickly the abundance of Art Deco buildings built in the 1920s and 1930s, brought to a climax with Amon Carter's Will Rogers complex and its soaring tower. Philip shared with Ruth a love of landscaping, and he noted admiringly the gardens she was creating around her new house to the designs of Californian Thomas Church. This enduring passion for horticulture of Johnson's derived from the childhood summers at Townsend Farms watching his mother attending her gardens and having the farm roads lined with elms.

Johnson and Ruth visited the property for the museum that the Carter Foundation had purchased near the Will Rogers Auditorium and Coliseum. It was a triangular site, between Lancaster Avenue and Camp Bowie Boulevard, that sloped downward from its apex, marred by a service station, to the flat blocks that flanked the forested river-plain park. Fort Worth's modest skyline of downtown buildings was silhouetted distantly to the east on the opposite rise above the river. But on this first visit, only the basic idea for a building came quickly to him: it would be a "porch," a great, monumental loggia that would, from its elevated position, lay claim to its site and the city skyline in the distance. For the time being, however, Johnson kept his counsel about the basic design concept and listened at length to Foundation board member

Katrine Deakins, Amon Carter's faithful, self-appointed keeper of his legacy. As Ruth points out, "Mrs. Deakins was devoted to Dad and was paying the bills and had to be reckoned with. Sometimes she drove us crazy, though."[16]

For several years, Johnson's thinking about architecture had been going through a change. The International Style of modernism, for which he had been such an articulate spokesman, had begun to lose its intellectual and stylistic lustre. Those young years of his, stretching back to his mother's Sunday afternoons of illustrated appreciation of European monuments, on through his many travels to the Continent as an intensely curious sight-seeing teenager and young adult, affected him deeply and lastingly.

The immediate and sharply felt experience of Europe's textbook of architectural eras—the Classical, Gothic, Renaissance, and Baroque, all the Revivals, and finally the Modern—left him with a passionate and protean sensibility, what Russell Hitchcock called his "catholic and relaxed attitude to all history, including the traditions inherited from the early modern architects."[17] No other practicing architect of the century had his reservoir of knowledge and affection for *all* architecture. It was bound to eventually affect his dedication to the strictures of Miesian philosophy. Mies van der Rohe had been his father-hero and international modernism his mother-church for almost thirty years. Now in his midfifties, in middle age, his nervous feet began to tap out a different rhythm. Hitchcock explained, "The result is that to Johnson architecture is not only an art, and an art of the present, it is an art that exists in time, with roots, selected roots, extending backwards, and feelers, antennae, reaching forward. It is an art of continuous evolution."[18]

Curving non-Miesian forms made appearances in his work as early as 1954 in the Kneses Tifereth Israel Synagogue in Port Chester, New York. An oval entry foyer under a shallow-domed ceiling attaches to a tall steel-and-masonry "box" of a worship space which is "roofed" by a shallow, taut ceiling-vault of plaster seemingly *stretched* to the columns in the long walls like fabric. It was the same kind of canopy ceiling he had added to his guest house's tiny bedroom in 1953 and was a clear reference to Sir John Soane's London breakfast room of 1812. It was a daring, new kind of sensual modern esthetic of subtle historic reference within a Miesian framework. Johnson was eyeing the door and leaving "home."

As late as 1955, however, he was still employing Miesian theology in the East Fifty-fifth brownstone apartment that he redesigned for himself. "It was a small apartment and it was *white,*" recalls Jay Presson Allen, a New York playwright who grew up in West Texas ranching country, who had cocktails there.

Walls, ceilings, floors, the slipcovers, were all white; the lighting was on the floor—white—and I went into the bathroom, which was white, and next to it was the bedroom, and it was pretty white, too. I said, "Philip, where do you keep a mop, or a vacuum cleaner or a dust rag? Where is all that *stuff?*" And he laughed and said "Oh!" and he had another small bedroom that was devoted to maintenance equipment; none of *that* impinged on the purity of the rooms that he had to look at every day. A little later, my husband Lewis and I were in an art gallery admiring some pieces of Trova "walking man" sculpture and I said, "You know who would just love these? Philip Johnson." And a voice behind us said, "Yes, I did—I do—and I just bought one." It was Philip.[19]

At Yale in early 1959, on the occasion of the first one-man show of his buildings and while he was at work on a number of break-away-from-Mies projects like the open-air church in Indiana and the museum in Fort Worth, Johnson said:

> My stand today is violently *anti*-Miesian. I think that is the most natural thing in the world, just as I'm not really very fond of my father. It is all very understandable; in these days of change, you have to thumb your nose, as you can, in order to exert your own poor little ego. Mies said it beautifully, "I'd rather be good than original." I suppose the rest of us aren't quite that great; and we all have our little egos, and we are damn well going to express them, and I think that is what's happening.
>
> I have always been delighted to be called *Mies van der Johnson*. It has always seemed proper in the history of architecture for a young man to understand, even to imitate, the great genius of an older generation. Mies is such a genius. But *I* grow old! No respect, no respect. This one-sided exhibition of mine is unfair, unfair to my work as a whole but maybe amusing to Yale undergraduates. My direction is clear: *traditionalism* . . . not academic revival; there are no classic orders in my work, no Gothic finials. I try to pick up what I like throughout history. We cannot *not* know history. How could the design for the Roofless Church exist without Bramante, or the Amon Carter Museum without the Loggia dei Lanzi? I have gone back to my own little way of looking at things, which is purely historical, and not revivalist, but eclectic.
>
> I must explain that my past is peculiar. I have spent much more time as a critic, an historian, than I have as an architect, because I didn't start architecture until I was thirty-five years old; so naturally my historical sense is overdeveloped.[20]

When work on the Fort Worth museum began, Johnson was heavily involved with Mies van der Rohe's design for the German-American master's

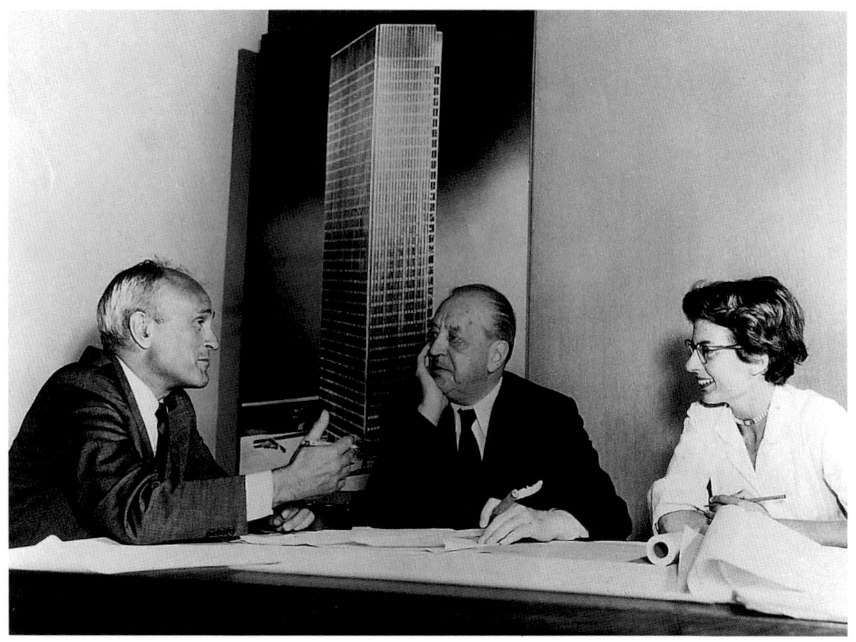

Philip Johnson, Mies van der Rohe, and Phyllis Bronfman Lambert with photograph of Seagram Building Model, mid-1950s.
Courtesy of the Museum of Modern Art, New York.

preeminent project: the Seagram Building on New York's Park Avenue, for Samuel Bronfman, president of Joseph Seagram and Company. The pupil became partner to his hero for the postwar period's most distinguished skyscraper.

In the mid-1950s, Samuel Bronfman's daughter Phyllis heard that her father had hired Charles Luckman of California's Perrera and Luckman to design Seagram's headquarters building in New York. She immediately flew home from Paris and talked her father into letting *her* hire the architect, which she did with her friend Philip's help. The top architects of the day were considered: Gropius and Breuer, Harrison & Abramovitz, Howe and Lescaze, Eero Saarinen, Louis Kahn, Minoru Yamasaki, Le Corbusier, Frank Lloyd Wright, and Mies van der Rohe. Mies's statement to Phyllis Bronfman Lambert— "*Form* is not the aim of our work, but only the result"—won the day for him over Corbu and Wright. He formed an association with the large New York firm of Kahn and Jacobs for the construction drawings and asked Johnson to be his New York design partner. It was ironic that as Johnson was experiencing this ultimate "submersion" in Miesian ideology with his longtime "master," his mind was wandering off down unorthodox modernist paths. Johnson's role as advisor was undoubtedly instrumental in getting this prestigious commission for his mentor.

Johnson's design responsibility ultimately involved the lobby areas, the building's lighting design, with Richard Kelly, and the deft steel-and-glass entrance canopies on the building's side streets. Johnson's most important contribution to the popular success of the building was the design of the bifurcated Four Seasons Restaurant on the ground floor. These elegant ancillary parts of Mies's masterpiece were personal triumphs for Johnson and his brilliant consultants and provided the stern and stately bronze-and-glass skyscraper with an enduring sex appeal. When the thirty-seven-story sheer-walled structure was completed and stood proud on its deep plaza amidst the stepped-back curtain-wall neighbors, a wag compared the Seagram Building to a very *soigné* lady in a room full of frumps. And Mies's famous maxim, "Less is more," caused Henry-Russell Hitchcock, upon seeing the sumptuous building for the first time, to remark, "I have never seen more of less."[21]

Four Seasons Restaurant, Seagram Building, New York City, 1959; with suspended Richard Lippold sculpture. Philip Johnson, architect. Photo by Ezra Stoller © Esto.

Though Mies, the dour master, was served well by his acolyte, the two of them more or less parted professional and philosophical company following the Seagram completion in 1959. John Manley was a young employee of Johnson's during this period and witnessed their working relationship in New York:

> Given a design problem, Mies would sit and think about it and think about it, and weeks would go by, or a month, then he would announce a solution and that was *it*. In all that time Johnson's light was flashing constantly; he would be suggesting dozens and dozens of solutions. This distracted Mies. The old German couldn't work that way, and soon they only communicated through a liaison. *This* upset Johnson. Mies' devoted go-between with Johnson was Gene Summers, a young, devoted Texas A&M graduate, whose twangy accent further irritated the New Yorker.[22]

Though Johnson later moved completely out of his early idol's shadow, in public he never referred to Mies as anything but a "master," and "one of the giants."

Curving, nonorthogonal surfaces, forms, and details entered Johnson's design vocabulary and became integral, identifying elements in the mode of modernism that he would practice with refined panache through the 1960s. But as early as 1955, while he was working with Mies on the Seagram Building, he was meditating openly about his conflicts over style and design in a speech at Barnard College:

> A style is not a set of rules or shackles, as some of my colleagues seem to think. A style is a climate in which to operate, a springboard to leap further into the air. The onus of designing a new style anytime one designs a new building is

> hardly freedom; it is too heavy a load except for the greatest of Michelangelos or Wrights. Strict style discipline hindered not in the slightest the creators of the Parthenon, nor did the pointed arch confine the designers of Amiens. . . .
>
> Rigid rules do help out bad architects but do not inhibit the imaginative. That is what is so *wonderful!* No single artist is conscious of the "rules" any more than he is of his *Weltanschauung* . . . the how-you-look-at-things. He just creates. Actually, he struggles the best he can *against* the style, *against* the known, *toward* the unknown, *toward* the original. Every modern architect being brought up with the modern style under his skin can struggle against it with all his strength. If he is great he will bend it. I use the future tense because so far none has done so.[23]

By 1960, it was clear that Johnson had become restless with the vows he had been observing with International Style modernism, particularly the personal breed of it practiced by Mies van der Rohe, and was attempting, with each new job, something more expressive. The Amon Carter Museum, finished in 1961, was a very visible design break with orthodox Miesian principles.

Ruth Stevenson (divorced from J. Lee Johnson in 1979) recalls, "Amon and Mrs. Deakins and I went up to New York in the spring of 1958 to see the first drawings. It was almost identical to what it looks like now. It was just the building sitting up there without the garden or the approaches, but it was the same *front* that you see today. There was no mention of stone or anything like that, but it was gorgeous and exactly what I was looking for. We approved it and asked Philip to proceed."[24]

Indeed, Johnson's initial schematic design for the building, its fundamental appearance, remained the same from the beginning. A service station at the western apex of the site and a north-south street on the east side of the site were built-in constraints; the street on the east was soon abandoned, creating a parklike space for the front of the building, and the service station was purchased later for the museum's first addition. Tom Seymour, superintendent for the contractor Thomas S. Byrne, recalls that one of the first things that Johnson did was to have a platform built to fully understand what the view would be like from the main floor of the museum he was planning.[25]

He located the simple, rectangular building, "a box with a porch," at the western side of its triangular site, with its "porch" on the east, fronting an all-glass wall and facing down the site's slope across a raised "front yard" to the skyline beyond. The museum floor was on a podium which he would connect with tiers of landings and steps, flanked by native shrubbery, to the large outdoor "room," on its own raised masonry platform. This large-scale open-air space anchors the building to its site and frames the bottom edge of the distant view. It is bordered by a stylized granite railing—like the one at Johnson's Glass House—and broad walks around a recessed lawn holding a group of native trees. Three monumentally abstract and vertical Henry Moore sculptures were mounted on a Johnson-designed, boldly scaled "table" of dark stone at the eastern edge of the podium. One might question the inclusion of a British artist's work at a museum dedicated first to Western art and later to American art specifically, but the Moores worked perfectly as foils to the terraces of the horizontally composed complex, and besides, Ruth Carter had picked them out herself in a New York gallery with Philip's approval.

The design of the building addressed the city in a simple fashion. In Johnson's words, "It was never intended to be a real *museum.* It was to be a memorial to Amon Carter and serve as a repository for his collection of Western paintings and sculpture. Katrine Deakins was running the show, and what she wanted was a *memorial,* not a museum. It was during construction that the idea for the museum shifted. That it should be for the *collecting* of Western art was suggested by Rene d'Harnoncourt, director of the Museum of Modern Art."[26] Later its purview focused on American art in general, and it was renamed the Amon Carter Museum.

The building's linear plan was an extension of the east-facing loggia space, which moved inside its great wall of bronze-framed, tinted glass to become a double-height "great hall" running the length of the building. This tall space, originally skylighted, was backed by a series of small galleries on two floors. The building's mechanical services were stacked in a small block on the building's rear west face. As the building evolved into a museum requiring more space, no structural changes to the original spaces have been made, but two building additions were designed by Johnson and a third large expansion was planned and designed in 1996.

With the exception of the great "window" facing the city, the blocky walls of the building were without fenestration but given sharp, minimalist details and faced with flush bands of creamy shell-limestone, first seen and admired by Johnson on the Houston City Hall in the 1940s. Several trips were made by Johnson to the quarries in Leander, Texas, to assure he got the right color. The interior details and finishes—teak, bronze, and a pinkish-grey Soames Sound granite from Maine—were in the same strict but elegant vocabulary as the Seagram Building, the most expensive high-rise building ever built.

Seymour says that Johnson was always the consummate professional who knew what he wanted but could bend when necessary, and Seymour's mechanical engineer recalls that Johnson was the politest architect that he ever worked with, always calling him "Mister" and cooperating fully with his requests. Richard Foster was Johnson's chief assistant, and one of his jobs was to approve or reject the granite flooring from Maine that, to everyone's surprise, had small, integral black flecks. Rather than reject the entire shipment, Foster resolved the issue by saying that if a quarter coin would not cover one of the dark spots, the piece of flooring had to be rejected. Ruth Carter Stevenson says, "Philip sort of had carte blanche with the budget. Mrs. Deakins was signing the checks and approving what he did, and we just stood back and admired the result."[27]

The strongly identifying elements of the finished building were the loggia's columns: refined and original and visually memorable, they were the most controversial points for critics. The five bays of tapered limestone pillars, concave on four surfaces, flared out from small bases to gracefully join the low segmental arches framing the bays. (The cut-stone column sections had to be threaded over supporting steel columns before the roof structure was erected.) Johnson's romantic maneuvering of architectural form within the modern canon gave rise to one critic's label of "toe-dance modern" for the Amon Carter and other similarly inflected buildings that were beginning to show up from the offices of Edward Stone, Paul Rudolph, and Minoru Yamasaki as these modernists began to play around with the "rules" of international modernism. (Johnson, himself expert at coining nicknames, gave a cheeky lecture in the spring of 1958 in which he analyzed the changing scene and described architects Matthew Nowicki and Eero Saarinen as "wavy-roof boys" and his Harvard mentor Marcel Breuer as a "peasant-mannerist.")

An "honest" structural detail of the Amon Carter building was the way Johnson designed the ceilings of the loggia and great hall. He had seen an industrial building in Houston designed by O'Neil Ford of San Antonio and Richard Colley of Corpus Christi which had a cladding of marble held in place with stainless-steel clamps. Interested in "heating up" his modernism, Johnson admired the decorative effect of the attachment system and in Fort Worth used bronze bolts to attach "tiles" of limestone to the ceiling structure of his loggia and great hall. The resulting bossed surface of subtle richness complemented the building's austerity.

The opening of the museum in 1961 was the major cultural event of Fort Worth's postwar period. Notables from New York and elsewhere flew to the city in a chartered plane on an icy January weekend for a big dinner and other events celebrating the building's dedication. *Time* gave it a story, and that was a first for a North Texas cultural institution. It was not just the memorialization of Amon Carter or his Western art collection that was newsworthy. For a city with the nickname of "cowtown," Amon Carter's children's tribute to their father, a sumptuously elegant memorial building designed by a high-profile

New York architect, changed the rules of architectural discrimination in that city as well as with its "nemesis" neighbor forty miles away. There was the gleaming classicized-modern temple up there on the crest of the hill for all to see and admire. Approaching from the east, you couldn't miss its silhouetted tapered-column portico, seemingly poised to spring.

There was not universal admiration for the design; it was just too new an image, and it is a universal sport to carp at the unexpected. One local critic compared its severity to a disposal plant. Even art guru Sam Cantey allegedly joked that its glassy, colonnaded facade resembled a set of TV screens. The tapered columns caused a British critic to label this turn in Johnson's esthetic as "ballet-classicism," though other architects like Le Corbusier in France, Oscar Niemeyer in Brazil, and Eero Saarinen and Minoru Yamasaki in this country had already begun breaking with International Style orthodoxy and taking expressionist liberties with rooflines, columns, and other support systems (tapered columns had been part of Johnson's formal language since his guest house's retrofitted interior of 1953 and Israel's Research Nuclear Reactor of 1960).

Yet there was still pride among most Fort Worth people in having a public building of such restrained, classy character, if puzzling to some, in their prominent midst. It was for *Mr. Fort Worth,* after all, and it outstripped anything in Dallas. Like it or not, Ruth Carter Johnson would not have gotten a civic structure of such distinction from one of the local architects. Her hiring of an out-of-town architect to design an important building worked well for Fort Worth and would become a routine custom there and elsewhere in Texas, often to the dismay of local architects. In the case of the Amon Carter Museum of Western Art, the majority of citizens were simply glad to see Mr. Fort Worth honored in a proper way. Wealthy Texans began to regularly hire East Coast architects to design their important buildings. It seemed to be culturally safe to stick with a well-known big-city Ivy League architect with design credentials. Later the range for esteemed-architect selection would broaden and become international.

Regardless of the local bemusement over the museum's design, Johnson's siting and planning of the building's relationship to the city and the two avenues that bordered it were repeatedly described as "flawless" by Dean O. Jack Mitchell to his Rice University students. Set back to the west between the south and north sides of the sloping site, the museum's east front is axially organized in a Beaux Arts fashion above the large, open ambulatory, the building's plaza. The northern, triangular section of land on Camp Bowie Boulevard is dedicated to landscaped visitor parking. From a circular vehicular drop-off, beneath large live-oak trees, the visitor begins Johnson's touted

Amon Carter Museum

Fort Worth, 1961

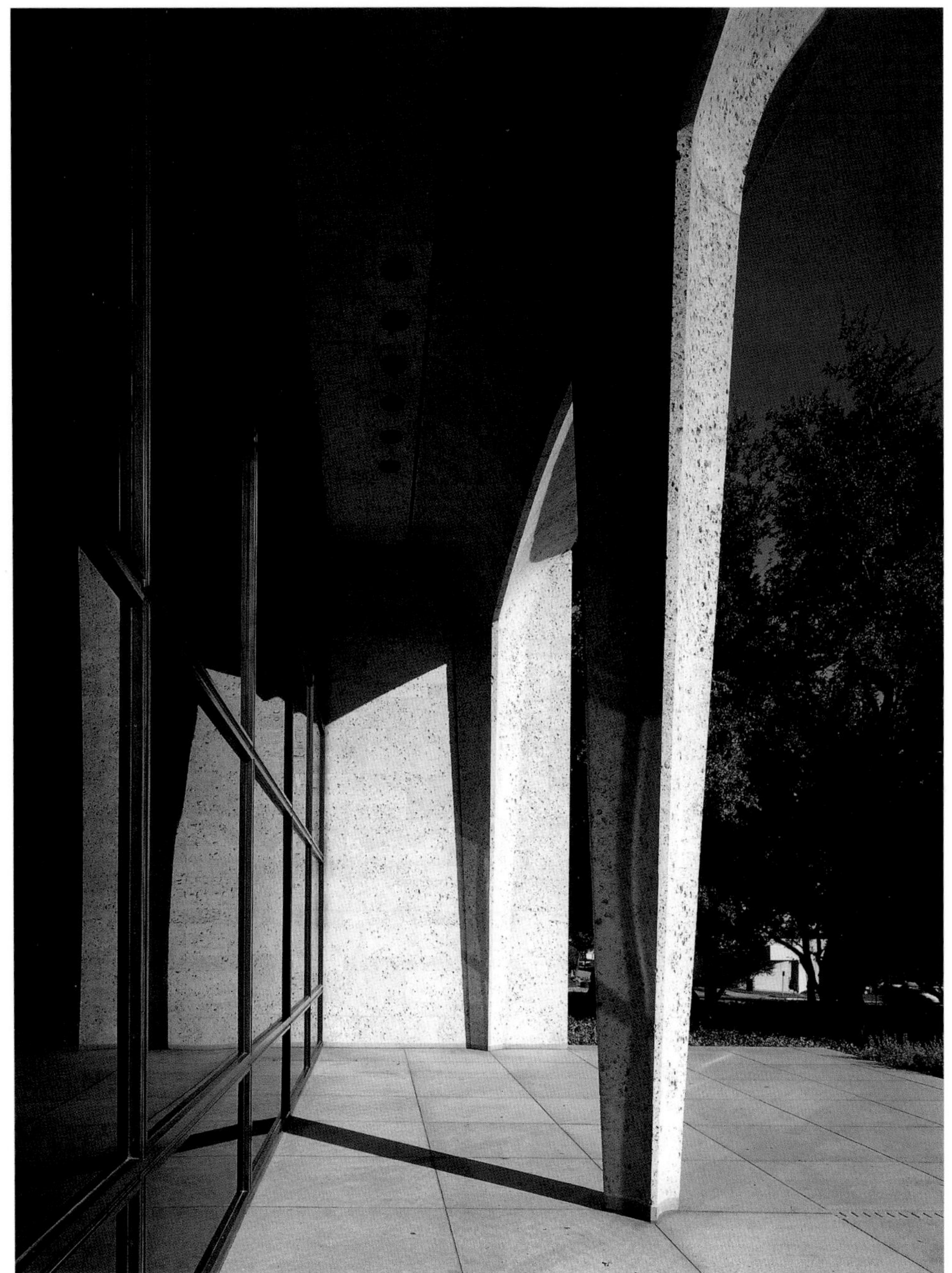

Loggia; tapered shell-limestone columns and arches, bolted limestone ceiling, and tinted glass and bronze window-wall.

PHILIP JOHNSON, ARCHITECT; JOSEPH R. PELICH, ASSOCIATE ARCHITECT.
PHOTOS BY PAUL HESTER, 1998.

Granite steps to loggia and entrance.

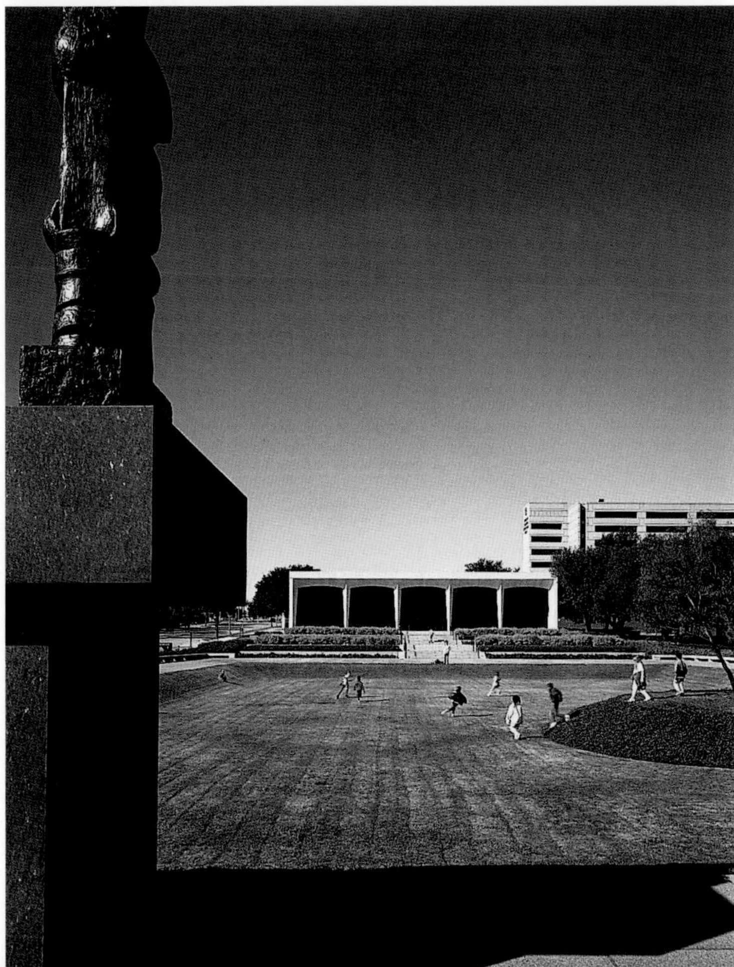

View from east across recessed lawn; in foreground: detail, three-piece *Upright Motives*, Henry Moore, bronze, 1956.

Fort Worth skyline from main gallery.

Main gallery, inside loggia.

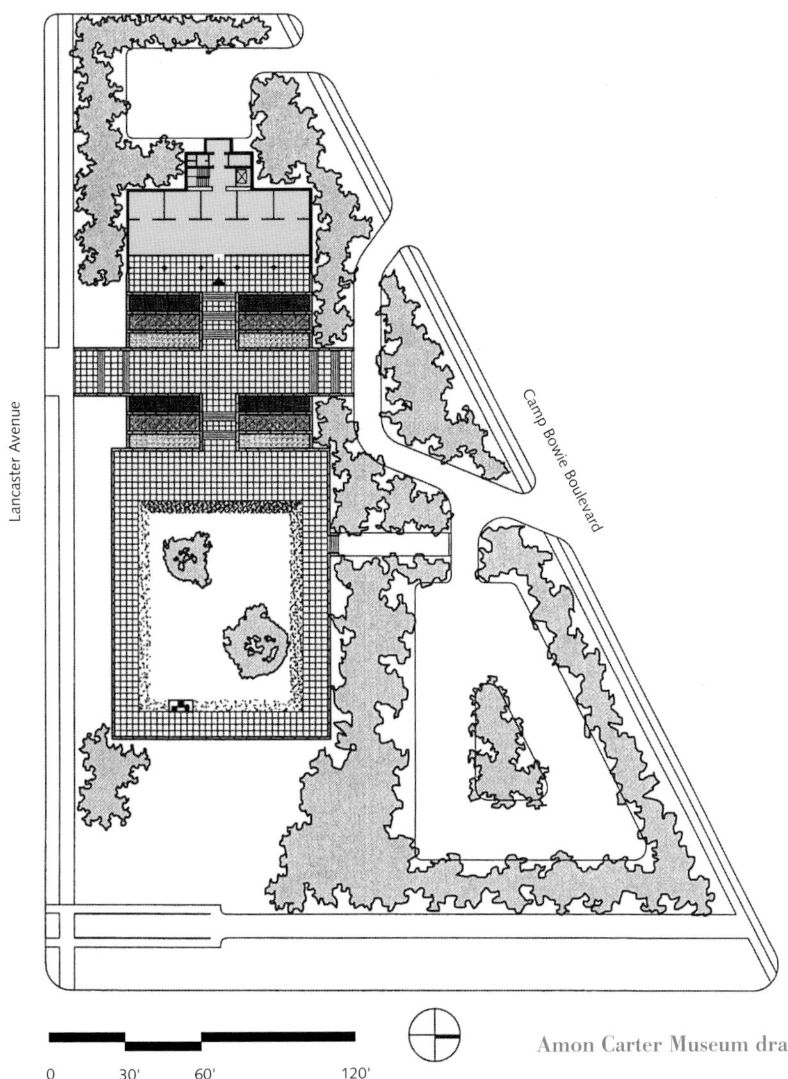

Amon Carter Museum drawing; site plan, 1961.

diagonal procession to the building's door. There are nineteen granite steps in five groups that ascend comfortably from the driveway to the portico. The groups of risers and deep landings of tawny aggregate-concrete lead south first in two sets to a broad, paved cross-axis to Lancaster Avenue. After a turn west, to the axis that unites the building above with the plaza below, a final three sets of steps, flanked by terraced planting, are traversed, to the building's five-bay stoa and entry in its wall of dark glass.

Responding to a question about the five arches in 1990, Johnson said, "Oh, I don't know where I got those. It was an attempt to not use *round,* thinking that was too classical, and the tapered column, ever since Knossos, in ancient Minoan architecture, was a well-known form. And then I wanted to be continuous, so I took the arris from the tapered column and carried it over the arch. The form is not new, but I'm damned if I can remember where I got it or why."[28]

Inside the door, the 24' x 24' x 120' great hall has a facing-wall of richly hued teak whose panels are strongly articulated with bronze-framed openings to smaller galleries on two levels. Turning around 180 degrees, the visitor has a wide view across the trees to the distant downtown that is striking in the way it makes the window-wall a visual frame of the city.

For the dedication, Johnson wrote:

> If it is true that sometimes civilizations are remembered by their buildings—and what else do we know of the people who built the Mexican pyramids or even the Egyptian?—today's buildings to be remembered may very well be its museums. Today we do not build—for whatever reasons—cathedrals and temples. May not future historians ask where our Bramante Churches and our Palladian Palaces are? Leaving aside the question of whether we have today architects as good as Bramante and Palladio, we certainly have no churches and no palaces to equal theirs.
>
> But the Museum is a new concept in building history. It is barely 150 years in the three thousand or so years of Western architecture since the first deliberately monumental museums were built, and now this year a museum has become the most important and the most talked of monument of the year: The Guggenheim Museum in New York by the late Frank Lloyd Wright.
>
> Museums, not city halls, palaces, state capitols, movie houses, opera houses, are the buildings we look to today. They play a new symbolic part in the life of our cities. Attendance goes up and up. Psychologists and sociologists may explain to us this phenomenon, but the duty of the architects, of the patrons of the city, is clear. We must build handsome museums.
>
> I can say nothing of the contents. It is true there must be Art in the buildings, but my particular part of the job is to make the museum building "art,"

in order better to view the Art inside, as well as to give pleasure of a public and communal nature.[29]

The March 1961 *Architectural Forum* wrote of the Amon Carter Museum:

> It is an exceedingly handsome building—beautifully detailed, beautifully sited (on one of the few hills in this flat land), and beautifully illuminated. And it is also a strangely incongruous building: although Johnson faced the structure with Texas-shellstone, he has given this local material the refinement of Italian travertine; although Fort Worth is "where the West begins," he has taken the theme for his latest museum from the great nineteenth-century classicist, Karl Friederich Schinkel, whose Altes Museum in Berlin is, in effect, a portico designed to decorate a public square—the "public square" in the Fort Worth case being a mutilevel, Johnson-designed plaza measuring about 140 by 300 feet.
>
> With all this apparent incongruity, the museum is a great success. The West is no longer quite as wild and woolly as some non-Texans believe, and a sophisticated, polished, vaguely "European" building looks no more out of place in Fort Worth than it might in Washington, D.C. or, for that matter, in Dallas.[30]

"I didn't have any idea about how to run a museum," recalls Ruth Stevenson, "had no notion of how to find a board or anything. But Philip, on a plane flight after the dedication of his Munson-Williams-Proctor Institute, said, 'That's not a problem; we'll get Jean de Menil, Rene d'Harnoncourt, your friend C. R. Smith, and I'll be on it; and you should get Ric Brown from Los Angeles, he's brilliant.' So we had a board!"[31]

Another museum building was soon to be built on a site to the east and down the slope from the Amon Carter Museum. In the mid-1960s construction on a community health center had begun on this prominent site when oilman Tex Moncrief noticed it one morning on the way downtown. Thinking the location inappropriate, Moncrief talked the city into moving the facility several blocks away and paid for the removal of the nascent construction himself. At about the same time, Fort Worth millionaire Kay Kimbell died, and his will specified that a museum in his name be built and funded from the heavily endowed Kimbell Foundation. The site selected was the one recently vacated by the Fort Worth Health Center; the first Kimbell director was Richard Fargo Brown, recently of the Los Angeles County Museum and a Carter Museum board member. Soon Brown was considering a list of name architects—excepting Johnson—and hired Louis Kahn of Philadelphia, who was teaching at the Yale School of Architecture.

Kimbell Museum, Fort Worth, 1972; Louis Kahn, architect. Sculpture pictured is *Figure in a Shelter,* Henry Moore, 1983. Photo by W. Mark Gunderson, 1996.

Kahn's reputation as a leading architect came during his middle age after he completed Yale's Art Gallery in 1953. Born in Estonia in 1901 and raised in poverty in Philadelphia, Kahn sketched and took free art lessons from an early age. He attended the University of Pennsylvania's ranking School of Architecture, under the French-American Beaux Arts classicist Paul Cret, to whom he remained indebted. After he designed Yale University's Art Gallery, Kahn's fame and commissions increased in the 1950s and 1960s, reaching a peak of accomplishment with the Salk Laboratory in La Jolla, California, completed in 1965. While he was teaching at Yale, he wrote and lectured extensively, expressing his feelings about architecture in obtuse but often poetic terms like "All matter is spent light—it is light when finished being light becomes material."[32]

Ric Brown, whose presence in Fort Worth affected the architectural culture significantly, grew up in Long Island and traveled abroad extensively with his importer father. A great-great grandson of the founder of Wells Fargo, he started as an English Literature major at Bucknell University but finished at Harvard, where he received a Ph.D. in Art History and met people in the arts that would be friends for life. He and his wife Jane (Polly, his first wife, died of postpolio complications in Fort Worth) settled well into Fort Worth's congenial society, and Ric's easy charm and personality fitted him comfortably for leadership in the city's art culture elite during the eleven years of his directorship of the Kimbell. A lot of credit for the success of the museum's design must be given to Brown; he led the process for the trustees with Kahn. His stated goals for the new building included his desire that the building be "a creative contribution to the history of architecture on the same high level and of the same esthetic quality as the arts it might house."[33]

"The total experience of a visit to the museum should be one of warmth, mellowness and even elegance," he further said. "The spaces, forms and textures should maintain a harmonious simplicity and human proportion between visitor, the building and the art objects observed."[34] Kahn's laborious process of achieving a design was nurtured and championed by Brown before the Kimbell board, a small group relatively inexperienced with architecture. The building's distinctive profile of arches in series and the luminous interiors beneath silvery concrete vaulting read as a dense poetry of structural and material expression, and when completed it received immediate critical and popular acclaim. The Kimbell further established Fort Worth as a world-class home for serious art and architecture. Sensitive to the fact that the new museum would stand between the Carter Museum and its view of the skyline, the Kimbell president of the board called Ruth during the building's design. She in turn called Philip and asked how *tall* the Kimbell should be; "forty feet!" was his quick reply.

Ric Brown's presence in Fort Worth, as an original Amon Carter Museum board member, was through Johnson. His subsequent role as the Kimbell's first director and selector of Louis Kahn as the museum's architect makes him one of the twentieth century's ranking patrons of architecture. (Johnson, the critic and scholar, had great respect for Kahn, ten years his junior, but also considered him a rival artist-architect for the kind of cultural institutions he excelled in.) Ric Brown died in 1979 after guiding Kahn's complex structural design to completion and launching the museum in 1972 as one of the world's most respected modern buildings.

In the late 1990s, many years after Kahn's venerated and show-stopping Kimbell Museum was built, there has been a heightened and revised appreciation, among Fort Worth people who care about such things, of the elegance and intimacy of the Amon Carter Museum and its connoisseur collection of American art. The Kimbell's "shadow" of celebrity still stretches far up the hill to Johnson's now mellowing building, but the intrinsic qualities of the earlier, watershed building are being recognized anew.

Several years after the Amon Carter Museum of Western Art opened in 1961, Anne Windfohr, a supporter and later a trustee of the museum and close to Ruth Carter Johnson though twenty years older, looked east for an architect as Ruth had done. She hired the Chinese American New York architect I. M. Pei to design a big new residence in Westover Hills as a fitting

Aerial view, Amon Carter Museum, Fort Worth, showing additions of 1964 and 1977. Photo © Craig Kuhner, 1997.

showcase for her art collection. Known for distinguished institutional buildings, Pei had just been selected by Jacqueline Kennedy to design the Kennedy Memorial Library in Boston and would soon be appointed architect for a new city hall for Dallas, winning the commission over competing firms Skidmore Owings & Merrill and Philip Johnson. Stanley Marcus was on the committee to select the city hall architect and describes the slight, self-effacing Pei as a remarkable salesman for his architecture, "absolutely *mesmerizing* in an interview; soft-spoken, diplomatic, and deferential of opposing views, but *never* losing an argument."[35] For contrast, when the assured, handsome, almost regal Johnson was queried why he wanted to design the new city hall, he replied that he wasn't sure that he *wanted* to, but that he liked Texas and had done some fine things there. He further confounded the committee when he added that his father had made him wealthy at an early age so he didn't need to work for the money. (His rival Pei, who was also independently wealthy, but *quietly* so, was a shoo-in for the city hall.)

Anne Burnett Windfohr Tandy, on receiving Patron of the Arts Award, Fort Worth, 1971. Photo by Gittings; courtesy of Burnett Foundation.

During the Windfohr house's construction Pei had trouble coordinating his professional activities in Dallas with activities in Fort Worth and his client's well-developed sense of *entitlement.* In Dallas once, Pei sent an assistant to Anne with drawings needing her approval, and she blew up. With a young Fort Worth architect in tow, she drove directly over to the Dallas hotel where Pei was staying. Steaming into his room she declared, "You have got a big nerve to send that kid over to Fort Worth after what I'm paying you! Mr. Pei, I'm here to tell you that you are *fired!*" I. M. Pei, the smooth, China-born Harvard graduate, had a well-developed reputation as a master at dealing with difficult situations, both architectural and social. He rubbed his hands together calmly and said, "Anne, I can tell that you are upset. Let me fix you a drink." In a few minutes, she was relaxed, leaning back on the couch and talking about the house.[36] There were other flare-ups between Anne and her architect when she felt he wasn't "listening" to her.

Pei's dramatic concrete and marble structure, nearly 20,000 sq. ft., was almost more museum than house; he had built a large scale model to study the effect of natural light on tiny renderings of Anne's major paintings. When completed, the house was a stunning addition to its expensive neighborhood and set a new standard in Fort Worth and Dallas for vanguard residential design. It featured concrete walls bush-hammered to expose a quartz and pink feldspar aggregate, and was a cool expression of the "brutalist" zeitgeist of the time, strong on geometrically bold and simple forms. A sharply raked, skylighted shed-roof rising over a spacious, marble-floored entertainment area, centered with a bar, gave the house its profile-identity. When *House and*

Garden ran a large picture story on the house, glamorous Anne, then married to Charles Tandy, was pictured in the sumptuous Benjamin Baldwin interiors, and described by Pei in the article as having special requirements which his design responded to. "Dividing the floor plan into two parts, one for entertaining and one for private living, was done partly because of her sense of a 'maintenance' problem," Pei said (apparently without irony). "She wanted to be sure she could live there without any help at all if necessary."[37]

Anne Tandy's house became a local landmark and was Texas's introduction to the Chinese American architect who would later achieve great fame there in the state and throughout the world. He would never design another private residence, however, nor would he design anything else in Fort Worth. Anne Tandy continued her patronage of ranking architects, talking to Mexico's celebrated Luis Barragan about designing a ranch house before she died in 1981. Her Burnett Foundation, administered by her daughter Anne Windfohr Marion, continues, with a few other wealthy Fort Worth foundations headed by Carters, Basses, and Moncriefs, among others, to provide essential and timely funding of local cultural initiatives. The big reservoirs of Fort Worth money for culture and education get passed around in tandem, each institution taking a turn. The primary recipient of Burnett Foundation money in the late 1990s is the Modern Art Museum of Fort Worth, which in 1997 held a competition to select an architect for a large new building in the Cultural District.

In 1967 Ruth Johnson, advised by her friend Philip, brought Paul Rudolph, Yale's School of Architecture dean, to Fort Worth to design an engineering building at Texas Christian University, funded by Sid Richardson's heirs, Perry Bass and his four sons. It firmly planted Rudolph in Fort Worth with the Basses. Also through Philip Johnson's influence, New York's Kevin Roche, of Roche/Dinkeloo, was picked by Ruth Stevenson (married to John Stevenson after a divorce in 1979 from J. Lee Johnson III) to design the large Moudy Visual Arts and Communication Building at TCU in 1980, funded by the Amon Carter Foundation. Ruth recalls being in Johnson's office when he picked up the phone and called his friend Kevin and told the reluctant architect that he simply *had* to do the building for Ruth. In 1997 New York's Hardy Holzman Pfeiffer continued the by now familiar incursion of East Coast architects into Texas by designing a new theater for TCU, a museum for San Angelo, and the Lucille G. Lupe Murchison Performing Arts Center at Denton's University of North Texas.

At the end of the century, Fort Worth was schizophrenic in its patronage of architecture. Architecturally it was Janus-like: looking backward and forward at the same time. The Bass brothers, Sid, Robert, Edward, and Lee, heirs to Sid Richardson's oil fortune, were Yale-educated entrepreneurs who came on the civic scene in the late 1970s as the major players in the city's architectural culture. In the mid-1970s, Sid, the oldest, had hired Paul Rudolph, introduced earlier to Fort Worth by Ruth Johnson through her friend Philip, who designed an exquisitely glowing, multilevel showplace house for him and his wife Anne near the Pei-designed Tandy house. Rudolph also soon designed two shaped and sculpted grey-glass office towers for the Bass brothers in the business district, as well as the engineering building at TCU.

Later, in a second marriage, Sid Bass built the most extravagant revival-style mansion Fort Worth had seen in years, while his brother Robert built a handsome modern house designed by Dallas's Enslie Oglesby. But it was Edward Bass who led the city into its retro-revivalist period with major infusions of Bass money for weaving mock neo-Classical and neo-Victorian construction into the downtown's handsome nineteenth-century fabric. This colorful and picturesquely rejuvenated downtown area, Sundance Square, filled with tourists and citizens looking for food and entertainment on weekends, and became the envy of Texas cities with moribund centers, like Dallas and Houston.

Ed Bass's enthusiasm for nostalgia culminated in 1998 with the Nancy Lee and Perry R. Bass Performance Hall, named after the brothers' parents. The huge, heavily eclectic limestone-and-stucco structure was designed by David Schwarz, a Yale acquaintance of Ed Bass's and architect for other downtown Bass projects. It fills a city block near the Bass brothers' glassy Rudolph towers and is adorned with two gigantic statues of angels holding gilded trumpets which extend over the street. The *Fort Worth Star-Telegram*'s front-page description of it as a European-style performance hall was accompanied by another story in the paper's inside pages announcing the results of the competition held to design a new Modern Art Museum of Fort Worth. Japanese modernist Tadao Ando's design was selected for the 130,000 sq. ft. building, featuring concrete, glass, and reflection pools, across the street from the Kimbell Museum.[38]

The Bass Performance Hall design was greeted with consternation by the city's modernist architects, while they and others cheered the decision of the Modern Art Museum's building committee. When the privately funded $67 million Bass Hall opened in May of 1998, David Dillon, the *Dallas Morning News*'s architecture critic, called it a "classical concoction" and asked, "Why, at the end of the 20th century, would anyone build a 19th-century opera house?"[39]

The community's patronage of architecture, which had produced the

Amon Carter Museum expansion model, exterior and interior, 1999; Philip Johnson/Alan Ritchie, architects. Courtesy of the Carter Foundation.

Carter Museum, the Water Garden, the Kimbell Museum, and other important modernist buildings, seemed to stumble and lose its bearings with the downtown performance hall, but almost immediately the community regrouped its sensibilities to choose Ando, an international, prize-winning architect, noted for his poetic minimalism, to design the city's next cultural monument.

In 1998, the Carter Foundation announced plans for a large expansion to the Amon Carter Museum designed by Johnson with his partner Alan Ritchie. The 107,000 sq. ft. expansion will triple the exhibition space and entails razing the existing 1964 and 1977 Johnson additions to the original building. The new wing, which will fill the site to the west, will be a three-level triangular block, clad in a brown granite, and will be a boldly striking, yet retroceding, foil to Johnson's original, creamy loggia. The flat roof will be topped with a low-vaulted, quadripartite roof, "a domed lantern," hovering above a dramatically scaled atrium. At century's end, Ruth Carter Stevenson continues the patronage of Johnson and modernism, so faithfully begun in the late 1950s as a memorial to her father.

Chapter 3

In Dallas, in the early 1960s, architectural competition for high-profile statements among the city's elite was not as intense as in Fort Worth, nor as personal.[1] Clients in Fort Worth hired out-of-state name architects before Dallas made it a custom. Dallas was bigger and its upper crust had many more layers than did Fort Worth's. Clients for modern houses in Dallas in the early 1960s also had a wider array of talented young local architects to choose from than existed in Fort Worth. Dallasites Patty and Henry Beck were having trouble deciding on an architect for a big house that Patty wanted to build, and though they, like others in their set, were close to local modernist Enslie Oglesby, what eventually led the Becks to Philip Johnson was a personal referral that, as was common in Fort Worth, ultimately went back indirectly to the Menil connection.

Downtown Dallas, 1955. Courtesy of the collection of the Texas/Dallas Archives, Dallas Public Library.

The Becks' large site was in North Dallas on a straight, flat, undistinguished street that later became noted for its extravagant dwellings. Patty and Henry were part of a gallivanting coterie of wealthy young Dallasites which included oilman John Murchison and his colorful, au courant wife Lupe. When in town, this group mingled and played at the Dallas Country Club or Brook Hollow Golf Club or downtown in posh business clubs on the top floors of the largest banks. When away from Dallas they usually stuck together at elegant retreats in East Texas or Colorado, or on the lower California coast.

Patty and Henry Beck Jr., Harbour Island, the Bahamas, mid-1960s. Courtesy of Kalita Beck McCarthy.

Henry C. Beck Jr., a smooth, dapper Dartmouth graduate with ancestral roots in rural Maryland, was a successful building contractor whose HCB Company, founded by his father, grew to nationwide prominence under his leadership. Like Henry, Patty Davis Beck grew up in Dallas. She attended Wellesley and had an avid love for horses and houses. She had stables in La Jolla, California, and Lexington, Kentucky, as well as France and raced thoroughbreds for years, while simultaneously looking after some thirteen dwellings including a chateau in the French Pyrenees. Patty Beck and her sister Camilla Davis Blaffer of Houston were daughters of Wirt Davis, a tight-fisted Dallas millionaire and president of Republic National Bank, with large landholdings productive of an oil and lumbering fortune.

The Becks spent a lot of time looking for an architect in California, Florida, and elsewhere. In Woodside, California, they saw and admired the work of Gardner Dailey, a San Francisco architect who, along with William Wurster and a few others, practiced a distinguished Bay Region style of relaxed modernism. Standing in her house in 1996 Patty Beck recalled, "We just loved the houses of his that we saw, they were perfectly beautiful and that's what we wanted, so we hired him on the spot. I have complete faith in what I'm doing. I don't need to ask someone what to do, so I told him what I wanted and this house here is exactly what he thought up, the gymnasium over there for the children and everything just like I wanted. But he never came up with what we were looking for as far as the *outside* was concerned."[2] Dailey developed a plan, to Patty's liking, for a two-story house with a symmetrically organized first floor having a large double-height reception hall at the center, flanked by a living room, dining room, library, and garden room. Henry Beck recalled, "Patty liked the floor plan from the beginning, but the elevations that Dailey kept showing us all looked like buildings at Stanford University. He couldn't seem to come up with anything else, so we finally had to let him go."[3]

The Becks kept a blueprint of the floor plan, which became dog-eared as Patty unrolled it over and over to show to their friends. Finally Jane Owen, Camilla Blaffer's sister-in-law and a friend of Henry's, heard of their search for an architect and called Henry to say that he should call Philip Johnson. Jane's shrine in Indiana had just been completed, and she was "thrilled with Philip," Camilla reported. When modern art collectors Lupe and John Murchison heard that Patty and Henry were vacillating about Johnson as their architect, Patty recalls John saying, "'Listen, if you can get that guy to do the house, go on and get him! *Do it!* He's just the finest thing in the world.' I said to John, 'But Mother doesn't approve, and Henry doesn't know what he thinks,' but finally I just went ahead and *did* it. If it hadn't been for John Murchison I never would have built this place."[4]

Johnson was soon back in Texas, in "Big D" this time, inspecting the large Beck site, which faced west and dropped off sharply to a creek on the east, and getting acquainted with Patty and Henry. He found the city dull and something of a contrast with both Houston and Fort Worth. While little of Wellesley had rubbed off on Patty Beck, who could not have been more East Texan and down-to-earth, most of the new, postwar people in Dallas were taken up with "image" to a greater degree than those in either of the other two cities. In the 1950s and 1960s Fort Worth related to the wide-open West with an informal social attitude, and Houston still bore the qualities of Southern agrarian society and its genteel social access.

Old Dallas was a tight society, marked by conservative, upper-middle-class values of appearance and the quiet sanctity of material success. *New Dallas,* of which the Becks and Murchisons were a part, was faster, younger, and more tuned-in to new ideas. Still, with a few exceptions, the new, eclectic houses of the rich and new-rich were grander, the clothes of the women had more couture cachet, and the downtown buildings were taller and topped with more attention-getting finials in Dallas than anywhere in the state. It is doubtful that a specialty store like Neiman-Marcus, with its goal of class in quality attire through extravagance, could have succeeded as well elsewhere in Texas.

In-the-know Dallasites took to modernism in the postwar period as many other urban dwellers throughout the country did. Frank Lloyd Wright and Edward Durell Stone and Harwell Hamilton Harris joined local architects O'Neil Ford, Arch Swank, Howard Meyer, and Enslie Oglesby in producing distinguished modern houses in Dallas for adventurous clients. The work of Harris and the Texans, while rooted in modern design precepts, reflected the Southwest through materials and planning and form-making in ways that the highly personalized designs of Wright and Stone did not. Johnson's house for the Becks would be another high-profile design by a celebrity out-of-towner that would be an anomaly in its setting.

"I didn't know that she gave all that credit to John, but we were great friends and I'm glad to hear what she said about him," Lupe Murchison says.

> She wanted a special house, and by hiring Philip, she certainly got a special house. Then the funniest thing happened after the house was finished. Philip knew that John and I were such good friends of Henry and Patty's, and he asked us to have dinner with him here in Dallas. He said, "What this is all about is that that house *requires* contemporary paintings! You've got to give Patty a piece of art to make her realize that that is what it needs." So John and I presented her with this George Ortman, which was a great piece of art. We went to the house and had cocktails, and we could tell something was wrong; Henry was wonderful about it, but Patty didn't know how to accept it, and John Murchison, being as smart as he was, said, "Now look, if you don't *hang* this, we want it back." Sure enough, a few months later, I was wrapping Christmas presents, and I saw this truck drive up and there was the painting. That was one thing that discouraged Philip no end—it was never furnished like he wanted. I agree with him that the house, with all those big walls, called for art.[5]

Patty Beck says, "We took the [floor] plan to Philip and said, 'This is what we want but we need a different *outside.*' He said fine, and then he couldn't make it work and came up with a plan shaped like a Greek cross, and we said that we didn't want a Greek cross, so he went back to my plan and worked it around a little and lapped it over with those arches so it would all go together."[6]

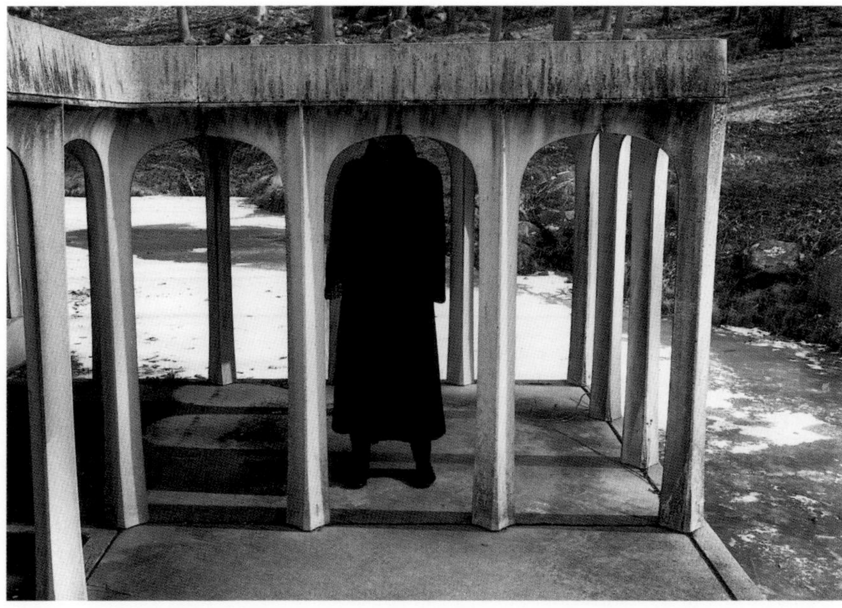

Figure in Pavilion. Photo by the author.

Pavilion at Pond (Kirstein Tower in background), New Canaan, Connecticut, 1962; Philip Johnson, architect. Photo by Paul Hester, 1994.

Johnson had recently built a folly at his New Canaan Glass House estate, the first of a number of buildings that he would add to the place through the years. Located on the edge of an artificial pond below the promontory where The Glass House sits, the little open-air structure of white concrete arches looks larger when viewed from above, but is only six feet tall, and one must stoop to enter it. The "floating" playhouse, laced with narrow watercourses, is a set of four open, colonnaded modules in a pinwheel plan. Surrounded by water and lightly moored near the pond's bank, the Pavilion gave a scale-jarring sense of a miniature Persian pleasure barge for dwarfs, enhanced with ceilings of gold leaf and a thirty-foot water jet nearby. The column-arch configuration is complex and inspired by the inward-curving toed columns of Robert Delaunay's 1909 expressionist painting of the Gothic interior of Paris's

Saint-Severin Church. From slightly flared column bases, the concave surfaces of the Pavilion's columns meld fluidly into narrow elliptical arches, which, in series, visually define the fanciful conceit on the water.

For the Becks Johnson magnified the scale of his Pavilion's arches and created a two-tiered system that he adroitly dropped over Patty Beck's scheme like a slipcover, making a cohesive whole of her archetypal plan. As the plan dictated and as Johnson nudged it, the advancing and receding ranges of white arches became airy loggias or arcades, or had infills of window glass and grey plaster. Johnson preferred a cast-in-place method of constructing the arches, but Henry Beck found an airplane maker in Fort Worth to make the intricate, curving forms for casting the concrete in parts and proceeded with this more economical method. A sample arch was mocked up for Johnson to inspect, and, reported Beck, "He ran his hands over the surfaces with eyes closed and declared the casting perfect."[7]

Patty called on Dallas architect and Johnson admirer Enslie Oglesby and others for help in completing the interiors of the house past the entertainment spaces around the grand skylighted entrance hall. (Johnson was quoted as saying: "I'm letting them do the upstairs.") Patty had Oglesby measure the Brook Hollow Golf Club kitchen to be sure she had adequate space for large-scale entertaining. Russian émigré Paul Raigorodsky told her that her entrance hall should have a double stairway like one he had seen in a Russian mansion. Patty put Oglesby on the search for the stairs, which he found in a book on Russian architecture. She slyly incorporated them into the design as products of Henry Beck's draftsmen, but Johnson surprised Patty by expressing delight with the twin Baroque stairways set in bays of curving glass. They became the sculptural centerpiece of the house.

Set far back from its street, the dense two-story range of repeating, sensuous arches—some open or glazed, some "blind"—stretches some 230 feet across the site. The house is centered by an attached entry loggia flanked by six perfectly pollarded yaupon trees. Young Peter Beck, sensitive to living in such an unusual house, called his mother and father "Mr. and Mrs. Arch." He and his younger sister Kalita, the two youngest Beck children, were seven and three when the house was finished and grew up there; each has mixed feelings about the experience.

The monumental interiors are detailed with Johnson's signature Miesian crispness and employ marble, walnut paneling, and parquet flooring, with peach-colored Fortuny fabric lining the dining room. The dining room is also "roofed," with a freestanding plaster ceiling supported by a perimeter of vaulted arches on slender columns. It suggests the Soane ceiling-canopy in Johnson's guest house bedroom, but without that room's finely scaled grace.

House for Mr. and Mrs. Henry C. Beck Jr.

Dallas, 1964

West facade, front.

PHILIP JOHNSON, ARCHITECT. PHOTOS BY PAUL HESTER, 1995–1996.

Detail, south facade.

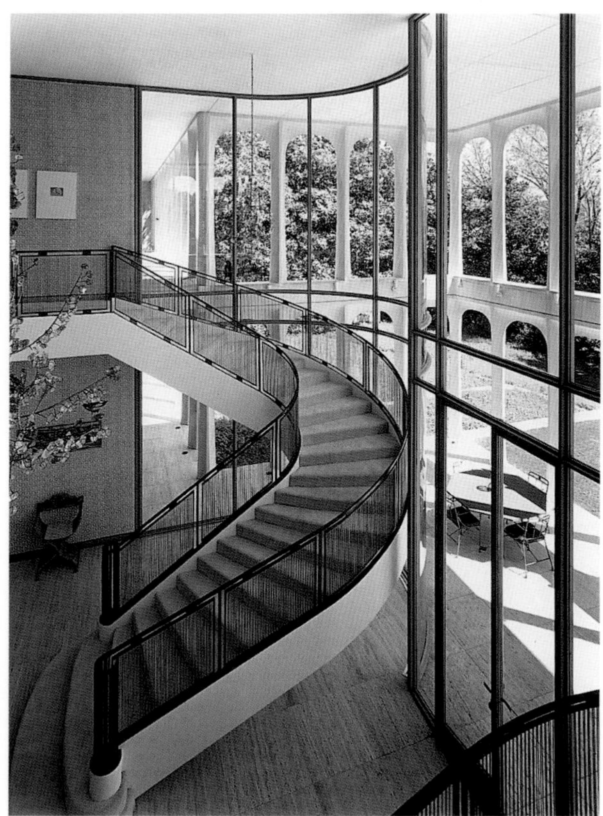

Detail, winding stairway, glass wall, and covered terrace on east.

Double winding stairways in entrance hall.

Dining room.

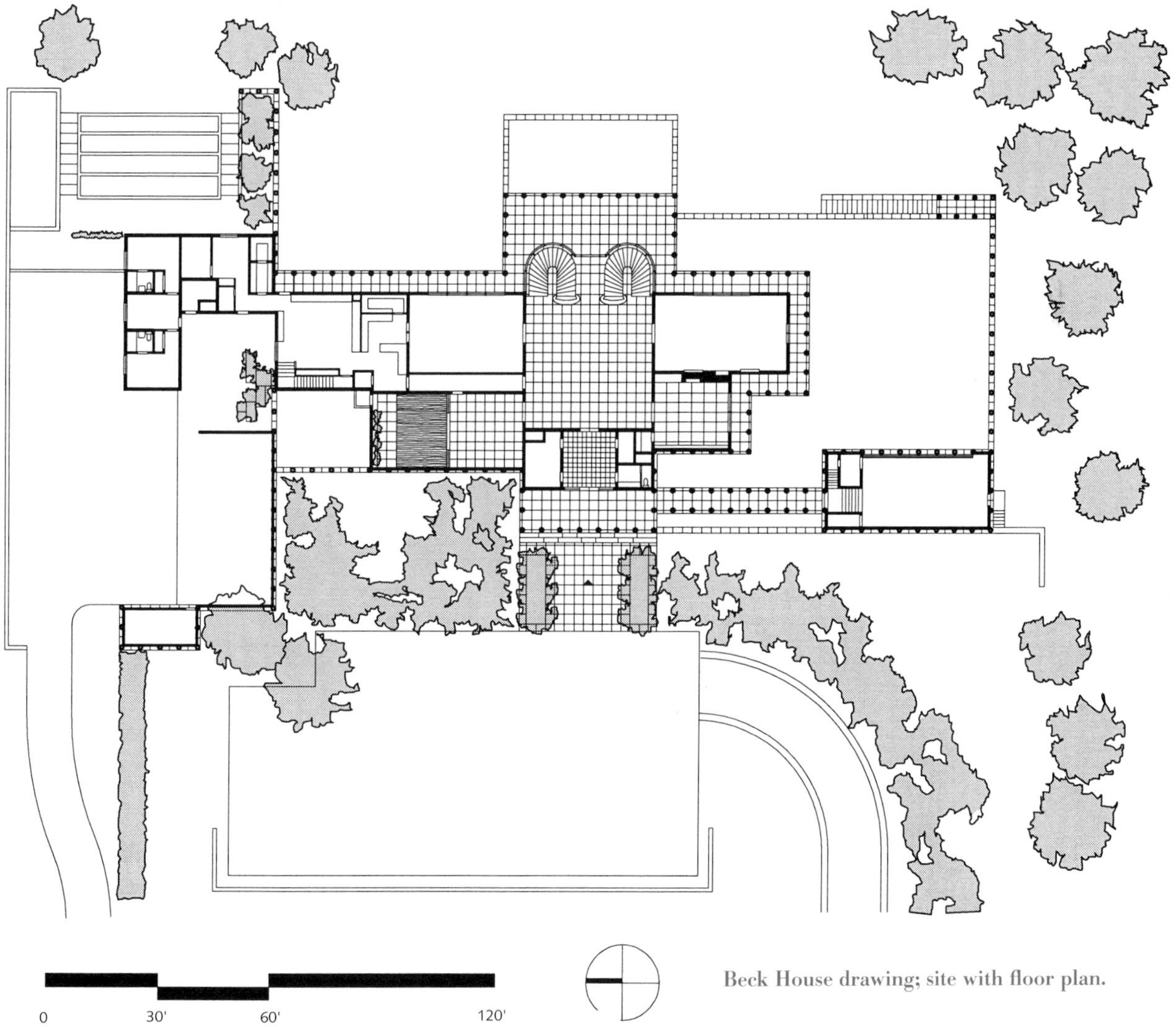

0 30' 60' 120'

Beck House drawing; site with floor plan.

Shortly after finishing the house (which for a time was called Kentmere, after Henry's palatial and historical thousand-acre place in Maryland), the Becks opened it up for a sparkling fund-raising ballet presentation on the garden terrace. Always wary of unwanted publicity, the Becks threatened to sue when *The Dallas Times Herald* hired an airplane and flew over the house for pictures. For years Patty Beck refused all requests to photograph Philip Johnson's largest house.

Patty and Henry Beck were divorced in the early 1980s, but she still lives in the house, keeping the large place in mint condition and attempting to sell it from time to time. Walking through the house and grounds in 1996, she reminisced:

> That's the hunting room over there, it used to be the gymnasium, which always drove Philip *nuts.* He'd say, "What do you want a gymnasium for?" And I'd say because I'm a mother and I have four children and I want them to have a gymnasium. I had one when I was a child, and I want one for my children. I said, "Philip, you don't have any children, and you have a house you can't even *feed* anybody in."
>
> He and I were very honest with each other. I stood up to him and didn't give him an inch, and he knew that! I'd go up there to New York on Sunday with my plans, maybe two or three times a month, spend the night at the Lombardy, and be at his office the next morning at nine o'clock, when he would walk in and say, "Why are you always here so *early?*" I'd say, "Because you've been home, had two days off, you're in a better mood, and it's before everybody gets to barking at you. You won't *fight* with me!" Everybody said we'd never get along, that we'd fight and tear each other apart, but it worked out fine.[8]

The Beck house design has always been a subject of controversy among Dallas's social *cognoscenti,* as well as with the city's architects. There is no affection for its site-swallowing broadside of unyielding, cagelike patterned facade. The constancy of detail of its double tier of advancing and retreating moulded arches begs perhaps for a void or a smooth plane to relieve the eye at the same time it heightens the delicacy of the narrow, finely moulded arches. Within and without, it is a handsome structure and, though redolent of the 1960s, stands in proud modern splendor among the recently built *faux chateaux* of its neighborhood.

Patty and Henry Beck's two youngest children, Peter and Kalita, were affected in different ways by growing up in the grand residence by Philip Johnson; in the late 1990s they each hired leading Texas modernists to design houses. Kalita Beck McCarthy, who was three when the house was finished and spent fourteen years there, recalls that the house's formality made it difficult to have friends over to spend the night:

> It sort of scared them—that very formal atmosphere—so I much preferred going to their houses. But it was a great house for a big party; I remember a New Year's Eve party when everyone wore masks and they opened the skylight in the atrium at midnight and released black and white balloons through the opening. I had a "sweet sixteen" birthday party there and made my debut there, so it was always perfect for big, fun parties. I must say that I have an appreciation and heightened sense of "space" that I would have missed not living there. My oldest sister, Patty, wrote a paper at MIT entitled "The Psychological Aspects of Space."[9]

In the 1960s, Lupe and John Murchison, along with Betty and Eddie Marcus and others, were in the vanguard of collecting contemporary art; they had helped found the Dallas Museum for the Contemporary Arts in the 1950s as a reaction to the conservative Dallas Museum of Art, which, among other things, wouldn't hang Picasso. In the meantime the Murchisons built a large, bold modern art collection; Lupe Murchison describes it this way:

> When John and I moved into his father's big house, we didn't have enough money to *furnish* it! John was busy in New York a lot, and I often went with him. We visited the galleries and the art was so *cheap,* such as Kenneth Noland and Helen Frankenthaler—they were fifteen hundred and some of them were eight hundred dollars. I said, "Let's just start putting them on the *walls,*" which we did—I thought, "We will never get that house furnished!" So we just started buying this art, which is unbelievable because they are all famous now.
>
> I can remember my mother saying, "I don't know how you can raise your children in all this"; she just thought it was the *worst,* and naturally she would, with Rauschenberg and Jim Dine with those hammers and saws. People have said, "You've got one of the greatest collections of the sixties period," and it was mainly because we didn't have any furniture to put in that house! And because of it maybe we had some influence. Howard Rachofsky[10] tells me that as a boy he can remember coming to the house with the young group down at the museum and says, "You inspired me."[11]

Philip Johnson and Eliza Bliss Parkinson at the Museum of Modern Art, New York City, mid-1960s. Courtesy of the Museum of Modern Art, New York.

During the early and middle 1960s Johnson was busier than ever, producing large and small designs that garnered publicity in the press. With that kind of popular exposure and his outspoken, pungent remarks, Philip Johnson became a celebrity. He continued an ardent social pace in Manhattan and at the Museum of Modern Art, frequently squiring the bright, attractive women of wealth, like Eliza Bliss, with whom he had always shared a mutual attraction, although, according to accepted wisdom, short of romantic intimacy. At one point, rumors were widespread in New York that Philip had succumbed to a smitten female client. When questioned about this at a dinner party, he cryptically retorted, "I would sleep with a *tree* for the job!"

Philip Johnson conversing with French painter Jean Dubuffet at the Museum of Modern Art, New York City, mid-1960s. Courtesy of the Museum of Modern Art, New York.

Besides the archly scaled Pavilion of colonnades on the pond, built in 1962, and the 1965 underground Painting Gallery, both at The Glass House, in the 1960s he designed the Miesian Munson-Williams-Proctor Institute museum in Utica, New York, and was architect for the New York State Theater at Lincoln Center, the East Wing of the Museum of Modern Art, the New York State Pavilion at the 1964 World's Fair, the Sheldon Memorial Art Gallery in Lincoln, Nebraska, a travertine-clad mansion for David Kreeger in Washington, the towering Kline Biology Laboratory at Yale University, and most importantly, the lapidarian Museum for Pre-Columbian Art, completed in 1963 at Dumbarton Oaks in Washington's Georgetown.

Changes of the capable right-hand men so essential to Johnson took place periodically. In the early 1950s Richard Foster had replaced Landes Gores, who left Johnson to start his own practice, and Foster became Johnson's trusted partner and man-of-all-parts until the 1960s. At about this same time, thirty-four-year-old architect John Burgee of Chicago became the new, trusted helper, replacing Foster and bringing with him big-office managerial skills from Chicago's C. F. Murphy and Associates, a successful interpreter of Miesian creed. The addition of Burgee would usher in a period of large projects. Johnson met Burgee, son of a prominent architect and a C. F. Murphy partner, when Johnson and the Chicago firm were competing for a large job in Philadelphia. Neither Johnson nor C. F. Murphy got the job, but Johnson got Burgee. The story is that after hearing Burgee make a presentation to the Philadelphia clients, Johnson jumped up, declaring, "You should hire that young man for the job!" and, following John Burgee out to the elevator, talked him into coming to work for him.

On the personal side, David Whitney, a young, erudite art history graduate of Rhode Island School of Design, entered Johnson's life as companion and confidant in the early 1960s and became the advisor on Johnson's growing art collection, a role Alfred H. Barr Jr. had filled for years. Almost coincidentally, in the private and professional realms, Whitney and Burgee became major, abiding influences in the fundamental parts of Johnson's life: art and architecture.

Johnson continued the pursuit of an astringent modernism inflected with historical reference in the New York State Theater, offering as precedent for its tall, paired columns the seventeenth-century east facade of Paris's Louvre by Claude Perrault. Even with its voluptuous Baroque-like interior details, his theater was the least mannered of the three monumental colonnaded structures facing the Lincoln Center Plaza, a fountain-centered classical space also designed by Johnson. The Museum of Modern Art's black-steel and glass East Building and the Sheldon Gallery in Nebraska continued Johnson's predilection for curvilinear, inside-corner details within a strict Miesian paradigm. The looming seventeen-story Kline Biology Tower, on a hill north of the Yale campus, was designed with partner Richard Foster and dominates the college town with its round base-to-cornice, purplish-red brick columns and red sandstone spandrels.

If there was a small-scale masterwork of this period, it was the Pre-Columbian Museum wing tethered to the venerated Dumbarton Oaks man-

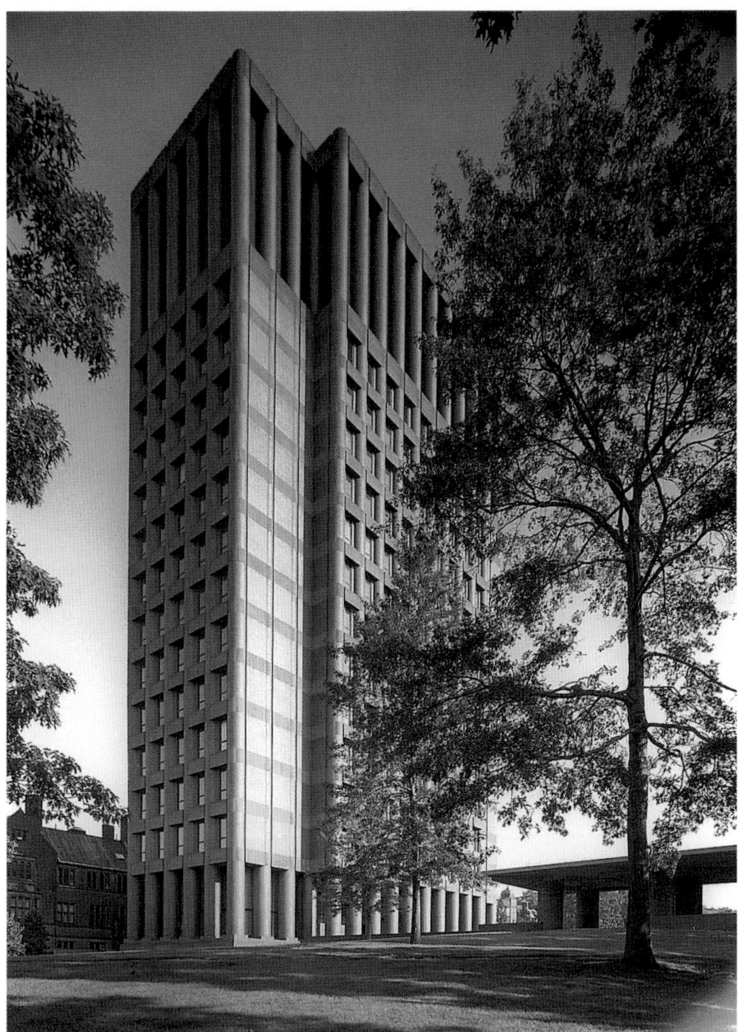

Kline Biology Tower, Yale University, New Haven, Connecticut, 1966; Philip Johnson and Richard Foster, architects. Photo by Richard Payne.

sion in Washington's Georgetown, which had been given to Harvard University by Mr. and Mrs. Robert Woods Bliss in 1940. Intended as a near-invisible addition to the Georgian mansion, Johnson's low structure is surrounded by planting and is linked to the older structure by a slender glazed passage. The museum is composed of nine contiguous, round modules, each topped with shallow metal-sheathed domes, except for the center circle, which holds a fountain and is open to the sky. The sinuously linked twenty-five-foot chambers, called "spools of space" by *Architectural Forum,* are topped with skylights and supported by hefty, round marble columns and enclosed with walls of curved glass. This sparkling little reliquary of a building, with its multiple domes evoking a Byzantine mosque, levitates with light and is lyrical in its single-minded concept and elegantly solemn in its tightly controlled execution. It has rarely been surpassed by Johnson.

While the Beck house was under construction in 1963, President John F. Kennedy visited Dallas at the end of a political swing through Texas and was assassinated by a sniper as his motorcade left downtown Dallas for a large civic luncheon. Texas Governor John Connally, riding with Kennedy in the open presidential limousine, was critically wounded. The news of the murder of the loved, but also reviled, young president ripped through the world and left the self-satisfied, conservative city where he died in a trauma of self-

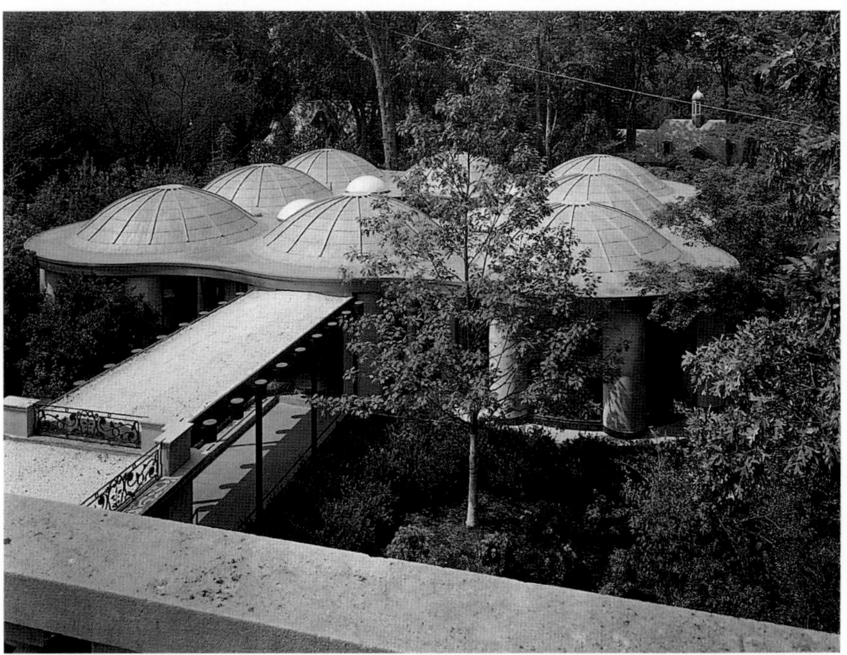

Museum for Pre-Columbian Art at Dumbarton Oaks, 1963; Philip Johnson, architect.
Photo by Ezra Stoller © Esto.

doubt and denial. The patrician Dallas merchant Stanley Marcus was an outspoken Democrat and one of the hosts for the Kennedy luncheon. Marcus felt deeply the shame and loss and was determined early that the city should respond with an appropriate memorial to the murdered president. A memorial commission was formed by the mayor to determine what kind, and where an appropriate memorial should be located, though a popular former mayor and city booster stated publicly that he was against the memorial and didn't want a reminder of the event.

The assassination site in Dealey Plaza was selected at first for a long, inscribed marble wall, an idea that was soon dropped. Deciding on the appropriate memorial and raising money for it became a daunting task for Marcus and other commission members. Marcus, the city's arbiter of taste and a Menil-like cultural leader, was also a political outsider, yet he served as leader of the group. Dallas writer Leon Harris, whose family's own specialty department store competed with Neiman-Marcus for many years, says, "Building the greatest fashion store in the world is, of course, an enormous achievement of Stanley's, but what I admire about him has been his powerful moral leadership in Dallas, for example with regards to race. Stanley stuck his neck out while the rest of us were hiding behind a tree. African-Americans were only allowed on the first floor of Neiman-Marcus when Stanley took over and threw out that policy."[12]

Stanley Marcus greeting Gabrielle "Coco" Chanel at Love Field, Dallas, 1957. Courtesy of Stanley Marcus.

Marcus and his commission colleagues faced another kind of hiding in trying to raise money. His committee was broad-based, but there weren't many civic leaders who were interested enough in a memorial to contribute much money. The city's conservative political establishment seemed to believe, like the former mayor, that ignoring the tragic event would erase its memory. As Stanley Marcus recalls, "There weren't many rich Democrats to approach."[13]

Stanley Marcus knew Johnson from the days when Marcus was a Harvard Overseer and was entertained at The Glass House, and with the commission's blessing, he asked Johnson if he would design the memorial. Marcus recalls that the New York architect was his only choice for the job; Johnson had recently completed the Amon Carter Museum, was a social acquaintance of the Kennedys, and had national prominence. Marcus immediately got Johnson's enthusiastic agreement to do the design, along with a waiver of his fee.

So the memorial commission had a well-known architect to attract interest in the project and soon got important support from Dallas County Judge Lew Sterrett, a good-old-boy politician who knew how Dallas's downtown business leadership wanted the city run. He offered a site on a county-owned block, east of the old red-sandstone courthouse, facing the new courthouse a few blocks east of the assassination site. Marcus's group still had to raise the money, but his committee had a site and an architect, so Johnson proceeded with a design. In late 1964 the memorial commission, according to *The Dallas Times Herald,* had raised $200,000 from fifty thousand donations (a lot of them from school kids), none of it from the city government. (Soon after the assassination, the State of Texas created its own memorial commission, which never went anywhere and was dissolved in 1970 for lack of interest and money.)

Johnson recalls:

> There was the square city block for the memorial, so a "square" form seemed appropriate. The idea of a sacred place, like an empty tomb, struck me as something fitting as long as it was abstract. A "room" with tall walls, open to the sky, would block out the surrounding city. Of course, it was essential that there would be no sentimentalizing of Kennedy; he would have disapproved anyway! So a spare, unadorned open volume, a geometric "cube," devoid of expression or moralizing, but monumental in its empty presence, presented itself in my mind. It was essential to me that whatever I did, it should only be a tacit interpretation of a memorial per se; it would be left to the viewers to find their own meaning.[14]

Stephen Smith, husband of Jean Kennedy Smith, represented the family in dealings with Johnson and the commission, and his communication was clear that the family wanted something very simple.

Dallasite John Schoelkopf was a young, energetic newspaper executive with an Ivy League education. He took over the chairmanship of the memorial commission in 1967 and became the contact with Johnson, picking him up at the airport and taking him to inspect the casting of the concrete for the memorial:

> He would run his hand over the bush-hammered surfaces, saying, "This is good" and "This is not good and won't do," until all of the finishes were acceptable for assembly. He was very polite about it, but his standards were high. I knew from zip about architecture and was sort of the "errand boy" for the commission. It was several years after the assassination, and while the original commitment was intact, the intense emotion of the early days after Kennedy's death was waning. Johnson was very kind to me—a junior executive with an afternoon newspaper—while he was probably wondering where the CEOs were.[15]

Johnson placed his "cube" in the center of the square block, which he made a minimally landscaped plaza, sloping it up to the centerpiece, which would be flanked with ranges of Texas live oaks. The 50' x 50' x 30' roofless volume is assembled from 30" square, chamfered concrete members with a rugged, white aggregate finish, bound together vertically with concealed steel cables forming rigid, enclosing planes. The cable ends are capped with round concrete bosses. Four pairs of the vertical members extend to the ground to form legs which lift and balance the assembly above the plaza floor. Concealed lighting, directed downward, causes the great cube to float at night, silhouetted above a pool of ambient light.

Two narrow, vertical voids, in opposite walls, split the chamber into two U-shaped cantilevers and provide access to the interior space, which is centered with a flat square block of dark granite, incised "John Fitzgerald Kennedy." Johnson adds, "I wanted the air to move *freely* through and under the structure; nothing ponderous in there and certainly no sculpture. Anyone can walk in and be separated from the life around. You can look up and see the sky, look down and see Kennedy's name, and most important, meditate in solitude."[16]

After years of fund-raising and foot-dragging, and a delay of several years for the construction of a parking garage beneath the selected site, the $125,000 memorial was dedicated in 1970, seven years after the assassination ($75,000 of the $200,000 collected for the project was contributed to the Kennedy Memorial Library in Boston). No Kennedy family members were present at the dedication, though Sargent Shriver, husband of Eunice Kennedy Shriver, came a week later and praised the design.

Johnson said later, "I wanted to design the simplest memorial and didn't want it to include any kind of architectural concept. A skyscraper is easy—there are no unpredictable parts," adding that this was the first monument he had designed. His original plan for the memorial to hold excerpts from the President's speeches became a controversial issue with the Dallas leadership and was dropped.

"Kennedy was such a remarkable man I didn't want to have a statue or hackneyed 'narrative,' but sought rather for something very humble and spartan. A major point for me was to raise it above ground level and keep it simple. It is a cenotaph, a memorial for one whose remains lie elsewhere."[17]

During the dedication, Johnson and various civic leaders spoke briefly and eloquently, but when his turn came, County Judge Sterrett forgot to mention Kennedy's name, dwelling on the benefit of the clearing of thirty-seven flophouses, beer joints, and liquor stores from the site, leading *The New York Times* to assert that Sterrett seemed to praise the memorial in urban renewal terms.

Response to the finished memorial was mixed, ranging from a fatigued

John F. Kennedy Memorial

Dallas, 1970

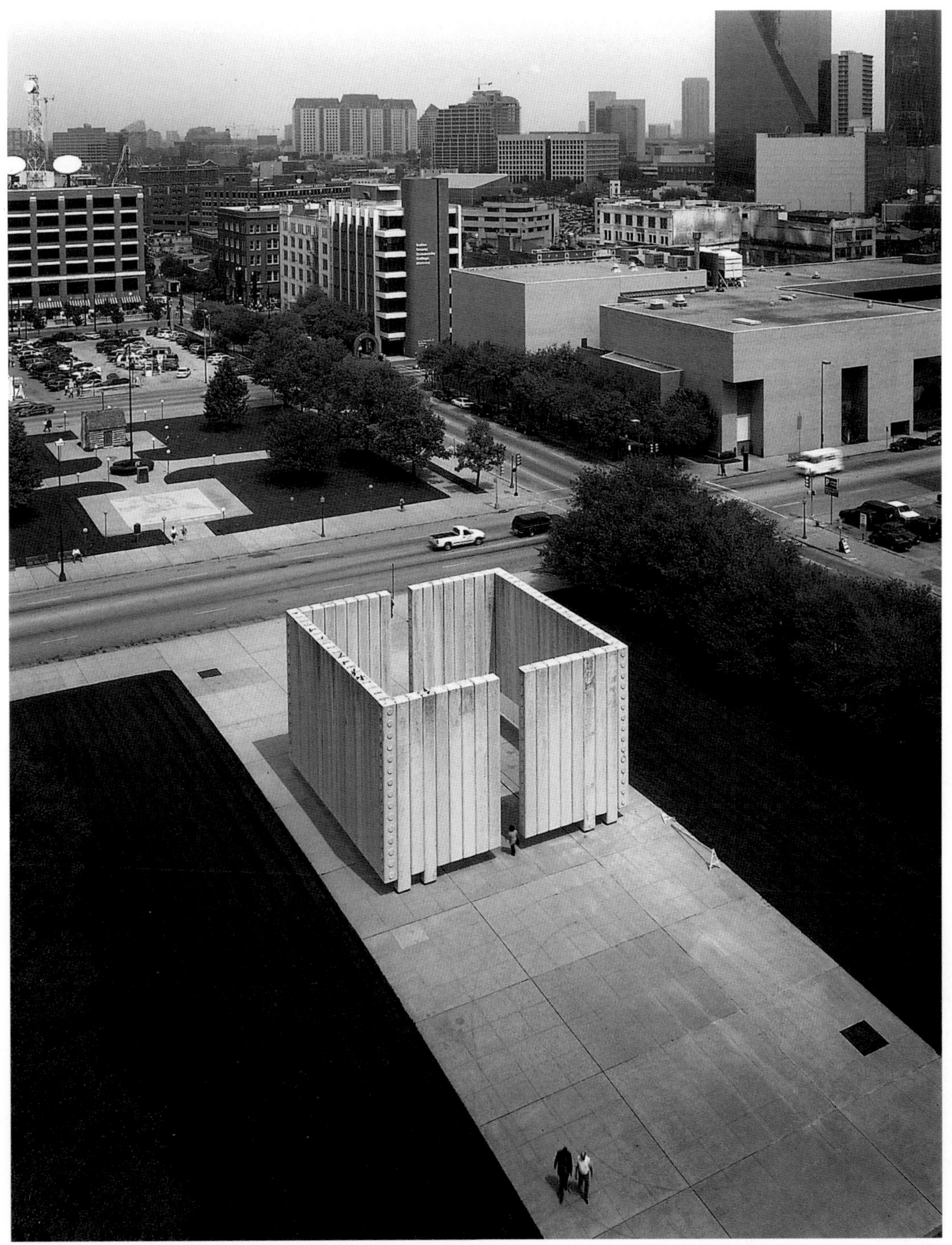

Kennedy Memorial Plaza from Dallas County Courthouse roof.

Entrance to the memorial.

Plaza from the south.

Memorial interior.

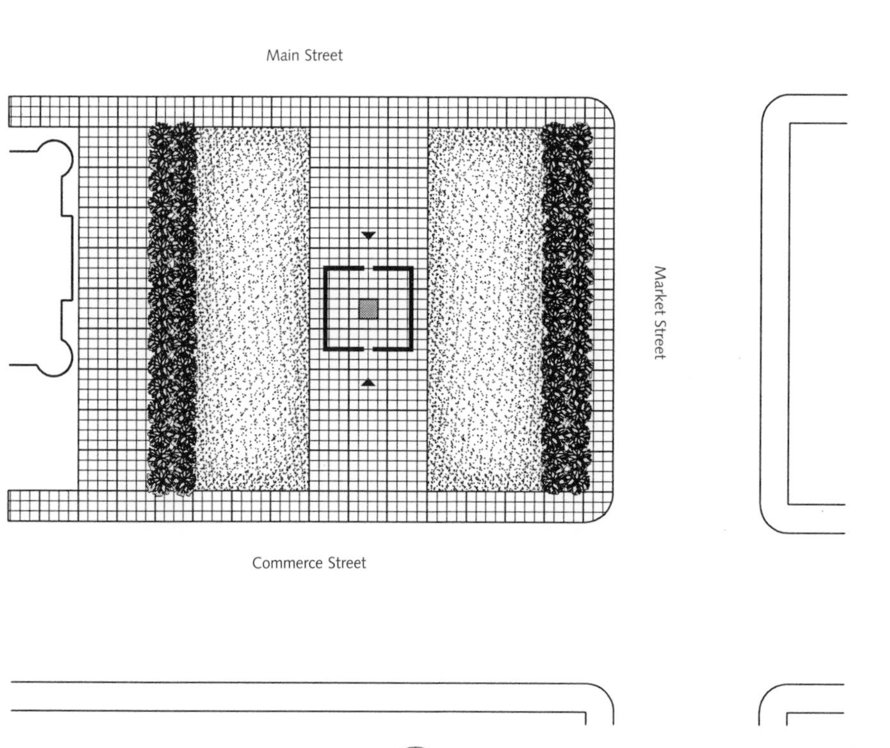

John F. Kennedy Memorial drawing; site plan.

civic pride to the bemused mutterings of some architects and ordinary citizens about the *meaning* of the memorial. It did not communicate much in a literal or a subliminal way. The massive volume floated on its tiny footings, leading one to speculate that the tentative quality of the mute structure was a metaphor for Dallas's quandary of grief and shame at the time of the assassination. Despite the balletic structural scheme and the reach of the light-catching surfaces, there is something somber about it. Hollow and emptied out, its lack of telegraphed emotion, while disconcerting to some, also brought to mind Robert Browning's line "true grief is passionless."

One of Johnson's detractors, and he had not a few, dubbed it the world's largest *urinoir* (*urinoirs* being Paris's freestanding street toilets). Years later Johnson joked about his friend Donald Judd, the minimalist sculptor known for his pristine "boxes," "Don has claimed for years that I owed him a commission for the design!"[18] More to the point perhaps was *Dallas Morning News* architecture critic David Dillon's observation: he pointed to the similarity of the monument to Mies van der Rohe's 1930 design to memorialize Germany's Great War dead, which featured a thick, square slab of dark granite centered in a lofty, marble-lined cube of space.

The Kennedy Memorial, while still controversial in the city where Kennedy's presidency was, and still is, a source of contention, has become, in the late

Donald Judd installation, South Artillery Shed, Chinati Foundation, Marfa, Texas.
Photo by the author, 1997.

Photo reproduction, Mies van der Rohe competition drawing for a memorial to the Great War Dead in Karl Frederich Schinkel's Neue Wache, 1930.
Courtesy of the Mies van der Rohe Archive, the Museum of Modern Art, New York.

1990s, an integral part of Dallas's history and its sparse downtown urban culture. The assassination site in nearby Dealey Plaza on the downtown's western edge draws several million visitors annually. The Sixth Floor Museum at Dealey Plaza, a handsome, moving, and scholarly exhibit dealing with the Kennedy presidency and his death in Dallas, is located in raw loft space in the building where a sniper's nest was found. Yet there is also, independent of The Sixth Floor Museum, an assassination Conspiracy Museum located across the street from the memorial, and a replica of Kennedy's open-top limousine is available for tours.

In 1983, twenty years after the assassination, David Dillon reflected on the lingering controversy about the memorial: "The differing responses to the Kennedy Memorial are as much emotional and cultural as esthetic. To many, Johnson's work speaks quietly and elegantly as a solemn, classical expression of grief for a lost leader."[19] However, the city and Dallas County have not maintained the memorial with care. The strength of the design is as a pristine, abstracted evocation of loss, and the stains and trash that accumulate at the memorial diminish its meaning. In 1998 a movement led by Jeff West, director of The Sixth Floor Museum, began a campaign for enhancement of the memorial. Johnson was asked for ideas, and his first solution called for a "cincture," a short wall to encircle and identify the memorial's precinct more distinctly within the contiguous urban scheme. In spring 2000, the memorial was cleaned of graffiti and restored to its original, stark abstract presence.

Before the Kennedy Memorial was finished and dedicated, Johnson had undertaken the design of another museum, a small one, this time on the Gulf Coast in Corpus Christi, Texas. Though Richard Foster continued awhile longer as an intermittent partner, John Burgee was now an integral figure and partner in Johnson's office, and the 1970s would be marked by the really large, influential commercial projects of high-profile design that the partnership of Johnson/Burgee became noted for. But first the decade was concluded with Johnson designing a modest-sized but finely modeled building for art on Texas's Gulf shore.

Chapter 4

Philip Johnson was widely quoted in the early 1970s that he longed to be *l'architecte du roi,* that he wanted to design monumental projects commensurate with the grandly scaled buildings of Europe: the sort of architecture with which his mother educated his young eyes in her Cleveland living room.

In the democratic era, the public decided the scale and character of its constructions, which were likely to be dams, highway systems, and other heavy, infrastructural components of a consensus society. The "palaces" of the modern mid-twentieth century tended to be privately funded buildings and complexes for commerce and trade, not an area that would ordinarily interest an art and culture figure like Johnson. That was where the monumental action of architecture lay, and Johnson was perceived as the expensive artist/architect outside the mainstream, used to hefty construction budgets and unsuitable where corporate programming and "bottom-lining" were essential components.

Working on the landmark Seagram with Mies and designing the high-rise Yale project whetted Johnson's taste for larger design tasks with grander effects. He was quoted as saying that he would work for the Devil himself if that's what it took. Further, he said that whoever commissions a building "buys me," while at the same time he was calling the design of buildings to suit a client "whoredom." He was also nearly sixty and turning more emphatically to the architecture of other architects, both contemporary and vintage, for inspiration. He described himself as an Eclectic Functionalist. But before he started receiving large commercial commissions, abetted by John Burgee, he designed one of his best buildings, the Art Museum of South Texas (AMST) in Corpus Christi.

Corpus Christi, Texas, from the bay, mid-1960s. Courtesy of Corpus Christi Business Alliance.

Corpus Christi, located on Corpus Christi Bay at the edge of a flat coastal plain, near the mammoth, legendary ranches of South Texas, called itself "the Sparkling City by the Bay." It was noted for tropical hurricanes, a petrochemical industry, and its proximity to the North Padre Island resort on the Gulf of Mexico. In the 1960s the population was under 200,000; one didn't pass *through* Corpus Christi to get anywhere—it was a provincial end of the line. Due to its subtropical character and its great, curving Ocean Drive, which wedded the city to its bay, Corpus Christi was the most picturesquely urbanistic city on the entire four-hundred-mile length of Texas's Gulf shoreline. It was sleepy and relaxed; the soft Gulf breezes swept sensuously through its hard, palm-dappled light. Nor was it a stranger to significant architecture.

Richard Colley was the town's maverick architect, with a creative, innovative modernist way reflecting the region's constraints and possibilities with stunning residential designs. His houses were shaded with deep overhangs and had freely flowing interior spaces surrounding lush courtyards. Colley had a contrary, opinionated personality. He considered himself an authority on everything from art to horticulture but had a real talent for developing articulated structural and mechanical systems before that became a vogue. In the mid-1950s he teamed with O'Neil Ford of San Antonio, Texas's best-known architect and a colorfully outspoken "folk hero," to produce a highly original manufacturing complex for Texas Instruments Company in Dallas. (Two other partners on the project were A. B. Swank Jr. and Sam Zisman.) By then, Colley, Corpus Christi's difficult but preeminent architect, had designed a number of the city's public buildings.

Patsy Dunn Singer, from an old Corpus Christi banking family, and her oilman husband Edwin Singer, a native New Yorker, determined that their languorous city on the Gulf was in a deprived state culturally, and Patsy Singer, an active amateur painter with an eye and a sense of quality, led the way toward improving the situation with her husband Eddie backing her. They and others on the city's Arts Council had been thinking for some time that Corpus Christi needed an art museum to replace the small, concrete-block Centennial Building where classes and local exhibits were held. One evening, after driving back from a big bird-hunt and barbecue in nearby Beeville, the Singers, over nightcaps with their friends Jane and Bob Flato, asked, "What kind of architect should we get for the museum? Should we get a local architect?" and Bob Flato replied, "If you're going to get an architect for something like a museum, for godsake get a *good* one!"[1]

Corpus Christi 1936 Centennial Museum. Photo by Frederick McGregor; courtesy of Art Museum of South Texas.

The Singers were acquainted with Dominique and John de Menil through the International Council of the Museum of Modern Art. Patsy knew what the de Menils were doing in Houston, and she contacted Dominique, who suggested they must first talk to Philip Johnson before they did anything about a new museum building. At about this time, in the mid-1960s, Patsy Singer and several other Corpus Christi ladies went up to Austin to attend one of Lady Bird Johnson's first Beautification Conferences. Johnson spoke to the gathering, and Sissy Farenthold, one of the ladies in the group, recalls that Patsy Singer was bowled over by him.

Not long afterward Johnson spoke at Massachusetts's Mount Holyoke College commencement and said, in part:

> Clearly our values are oriented toward other goals than beauty. Two goals stand out, two goals that we Americans think more important than beauty. Money and utility.
>
> What use, my friends, is beauty? Why did the Athenians bother to take thirty years and the talent of every Athenian to build the Parthenon? . . . should we not appropriate some of our billions to make . . . our cities beautiful, if not for posterity and immortality like the Greeks, then for ourselves?
>
> As you have guessed I am being somewhat fanciful. But I am convinced that Americans can do what they want. And I have it on the authority of Pericles, the leader of the Athenians, who built the Parthenon, that Athens (and we) could have guns and butter—and great buildings.[2]

John de Menil sent a list of architects to Eddie Singer which included Johnson, Charles Moore, Louis Kahn, and Mies van der Rohe, but Patsy wanted to talk to Philip Johnson; along with the charismatic impression he made on her in Austin, his longtime connection with the Museum of Modern Art impressed her.

She went to New York to see Johnson, and he received her with his customary charm and interest in a new building. But when he asked how much money they had for a museum and what kind of art they had, Patsy Singer replied that they didn't have any of either. Johnson was stunned by her bravado: they wanted a museum but had no *money* and no *art!* Johnson at first demurred, saying that the project was too small and he was too busy on larger projects, but Patsy Singer countered by saying, "Some doctors make a lot of money on rich patients and give charity to their poor patients; well, we're a poor patient." Johnson retorted, "You Texas women have an answer for everything! Go back to Corpus Christi and raise some money and then come back to see me. You might also think about where the art is coming from for a museum."[3] (He had seen his share of people who simply wanted to meet "the famous architect," without real intentions of building.)

Returning to Texas, Patsy Singer and her husband soon raised enough money, $700,000 toward a projected $1,000,000, for Patsy to return to New York. Cultural philanthropy for the fine arts was something most of the well-heeled of Corpus Christi in the late 1960s had never heard of, but with support from area ranching families, they all pitched in and Eddie Singer's business connections across the country made up the rest. This time when they went back to Johnson, they had money but only the barest list of needs for a museum.

Blissie Blair was president of the Corpus Christi Art Foundation (which operated the little Centennial Museum) when things started happening to raise interest and money for a new building. She recalls attending lunch with other museum ladies at the city's premier Town Club, when Patsy suggested that they try to get Philip Johnson as their architect. As Blissie Blair tells it, "Their eyes simply rolled around at the very idea of getting someone like Johnson to come all the way down to Corpus Christi!" Blair adds that later "Johnson loved to regale everyone, describing Patsy's coming up to New York with her 'golden curls,' batting her big lashes, and talking so soft and sweet."[4]

Derelict buildings had been cleared from a raw, flat site—on Corpus Christi Bay a mile north of the downtown at the end of Ocean Drive—which Eddie Singer and others had put together. It was edged with the 1930 Seawall, designed by resident Gutzon Borglum, which had been built as a hurricane bulwark. The museum would be the first building erected on this reclaimed waterfront acreage at the confluence of the bay and the intracoastal canal, in the shadow of the great Harbor Bridge. The point of land was envisioned by Singer and others as a future science and art center. Talks were resumed with Johnson, who agreed to go ahead and took it on himself to write the program for a new building as his schematic designs developed. It was a very informal way to get a public building designed, but the Singers, particularly Patsy, were in a hurry and captivated by Johnson's magnetic, confident way. They did not consider another architect.

Patsy and Edwin Singer in front of the newly completed Art Museum of South Texas, 1972. Courtesy of Edwin Singer.

Eddie Singer, a shrewd businessman, developed great admiration for Johnson. Singer recalls:

> He was amazing. There was that great energy and the obvious talent and intelligence, but the thing that impressed me the most was his ability to *sell* his ideas. He would come down here and it's a long way from New York, he would certainly be tired. He would go into a meeting and immediately charge up everyone with his enthusiasm. People were dazzled by him. This was not a great big job for Philip and John, but he made us believe it was the most important job he had ever undertaken. And he could disarm criticism with a sort of smart-aleck confidence; at one meeting when he was describing the building, some lady raised her hand and asked if the skylights would leak. "Of course they will," he came back, "*I'm* not going to *install* them!" It got a laugh; they ate it up. I never knew anyone like him![5]

The local professionals were not happy when Johnson, the breezy, brainy New Yorker in the fancy suit, was chosen; Richard Colley, the proud and talented local architect, resigned from the Arts Council, while others grumbled. One architect suspected that Patsy Singer chose Johnson because of his con-

Philip Johnson lecturing a group during construction of Art Museum of South Texas, 1971. John Burgee, in a dark suit with a cup in his hand, is in the center of the group. Photo by Blackwell Photography; courtesy of Art Museum of South Texas.

nection to the Museum of Modern Art, where she prized her place with other MoMA devotees. She wasn't the first or last Johnson client attracted to New York's glamour as the culture capital of the country. At least haggling was avoided between the Singers and the few Corpus Christi firms who considered themselves qualified for the prestigious job; difficult choices for the Singers to make among them were precluded. *All* the locals were miffed.

Johnson already had a team in mind to help out as soon as he had worked out a design. Howard Barnstone, the dedicated Johnson admirer, and Barnstone's young partner Eugene Aubry were Johnson's—and John de Menil's—choices to implement work on the building from their Houston office. Barnstone was still on close terms with his New York mentor even after Barnstone and Aubry had taken over Johnson's uncompleted work on the Menil-conceived and -funded Rothko Chapel, completed in 1971.

"When preparing a new building design," John Manley, of Johnson's office, recounts:

> Mr. Johnson typically would come in on Monday morning with dozens and dozens of pieces of thin yellow tracing paper. There would be rudimentary schemes—just little raw sketches really—which he would give to someone to interpret. Developed ideas were later looked at on the drafting room tables by

him and often discarded over and over when there was something that he didn't like about one scheme or the other.

He was very quick in making a decision, but proportions developed gradually on the schemes he favored. Nearly all his conceptual ideas were developed on weekends at The Glass House, and each Monday morning we waited anxiously for his arrival with all those little yellow pieces of paper. The concept for the art museum in Corpus Christi, however, never changed much from the initial concept that he had.[6]

Gene Aubry, living in Maine in the late 1990s, recalled:

Philip's original scheme was to have the building sitting out in the water, but we had to settle for putting it on the Seawall; it still ended up being pretty spectacular. You have to remember that there was absolutely *nothing* there! That conglomeration of civic buildings out there hadn't been built yet; they followed the museum, unfortunately. It was an absolutely blank site and there was this gigantic long concrete seawall stretching back to Corpus and the wind was blowing forty miles an hour all the time. So very early Philip got Robert Zion of New York involved to do the landscaping and got Howard and me involved to do the working drawings and watch the construction.

We did the construction drawings and built this big study model of the building and took it down there—we were under construction—and had it in the contractor's shack when this horrendous hurricane struck, Carla I believe, and everything, I mean *everything*, was blown away; the shack with the model was never found. It ripped us up and we basically started over again.[7]

Frank Stella, "Irregular Polygrams" exhibition, Leo Castelli Gallery, New York City, 1966.
Photo by Rudolph Burckhardt.

The design of the Art Museum of South Texas was a formal departure for Johnson. It had multiple sources of derivation, but the provenances were varied and more contemporary than before. A few years earlier, he had designed a gallery for sculpture on the grounds of his Glass House compound. It was, until the construction of his Gate House in 1996, the most unusual, freewheeling structure in his personal collection of design experiments. Located on a slope on the north edge of the sloping property, the Sculpture Gallery in plan and form was an abrupt shift for Johnson.

Frank Stella was a friend and artist whose abstract paintings Johnson had begun collecting. In the 1960s Stella had turned from the austere Stripe Paintings for which he was famed to asymmetrically shaped canvases that he called Irregular Polygons. The plan for the gallery reflects the sliding, shifting planes of the angular, nonorthogonal geometric shapes of Stella's newest work. Johnson called his plan "Two rotated rectangles with wedges cut away to create distinct spaces for the sculpture." It was a radical turn from Johnson's

Exterior of Sculpture Gallery, New Canaan, Connecticut, 1970. Photo by Paul Hester, 1994.

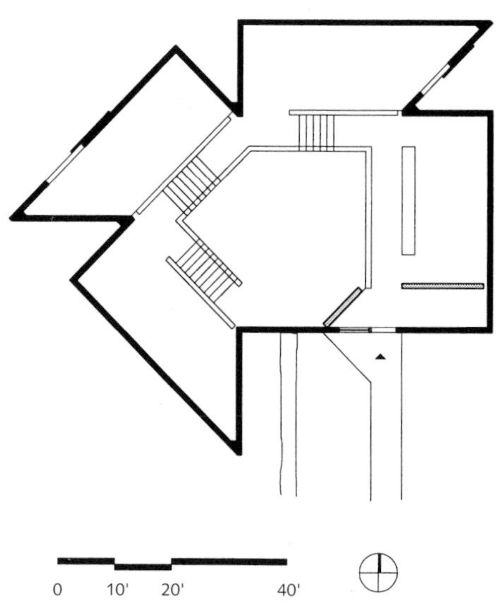

Floor plan of Sculpture Gallery. Courtesy of Philip Johnson.

familiar orthogony of form: a light-filled barn conceived in formal terms that could be likened to Japanese origami. From a distance, the white painted-brick building, imbedded in the slope, is striking with its low, gabled form; yet as one approaches, it becomes surreally sculptural with its glistening, all-glass "greenhouse" roof and the shifting, unexpected angles of the wall and roofline. The dramatic interior is a scooped-out, pivoting vortex of descending steps and platforms on three levels.

The *whiteness* of the Sculpture Gallery and the Corpus Christi museum was Johnson's nod to the group of ambitious young architects—protégés of Johnson's—who were called "The Whites": Peter Eisenman, Michael Graves, Charles Gwathmey, John Hejduk, and Richard Meier, all New Yorkers except Graves, who taught at Princeton. Their well-publicized high-style designs were rendered with the light-catching surfaces and forms associated with the Swiss master Le Corbusier. "Corbu" and the others were certainly in the wings of Johnson's mind when he conceived the museum for Corpus Christi.

Art consultant Cathleen Gallander grew up in a small South Texas town near Corpus Christi and served as the museum's first director. She recalls hearing from David Whitney that, one weekend in New Canaan, when Philip was working on the study model for Corpus Christi, Whitney, with his unerring eye, suggested that the building would look better if it was flipped around, so Johnson took it in the bathroom and looked at it in the mirror and agreed with Whitney; the design's facade was reversed.

"Several of us went to New York to see Johnson's presentation of the design," Gallander recalls.

> Howard Barnstone was there. Johnson was charming and attentive as always, and when he brought in this beautiful white model we were all just knocked out. I couldn't believe it and knew we were seeing something very special. We all understood that it was a major, major statement. Eddie and Patsy said from the very beginning that this building was not going to be a museum built by a *committee* but a museum built by a *great architect.* That was brilliant of them, and I believe that's the reason for its success. There were no fundamental changes made to the original design.[8]

Eugene Aubry talks about what it was like working with Johnson:

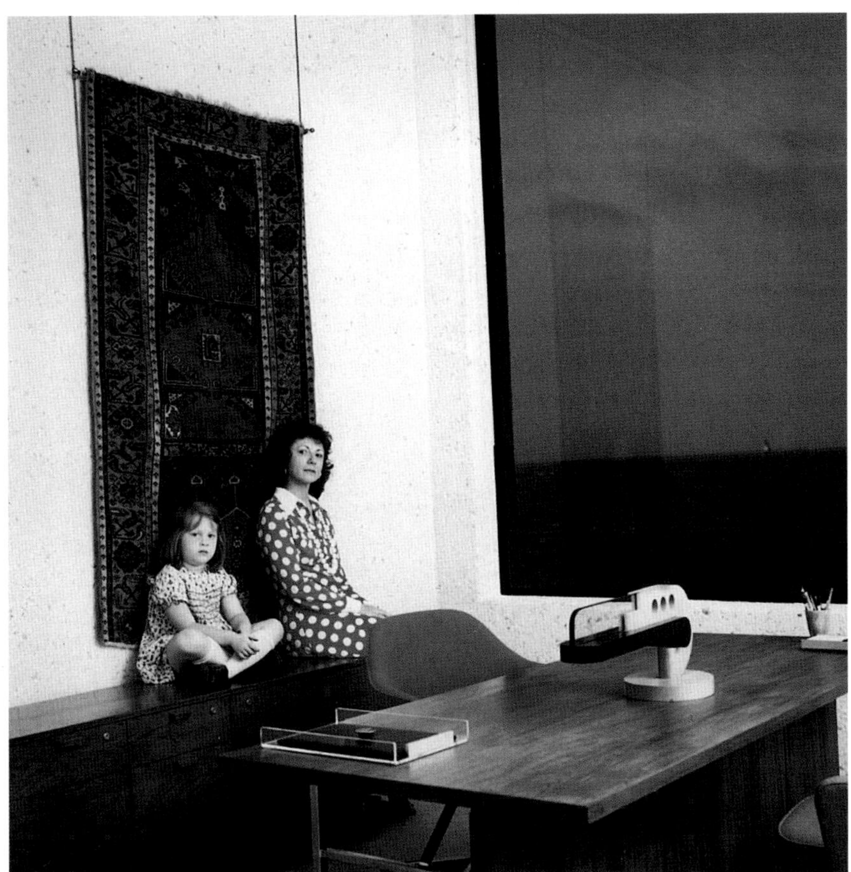

Cathleen Gallander and daughter Melissa in the director's office, Art Museum of South Texas, 1974. Photo by Hans Namuth for *Fortune;* courtesy of Cathleen Gallander and the Hans Namuth Archives, Center for Creative Photography, University of Arizona.

> Whenever we worked with Philip, we would always get these very beautiful, carefully drawn schematic building designs from Johnson's office, drawn by John Manley, and then we would take these wonderful drawings and develop and correct them and send them back to New York. Johnson's bunch had absolutely no "give-a-damn" attitude about flashing details and things like that, other than that they wanted to be *sure* of everything! Manley would check all our stuff out, and he was really good—I mean he was top-notch and the heart and soul of that office.[9]

The building design that evolved was weighty, all-concrete, and absolutely white, an effective foil to the shoreline's blue water and the vast coastal sky with its drifting cumuli. Two levels of galleries and public space were placed above the entrance grade, with a third, lower service level located on the Seawall, which the building straddled. The articulated parts of the plan were pulled apart and composed asymmetrically, creating large and small openings in the exterior wall for access and deeply embrasured views of the bay.

The broad dark-glass entry provides a vivid enticement to enter the chalky, windowless front facade. Low, sloping roofs bracket each side of the main entrance block. The building contains a cool and lofty great hall spanned by a sixty-foot bridge from the curving towerlike stairwell to the second-level galleries. The first impression upon entering the building is that of a pale, pristine cave with glowing alcoves radiating natural light from concealed sources. The polished floor is white concrete, as are the bush-hammered walls. The carefully orchestrated ambient light articulates the interior in a luxurious way. The building is unlike anything Johnson ever produced.

The carefully composed window openings are few, due to the brilliant coastal glare. Compensating for the lack of windows in the second-floor galleries are angled industrial-type light monitors on the roof, which give the building a serrated profile and cause those upper galleries to glow. Everything is pared down, with no superfluous parts. The overall effect is one of pure and assuring sculptural strength. Bleached and radiating light, the building claims the shoreline as if carved from a giant gypsum block.

"Philip came down with John Burgee from time to time to look at the building and check the concrete forms and the concrete finish," Aubry recalls.

> At one point he became worried about how the roof of the building looked from the Harbor Bridge that hovers nearby, and that you would see all those air-conditioner units sitting up there, so he had the whole top of the central part done in galvanized subway grating so you can't see anything.
>
> We would do big wall samples and get these Mexican guys with hand-held pneumatic, steel-pronged things that ground and roughed up the walls,

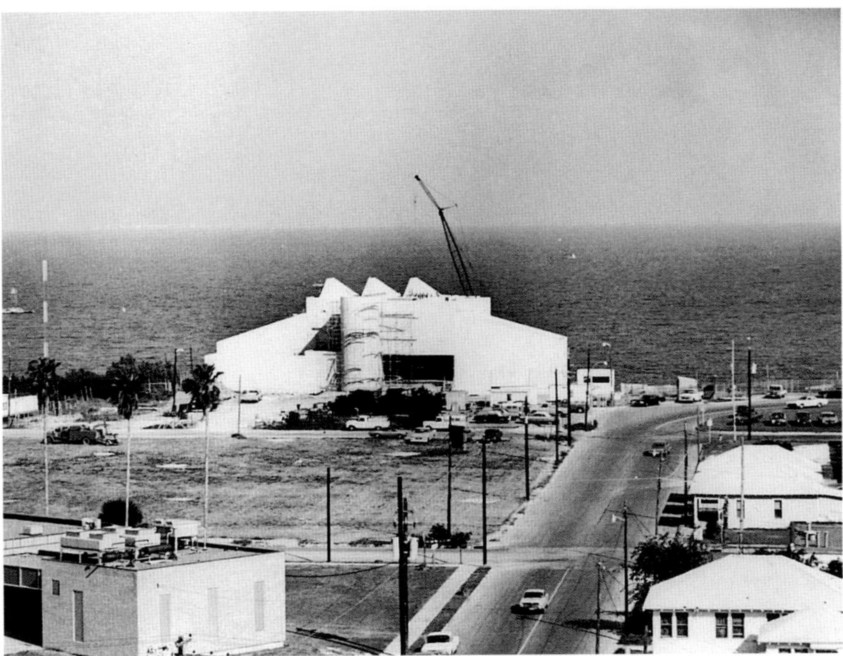

Construction of Art Museum of South Texas, 1971. Photo by Blackwell Photography.

all of which had rounded corners. When finished, the building was beautiful and very, very dramatic there on the water: all-white concrete, made with white cement, white sand, and white aggregate. The walls are fourteen inches thick, so it's not *going* anywhere; it doesn't make any difference if it floods! You didn't need any art inside because the paintings were the *windows:* You would stand there and these huge ships would come by, and there is one spectacular window that looks down the long Seawall to the city's skyline.

Reflecting on Johnson the architect and cultural figure, Aubry continues:

Philip is one of my favorite people in the world. I came very close to going with him when Howard and I divided up. His whole mind and his whole life are an interesting study, and I mean it is fascinating how that mind operates and how he has been able to stay in complete control. Nobody maneuvers Philip, and if you study the life that he's had, it's all very carefully orchestrated. I think he has more than a special place in architecture, other than what he does as an architect; he has a much, much bigger role.

He is all over the board: he's the Andy Warhol of architecture! When you think you've got this sucker nailed down you find out he's slipped out the window! He's gone, you can't find him! And so all us stupid architects sit around and try to figure out what Philip is going to do next year.

He's the ringleader of a young bunch of so-called disciples, or whatever

> you want to call these hangers-on, who actually sit around and believe everything he says. But he's always a jump ahead of them! I was in his office once and there was this big stack of manuscripts on his desk and he was complaining and name-dropping, "Jackie keeps calling me to read this book and that book but I am so busy! I've got this show to do over at the museum and when it opens, Michael Graves is going to be history!"[10] He likes all these young guys, they're all friends, but he kind of leads them on.[11]

In 1981, for the convening Texas Society of Architects, Corpus Christi architect John Dykema Jr., calling the museum a continuing source of civic pride for the city, described it this way: "An agglomeration of hard-edged forms carefully crafted in pure white concrete, the museum is the epitome of building-as-sculpture. Its success derives from the juxtaposition of forms to create rich spatial experiences, as well as from the deft manipulation of light and view. The whole evokes a range of associations, including the white-against-blue of a Mediterranean setting and the thick-walled, punched architecture of the Pueblo. From outside and within, one experiences a pervasive sense of coolness and shelter."[12]

Paul Goldberger wrote about the museum in a 1973 special issue, on Johnson, of *Architectural Forum:*

> Here in Corpus Christi it was not the greenhouse roof of the Sculpture Gallery that Johnson picked up but the sense of sharp, angular forms in tension with one another. Like the Sculpture Gallery, the museum is an all-white building too, suggesting comparison with the "pure esthetic objects set down in the landscape" (to use Reynar Banham's term) of early Le Corbusier, or perhaps with much of Richard Meier's current work. But at least as relevant a comparison is to Charles Moore's Sea Ranch of 1965, a casual, almost slapdash structure of wood without the elegance of early Corbu or Meier, but with sharply sloping roofs whose diagonals possibly prefigure the overall form of the Sculpture Gallery and the museum at Corpus Christi.[13]

Dallasite Ellis Shamoon, who designs and manufactures sleek consumer products, grew up in Corpus Christi and recounts the effect that the museum had on him: "I left Corpus when I was eighteen and went away to school and military service, and when I returned this incredible building had been built north of town on open land near the water; it utterly changed how I looked at things. You might say that the appreciation of *design* with a capital 'D' entered my life and never left. Returning to my hometown and finding that gleaming building with its abundantly glowing interior was a shock."[14] In 1972 Cathleen Gallander opened the $1,300,000 Art Museum of South Texas in tandem with the opening of the majestic $6,500,000 Kimbell Museum in Fort

Worth. The nation's art crowd came to Texas focused on Louis Kahn's masterpiece, but they also traveled down to Corpus Christi. The opening exhibition, curated by David Whitney, was an eye-opening, colorful show of Frank Stella, Jasper Johns, and Andy Warhol. It was a stretch for most of the South Texas crowd. But not the stretch that a later show of Whitney's for Corpus Christi proved to be; one of the museum's benefactors was enraged by a guard who asked her to remove her highball glass from one of Donald Judd's minimalist plywood cubes. Also included in this exhibition was *Skyway,* Robert Rauschenberg's epic 18' x 16' painting, which Johnson had commissioned for the 1964 New York World's Fair. John Kennedy's image in the painting contributed to the controversy over the piece, and AMST's board decided against its purchase; today it hangs in the Dallas Museum of Art.

Philip Johnson lecturing about Jasper Johns during the Art Museum of South Texas opening, 1972. Courtesy of Art Museum of South Texas.

Gallander is unstinting in her praise of both Johnson and the building:

> I think he is wonderful, with an incredible mind, and the building, well, to me the experience of that building was almost religious; I never got tired of walking into that great volume every day with those great windows framing views of the Gulf or Ocean Drive or these great ships that look like they are coming right into the museum; it was like being in a Fellini movie! I think he was a genius in what he did in that building. He really understood the harsh Texas light like nobody has ever done: the way it filters into the building down those concrete walls is poetic and makes art sing.[15]

Terrell James is a Houston artist whose paintings were exhibited at the Art Museum of South Texas in 1997 and recalls:

> I went to Corpus five or six times in the process of getting my show organized and installed, and I gave talks to docents who would be taking schoolchildren through. I met three different women who had lived in other parts of the country and world, and they were in out-of-the-way Corpus Christi because they were married to someone in the oil and gas business who had been transferred there. They were all saying how much it meant to them that there was a museum of that caliber there. One woman actually said to me that she came down there with her husband to decide whether or not she could really live there, and the museum made her think, "It would be all right."
>
> I think that it's interesting that it has this kind of symbolic meaning to people arriving from far away: "There's an important museum that's trying to be serious here—I guess I can take it." They could identify with some kind of *effort.* Hearing this was gratifying to me as an artist. And as an artist my experience of showing in that building with that wonderful upstairs space filled with natural light was an incredible one. It's almost like there's a different three-dimensionality to the paintings because the light is so beautiful.[16]

Art Museum of South Texas

Corpus Christi, 1972

Detail, west facade.

JOHNSON/BURGEE, ARCHITECTS; BARNSTONE & AUBRY, ASSOCIATE ARCHITECTS.

PHOTOS BY PAUL HESTER, 1994.

West and north facades.

View to north along seawall; Bayfront Plaza Convention Center (1979–1982) on left, Harbor Bridge in distance.

View of galleries.

Window to east and Corpus Christi Bay;
skylighted planting areas.

Detail, second floor terrace on north facade.

Skylighted stairwell.

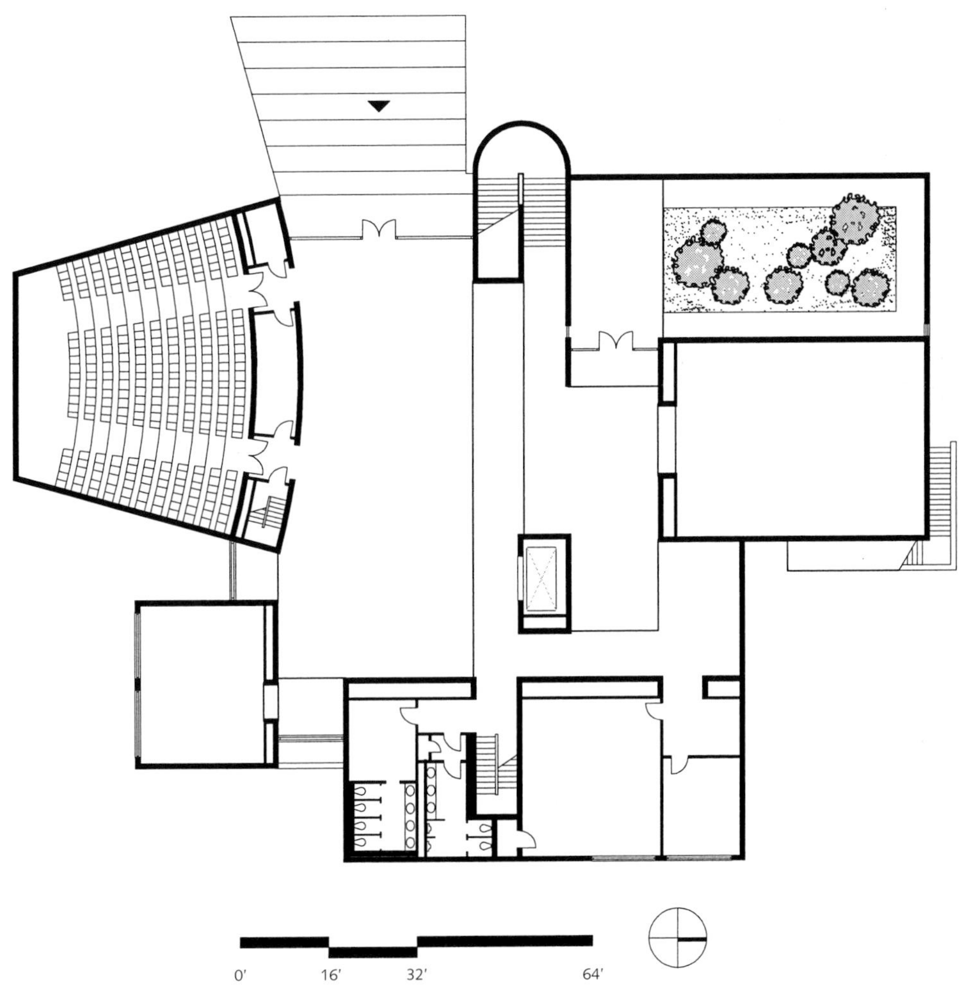

Art Museum of South Texas drawing; ground floor plan.

"Philip did a lot more for us than his contract called for," Eddie Singer says. "He volunteered his time to help plan the entire bayfront complex, appearing before the city council several times. But as far as I know his effort to apply some coherent urban design to the future complex never went anywhere; he might have been a little rich for their blood."[17]

A few years after the museum opened, when plans were developing for a big multipurpose civic building to be built near the museum, Patsy Singer went down to the city council and did battle. She said, "We need more *room.* You are *not* going to build this enormous building smack up against the museum!"[18] It took several more appearances by her before the planners shifted slightly the location of the building, called Bayfront Plaza (SWHC Inc., Corpus Christi, and CRS, Inc., Houston, associate architects). Its resultant brutalist mega-scale dwarfs Johnson's sculptural building, on which it turns its back.

"I think Johnson sort of adopted us," Eddie Singer continues.

> We were having trouble getting someone to put together a show for the museum's grand opening; James Johnson Sweeney had backed out as curator when one of our board members—and we were all Anglos then—reminded Sweeney that Mexico was our neighbor and should be recognized in the show; Sweeney wasn't going to be told what to do and quit. There was this cultural divide in Corpus Christi then that exists even today, but it has moderated a great deal.
>
> Johnson leaped into the breach brilliantly! He got David Whitney to organize the inaugural exhibition of three high-profile New York artists: Johns, Stella, and Warhol. All were friends of Johnson's and Whitney's, and Warhol made a big multiple portrait of Philip for the show. The exhibit's sophistication definitely made a mark nationally for Corpus, but I guess the citizens were a little ambivalent about all that color and abstraction. Johnson loaned pieces by all three artists from his private collection. [Mexican-American presence in the museum came later.] In that white building it was very beautiful.[19]

Yolette Garcia, an executive producer with the public television station in Dallas, is a third-generation Mexican-American Texan, with Spanish land grant ancestors. She grew up in Corpus Christi and says that discrimination there has ebbed since the early 1970s, when the museum opened and the minority community began asserting itself for a place at the civic table. Even before the change, her grandmother and mother were active in many cultural affairs, and her father was one of the first Mexican Americans to be elected to the Corpus Christi city council. She remembers the excitement that her family felt for the huge event of the museum's opening and the pride they had.

"There is an unworldly aspect about the building," Garcia reflects. "For Corpus Christi it is a cultural beacon there at the water's edge in a way that a lighthouse could never be. Inside, it's like a holy place; it has the feel of a Greek temple with openings in the walls looking out to the ocean."[20]

The lowest level of the building, near the level of Corpus Christi Bay, proved problematical with the high surges of water from the hurricanes that visit the Gulf Coast. Paintings and material in storage have to be moved when this occurs, presenting the museum with the decision about how best to add a needed facility above the surge level, and whether that should be attached to the building or separate. Any appropriate way to add on to Johnson's sculptural structure is inconceivable, so a separate, complementary structure nearby, connected by tunnel, appears to be the viable option; Ricardo Legoretta has been commissioned to prepare a design.

Meanwhile, for Johnson and his new partner John Burgee, in Minneapolis, the diagonal as a driving design element was figuring even more prominently in their biggest project yet. Burgee's ease and experience with the corporate world began to pay off. It was the building complex that would provide Johnson and Burgee with entree into the big time of commercial building. While Johnson/Burgee was completing a large addition to the Boston Public Library, with no important new work in view, a group of Minneapolis businessmen hired Johnson and his partner to take over the design for a big office building on Minneapolis's downtown Nicollet Mall. The 1967 mall was a successful redesign of the city's main street by San Franciscan Lawrence Halprin, the deliberative and innovative planner of Sea Ranch, Ghirardelli Square, and striking civic spaces for Portland, Oregon. The initial program for the project's development expanded beyond a single building, and the resulting complex of tower and lower, ancillary structures, on an entire city block, changed the skyline and urban life of Minneapolis as it altered the perception of what Philip Johnson and his partner were capable of. Johnson was finally qualifying for the position of *l'architecte du roi,* with John Burgee as point man, and the sixty-seven-year-old architect liked it.

John Burgee and Philip Johnson in Johnson/Burgee office, New York, 1980. Courtesy of Hines Interests.

The IDS Center in Minneapolis, a mixed-use complex of great urban richness, is linked to adjoining blocks by pedestrian bridges and marked by a glittering, faceted fifty-one-story office tower and a large enclosed plaza roofed with a spectacular, cubistic construction of steel and clear acrylic: a greenhouse roof as a Lego construction. Department stores, a bank, and a hotel huddle at the base of the reflective-glass tower, which is octagonal in plan and serrated on its angled walls, creating banks of corner offices on four of the building's sides that make a vertical sweep up its facades of enormous visual impact. For an architect who had a longtime record of disparaging social agendas for architecture, there was irony, in that his IDS Center was such an enormous social and urban achievement and the most successful thing of its kind for American city life since New York's Rockefeller Center of the 1930s. The architecture was good; what it did for the city was better.

In 1973, after it was completed, Johnson wrote about IDS in *Architectural Forum* in a piece entitled "A There, There":

> John Burgee and I are perhaps the luckiest team of architects around.
>
> Consider Minneapolis: A city before we arrived with (1) a handsome, successful pedestrian Mall through the center of town; (2) a network of bridges connecting many of the downtown blocks at the second level; (3) two great department stores located on the Mall; (4) a client, Investors Diversified Services, with vision to choose the Mall's center block—I would almost say the epicenter—to build its complex on.
>
> An architect's dream.
>
> With all this given, we tried to improve on it. We aimed to put into practice our theory, in no way original, of a new kind of City Square. We had the

IDS Center, exterior and interior, Minneapolis, Minnesota, 1973; Johnson/Burgee, architects. Photos by Richard Payne.

people, we had the location, but a normal open plaza was out of the question. Much of the weather in Minnesota is similar only to Siberia—cold, very cold, in the winter but hot, very hot, in July and August. Strolling in Piazza San Marco is impossible nine to ten months of the year. So, with a similar situation, a "solution" was obvious: We enclosed our square with buildings and roofed its 20,000 square feet with a trussed grid of clear plastic. Everyone in Minneapolis passes through it; splendid for girl watching and ice cream buying—both in air-conditioned comfort. The plaza is dead: long live the climate-controlled court!

The shape of the court itself is pentagonal, not rectangular, making an easier more informal pedestrian flow around corners. The four entrances to the space are not symmetrical, are not opposite each other. Some little mystery remains. One crosses the "clearing" in a casual, diagonal manner. The *procession,* the on-foot circulation was indeed the main preoccupation. Our aim of making a popular plaza has succeeded. The combination of hotel, office tower and shopping center works: high density suits a city center; and the tower is a beacon, visible from everywhere. The bridge system works so well that many Center citizens drive to work in the winter, bringing no overcoat with them. Minneapolis, always one of the more delightful cities of the world, is now one of the most walkable cities, one of the easiest to move in, one that rewards movement with varied experiences and encounters. We hope there is more of a *there, there* now.[21]

Johnson the "sociologist" was not exaggerating the effect of IDS Center on Minneapolis: it dramatically "leavened an already lively downtown" and won national praise from the architectural critics and urbanists alike. As it became the place where the city's quickened pulse was felt, Johnson and Burgee were on their way to becoming the country's most publicized architectural firm, noted for large, imaginative urban projects. Like the "Drawing Room of Europe" that was Venice's Piazza San Marco, Minneapolis's Crystal Court evolved quickly into that city's magnetic "Town Square," where all paths crossed.

As successful as IDS was in urbanistic terms, Johnson nevertheless turned down an opportunity to design an entire block in the center of Paris. Texan Robert Cadwallader, president of Knoll International, was asked in the mid-1970s by the Dubonnet family which American architect should design an entire block of buildings in the French capital to replace one which the venerable distiller family owned and planned to raze. Cadwallader recommended Johnson, who refused the commission, declaring, "You can't do what you want to in Paris; there are too many rules and restrictions!"[22]

In 1970 Johnson was called back to Fort Worth by Ruth Carter Johnson for a wide-open urban design project free of design restrictions. This would further alter the perception of Philip Johnson as an exclusive and deft designer of elite, high-style small buildings. Lady Bird Johnson's agenda for civic beautification inspired Ruth Johnson to get the Amon Carter Foundation to purchase several blocks of rundown property on the southern edge of downtown for a park and make it a gift to the city. Ruth did not consider any other architect for the job; she and Johnson remained close friends after the completion of the Amon Carter Museum and its subsequent additions. The four-and-a-half-block site purchased by the Carter Foundation for the park lay between the Tarrant County Convention Center and railroads beside an elevated freeway in a fringe area of the downtown receiving only occasional redevelopment. Ruth Johnson had no ideas about the project beyond her desire that it be an asset to the city, something that would enhance a part of downtown that needed an esthetic boost to its civic morale.

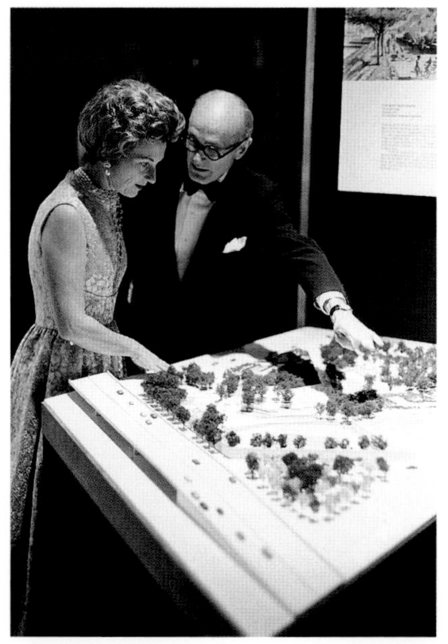

Philip Johnson and Ruth Carter Johnson inspecting model of the Water Garden, the Museum of Modern Art, 1971. Photo by Jan van Raay.

Johnson's first design did not appeal to Ruth: she recalls that there were built-up berms of land on the flat site, with a belvedere-type structure as an overlook. There was nothing particularly original or striking about it; neat, but without a pervasive idea. Johnson went back to work. This time he proposed dramatic changes in level of concrete surfaces holding a variety of water features. In the much smaller Museum of Modern Art Sculpture Garden that he designed in 1953, Johnson had created an illusion of spaciousness by subtle level changes in the garden floor, with its crisp orthogonal islands of planting and pools of water. At the four-and-a-half-block site in Fort Worth, Johnson sharply and dramatically upped the ante in levels, fountains, and masses of planting. Ruth Johnson was thrilled with what she saw in his revised design: she called it the Water Garden.

Johnson's plan for the Water Garden was a free, abstract composition of angular, shardlike polygons seeming to shift and slide past each other in a fixed pattern of kinetic movement. Three large irregular sections were planned for water features; the balance of the site was given over to walkways leading to a large "plaza" and banks of platforms and tiers of retaining walls for trees and greenery in raised and sunken planes. Commenting on the Fort Worth Water Garden soon after it was completed, Peter Papademetriou said in *Progressive Architecture,* "The form of the Water Garden relates to Johnson's latest work, consisting of a geometry more activated and dynamic than that of his so-called 'Miesian' period. Ever unabashed to use a good idea, Johnson might be said to be 'Learning from Larry'—Halprin, that is—yet the result bears Johnson's touch."[23] Before Johnson began the design for the

Aerial view, looking northeast, Water Garden site, Fort Worth, early 1970s; elevated freeway at lower edge, Tarrant County Convention Center at upper left. Courtesy of W. D. Smith, Inc. Commercial Photography Collection, the University of Texas at Arlington.

Water Garden, landscape architect Lawrence Halprin had received accolades in the architectural press for his urban design work for Portland, Oregon. Born in Brooklyn in 1916 and educated at Cornell, the University of Wisconsin, and Harvard's Graduate School of Design, where he knew Johnson, Halprin settled in the Bay Area after World War II and worked for Thomas Church. Halprin became noted for his understanding of the spatial experience of human movement in the environment, calling it "motation," a system of motion choreography worked out with his wife, Anna Halprin, a dancer. For Portland, Halprin created three distinct open spaces, with unique water features, in the city's center, which undoubtedly caught the ever-inquisitive, design-voracious eye of Johnson.

One of Halprin's plazas was a conventional civic park of trees, paving, and sedate fountains. The other two spaces employed a freewheeling and brutalist palette of raw, monolithic concrete combined with a sensationally theatrical use of water. These unique urban spaces, where water is used as coarsely falling cascades from massive escarpments, brought, in Halprin's words, an "experiential equivalent" of mountain crags and waterfalls into the city's heart. Halprin plotted pedestrian movement through Portland's strikingly original spaces as in a modern-dance ballet, with broad, angular changes of movement and level. Many felt that Johnson was given a creative cue from

(left) **Lovejoy Fountain, Portland, Oregon, 1968; Lawrence Halprin, landscape architect.** Courtesy of Lawrence Halprin.

(right) **Ira's Fountain, Portland, Oregon, 1968; Lawrence Halprin, landscape architect.** Courtesy of Lawrence Halprin.

Halprin's work in Portland. With a license common to creative people, he went for something even more dramatically scaled and nontraditional for the four and a half blocks he had in downtown Fort Worth.

In 1976, Halprin's Heritage Park, a small but distinguished mazelike plaza of trees, pools, and waterfalls in a blocky, concrete infrastructure, was dedicated north of Fort Worth's Tarrant County Courthouse. Ruth Johnson knew Halprin from his urban planning work for Fort Worth and was responsible for his getting the job; the Carter Foundation helped pay for the park. Honoring the nation's Bicentennial and the city's founding as a nineteenth-century fort, this jewel of an urban space overlooking the Trinity River is woefully hidden and surrounded by fast-moving traffic. At the time of the park's dedication, Halprin began work on the Franklin Delano Roosevelt Memorial in Washington, which took twenty-five years to get built and is the apotheosis of Halprin's special vision.

The completed Water Garden employed three elements in its design: concrete, water, and densely treed vegetation beneath a fourth encompassing entity, the broad Texas sky. The parts of the plan composition are angular, not rectilinear, as in Johnson's garden at the Museum of Modern Art. And where the New York garden, a patio really, is staid, urbane, and static, the Fort Worth space is dynamic: it *moves.* The broad, flat space is made to twist and straighten, close and open, dip and rise in an almost infinite variety of unexpected experiences. One enters the park at an angle between stepped concrete retaining walls holding live-oak trees and a small cascading sheet of water. On the right, leading one straight and diagonally into the park, is a long, narrow brimming channel of water which overflows a tall, battered wall to a sunken, irregularly shaped still pool ringed with bald cypress. Directly ahead, past another sunken polygonal pool with forty aerating fountains, one reaches Johnson's large space, his plaza, paved in the same rugged pale-roseate concrete as all the surfaces. To one side of the plaza is the highest point, a twenty-five-foot concrete "mesa" for speech and performance. It is reached by steep, twisting asymmetrically tiered steps, formed from stacked concrete "layers" which imbue it and the myriad retaining walls in the park with a subtle flavor of the Incas. Behind this pyramid an amphitheater with the park's only green lawn is walled away from street and freeway traffic to the south.

On the east side of the Water Garden's plaza is the pièce de résistance of the park: a great, almost angry, "subsidence" of the park floor has been transformed into an exhilarating, memorable sensory experience. When first seen at the plaza's edge, there is something menacing and unsettling about the way that the water flows, as if from a broken main, and rushes from all sides across tiered, undulating slopes of concrete to a foaming, roaring vortex forty feet below. It is a man-made flooded *erosion,* an evocation of violent nature. The palpable sense of danger permeates this gorge of overlapping geometric plates, awash and rushing downward to a roiling sinkhole which has to be the quintessential threat of architectural engulfment. Johnson's often vaunted sense of a portentous quality in architecture—exciting wonder and awe—is present here in spades! For the strong-hearted, a meandering series of blocky, freestanding steps, elevated above the water, descends the

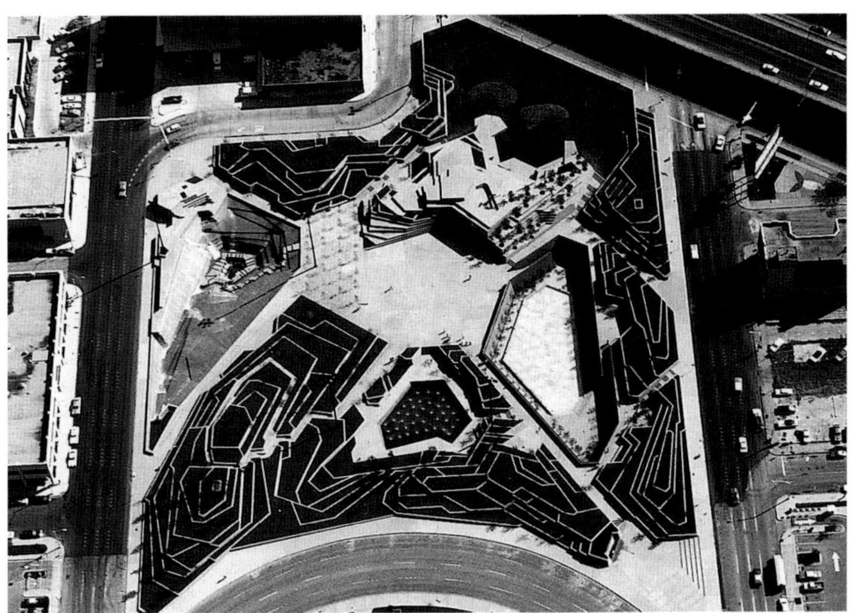

Aerial view, Water Garden, 1975; elevated freeway at upper right. Courtesy of W. D. Smith, Inc. Commercial Photography Collection, the University of Texas at Arlington.

glistening ravine of rushing and flowing water, which disappears in gushes through a dentil-edged basin at the bottom. It is a design and psychological tour de force.

"The result of the Carter Foundation's gift may serve as a potential *agora* for central Fort Worth," Papademetriou continued in his 1975 piece in *Progressive Architecture.*

> The Water Garden and its opening are very much in the Fort Worth tradition. Rarely in American cities is the direction of public life so clearly the result of efforts by civic-minded individuals who are concerned about making the urban setting unique.
>
> The design's "big splash" aspects are a reflection of the achievement-oriented pride characteristic of Fort Worth. The city received the gift from the Amon Carter Foundation and for its patrons, the Water Garden opening also was the occasion of Ruth Carter Johnson's birthday. It stands not only as a gift to the city of Fort Worth, but also as a happy event for a devoted group of people who have proved that intervention can better the urban scene.
>
> Philip Johnson probably would have kept the garden closed for five years, during which time the tiers of plantings and groves of small trees would have grown to the necessary mass to function as space makers. Fortunately, he did not have his way."[24]

Philip Johnson undoubtedly didn't hear Ruth Johnson's later plea before a group of architecture students for quality materials in civic construction: "It's better to plant a ten-dollar tree in a hundred-dollar hole than a hundred-dollar tree in a ten-dollar hole!"[25]

"What they created was a miniature landscape of mountains, forests and lakes in the image of an architect's contour map rendered in angles," Nory Miller wrote in 1979 after the park matured.

> They maintained an extreme economy of means and manipulated these few elements within a restrictive geometric order. Within these limits, however, the architects set about introducing every type and shape of variety that could be squeezed in. Layers of concrete edges and soft plantings pile up quickly for mountains or more gradually as cultivated hillsides. There is constant variation of lushness and hardness, simpler and more frenetic configuration, height and depth. There are so many vectors of movement that it is intriguing and animated and vivid, but the palette is so restricted that it never loses continuity.[26]

Before the Water Garden was dedicated in October 1974, Philip Johnson and John Burgee had become involved with a Houston developer whose entrepreneurial genius would elevate the New York architects into an empyrean

Fort Worth Water Garden

1974

Recessed Quiet Pool surrounded by bald cypress trees.

JOHNSON/BURGEE, ARCHITECTS. PHOTOS BY PAUL HESTER, 1998.

Vortex of Active Pool.

Westerly view of Water Garden from above; elevated freeway on left, Tarrant County Convention Center on right.

Entrance walkway, looking north, next to sloping water wall above Quiet Pool.

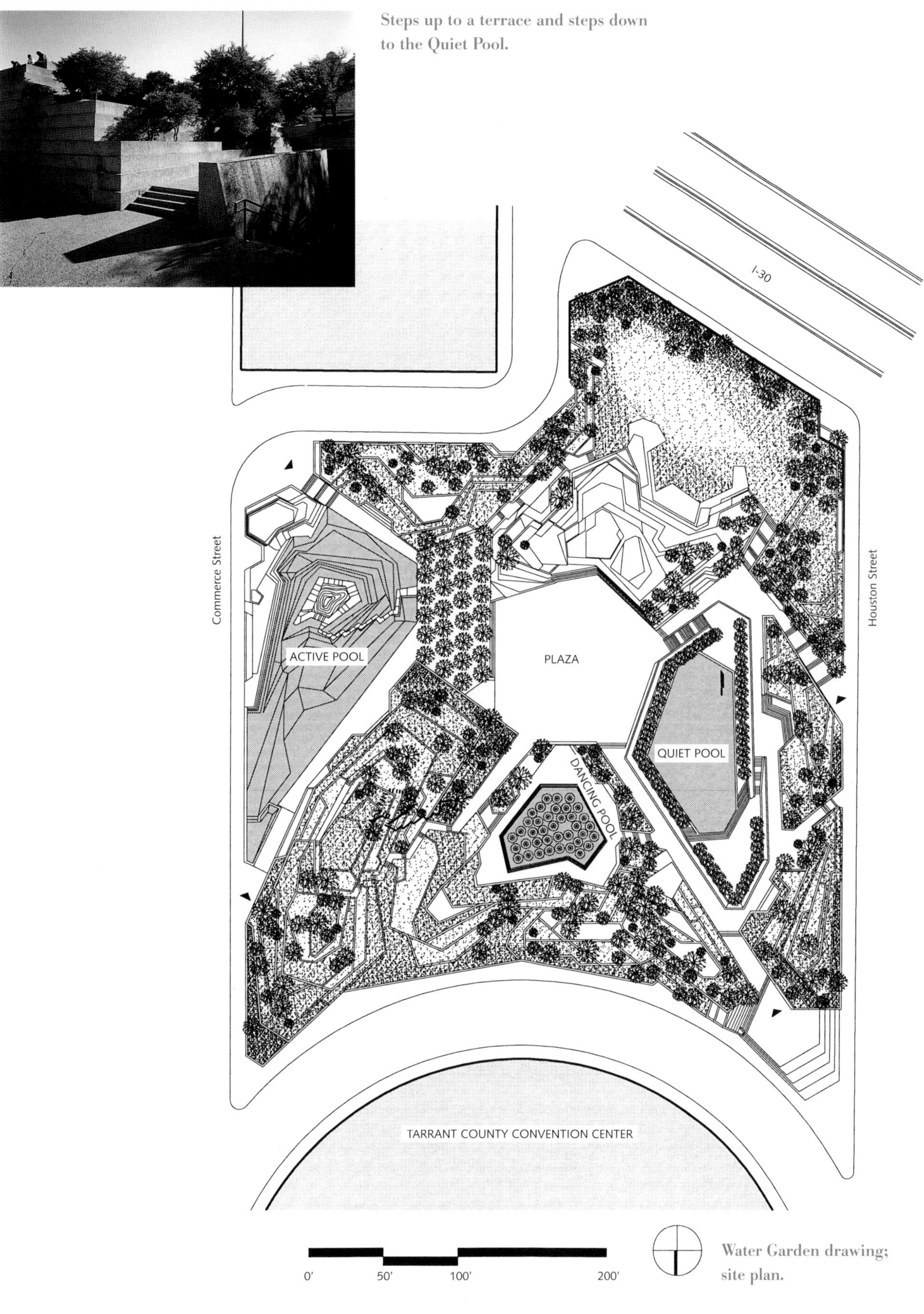

Steps up to a terrace and steps down to the Quiet Pool.

Water Garden drawing; site plan.

realm of income and fame, changing the skylines across the country and the public's perception and expectation of architecture. When he teamed up with Burgee, Johnson, the artist/architect, made what amounted to a Faustian pact, eschewing finely wrought elite architecture for big, impersonal projects. Johnson jumped into the fray of competition with large commercial firms with a gusto that surprised everyone who knew him as the cultural connoisseur. During this lengthy period of partnership with John Burgee, there would be high points of accomplishment for Philip Johnson, but far more low or middling points. The period began in the 1970s not long before Johnson suffered a great professional disappointment.

After more than forty years of intimate reciprocal association with the Museum of Modern Art, Johnson was rejected as a prospective architect for the museum's expansion in the mid-1970s. He had certainly benefited from association with the institution he had helped start in the 1930s, besides serving, without pay, as first Director of the Department of Architecture and Design and paying a secretary and the librarian himself. He had been hired to design all of the museum's additions since the beginning, including the celebrated Garden. Serving as a trustee since 1957, he had also made numerous gifts of art—more than anyone except for cofounder Lillie P. Bliss—to the establishment that had been his emotional and intellectual home for most of his life.

While there were other architects serving on the museum's board at the time, Johnson was considered the "house architect," and that assumption caused his being passed over for what could have been a major achievement at the apex of his career. Cesar Pelli was selected as architect. It was an enormous blow to Johnson's pride and sense of worth at a vulnerable point in his years. Punishment for good deeds must have crossed his mind, but it didn't help the pain that endured. Ever the pride-swallowing pragmatist, Johnson, with Whitney, bought an apartment in the museum's Pelli-designed residential tower, which adjoined the expanded museum; its windows looked down on the Museum Garden.

The entry of Johnson and Burgee into the commercial, big-building marketplace represented a symbolic exit for Johnson from the intense and rarified cultural world of New York that he had enjoyed and cultivated since his twenties. Johnson and Burgee's affair with "trade" lasted until the country's building boom crashed in the mid-1980s, as Johnson himself turned eighty and the Johnson/Burgee team simultaneously unraveled. But in 1974 Johnson was sitting pretty—he had his *roi* at last! Yet in 1992, standing by his office window, he looked down on the Third Avenue traffic and, rubbing his chin, mused, "Gerald Hines! Where in the world did *he* come from?"[27]

Chapter 5

Developer Gerald Hines's eminent place in Philip Johnson's career was the result of twenty years of luck, circumstance, and friendships that led back to Dominique and John de Menil.

The track led through Ruth Carter Johnson, who had been introduced to Johnson by the de Menils. During construction of the Amon Carter Museum, Johnson insisted that the teak paneling in the design be fabricated by the New York firm that had furnished the millwork for the Seagram Building. Thomas Byrne of Fort Worth wanted to use I. S. Brochstein's millwork company in Houston; Brochstein had recently furnished the millwork for the Fort Worth National Bank, which Byrne built. Johnson was skeptical. He didn't think that there was a good woodworker west of the Hudson River but eventually bowed to Byrne's advocacy of Brochstein. Johnson was so impressed with the Houston company's perfectionism on the Carter Museum that he selected Brochstein to furnish materials for many other buildings, including the Beck house in Dallas and the Kreeger house in Washington.

Gerald D. Hines, mid-1970s. Photo by Marc St. Gil.

Gerald Hines grew up in the Midwest and after graduating from Purdue University came to Houston and went to work for a refrigeration company. He started building speculative office buildings in the late 1950s designed by Harwood Taylor, a recent University of Texas graduate, and his partner J. Victor Neuhaus III. The modernist, low-rise buildings that Hines built to Neuhaus & Taylor's modern designs along Richmond Avenue in southwest Houston were eye-catching in their visual freshness. (Cleverly planned in response to specific conditions, they rented easily.)

Taylor and University of Houston teacher Howard Barnstone were two of the leading young modernist architects in Houston in the mid-1950s, with a clientele for small-scale elite residential projects. Recognizing Taylor's reputation and value, Hines sought him out. Vic Neuhaus, whose firm, Neuhaus & Taylor, eventually became the huge six-hundred-member 3D/International, recalls, "Gerry just walked in the door sometime in 1956—Harwood and I hadn't had our office too long—and said he wanted to build a warehouse with an office attached. We were delighted to get the job, and it turned out to be the first building that Gerry built. Later we designed a large number of office buildings and hotels for him before he turned to high-profile national firms."[1]

Cynthia Rowan Taylor, Harwood Taylor's wife at the time, recalls, "Harwood was very persuasive and really was Gerry's teacher about good design. He convinced him that quality architecture did not have to be expensive, that you could achieve architectural distinction while controlling construction costs if your design was up front where it counted, where people could see it. Gerry was an ambitious newcomer to Houston, and he wanted to be identified with the good things, design-wise, as long as the numbers worked. He and Harwood and Vic made a good trio."[2]

Gerald Hines was successful with the buildings on Richmond Avenue, and in the mid-1960s he hired Neuhaus & Taylor and Hellmuth, Obata & Kassabaum (HOK) of St. Louis to design a big retail complex, the Galleria, near the western edge of Houston's inexorable spread into the plain of ranchland and rice farms. The commission developed because Neiman-Marcus wanted HOK for its anchor store; Neuhaus & Taylor worked with the St. Louis firm as associate architect for the multilevel complex with an ice rink below a vaulted, skylighted roof. The Galleria, with its central space fashioned somewhat after Milan's famous arcade of the same name, became a national trendsetter and prototype for the suburban, mixed-use enclosed mall with a unified architectural design.

I. S. "Ike" Brochstein, who immigrated to Galveston from Palestine in 1912 at age fifteen and went to work for a cabinet shop, had, by 1960, the leading millwork firm in the Southwest and owned acreage on Post Oak Boulevard near the Galleria. In the late 1960s Hines, sensing Brochstein's desire to build a competing shopping center, approached him to make a deal: let Hines lease the land and build a complex of high-rise office buildings in partnership with Brochstein. Brochstein's son Raymond was an architecture graduate of Rice University and, though an important part of his father's firm, retained a strong and refined sensibility about architecture. Andy Todd, the ardent disciple of Mies van der Rohe, had been his professor at Rice and later said, "Ray Brochstein was the best student I ever had!"[3] Indeed, young Brochstein's position of influence with his father played a big part in the history of late-twentieth-century architecture by further promoting Gerald Hines's emergence as a developer-patron of quality design. Through young Ray Brochstein, Johnson/Burgee's ascendance to top rank among the nation's architects became wedded to Hines's success.

Raymond Brochstein. Courtesy of Raymond Brochstein.

"I think Dad's position with Philip Johnson crystallized during the construction of the Amon Carter Museum," Ray Brochstein recalls.

> Johnson, you know how he is: it must be *perfect,* and Dad was a perfectionist, too, with a sharp eye. Johnson had specified South American teak veneer for the plywood paneling in the museum. Dad discovered that our supplier had shipped some nonmatching flitches of the teak that were going to cover that long, tall wall in the main gallery of the building. Dad called him on it and the supplier argued about it, so Philip sent his partner Richard Foster to Houston and Foster confirmed what Dad said. Another teak log had to be found and Johnson never forgot it, and later pushed work in our direction.
>
> Sometime in the late sixties we were making plans to develop some acreage that Dad had accumulated on Post Oak Boulevard, an area which was getting hot with development. Well, when Gerry Hines heard that we might build a shopping center that near his Galleria, he approached us in 1969, proposing an office building complex instead. We decided that if we were going to work out a deal with him, we wanted a say-so about the architect. Dad liked the buildings that Harwood Taylor was designing in Houston, but though Hines had used Taylor and his partner Victor Neuhaus many times, he said he wasn't going to be held to *one* architect; he insisted on a nationally known firm, which was all right with us if we got to okay the selection. Hines came up with a list that included one local firm, Neuhaus & Taylor; Hines' personal favorite, Bruce Graham of Skidmore Owings & Merrill of Chicago; I. M. Pei of New York; and Roche/Dinkeloo, Eero Saarinen's surviving firm based in Connecticut. Dad liked Philip Johnson a lot and asked Hines to add his name to the list of possible architects for the job.

> Well, Skidmore was doing these nice buildings everywhere that all sort of looked alike, so they got scratched, and Pei and Roche/Dinkeloo both said that they didn't *do* speculative office buildings. Johnson was the last one called, and he and his partner John Burgee said, "Of *course,* we would be *happy* to talk to you!" They came right down to Houston for an interview with Hines and got the job. They had Minneapolis' successful IDS job under their belt and that impressed Gerry.[4]

What followed is architectural and entrepreneurial history.

Gerald Hines is something of an enigma. He has a rather flinty persona and doesn't give off many signals about what's going on inside his head that makes it tick so efficiently. Born in Gary, Indiana, in 1925, his college degree was in mechanical engineering, and that perhaps explains his no-nonsense, cerebral engineer manner. When he came to Houston after graduation he worked first as a salesman for air-conditioning equipment. He soon started in construction with small commercial remodeling, warehouses and office buildings, and moved to larger, successful projects marked by a tight rein on construction costs and dollar-saving maintenance costs. He also soon learned the value of marketing, of both the research and selling varieties. He made some painful market-research mistakes along the way, particularly in housing, but learned from the errors. "Careful homework" became synonymous with Gerald D. Hines Interests. He was not a handshaking, showboating kind of promoter in the mode of, say, William Zeckendorf, the high-profile developer of New York's booming 1950s. (In the late 1940s Zeckendorf put I. M. Pei, the Chinese American Harvard graduate, on his staff as company architect.) Hines, the buttoned-up cool calculator of men and money, liked the idea of a vacation of mountain climbing, alone. (He is at a loss to explain how he became a patron/developer of high-profile architecture beyond remarking that he had a grandfather who built churches in Nova Scotia.)

The first concept that Johnson/Burgee came up with was very conventional stylistically and, according to Raymond Brochstein,

> looked like every other building in Houston; I thought my father was gonna have a stroke when he saw it. They had a group of three towers, clad in precast concrete sort of like the Galleria buildings a few blocks away. The corners of the buildings were chopped off at forty-five degrees, making octagonal floor plans, and the whole thing was on a gigantic megastructure that held parking, retail, and some housing. Dad just hated it. Of course it was never built, but Hines had some promotional brochures printed to pass around. The project sat for a while because Gerry was stretched out with other irons in the fire, building three or four buildings simultaneously. It delayed starting our project, and we were anxious to get going.

> Finally it became clear to everyone that Hines, with all he had going, couldn't build all the buildings at once, which Johnson/Burgee's scheme required, because the megastructure at the base was integral to the design. So he went back to Philip and asked him to rethink his design, making a group of economical buildings that could be built one at a time. He also asked for a more distinctive design language for the buildings.[5]

Johnson welcomed the opportunity to revise his design and this time took a big leap away from the modernist orthodoxy of the Skidmore Owings & Merrill sort. He not only cut corners for Gerald Hines, he *rounded* them. The inspiration for his revision was a 1931 building near the Hudson on New York's midtown West Side, the Starret-Lehigh Building by Cory and Cory, a landmark ribbon-windowed Art Deco industrial building which became a model for postwar office buildings in New York and elsewhere.

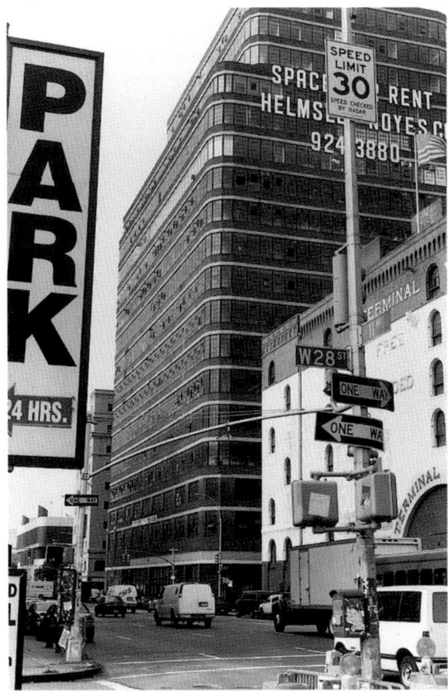

Starret-Lehigh Building, New York City, 1931; Cory and Cory, architects.
Photo by the author.

The new design, which everyone liked, particularly the Brochsteins, evoked stepped-back New York office buildings which had evolved from the Deco style that Johnson attacked in the 1930s as he trumpeted the artistic merits of the newer European import, the International Style. But, following his own oft-quoted exhortation, "One cannot *not* know history!" he made peace with the dated Deco style, but in a minimalist, stripped-down mode. With Hines, construction costs were critical, so, as John Burgee was quoted, "We thought of the cheapest thing you could do and they were ribbon-windows, set-backs and curving corners."[6]

Johnson/Burgee employed a thin tensile wrapping of charcoal curtain-wall, silvery glass, and polished aluminum in continuous, horizontal bands that curved around the outside corners with streamlined zip. When the first twenty-four-story unit, called Post Oak Central I, was completed in 1975, it proved to be a strikingly profiled tower and rented rapidly. The second building, Post Oak Central II, was built in 1978 and is a parallelogram in plan but with language identical to the first tower's; Post Oak Central III, built in 1981, has a triangular floor plan and the same facade treatment and twenty-four-floor height as its siblings. That completed the three-building composition, flanked with parking buildings, on the Brochsteins' seventeen acres.

By the mid-1970s Gerald Hines had gained a national reputation for his success in Houston with speculative office buildings of architectural distinction. In 1971 he completed his first building in downtown Houston, the fifty-story One Shell Plaza, with Shell Oil Company as the stellar tenant. It was also the first Hines project to use a nationally known architect, Skidmore Owings & Merrill (SOM) of Chicago, with Bruce Graham as principal designer. The travertine-clad shaft, which became an immediate Houston landmark, had

Post Oak Central One, Two, and Three

Houston, 1975–1982

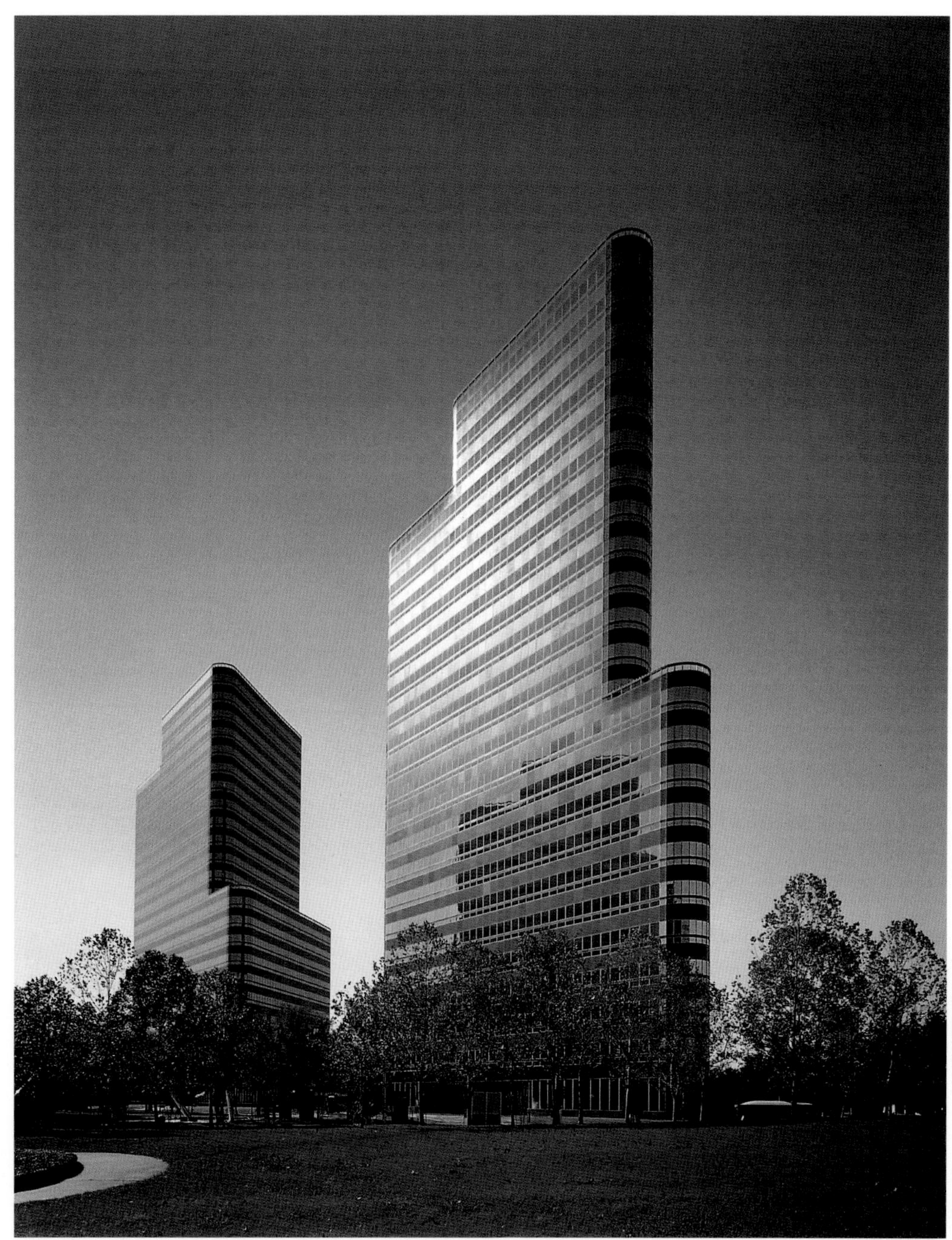

Post Oak Central Two and, in background, Post Oak Central Three.

JOHNSON/BURGEE, ARCHITECTS; WILSON, MORRIS, CRANE & ANDERSON, ASSOCIATE ARCHITECTS (BUILDING ONE); RICHARD FITZGERALD & PARTNERS, ASSOCIATE ARCHITECTS (BUILDINGS TWO AND THREE). PHOTOS BY PAUL HESTER, 1981–1998.

Post Oak Central group from hotel across Post Oak Boulevard.

Post Oak Central Three with One in background and parking garage on the right.

Base detail, Post Oak Central One; Transco Tower in distance.

Entrance, Post Oak Central One.

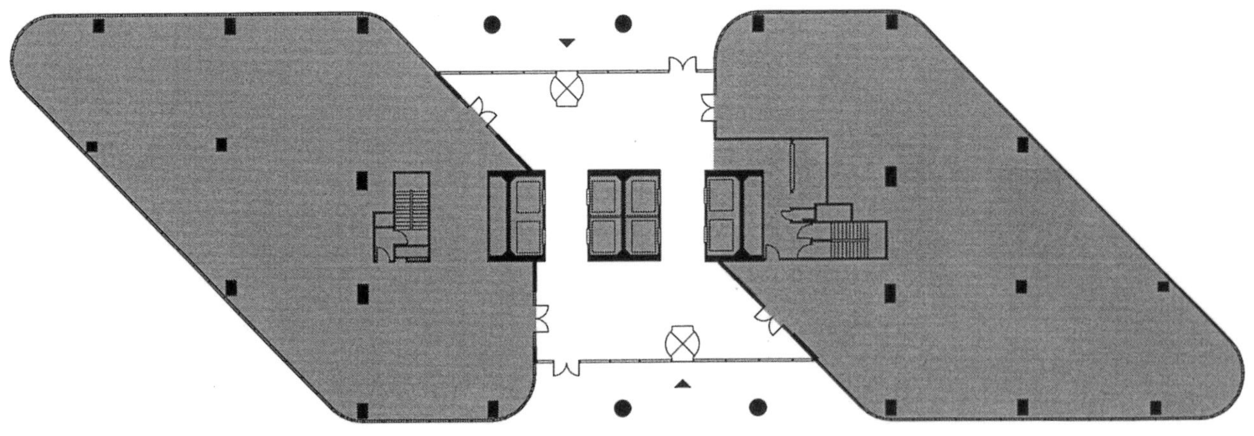

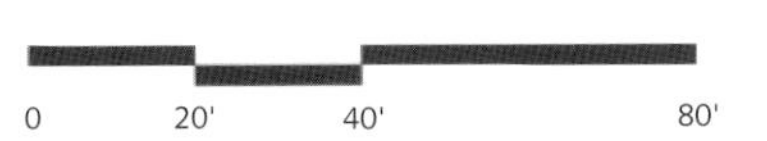

Post Oak Central Two drawing; ground-floor plan.

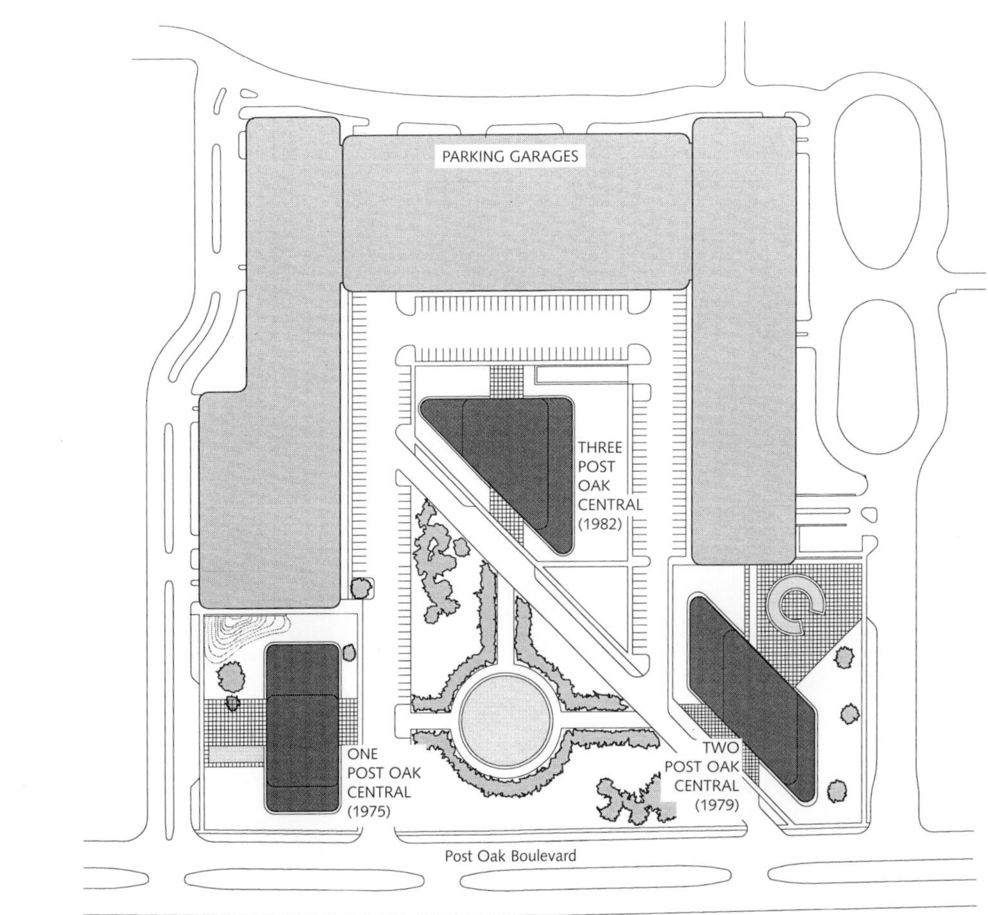

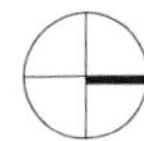

Post Oak Central drawing; site plan.

Chicago School overtones in the expressive way that the structural envelope, designed by engineer Fazlur Khan, flared at the base and corners, reminiscent of the load-bearing walls of Burnham and Root's 1891 Monadnock Building in Chicago's Loop.

Hines's insistence on careful cost control, market analysis, and high-profile architecture became his path to preeminence as a developing landlord. In 1978 he had completed projects in excess of $1 billion in value and had another $200,000,000 worth of projects under way. But back in 1970, before the first Post Oak Central building was started, Hines was approached by the chairman of the Pennzoil Company to develop a headquarters building for his company in downtown Houston.

J. Hugh Liedtke is a direct and plainspoken Oklahoman who told Hines he didn't want another cigar-box building standing on its end and "none of that shiny glass," but something special-looking, not just tall. He reasoned the tallest building soon becomes the second-tallest and then third-tallest. Liedtke and his brother Bill, who was president of Pennzoil, once operated out of a windowless basement in the West Texas oil town of Midland, and he was insistent on having "plenty of light." Hines hired Bruce Graham of SOM for the job but soon got Liedtke's message demanding something other than the familiar corporate designs that SOM produced. So Hines, with the two Liedtkes, interviewed other architects and selected Johnson/Burgee. (The first Post Oak Central building and the Pennzoil building were built simultaneously.)

J. Hugh Liedtke, mid-1970s.
Courtesy of J. Hugh Liedtke.

Hugh and Bill Liedtke grew up in Tulsa, and both attended Amherst College; Hugh graduated from Harvard Law School. The elder brother kept emphasizing to the cautious Hines that he wanted something *distinctive.* He had spent many hours in Frank Lloyd Wright's Price Tower in Bartlesville, Oklahoma, making oil deals with his friend Harold Price and liked Price's curious building, which stood out like a sore thumb on the Oklahoma prairie. Hugh Liedtke thought that if he was going to all the trouble to build a building, he wanted something *different.* Hines coincidentally concluded, "Allen Center, a superblock located a few blocks west, was recently built and those series of slablike towers were not renting well. Something unique in design in Pennzoil's part of downtown seemed like a viable option."[7]

The site, assembled from six parcels of land after a year of negotiation, was a square block somewhat north of downtown Houston's concentration of important new construction but next to the Jesse H. Jones Hall for the Performing Arts, designed by Caudill Rowlett Scott in 1966. There were no looming office buildings nearby. Liedtke contributed to a problem for Hines: he wanted only 400,000 sq. ft. for Pennzoil, so Hines needed another major tenant to make the deal work in this part of downtown Houston. After lining up

Zapata Oil for ten floors in the building, Hines asked Johnson for a building with a dual image to reflect his major pair of tenants. Johnson's first schemes were very conventional, one being very similar to the Seagram Building. They were rejected by Hines and Hugh Liedtke, who objected by saying that he wanted the building "to soar, to reach and a flat top doesn't reach."[8]

Johnson was frustrated in trying to create a path through the 250-foot-square block to connect older downtown to Jones Hall and Ulrich Franzen's Alley Theater on the other side. John Manley, Johnson's chief designer, recalls picking up a pencil and drawing a diagonal line through the block from one corner to the other as Johnson leaned over his drafting table. So instead of a building with two identities to serve Hines's two tenants, Johnson now proposed two *buildings,* webbed together at their bases by a soaring, greenhouse-type lobby. The model of this proposal was shown to Liedtke and he said, "The buildings still have flat tops." Johnson quickly picked up the sloped-roof lobby part of the model and placed it on top of one of the buildings: "Is this what you have in mind?" Liedtke answered, "Yeah, *that's* it!"[9]

The extraordinary thing about Johnson's final scheme was the *shape* of the two buildings. When he sketched the plan he had in mind on a cocktail napkin for Hines, the developer thought it looked like the logo for NBC.

Johnson's buildings had become increasingly abstract in character. Two recent, large office-building projects had been designed but not built, one for New York's Wall Street and another for Philadelphia. They featured strongly modeled geometry of large-scale shapes. The boldly sculptural New York project for Lehman Brothers had triangular indentions in the soaring outside corners of its shaped mass, and the Philadelphia project on Logan Circle arranged two different-height towers with stacked and rotating blocks of floors, which reflected the project's curving site. But for Pennzoil, which began construction in 1972, Philip Johnson seemed to have taken a leaf from the minimalist architectural sculpture of Tony Smith and managed to design his most abstractly startling building to that point. *The New York Times*'s architecture critic, Ada Louise Huxtable, heaped praise on it, naming Pennzoil the "building of the decade." Writing about Smith and his sculptures in the *Times* twenty years later, critic Grace Glueck seemed to be describing Johnson and Pennzoil when she said, "Smith, attuned to mathematics but with an artist's pitch, looked to geometry for his sources, the geometry of nature and pure ones plotted by man. He was particularly interested, he once said, in the mathematics of surfaces, Euclidean geometry, line and plane relationships."[10]

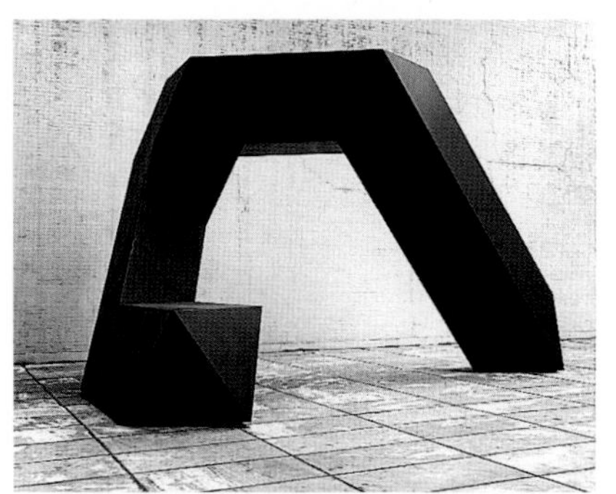

Tony Smith sculpture, *Cigarette* (1961, fabricated 1971). © 1999 the Museum of Modern Art.

The two towers of Pennzoil Place are trapezoid-shaped, with the tops sliced off at 45-degree angles. The bronze aluminum-and-glass curtain-wall, fabricated on the thirty-inch module Johnson/Burgee adopted for IDS in Min-

Pennzoil Place

Houston, 1976

Pennzoil Place looking northeast; Neils Esperson Building (1927) in foreground, RepublicBank Center in background.

JOHNSON/BURGEE, ARCHITECTS; WILSON, MORRIS, CRANE & ANDERSON, ASSOCIATE ARCHITECTS. PHOTOS BY PAUL HESTER, 1984–1999.

Detail, peaks of Pennzoil towers.

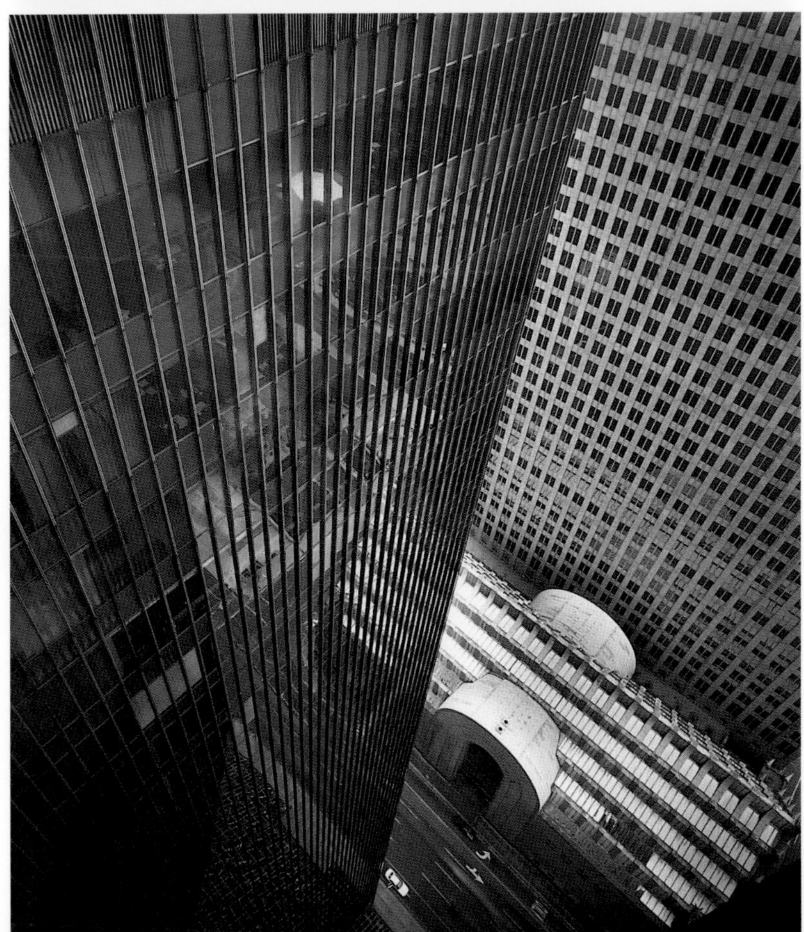

Street between Pennzoil Place
and RepublicBank Center from above.

Pennzoil Place, looking west.

Glass-roofed atrium plaza connecting towers.

Atrium escalator, looking toward 10-foot slot between towers.

Houston skyline around Pennzoil Place: RepublicBank Center, Neils Esperson Building, 75-story Texas Commerce Tower (1981, I. M. Pei & Partners), 36-story Gulf Building (1929).

Office beneath sloping facade.

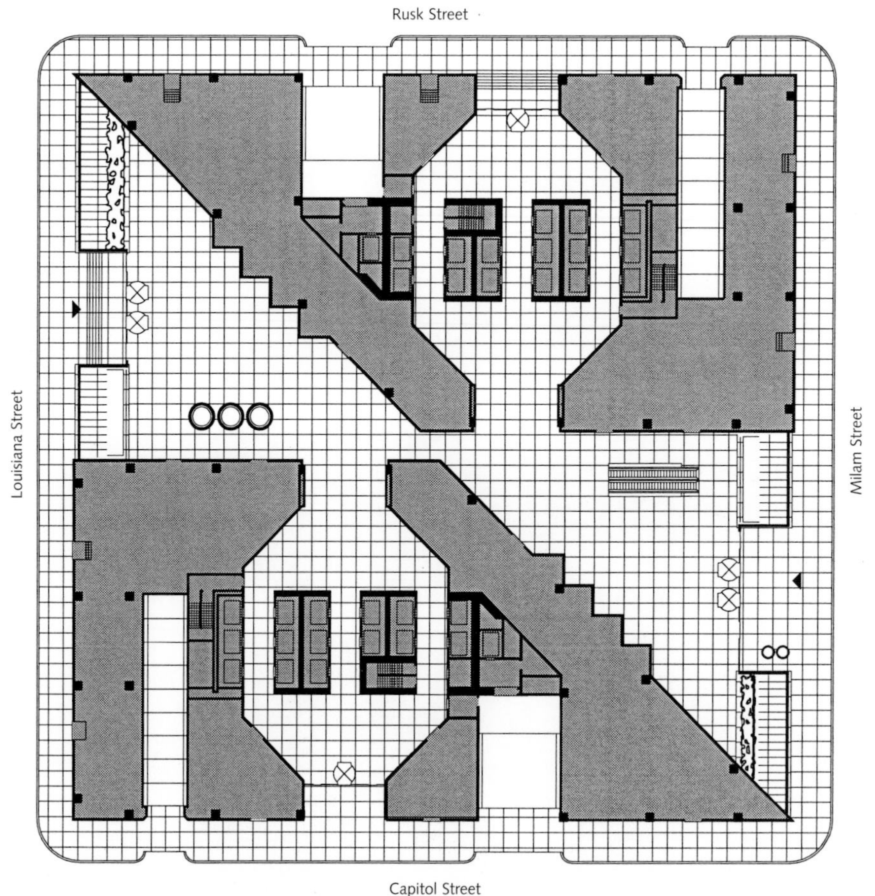

Pennzoil Place drawing; ground-floor plan.

neapolis, imparted a richer, finer grain to the sheer wall surfaces than the conventional five-foot module of other curtain-walls. One of the delights of Pennzoil is watching the relationship of its geometric shapes evolve, overlap, and separate as one travels on the nearby freeway. The two identical towers are rectangles in plan, with one outside corner of each cut off at 45 degrees like the tops. The peaked, thirty-six-story shafts are separated by a ten-foot sliver of space between two 135-degree corners; it forms the passage between two triangular greenhouse lobbies, which bracket the buildings' bases and fill the balance of the site. These are tautly roofed with white steel and glass, which slopes tentlike to the ground from the buildings' signature slot. The visual metaphor is one of repelling and attracting magnets at the ten-foot interval between two pure, somberly glistening prisms. From bottom to top the composition turns kinetically in visual tension.

Nory Miller wrote in 1979: "Pennzoil is as distinctive on Houston's skyline as IDS is on Minneapolis', despite its being shorter than several of its neighbors. It is distinctive because it is slanted on top, sides and bottom; because the closeness of color between its bronze-tinted glass and bronze-anodized aluminum as well as the severity of its geometry gives it a starkness unmatched by anything around; and because void as well as solid is tightened so resolutely in place as to exact the one quality that distinguishes fine art from attractiveness: tension."[11]

In 1981 Paul Goldberger wrote of Johnson/Burgee in *The Skyscraper:* "Rarely did they equal IDS's brilliant combination of formal beauty and urbanistic appropriateness. But Pennzoil Place, in Houston, completed in 1976, became the best-known building in that booming city's downtown with good reason. This was pure abstraction, but it was dazzling—a city had not seen so recognizable a skyscraper top since the Empire State Building's. And the twin trapezoids, for all their energy, had a certain dignity, too. . . . it was Johnson's gift that he was able to create an eye-catching form just right for the image of this city, a place eager to make its mark yet desirous of appearing strong and stable at the same time."[12]

Gerald Hines had been skeptical of the market value of the sloping-glass offices at the top of the buildings, but when these spaces rented faster than the floors below and popular notoriety focused on the buildings' unusual design, it caused Hines to add two extra floors to each tower during the construction. For marketing the building Hines spent $300,000 to display models and office mock-ups in the building next door to the construction site, with Johnson the "undisputed star" of a nine-minute video articulating the merits of the bifurcated building; his way with words was part of Hines's package. Later Johnson commented dryly, "Gerry now thinks architecture can make the difference between *renting* and *not-renting!*"[13]

Pennzoil Place was not the first modern building of distinction designed as an abstraction; I. M. Pei's enormous rhomboid-shaped John Hancock Tower in Boston's Back Bay, designed by Harry Cobb, had been completed in 1972 before developing its well-publicized problems with falling window-glass. In Chicago, Skidmore Owings & Merrill had designed two landmark skyscrapers, John Hancock Center in 1969 and the Sears Tower in 1974, as looming abstract "objects" in the cityscape. There was also the nonabstract, figurative Transamerica Building in San Francisco by William Pereira in 1976, which gave that sophisticated city an Eiffel Tower silhouette it didn't need. And in 1978 Dallas got a cluster of scaleless mirrored blocks for its Hyatt Regency Hotel by Welton Becket. Indeed, developers, enjoying boom times, saw Pennzoil's handwriting on the wall and quickly concluded that its unique angular design "sold well." Following the building's sensational acceptance nationwide, architects seemed to consider it a license to let it all hang out, and the country's cities were, over the next ten years of intense construction activity, inundated with awkwardly shaped buildings, many with look-at-me "party hats" for crowns. Miesian-modern office towers, having been reduced to a banal formula, were replaced by freewheeling designs which finally led to architects' playing with historicism; critics named it postmodernism and its defenders liked to recall Johnson's 1961 entreaty to his Yale students: "We cannot *not* know history!"

Pennzoil Place, Johnson's celebrated initiative with abstracted building form, opened a Pandora's box of indulgent form-making by architects without the background, knowledge, or feeling for the art potential in a modernism that deviated from Miesian purity. One singular exception was Harry Cobb's prismatically abstracted Fountain Place building, completed in Dallas in 1986. Designed to be a pair of identical towers, playing off each other's twisting, reflective dynamics, the Pei Cobb Freed building, sheathed in a fine-textured green-glass skin, stands alone, lifted on stout legs above a Dan Kiley–designed plaza of fountains and trees. The 1.2 million sq. ft. tower, of which Pennzoil Place's geometry is the precursor, is the Dallas skyline's most defining structure.

At the time Pennzoil Place was completed, the ten-year-old Hines company employed 280 people, had a $4,000,000 overhead, and owned more than 20 million sq. ft. of space, the equivalent of three World Trade Centers, then the largest skyscrapers in the world. Hines explained that it was "a totally integrated manufacturing organization, just like Ford Motor Company. We do design, development, marketing, finance, leasing and construction."[14]

When Trans World Airlines was considering putting up a headquarters building in Kansas City, it figured the cost to be $18.5 million, but Hines convinced TWA that he could build the same building for only $12.6 million and did, on time, too. With that kind of reputation Hines decided to pick and choose his clients, concentrating on big banks and corporations, what he called "the Medici of today."[15] A few years after Pennzoil was completed, Hines hired I. M. Pei's firm to design the seventy-five-story Texas Commerce Tower, a block away and for a while the tallest building west of the Mississippi.

Through the years the Hines organization has produced a number of "graduates" who started up new companies that competed against the tightly controlled father organization. One of the Hines alums said that Gerald Hines changed the way real estate development was done: "In order to compete with him, you have to do things the way Gerry does them: you have to believe that the product is the thing."[16] The product for Hines was "quality goods," in the sense that by hiring design leaders in architecture, or at least those architects with a substantial name or style identification, he felt assured that the public would respond by renting his buildings; there was some reflected glory in having offices in a building that had at least a semblance, and sometimes it was only a veneer, of design distinction. Hines still carefully controlled the costs.

People in the architecture world were continually surprised that aristocratic Philip Johnson, long associated with high-style buildings and the haute monde of art culture, would "stoop" to working with a commercial developer. But Johnson's swift and sudden enthusiasm for working in the nuts-and-bolts marketplace was consistent with his restless and adventurous, but realistic, nature; he was still seeking his *roi*. In 1976 he said, "Hines is enough of a businessman to know that he has got to push his architect in certain directions, but he's also enough of a patron to know where to stop. No developer interested me until he came along, because no other developer I've ever met had this combination."[17]

While Pennzoil Place and the first Post Oak Central buildings were being completed, Johnson had been approached by businessman Peter Stewart of Dallas to design a small public square in the heart of downtown Dallas. It was Stewart's dream to build a public place of ecumenical worship commemorating the world's gratitude for its blessings and reflecting the nation's two-hundred-year-old history of the official observance of Thanksgiving. Peter Stewart had an interesting background. His mother died when he and his brother were very young, and their early years were spent first in Galveston, then with their grandparents in the Midwest and in Houston. Peter and his older brother Waldo went to Harvard at the insistence of their grandfather, who was a poor orphan but self-educated, with an avid intellectual interest in world religions.

Peter Stewart, 1985.
Courtesy of Peter Stewart.

Peter Stewart's father was a wide-ranging entrepreneur who was married briefly to Mellie Esperson of Houston, an important developer of that city's downtown in the 1920s and 1930s. The boys also lived in Cuernavaca, Mexico, with their father before coming to Dallas in 1930. Colonel Harry Stewart bought the landmark Stoneleigh Hotel, where he added a penthouse floor for his residence de-signed by John Wisne, a New York architect with Dorothy Draper's company. The Stewart Company, which sold tractors, built a prize-winning modern headquarters building in 1953 under Peter and Waldo's initiative, with a large mosaic mural, *Genesis,* by the Mexican artist Miguel Covarrubias, on the wall facing an expressway in North Dallas. Waldo Stewart was instrumental in getting Frank Lloyd Wright's Dallas Theater Center built in 1959; Peter came by his interest in art and design through an architecture course he took at the University of Texas one summer in the 1940s. Raised as a Christian Scientist, Episcopalian Peter Stewart holds deep spiritual feelings that developed at the knee of his grandfather. These came to life with his project for downtown Dallas. He and his brother are noted in the city for their generosity and ardent support of a broad range of community activities both secular and religious.

With other Dallas businessmen Peter established the Thanks-Giving Square Foundation in the late 1960s and purchased a site in the Dallas business district, clearing it of a ragtag collection of two-story buildings from the once vital, colorful core of downtown Dallas. For years Stewart and his board did far-flung research to select the right architect for their square, traveling to England to meet Sir Basil Spence, the architect whose modern addition to the bombed-out Coventry Cathedral had impressed Stewart. Spence advised them to hire an American architect, but before they finally did, they visited Japan to meet Kenzo Tange, Japan's leading modernist, and went to Mexico City to see Luis Barragan, the ailing leader of modernism in Mexican architecture. In the United States they interviewed I. M. Pei and Kevin Roche and other leading American lights (including Lloyd Wright of Los Angeles, who did a design). But Peter Stewart kept putting off meeting with Johnson, who, according to Stewart, seemed "almost too obvious a choice" after the Water Garden and the Kennedy Memorial.

Stewart says, "A symbolic structure was the key part of the program for the square, and it became obvious pretty soon that some of these top architects didn't have the background or feeling needed for the building that I envisaged would carry great meaning for another two hundred years."[18] Stewart felt that the universal idea he was after needed to be expressed *cosmically.*

Meeting with Stewart's group, Johnson was quick to point out that though he didn't train as an architect and though he didn't have any religious affiliation, his first important building was a synagogue in 1956. (Stewart says that he failed to mention his teenage epiphany when he entered Chartres Cathedral with his mother.) But according to Stewart:

> From the beginning it was clear to us that Philip had the symbolic sense of what we were seeking and obviously the historic sense from his years as critic and scholar. Yet strangely enough the first chapel designs he showed us were *awful:* just cubes—imaginative cubes—but still just cubes. They weren't the right thing at all. We told him his concept wasn't working, so he retreated to restudy the design.
>
> In the interim of several months, I had seen an essay by a Benedictine monk on the symbolism and interpretation of *gratitude:* the thesis being that gratitude is best expressed, not as a closed circle as was supposed, but as an *ascending* circle, that a gift always returns to the giver on a higher plane. The board and I thought that was an inspired interpretation, and so it was a providential coincidence when Johnson came back with his spiral scheme for the chapel. Much has been written on the mysticism of the spiral, and we were thrilled that the spiritual and the design people were on the same wavelength.[19]

The site for Thanks-Giving Square is a sloping, three-acre triangular block in downtown Dallas, whose short side fronts the Republic National Bank Building's thirty-four-story facade of embossed aluminum panels, designed by New York's Harrison & Abramovitz in 1955. Johnson located the chapel, formed as a spiral of white concrete near a street-side walk at the highest part of the site, below the bank's tall grey facade. Access to it from the lower parts of the square is by a long, ramping bridge over the plaza, framed by angled walls retaining slopes of lawn and trees. From the sharp acute corner at the lower part of the block, beneath a large, white concrete gantry holding a carillon, an entry walk slopes down through angular, grassy areas to the central plaza of the space. Roseate concrete with exposed aggregate of Texas pink granite is the material used for all surfaces and retaining walls except for the chapel and carillon tower. Walks from all sides ramp down to the central area, which is tied to other parts of the square by channels, pools, and a large, sloping triangular rapid of water that tumbles over a "washboard" of granite at one side of the chapel. The angular plan elements of the square are derivative of the Water Garden, but here the assembly of "jumbled" parts descending to a paved plaza is organic to its triangular site, though still resonant of the

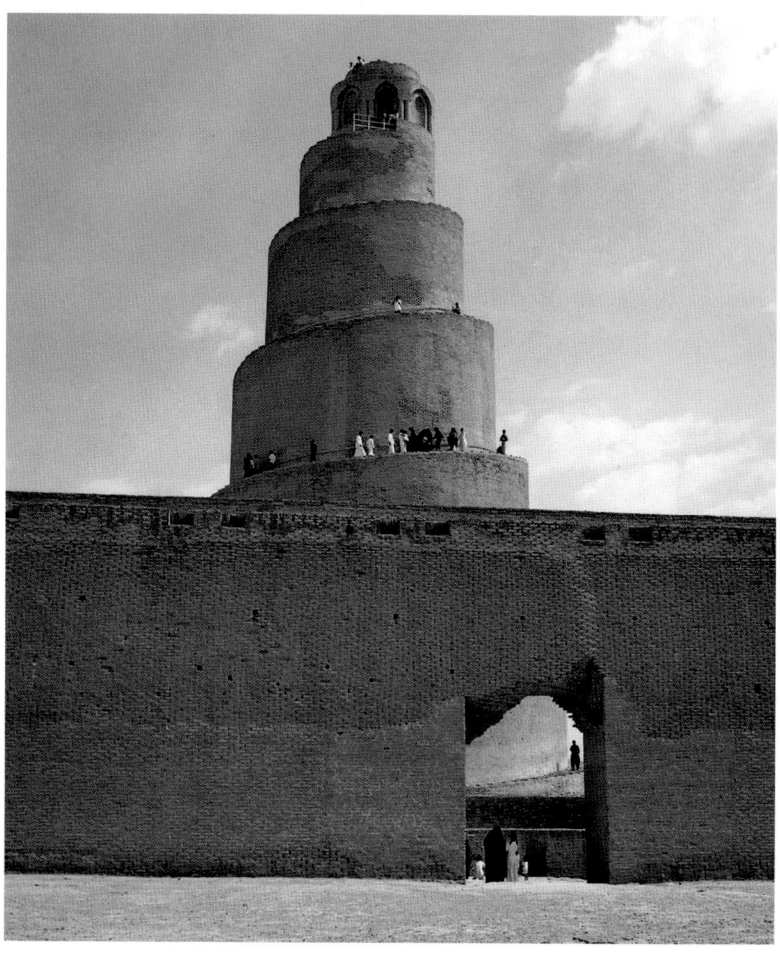

Ninth-century mosque, Samarra, Iraq. Photo by Carolyn Brown, 1991.

abstract art language that the Fort Worth design embodies. Thanks-Giving Square is a *sculpting out* of a limited site; the Water Garden is a *building up,* with layers of varying heights as offsets to water features cut into the site.

The chapel's interior is skylit by stained glass in a continuous spiral of color between the ascending, coiling walls of the ninety-foot-tall structure; an altar-cube of white marble is centered on its floor. The scale relationship of the thirty-foot-diameter floor to the chapel's height is awkward, giving a misleading impression of a diminutive space when actually the structure soars, abetted by a spiraling ramp that rises a short way up one side. It is a totally abstract space, confounding its function as a *chapel* for more than a few people. It is also unforgiving of the odd chairs, velvet ropes, and framed certificates on the wall. The formal "objectness" of the chapel at the crest of the slope of fractured planes is Thanks-Giving Square's raison d'être: its symbol and centerpiece.

Thanks-Giving Square

Dallas, 1977

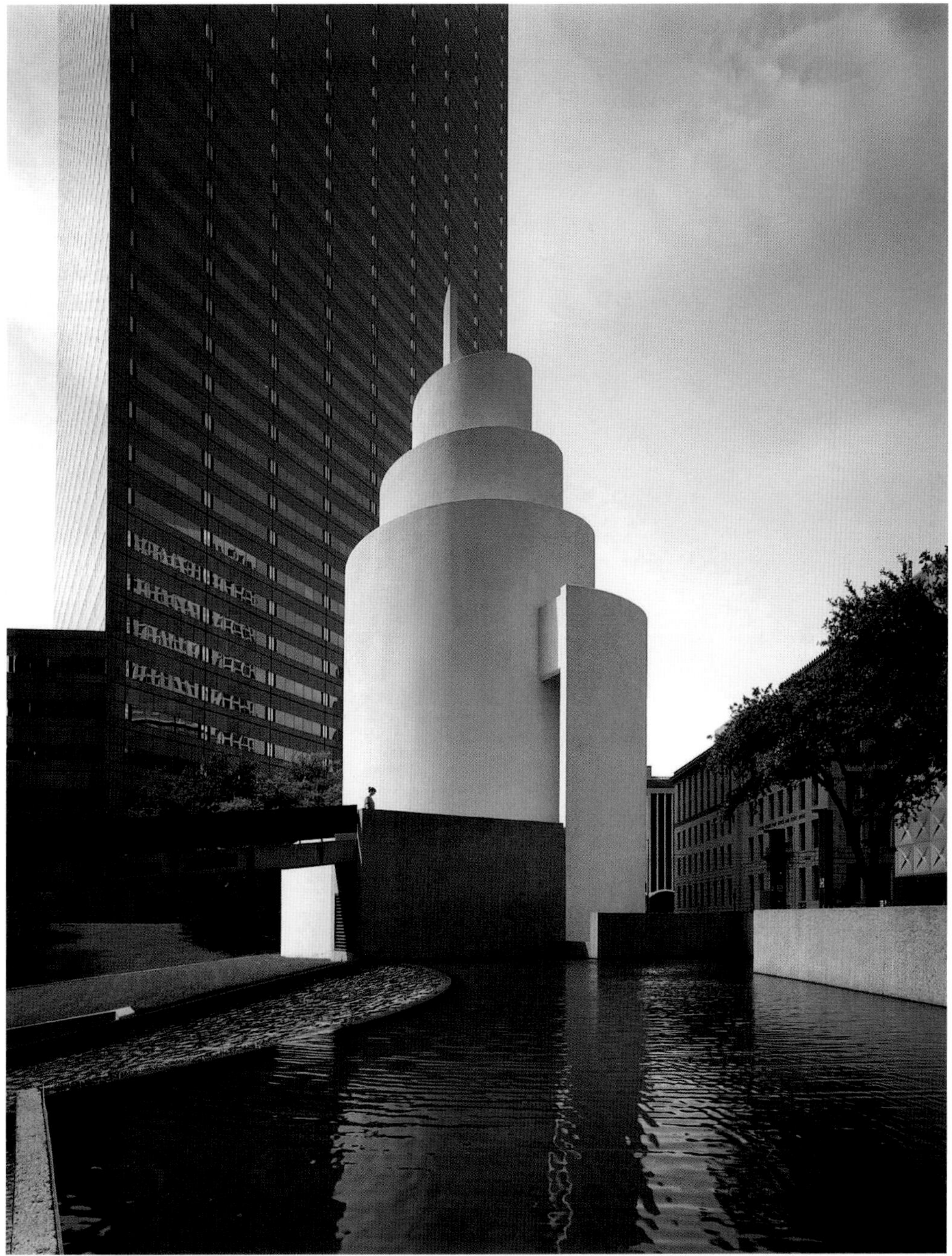

Thanks-Giving Square Chapel; 49-story Energy Square in background (1984, I. M. Pei & Partners).

Summer view of square.

Winter view of square.

Thanks-Giving Square from above.

Ascending spiral of stained glass in chapel ceiling.

Concrete carillon at lower point of square; behind chapel: 36-story Republic Bank Building (1955, Harrison & Abramovitz).

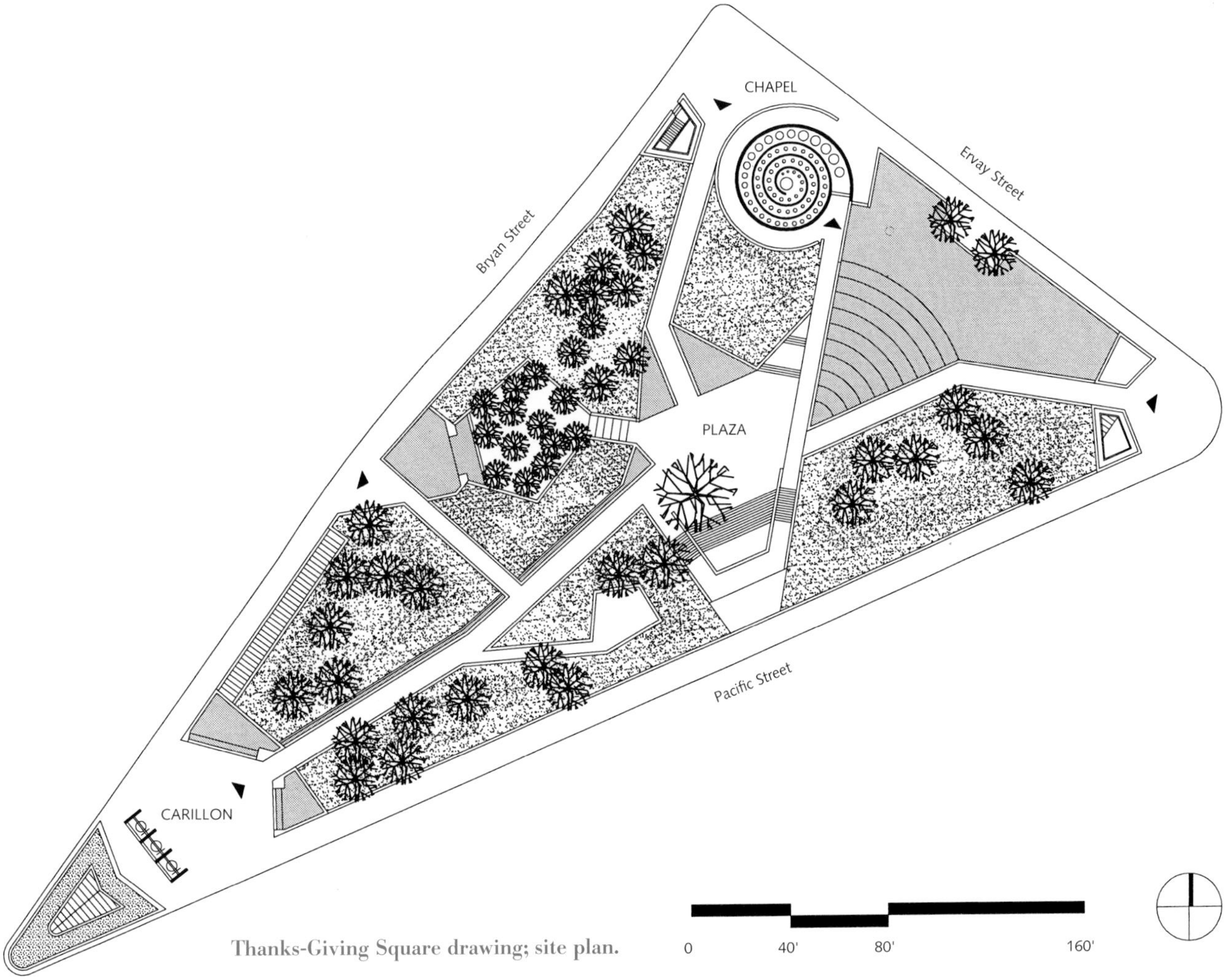

CHAPEL

Ervay Street

Bryan Street

PLAZA

Pacific Street

CARILLON

0 40' 80' 160'

Thanks-Giving Square drawing; site plan.

Peter Stewart says that Johnson selected everything personally, "down to the last piece of hardware." Dallas architect Reagan George recalls passing the Square on a cold winter day in 1977:

> There was a group of workmen there down at the tip of the Square under the carillon, so I stopped to see what was going on. The cascading pool of water there, which is circulated through the park, had been dammed up with a piece of plywood to create more water depth; the pool as built was too shallow and overflowed on the walk. Philip Johnson, dressed in a dark suit and overcoat, was stooped over in the midst of the workmen with a carpenter's rule measuring the water depth. A problem of circulating water volume had to be solved, and he was there to tell the contractor's men what to do. When I introduced myself, he pleasantly allowed that there were always problems with every job that had to be resolved after completion.[20]

When the Square opened in 1976, it was met with criticism and controversy in Dallas and elsewhere; some local citizens decried the bronze gates that closed it off at night, making it elitist and exclusionary. Robert Campbell, architecture critic of the *Boston Globe,* visited Dallas and didn't like the Square, reputedly remarking that "The chapel seems designed to commemorate Liberace's ascension into Heaven."

It had been difficult enough to see the completion of such a project in the midst of the business district, but Peter Stewart, a patient and determined "detail man," saw it through almost single-handedly. The Square had bronze gates that were closed at sunset, drawing criticism from groups who considered it public property. In the midst of the reactions to Stewart's achievement, Johnson told someone that the people of Dallas thought they were getting a park and what they got was a church.

A few blocks away Dallas developer Vincent Carrozza purchased a block and, catching I. M. Pei in a lull following the scandal of falling window glass from Boston's John Hancock Building, found him receptive to designing a speculative office building on short notice and a tight budget. In addition to needing the work, Pei needed to recover his footing and put his partner, Harry Cobb, to work on Carrozza's One Dallas Centre. Only one of several planned buildings was built, but its sleek minimal style freshened the air in downtown Dallas. The taste for designing carefully budgeted commercial structures caught on in the Pei firm temporarily and increased its presence in Texas, rivaling Johnson/Burgee's activity with large projects, but not the variety and size of things that Philip Johnson and his partner tackled.

In 1978 Gerald Hines asked Johnson/Burgee to design a facade for the Marshall Field store (later Saks Fifth Avenue) he was building in his Galleria II

Marshall Field facades

(now Saks Fifth Avenue) Houston, 1979, and Dallas, 1982

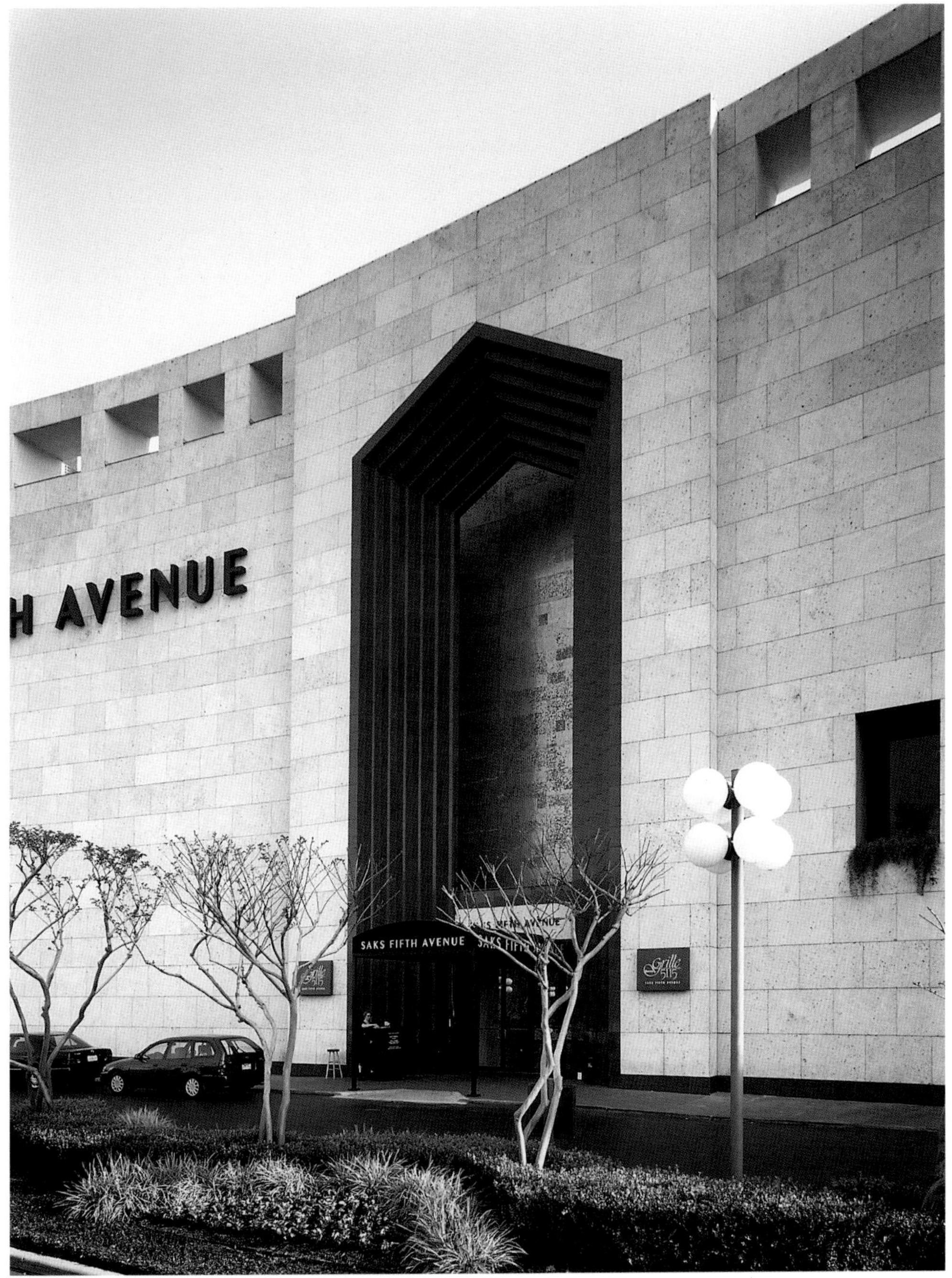

Detail of entry, Houston Galleria.

JOHNSON/BURGEE, ARCHITECTS. PHOTOS BY PAUL HESTER, 1999.

North facade, Houston Galleria.

West facade, Dallas Galleria.

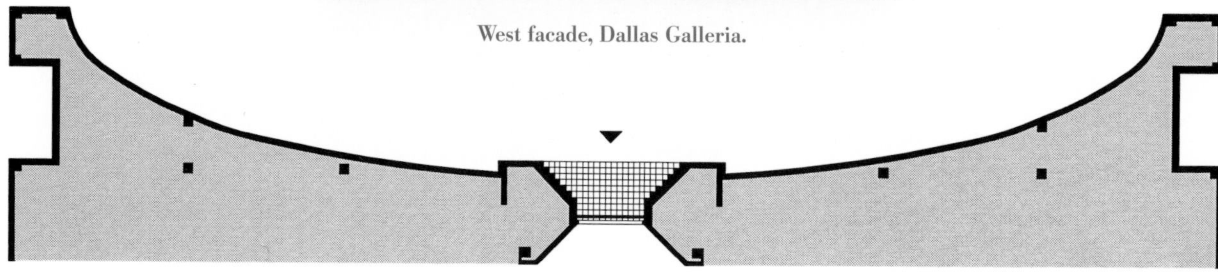

0 16' 32' 64'

Marshall Field facade drawing; floor plan.

expansion. He figured that Johnson would give the store some needed identity amid the sprawl that the Galleria complex was becoming at Westheimer Road and Post Oak Boulevard. Johnson used classical urban models, in a stripped version, to make an eye-catching curving screen of Texas shellstone with deep, punched-out openings. It seemed to peel away from the ordinary box-building behind. The facade is centered with a tall pointed-arch entry framed in dark granite and faced, on its shallow foyer walls, with gold mosaic tiles. The peeled-back wall was inspired by the designs of SITE, the avant-garde design firm responsible for a series of buildings in metamorphosis—crumbling, collapsing, decaying. (SITE's buildings appeared to be falling apart.) As seen across the Houston Galleria's vast parking lot, the Marshall Field building face, more like a mask, was both assertive and bland. Johnson's idea to hire artist Claes Oldenburg to install large, free-form splatters of primary color across the building was rejected by the Hines people. The resulting building, though certainly striking, would have been more Oldenburg than Marshall Field *or* Philip Johnson. A duplicate Marshall Field facade was built in Dallas's Galleria Mall when Hines moved into the far-north part of that city in the 1980s.

Johnson came to Dallas in the spring of 1978 to receive the Gold Medal, the American Institute of Architects' highest honor, before a packed awards luncheon in the Fairmont Hotel. Peter Eisenman, a Johnson acolyte, was his escort. Johnson's extemporaneous remarks charged up the crowd, dwelling mostly on the shift in architectural thought—postmodern design controversy was in the air—along with a genteel defense of Johnson/Burgee's design for New York's AT&T headquarters building; it had recently been published, creating a "furor" among modernist architects. He called the award "a vote for the art of architecture, which is my passion," and concluded with the following:

> The whole world ideology is taking a subtle shift, and we're the last, the architects, as usual, picking up the caboose. But there is no doubt about the feeling—the groundswell all over—that there's a new shuffle. There's a new interest in history, a new interest in symbols, a new interest in preservation.
>
> And the "kids," of course, are having a marvelous time, the people under fifty, and I'm enjoying it with them. We are entering a new era, that I don't have the name of and you don't know the name of and the "kids" don't know the name of. But it's a great, wonderful future. I use the analogy best of a river: when a river runs through a gorge it runs fast and straight and deep and single, that was the International Style. But rivers do lots of things, rivers also go through plains, they wander, they take new courses, they take maybe five or six courses at the same time. *All* are right. Goodness sakes!—the Bible says,

"The house of my Lord has many mansions," or as the more contemporaneous Chairman Mao said, "Let a thousand flowers bloom."

> Diversity is the name of the game, the pluralism of our culture; this pluralism also applies to architecture, and we can welcome it. There isn't one single one of the "kids" here today, testifying about whatever they are doing over there at the convention, not one of them would do the AT&T Building the way John Burgee and I did. But they all respect enormously our privilege and right and beauty to design it exactly that way. God bless the "kids" and God bless architecture![21]

In 1981, Johnson/Burgee was interviewed for a new Dallas symphony hall along with several other well-known firms. I. M. Pei got the job, though he had never designed a music hall and wasn't sure that he wanted the commission; in fact, he ignored the building committee's request for an interview. Stanley Marcus went to great lengths to talk Pei into coming for a meeting with the selection committee, where Pei won the commission with his patient, low-key authority. Eugene Bonelli, a member of the selection committee and Dean of the School of Music at Southern Methodist University, recalls that Johnson made a very impressive presentation, but one can speculate that Pei's reluctance only contributed to his being the choice, with Marcus's backing, of course.

The resulting building, named the Meyerson Symphony Center, was designed under Pei's hand and, from a formal standpoint, is the most unique work that Pei and his partners ever produced. Rigorously astringent as always, the building, completed in 1989, is a large-scale "playing against each other" of massive geometries—the cube, the circle, and the cone—that the Pei firm had a longtime devotion to, but this time in a big, controlled overlapping "collision," reminiscent of the smaller-scale polyphony of forms coming from Frank Gehry's office. The building's soaring, sweeping light-filled lobby contrasts dramatically with the warm tones of finely detailed wood finishes in the McDermott Symphony Hall.

Johnson/Burgee's major building of the early 1980s was in California for the Rev. Dr. Robert Schuller, the charismatic evangelist who began his career preaching from the roof of a drive-in movie snack bar. He hired Richard Neutra in the late 1940s to design his first church in Garden Grove, California, which uniquely opened up to the parking lot so worshipers could stay in their cars during services. He became the nation's leading evangelist on television and in the late 1970s planned to build a bigger church to hold three thousand people. Schuller had big dreams.

After reading a magazine article about Johnson, Schuller went to New York to see him, and they hit it off perfectly, after some initial confusion.

Garden Grove Community Church, Crystal Cathedral, exterior and interior, Garden Grove, California, 1980; Johnson/Burgee, architects. Photos by Richard Payne, 1990.

Schuller went to the office without calling first. Johnson was gone and Burgee turned him away, thinking that Schuller's request to discuss a job meant that the Californian was seeking employment. Schuller returned and finally met Johnson. Eli Attia, an Israeli-American architect who was with Johnson/Burgee for ten years, was Johnson's design arm on the Garden Grove church. Their first design proposal fell flat with Schuller; it was closed in with few windows. Johnson felt that you needed to get away from all the California sun. "When I showed him the design there was this dreadful silence. He's not a silent man; *quiet* isn't one of his goals. I thought, God, what have I done?" Schuller wanted to see the sun and the sky and the highway traffic, to be a *part* of the environment.

"Look, you have to understand, this is California," Schuller said. "We like to be outdoors, and why not? I preached outdoors for many years, on top of a truck. I think I want to go on preaching that way."[22] He wanted a *glass* building, and Johnson was ecstatic about that and started working with Attia, who developed the basic form, which he envisioned as a hard, geometric crystalline shape. It evolved into a great glass *tent,* through compressing the volume and stretching the lateral axis to fit the site, into a plan that caused Johnson to remark, "It's the Star of Bethlehem!"[23] Dr. Schuller loved it.

When Schuller's building, popularly known as the Crystal Cathedral, was finished, the evangelist said about Johnson: "It's so rare to find a person who's sensitive and sophisticated but who hasn't become emotionally frigid. I think Philip has the same quality that Walt Disney had: the enthusiasm of a boy who's never grown up. Philip and I are just like peas in a pod, I found. Although he says he's not a religious person, I feel that Philip Johnson and I are on a very harmonious wavelength, and one that is transcendent enough to be labeled a spiritual relationship."[24] The building became a landmark in Southern California and a benchmark in Johnson's career.

Before the church in California was finished Johnson was hired for the AT&T Building in New York, the project that would catapult Johnson/Burgee more deeply into popular consciousness and land Philip Johnson on the cover of *Time* magazine cradling the building model in his arms. In 1978 the executives of the American Telephone and Telegraph Company made plans to build a new skyscraper in Manhattan and sent out requests for qualifications to twenty-five of the nation's top architects, including Johnson/Burgee. The inquiry was ignored by the busy pair (Johnson saying, "We don't like questionnaires"). The AT&T people made a second inquiry, and Johnson invited them to come for a visit. Shunning the overwritten volumes extolling their qualifications that all the big firms had furnished AT&T, Johnson had a cordial meeting with the small group of executives without so much as a piece of paper on his small, round marble table. When the meeting was over, Johnson/Burgee had their most prestigious commission to date in the center of the city of celebrity and fortune.

Completed in 1984, the AT&T Building, with the broken-pediment roof, defined the postmodern trend of employing historic sources to energize modern architecture. In 1961 Johnson had told a London audience of architects to "choose from history whatever forms, shapes, or directions you want to, using them as you please."[25] In the base of the 648-foot slablike tower was a

60-foot-high arcade, inspired by Filippo Brunelleschi's Renaissance Pazzi Chapel. This lofty loggia turned the corner in a generous urbanistic move, but ultimately proved to be too dark and windy. The majestic arched entrance on Madison Avenue and the moulded oculi in the building's base are reminiscent of Forty-second Street's 1923 Bowery Savings Bank by York and Sawyer, as well as the Florentine chapel. Young architects from Johnson/Burgee's office could often be seen wandering around Manhattan with sketchbooks in hand.

AT&T Corporate Headquarters (now Sony Building), New York City, 1984; Johnson/Burgee, architects. Photo © Peter Mauss/Esto, 1985.

Above the base, the shaft of the building was not unlike sedate New York skyscrapers of the 1920s and 1930s: articulated fenestration with pilasters, mullions, and spandrels crisply rendered in one material: thirteen thousand tons of pink granite. In that sense, the building and its distinctive top were "regionalist" in the broad sense, reflecting the traditions of their setting. The gable roof of the building, with its decorative, scooped-out pediment, was the shot that got the critics. At the same time, it caught the eyes of developers and corporate executives. It attracted a Tennessee bank executive who showed the *Time* cover to his New York architects, Kohn Pederson Fox, and said he wanted a building like *that.* The resulting skyscraper in Nashville has an overscaled, gridded facade of pink masonry with a timid pediment roof and a base of "Egyptian" details intended to respond to a nearby nineteenth-century church by William Strickland.

After initial doubts, Paul Goldberger of *The New York Times* praised the building, but according to an article in *Esquire* equally reputable critics "damned the building, from broken pediment on down, as a display of extravagance, arrogance, and perversity. Johnson, they said, was less an architect than an aging couturier desperate to remain in fashion. The largest corporation in the world, as it was before its court-ordered breakup, had spent at least $175 million in the hope of getting a great building. What it had got, they said, was merely one of the most expensive buildings, in terms of square footage, ever constructed, and one that resembled nothing so much as a Chippendale secretary or a grandfather clock."[26]

While the building's controversial roof created a flurry of debate among old and young architects and critics, it remains a rather conservative New York building, executed with the kind of consummate skill and taste one would like to associate with the cultural and financial capital of the Western world. Most of New York's big buildings of the 1980s building boom were uninspired by any sense of artistic form or contextual fit. Almost simultaneously with the AT&T contract, Philip Johnson and John Burgee received a commission from Gerald Hines for a similarly prestigious building in Houston that would define that booming city's skyline in terms of architectural showmanship as it underscored Philip Johnson's position as Texas's "favorite out-of-town architect."

In 1979 Hines decided to build a place-marking building adjacent to his burgeoning Galleria complex of specialty stores, shops, offices, hotels, and restaurants. He selected Johnson/Burgee for their success in designing buildings that created "a sense of place and a sense of excitement." Houston is located on an unendingly flat coastal plain, and Hines wanted a tall, punctuating building, visible for miles around, that would pridefully mark his Galleria, becoming the jewel in the crown of Hines's commercial development. Again Johnson went to the history books for stimulus, but recent history was the source this time. Earlier in the century some remarkable foursquare towers were built in the United States employing the Art Deco style. In addition to the most prominent example, New York's Empire State Building by Shreve, Lamb and Harmon, there were Fort Worth's Will Rogers Memorial Coliseum and Tower, by Wyatt Hedrick, of 1936, Nebraska's 1916 State Capitol by New York's Bertram Goodhue, and the Goodhue-inspired Louisiana State Capitol in Baton Rouge by Weiss, Dreyfous and Seiferth, known as "Huey Long's Capitol." John Manley thinks the strong verticals and modeling of the top of the building for Hines derived from William Mead Howells's 1928 Beekman Tower Apartments, which Johnson could see from his office.

For the Galleria, Houston's mammoth "town center" in the suburbs, Johnson provided a slender, sixty-four-story campanile surfaced with a taut, "stretch-wrapped" mirrored glass-skin and topped with a shallow, dark pyramidal roof. The hard, mirrored skin is modeled with inset and reentrant corners and setbacks above a cruciform base; Johnson's original schemes were richer in form and surface detail, but Hines's budgeteers prevailed against his more lyrical proposals. Rectangular and triangular bays of dark glass articulate the sheer, reflective surfaces and add velocity to the tower's upward movement. Transco Tower, named for Hines's major tenant, has a curtain-wall of square glass panels that does not differentiate between the wall's spandrel and view sections, seemingly *bound* by a relentless grid of white mullions, relieved by the dark, upward streaks of the triangular glass bays. A 60-foot-tall, classically arched ceremonial entry of pink granite nudges the building's glass base uncomfortably, as if it is mobile and could be wheeled away; people *enter* the building from a parking garage on the opposite side.

The pristine, priapic 900-foot shaft, rising abruptly from a low polyglot of commerce near the Galleria, is best enjoyed from a distance: up close its abrupt, chilly meeting with the ground lacks the finesse that some scaled-down elements would have given it. But nearby is the building's pièce de résistance, the Transco Fountain, a monumental "folly" of grandly scaled falling water and classical architecture that serves as gazebo to the 360-foot dished-out lawn stretching, parklike, south of the building. The curving double-faced

Transco Tower and Fountain

Houston, 1983

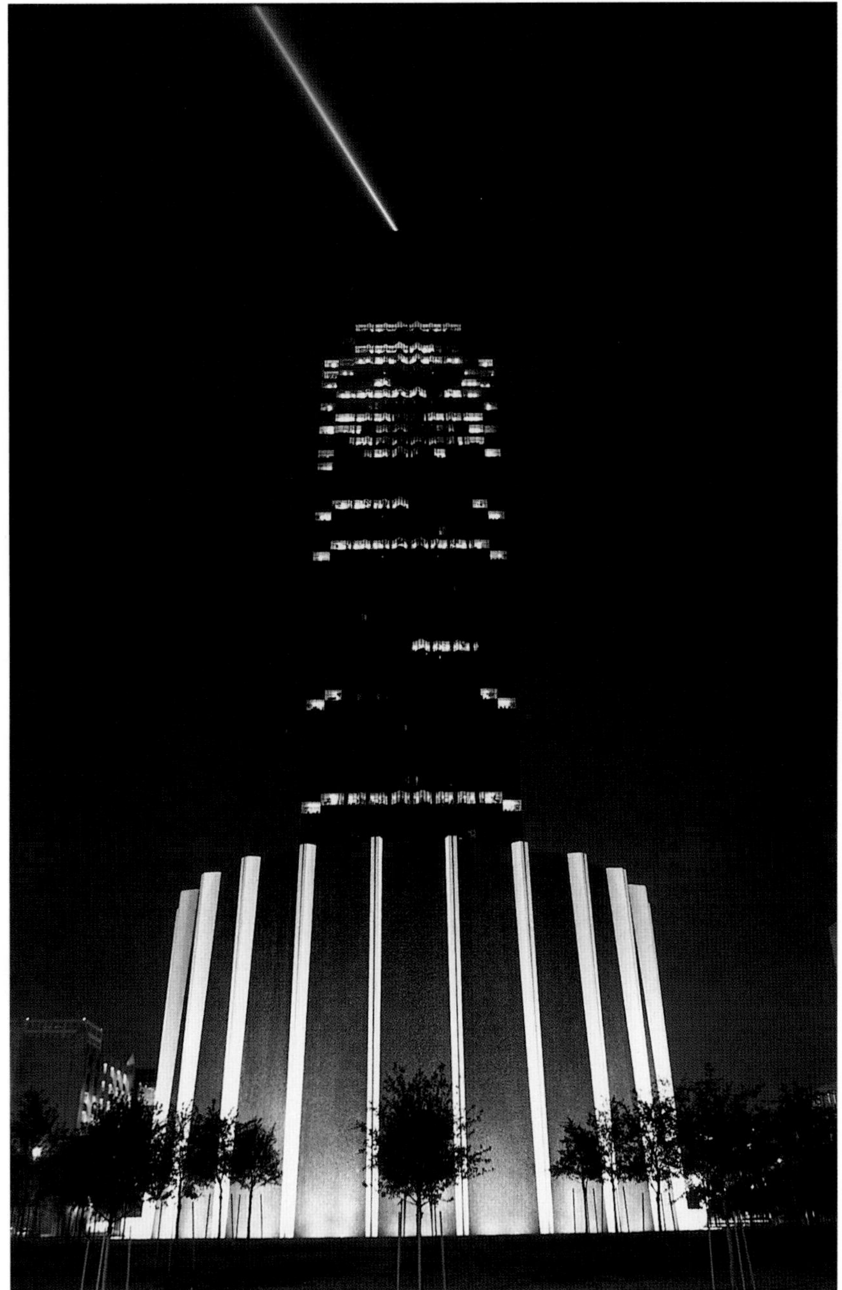

Night view of Transco Fountain and Tower from the south (1985).

JOHNSON/BURGEE, ARCHITECTS; MORRIS*AUBRY, ASSOCIATE ARCHITECTS. PHOTOS BY PAUL HESTER, 1985–1999.

Shaft of Tower from southeast.

Transco Tower as campanile for the Houston Galleria and southwest Houston; Loop 610 in foreground.

Southeast corner of base and building entrance.

Tower lobby.

Lobby escalator.

Concave side of the fountain at night.

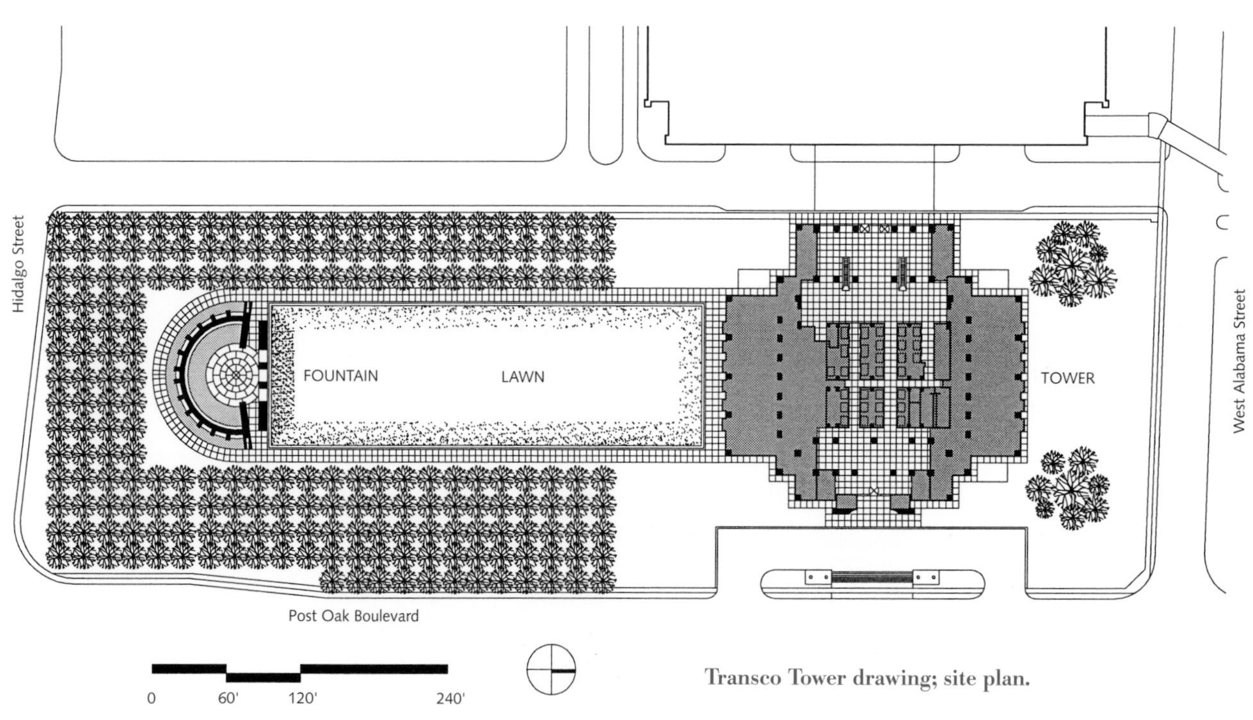

Transco Tower drawing; site plan.

wall of rushing water is a destination spot and resting place that Houstonians and tourists love (architect and University of Houston professor Peter Zweig always takes visitors to Houston there first); weddings are held in front of its thundering 60-foot-tall, curving waterfall behind a Palladian, triple-arched masonry screen. Completed in 1983, the Transco Tower is the orienting landmark for southwest Houston and the country's tallest building outside a central business core.

If the AT&T Building was the defining building for Philip Johnson in his adopted hometown of New York, and the Transco Tower his most visible accomplishment, the RepublicBank Center (now Bank of America Center) in downtown Houston, for Gerald Hines, was an exemplary architectural achievement in Texas. Design began in 1979, and the building was completed in 1984. The site was a block across the street from the dark and prismatic Pennzoil Place. Johnson's first impulse for the new building's design was a diplomatic one: he proposed a building sympathetic to the heralded Pennzoil. He thought it should be complementary in massing and minimalist in detail. Hines thought that was a terrible idea; he told Johnson that the RepublicBank building had to have its own identity, totally different from Pennzoil's. Always relishing the challenge of a new direction, Johnson responded by producing a tour de force of boldness and delicacy.

Johnson recalls, "Russell [Hitchcock] had just published a lovely book on sixteenth-century Dutch Gothic gabled architecture and, fishing around as I often do, [I] thought some ideas there could be adapted to a really big building."[27] Johnson/Burgee had recently completed a reflecting-glass-clad headquarters for the Pittsburgh Plate Glass Company whose silhouette was reminiscent of the Gothic Revival Houses of Parliament in London. And in Cleveland, work was under way on additions in a Romanesque style to the Cleveland Playhouse, with an entrance rotunda inspired by a domed seventeenth-century church by Gian Lorenzo Bernini. Through the mid-1980s these historicist exercises were paralleled with freewheeling modernist geometry employed for Hines high-rises throughout the country. One in Denver was dubbed "the mailbox"; another, in Virginia, was called a "shopping bag." But the RepublicBank Center, located next to the iconic modern monument of Pennzoil, had to be something special.

Two constraints, one personal, one practical, imposed some limitations but created opportunities for the new bank building. J. Hugh Liedtke, chairman of Pennzoil, had his office high in the slope-top reaches of the Pennzoil Tower and let it be known to Hines and Johnson that he didn't want anything to spoil his view when the larger, taller building went up next door. The other constraint was a lease to Western Union for a switching station on one-quarter of

Photo reproduction, Dordrecht, Reitdiksche Poort, 1590, from an eighteenth-century watercolor. Frontispiece to *Netherlandish Scrolled Gables of the Sixteenth and Early Seventeenth Centuries*, Henry-Russell Hitchcock, New York University Press, New York, 1978.

the site that could not be broken, so the station had to be incorporated into the use of the site.

Johnson divided the site in half, one part for an office tower, the second part for a connecting lower element to hold the banking room and the locked-in lease space. He located the banking room wing next to Pennzoil, giving it some distance from the planned tower. The building composition that resulted became, as with the earlier Pennzoil Place, a stunning feature of the Houston skyline. The two proud buildings, one dark glass, the other red granite, could not be more dissimilar, and yet they are compatible, each playing off the other with grand-scale irony. What they shared were fully realized ideas with a deeply focused feeling for *form* in unities of materials, one abstract, the other decorative and eclectic.

RepublicBank Center

(now NationsBank Center), Houston, 1984

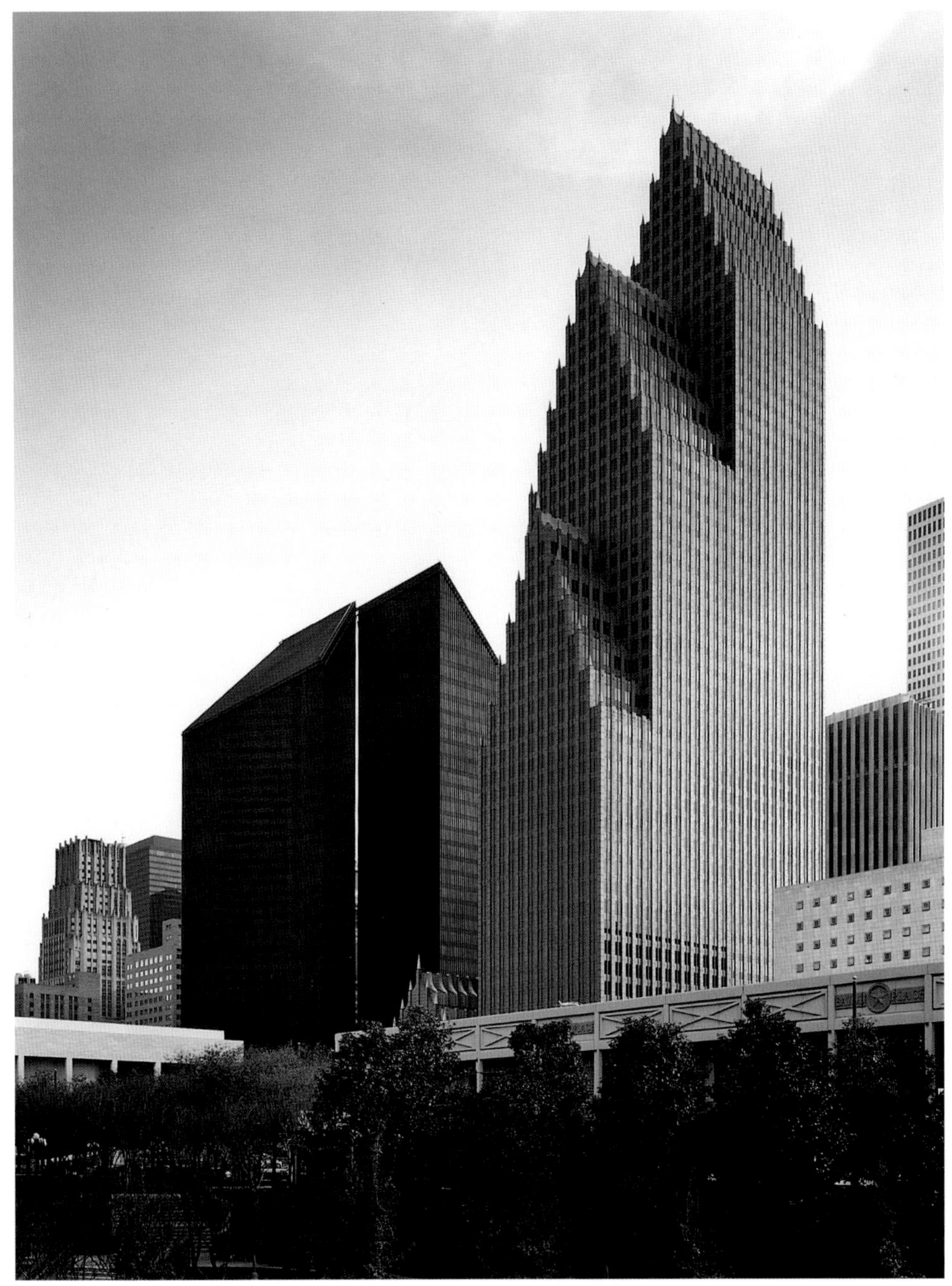

View from northwest; Pennzoil Place in background, Buffalo Bayou in foreground.

JOHNSON/BURGEE, ARCHITECTS; KENDALL/HEATON ASSOCIATES, INC., ASSOCIATE ARCHITECTS. PHOTOS BY PAUL HESTER, 1984–1998.

North entrance on Smith Avenue, facing Federal Office Building and U.S. Courthouse (1962).

Skylighted banking room.

Banking officers' area.

East-west cross axis through the ground floor.

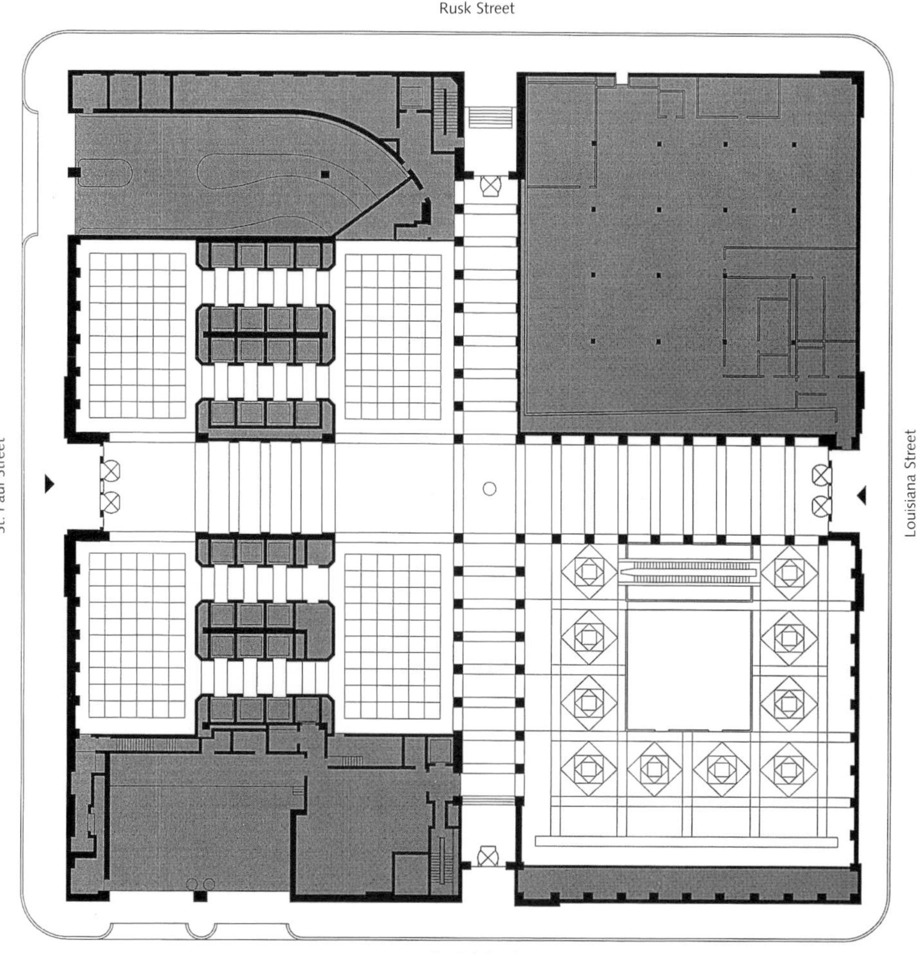

RepublicBank Center drawing; ground-floor plan.

The RepublicBank Center's tower is a thick slab with its upper massing cascading down in a corbiestep of steep, decorative gables, recalling the Low Country municipal buildings in Hitchcock's book. (The lowest gabled tier of floors was dropped sufficiently by Johnson to preserve Liedtke's view.) In turn, the raked roof-plain of each gabled tier is stair-stepped down in double floors of windowed offices. Window-framing pilasters on the gable facades are topped with lead-covered spires giving the building a spiky profile. The similarly gabled and decorated banking room wing, with a mammoth, Ledoux-like arched entry on the street facing Pennzoil, recalls sixteenth-century Dutch guild houses. Its lofty, skylit banking hall soars, marked by rising ranges of plaster arches which evoke the eighteenth-century fantasy renderings of Giambattista Piranesi. Not surprisingly, the architectural historian Henry-Russell Hitchcock told his friend Johnson that it was his best building.

Ann Holmes, longtime art critic for the *Houston Post* and the *Houston Chronicle,* is writing a book on the history of the art scene in Houston and credits Gerald Hines with the creation of the city's distinguished collection of high-rise buildings: "He hired high-profile architects, like Johnson, to design his office structures, bought important sculpture for the buildings, and always listened to the experts, the architects and the critics. Johnson and I. M. Pei 'worked' on him a lot. Design-wise, he upped the ante on himself over and over again. 'Good design was good business.' Holmes calls Houston Philip Johnson's 'showcase city' and says that he 'blossomed' there because of Gerald Hines. For Hines, good architecture—exciting architecture—made people want to come, and pay for it, too."

Holmes recalls:

> Gerry called me one time to come for a brown-bag lunch at his office; he wanted to show me a sculpture for the plaza in front of his latest office building on Main Street by Skidmore Owings & Merrill. I looked at the photograph of the sculpture; Gerry said, "What do you think?" I replied that it was "costume jewelry." He said, "Would you say that in the paper?" And I said, "Of course." Later the architects asked me to look again at the piece, but I said nothing had changed my opinion, and before long Hines had bought the magnificent Dubuffet that stands there now.

About Johnson, Holmes says:

> When Philip first started coming to Houston in the 1950s he would get together in the evening with young architects like Barnstone and Keeland and tease them and stir them up by telling them that "we've got to give up this idea of letting the client tell us what they want; all they want is kitchens and

> bathrooms, and we don't have to fool with that stuff." That really popped everybody's eyes open, but it was really only him being his usual mischievous self; he's more of a theoretician and esthetician, certainly not interested in Martha Stewart–ism. I have always loved that fact about him. He's very refreshing and stimulating; if you sit down with him and have a drink, he is just so much fun with that puckish sense of humor. He has been criticized by many in Houston for being a Harvard snob with a failed loyalty to his god Mies, but I think he redeemed that by his loyalty to his partner Burgee; he always insisted on including him during our interviews—Philip, of course, was the one with the ideas.[28]

While work proceeded on RepublicBank Center, Gerald Hines hired Johnson/Burgee to design a group of office-park buildings in Sugar Land, eighteen miles southwest of downtown Houston. The Hines group was developing a large upscale residential area on a plain where there were once large fields of sugarcane. Charles Moore designed a country club for the development of traditional-styled two-story houses. Johnson/Burgee's master plan for the office park called for three classically inflected, three-story buff brick buildings with angled tripartite plans, each of the three parts crowned with a shallow "false-front" pediment on each face and marked with regularly spaced windows above cast white-stone spandrels. The buildings are abstracted reminders of small-town commercial and institutional buildings of mid-nineteenth-century America; Johnson's stated inspiration for the basic design was the ordered facade of Schinkel's 1829 Feilner house in Berlin.

FAÇADE DES HAUSES WELCHES DER OFENFABRIKANT FEILNER IN DER HASENHEGER- GASSE IN GEBRANTER ERDE AUSGEFÜHRT HAT.

Photographic reproduction, *Feilnerhaus*, Berlin; R. F. Schinkel, 1829.

One Sugar Land Park Building

Sugar Land, Texas, 1982

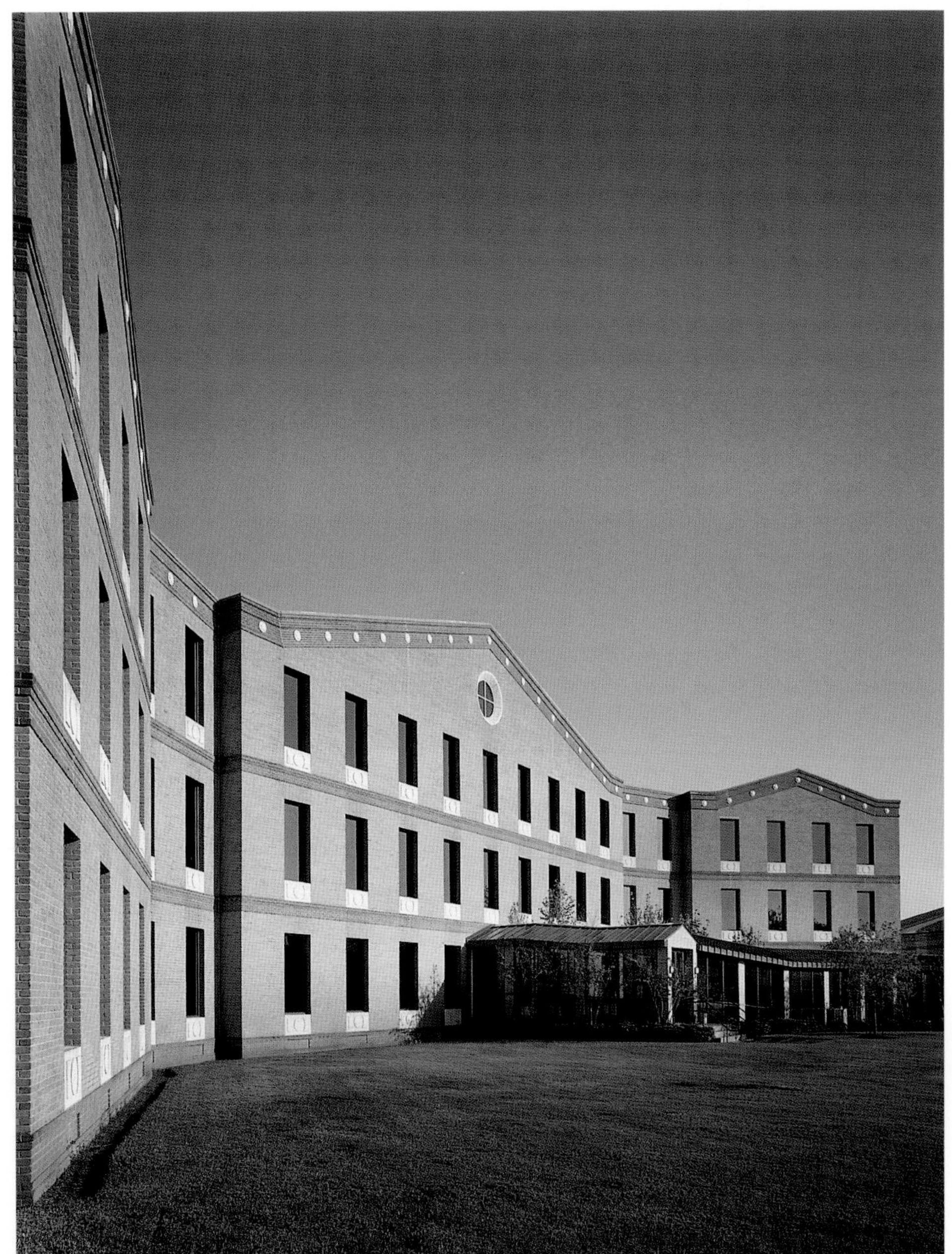

West facade with 1996 first-floor addition, Watkins Carter Hamilton, architects.

JOHNSON/BURGEE, ARCHITECTS; RICHARD FITZGERALD & PARTNERS, ASSOCIATE ARCHITECTS; 1996 ADDITION, WATKINS CARTER HAMILTON, ARCHITECTS. PHOTOS BY PAUL HESTER, 1998.

View from west across canal.

1996 building added by Watkins Carter Hamilton, architects.

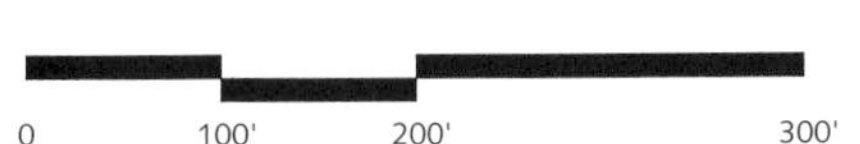

Sugar Land Park drawing; master site plan.

He intended that the three crescent-shaped buildings—each bisected by a lobby—would be strung along the bank of the site's man-made canal as a necklace. Only one 65,000 sq. ft. unit of a planned group of six buildings was built in 1981. It was sold by Hines in 1992 to a managed health care company, which added a porte cochere and made other alterations, converting the building to medical offices, and in 1996 added an architecturally assertive surgery-center wing, by Houston architects Watkins Carter Hamilton.

In 1983, Howard Barnstone, the most esteemed professor of design at the University of Houston, was, as always, a steadfast Philip Johnson devotee, having asked him to make repeated visits to lecture the architecture students since the early 1950s. Burdette Keeland Jr., a faithful colleague of both Johnson's and Barnstone's, was also a respected professor teaching design in the College of Architecture when the university decided to build an architecture building. The school had $20,000,000 of state-authorized money for the project; the College could move out of the metal "barns" it had occupied for almost forty years. (By contrast, the city's private companion university, the richly endowed Rice University, had housed its architecture school in a two-story building fronting on that school's academic court, to which the London architects James Sterling and Michael Wilford had made extensive additions in 1961.) A building committee was formed at UH to begin deliberations about an architect for the new building. Keeland, particularly, lobbied for Johnson, a longtime visitor and lecturer at the school, but the job was not to be handed to him outright.

"For one thing," according to Keeland,

> Burgee did not want the job in the office. They were doing these huge projects, AT&T and whatever, and our building was just a "little puddle"; Burgee also knew that Johnson would involve the staff to an inordinate, unprofitable degree on a building he had his heart set on. Johnson told me that Burgee wouldn't let him do it. But about this time, I saw Philip at a party at the de Menils' and cornered him and said, "If I wrote you a letter about the building saying we wanted you to do it, would that help?" And he said, "Write the letter." And I did and he responded that he seriously *wanted* to do the building.[29]

William Jenkins, dean of the architecture college, suggested to the thirty-member faculty that the school conduct a design competition, but Keeland stood up and tried to convince the teachers, most of them practicing architects, that Johnson should be chosen because of his fame, his lengthy and loyal association with the school (Johnson only lectured at Rice once), and his close, successful relationship with Gerald Hines, a potential benefactor to the school. Faculty member Robert Timme, one of the prize-winning Taft

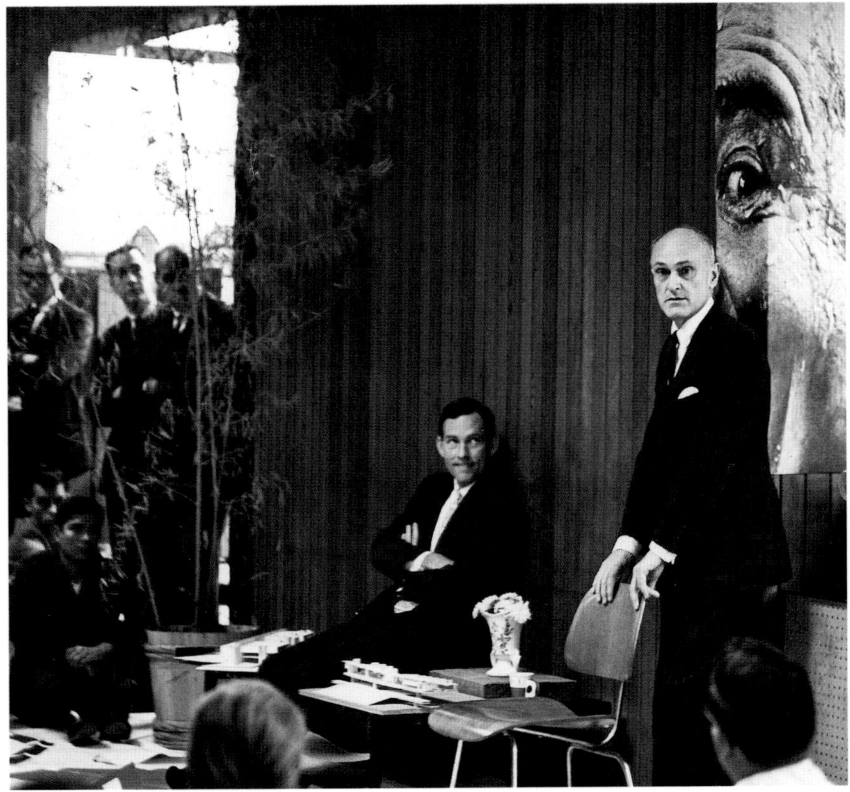

Philip Johnson and Burdette Keeland Jr., University of Houston College of Architecture, 1964. Courtesy of Burdette Keeland Jr.

Architects partners, remonstrated with Keeland, asking why there was only Johnson to consider and suggesting a limited, three-architect competition. Keeland recalls, "I said no. The chances are too great that a mistake will be made, which is usually the case with competitions; they always pick the wrong architect!" These meetings of argument and negotiation went on for a year—Jenkins hated faculty meetings—and finally it was put to a vote, with each faculty member writing down a choice for the architect, and Johnson won.[30]

The building's design was a paraphrase of an unbuilt project by an eighteenth-century visionary, a "House of Education" by French architect Claude-Nicolas Ledoux. The Ledoux model was adapted freely by Johnson for a 153,000 sq. ft. building for 640 students, with a central atrium whose four stories of design studios share a view across a grand skylit space. It is marked with a colorful terrazzo floor in a classical pattern, decorative Greco-Roman-style X-railings, and symmetrical stairways beneath a glass ceiling, which is surrounded by a square, open-roofed *tempietto.* Johnson submitted only one design proposal, and it was enthusiastically endorsed by the university's Board

Photo reproduction, ***House of Education***, 1773–1779. From Claude-Nicolas Ledoux, ***Visionary Architects***, University of St. Thomas, Houston, 1968.

of Regents. In 1983 he and Burgee flew to Houston for a meeting to make their presentation. Keeland, Barnstone, and Jenkins sat in on the unveiling.

Keeland recalls the meeting with relish:

> Philip and John had come down from New York carrying one of those big Bloomingdale's shopping bags. It was great the way Philip did it: he came in with this bag and set it down on the table and said to the Regents, "Gentlemen, I have your building in here." None of us had seen what he had until he took this exquisitely made little model out of the bag and put it on the Regents' conference table, and somebody went, "Oh, great!" I felt good because everybody was saying, you son of a gun, you've gone and pushed this guy and he's going to give us some glass palace that's all wiggly and ugly, and so when he pulled out this "Ledoux," everybody went, "A-h-h-h!" Philip, excited that he had scored, completely ran the show, did all the acting while Burgee sat quietly. It was a totally unexpected thing; few of us were that familiar with Ledoux. One guy said, "Look! It's got a *roof!*"
>
> Johnson laughed and all of a sudden said, "You don't have to be reminded that you have to spend 2 percent of your budget on art or sculpture for any building you build. Well, that won't be necessary," and reached in his pocket and took out a velvet Tiffany bag from which he drew a model of a tiny temple and, placing it on the roof of the model, said, "You now have your *art!*" It brought the house down.[31]

But the design that Johnson proposed and the Regents heartily endorsed met with strong opposition from some of the architecture faculty; even local architects wrote letters of protest. Some of the UH faculty organized student demonstrations against the building's design, and posters were put up asking, "Why Does an Architecture Building Have to Be a COPY???" and "Why Does $20,000,000 Have to Be Spent on a COPY???" and "Ledoux or Not Ledoux?"

For the ground-breaking ceremony, where Keeland had Johnson bursting through a banner depicting the building's front elevation, students hassled the nearly eighty-year-old architect. They wore mock "Philip Johnson" black frame glasses and carried placards that read, "How can you accept $1,000,000 for a COPY?" and "Why weren't the students consulted about this design?" Johnson handled it all with his usual wit and good humor—confrontation particularly from students never bothered him—and later gave a rousing thirty-minute lecture on the value of the art of architecture. Everyone went home happy, but the building would remain controversial.

Martha Seng, a 1975 University of Texas graduate in architecture, was working for Johnson/Burgee's local associate architect, Morris*Aubry Architects, and was the project architect for the architecture building. She remembers Johnson as "terrifically humorous," and when he would come to town his cadre of admirers would gather around him for drinks and dinner, enjoying his wit and magisterial charm. Johnson was "definitely the leader of the pack," which included Barnstone and Keeland and Gene Aubry, and reveled in the warmth of their gathered admiration, with one exception. An architect in the Morris*Aubry office, noted for his dry humor, irritated Johnson with his attempts to co-opt the master's spotlight with *his* witticisms, causing Johnson to dismiss him as "that guy that keeps trying to be funny."

Seng recalls that Johnson liked being the New York architect bantering and holding court, but he could also be forgiving of the human glitch. Seng recalls her terror when she realized she had made a major mistake with the shop drawings for the fabrication of the cast-concrete columns of the rooftop *tempietto.* Checking the drawings for accuracy, she missed the fact that the fabricator planned to cast the abacuses topping the column capitals as *round* instead of the classic *square* and had to face Johnson with the news. He looked up at the unorthodox column caps, more Minoan than Greek, and said, "Don't worry about it Martha, I like them fine."[32]

The highly visible campus building is faced with the same soft grey-pink brick used at the University of St. Thomas and is a copy of the Ledoux archetype, although much larger in size. (Johnson did battle for the brick with the university's construction office, which insisted on the campus's regulation brown brick.) Like Ledoux's original concept, the four-story facades are a mixed assembly of barrel arches and square and rectangular window openings beneath overhanging roofs, here covered in standing-seam copper, and topped with the roofless stone temple surrounding the atrium's skylight. The building's location on axis with a large student parking lot and a primary pedestrian mall makes its atrium a natural crossroads from car to campus.

Critic Stephen Fox summed up the building this way: "Philip Johnson's *jeu d'esprit* at the University of Houston was to expropriate the French architect Ledoux's 18th-century never-built design, inflate it to Texas proportions, and drop it on axis with the campus's major parking lot entrance to become the university's new architectural set piece. The frontality, figuration, and symmetry of the building are a relief compared to its trivial or merely anonymous neighbors. But in its perfunctory detailing and concern with superficial image, it is more like its neighbors than it would have us believe."[33]

Award-winning modernist architect William Stern is a professor at UH and takes an admire-disparage stand on the building, and Johnson.

> I should say in the beginning that there are several positive things about the building. It does something that very few recent buildings on the campus have done: it's a point of connection; in some ways it harks back to the original plan of the campus, where the buildings were joined to form a kind of a quadrangle, and what this building does is that it's on axis with the central part of the campus, and that axis actually passes through the building, so in terms of its organization on the campus, it is an anchor at that end and helps to give a sort of orientation as well.
>
> It's clearly a landmark, people can *see* it, it's easy to find, and on that campus, buildings are hard to find. It's easy to see from the freeway—taxi drivers point it out—and is easy to find, in my view, not so much because of its appearance but mainly in the way it is sited on the campus. The other aspect of the building that I think of as positive is the central space; it's the most public interior space on the campus and is used not only by our college but by many others. It is a sort of a campus agora and is clearly the most successful part of the building.

Stern, however, has few good words for the building as architecture:

> I find Johnson's premise for the building false, very glib and cynical. Johnson, tongue in cheek, condescendingly thought, we'll give the students a history lesson, copying almost verbatim a design by Ledoux for a building that had a much more complex program and set of needs than the eighteenth-century model could possibly embody. I must admit that the basic diagram of the big central space with the studios opening onto it, connected by flights of

Gerald D. Hines College of Architecture

University of Houston, 1985

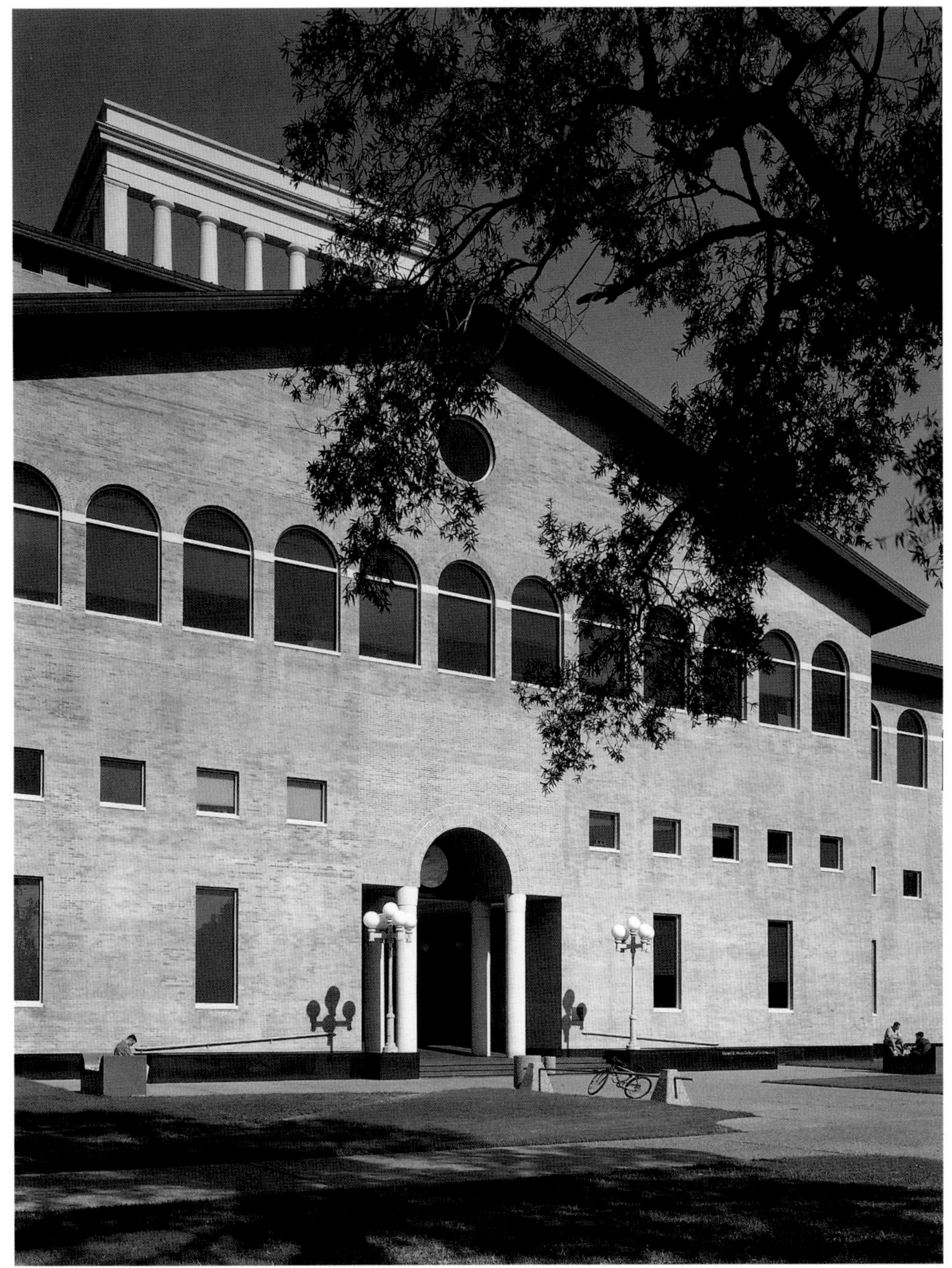

Detail, south facade.

JOHNSON/BURGEE, ARCHITECTS; MORRIS*AUBRY, ASSOCIATE ARCHITECTS.

PHOTOS BY PAUL HESTER, 1998.

View of building from southeast; rooftop tempietto surrounds a skylight.

View across atrium from fourth-floor studio.

Three studio levels open to the atrium.

Atrium floor from above.

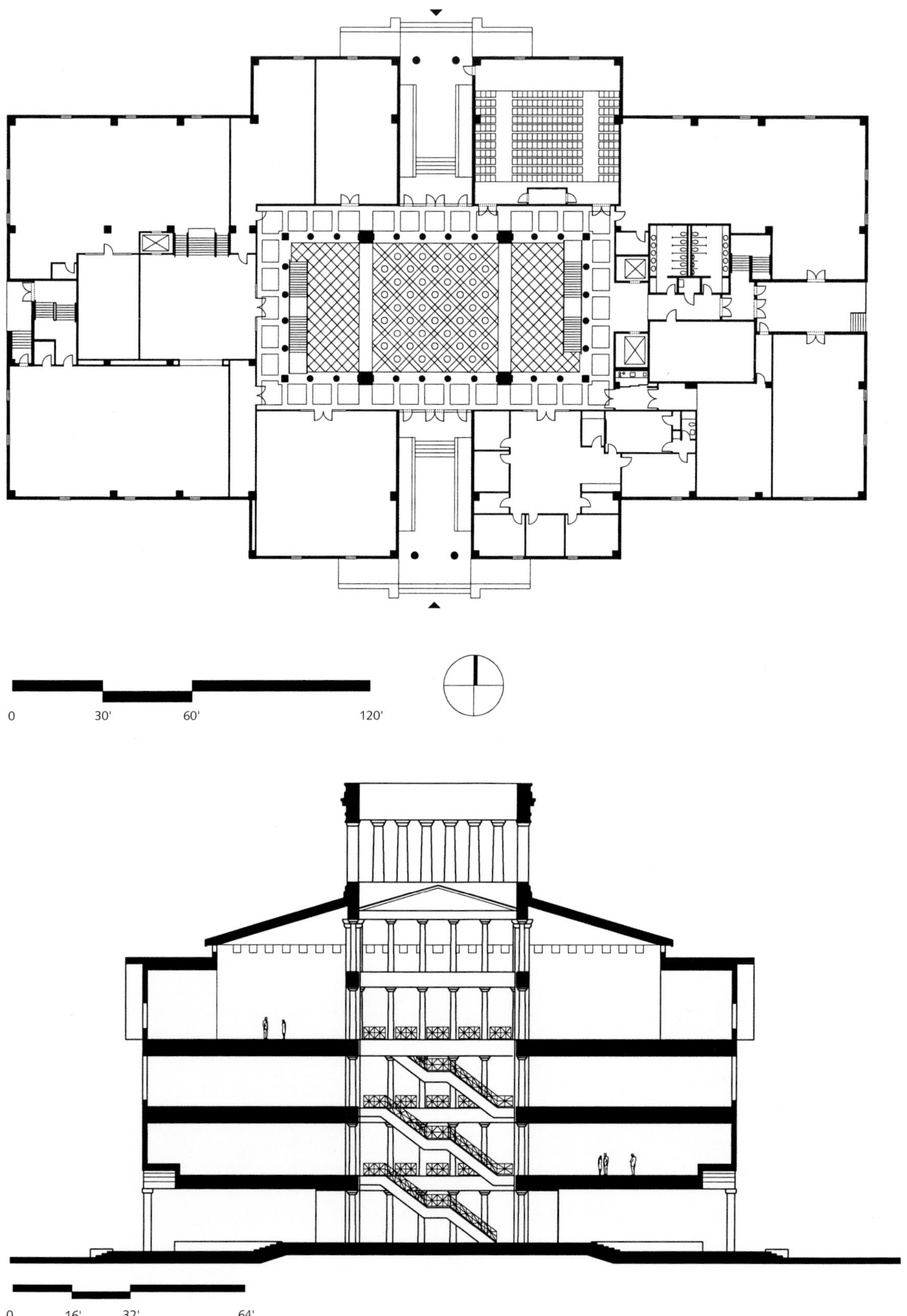

College of Architecture, University of Houston, drawings; floor plan and building section.

> stairs, is successful and makes a sort of sense, though for me the negatives outweigh the positive aspects of the building. On the other hand, the "citizens," as my father calls them, love the building; it's popular with the *people!*[34]

Populist is not an adjective that comes to mind with Johnson.

While not everyone is in love with the building, most *like* it and agree that the openness of the multilevel studios arranged around the skylit atrium works extremely well to unite the school in a common, light-filled spatial experience. When Johnson returned to the school in 1991, he received the students' applause and cheers as he stood in the atrium looking up to the tiers of studios. In 1996, ten years after the building's dedication and after cajoling by Keeland in Houston and a Four Seasons lunch with Johnson in New York, Gerald Hines and his son Jeff gave the school $7,000,000, and it was renamed the Gerald D. Hines College of Architecture. Hines had begun big development work in Europe and elsewhere and had more or less decamped from Houston and the Robert A. M. Stern mansion he built in River Oaks in 1990. His European headquarters was London, where he and his wife lived a good part of the time.

For many years, Johnson has befriended and encouraged younger New York architects with avant-garde agendas. A New York group formed in the 1960s and began to meet regularly; Johnson patronized them by sending them clients. "Philip's Boys" was the pejorative name given to this coterie of New York architects, which formed a clique and paid court and exchanged gossip with the old insider and master of spin during dinners at the exclusive Century Club.[35] In the 1980s Frank Gehry was included when he was in town from Los Angeles. Other stars of the moment like Rem Koolhaas and Zaha Hadid would come from Europe and join the New Yorkers for evenings of shared insiderism.

Johnson's patronage of young talent extended beyond New York to Texas. In 1981, Dick Moncrief, the young member of an established Fort Worth oil family and a friend of Ruth Stevenson's, was hastily made chairman of a building committee to find an architect for the prestigious River Crest Country Club after its clubhouse had been destroyed by fire. He went to New York and met with Johnson and Burgee, who were too busy with skyscrapers to take on the project. On the elevator going down to lunch, Johnson counseled Moncrief, "You don't need us. There's that firm in Texas; why don't you get them? It's Taft Architects, isn't it, John? They are winning awards all over."[36] Johnson had never seen a Taft building but knew of their colorful postmodern designs through Robert Stern, who had lectured on the Rice University campus and knew the three young architect partners.

Moncrief flew to Houston and met the Taft trio, John Casbarian, Danny

Samuels, and Robert Timme, and cavalierly asked for a sketch of a country club to show his committee. The young idealistic architects, all teaching design at either Rice or UH, demurred, since they had not been hired formally. Moncrief then suggested that they come to Fort Worth and meet the club's board, which they did, armed with a projector and slides of images of English country mansions and grand houses by Sir Edwin Lutyens and Andrea Palladio. The borrowed images of past architectural glories reflected warmly on Taft Architects, and they were hired on the spot. Completed in 1984, the award-winning and colorful River Crest Country Club, of red brick and green terra-cotta, evokes great-house grandeur and is a Fort Worth landmark.

The three young Taft partners later flew to New York with the best bottle of champagne they could find and visited Johnson, who gave them the treatment with lunch at the Four Seasons. Danny Samuels recalls, "It was *the* experience! When he came into the restaurant, it was as if the Prince had arrived. He went around greeting people like Henry Kissinger with everybody in the place leaning over and whispering to each other before we sat down at his personal banquette. Johnson loved it!"[37] Only a person in politics or show business could work such a staid Manhattan public room with his fluid ease. (Midwestern boosterism was in Johnson's bones, part and parcel, and would last him forever.) During lunch, Johnson said that he had recommended the young architects to Jayne Wrightsman, a reigning Manhattan social figure, who needed an architect for a house in Palm Beach. Mrs. Wrightsman soon visited Houston, in a downpour, and was incredulous ("Is *this* the place?") when she arrived at the Taft Architects' modest office in an old residential neighborhood. Stepping over a water-filled street gutter, she made it to the door, where she met the young, anxious Taft partners briefly before fleeing the scene in her chauffeur-driven limousine.

Phillip Shepherd is a Dallas architect whose firm, Shepherd & Boyd, designed the fashionable Mansion on Turtle Creek in the early 1980s for Caroline Hunt Schoelkopf, a daughter of legendary oilman H. L. Hunt, described by *Life* magazine as "the richest man in the world" during his heyday in prewar oil-boom Texas. In the 1930s, Hunt bought a big house, "Mount Vernon," on a prominent site facing Dallas's White Rock Lake; it bears a vague, pumped-up resemblance to the original.

Caroline Schoelkopf's Rosewood Corporation now specializes in developing and managing luxury hotels, of which the celebrated Mansion on Turtle Creek was the first and best known. Shepherd had been a partner in Harwood K. Smith & Partners, Dallas's largest firm, with personnel numbering in the hundreds. Like many other ambitious HKS architects, he started his own office with a foothold of experience and client acquaintance acquired in the father firm. Another HKS alumnus, Bobby Boyd, joined Shepherd as production partner.

Phillip Shepherd and Steven Sands, Caroline Hunt Schoelkopf's oldest son, were neighbors and friends in Dallas's affluent Highland Park, and through his friend, Shepherd got the job of architect for Rosewood's first high-profile venture. The Mansion on Turtle Creek was also Shepherd & Boyd's first important job, and it was a resounding success, setting a new standard in Dallas and the Southwest for food, comfort, and an ambience of wealthy well-being. Its name derived from the 1920s Mediterranean-style villa existing on the property, which Shepherd remodeled as a restaurant, integrating its style with Rosewood's new multistory hotel. Today the restaurant and hotel remain Dallas's nonpareil social center for the rich and famous.

When the Rosewood company, flush with the success of the Mansion, bought a large triangular tract of land prominently positioned near, but not in, the downtown business district, Caroline Schoelkopf's son Steve, now running Rosewood for his mother, approached his friend Shepherd about developing a large mixed-use complex on the ten-acre property. He envisioned an office building and a luxury hotel with attached upscale retail shops. Shepherd became a general partner in developing the property. Knowing better than to take on the design job single-handedly, he selected Johnson after interviewing some of the nation's best-known architects with Steve Sands. It was unique for Johnson to have a client who was also a partner-architect. Shepherd recognized Johnson and Burgee as the architects with the name and experience necessary to promote the project and attract national as well as local tenants. This was after the AT&T publicity and the big, highly publicized Hines projects in Houston. Sands remembers Johnson's enthusiasm for the project. Far less circumspect than the other architecture stars, Johnson *liked* Texas, for obvious reasons, and that gave him an advantage.

Phillip Shepherd is a plainspoken West Texan and graduate of Texas Technological University in Lubbock. He is expansive about his relationship with the nearly eighty-year-old architect:

> I was the architect doing the working drawings and hired Johnson and Burgee to collaborate with us on the design. I felt that Johnson could work with me in a way that was economically feasible rather than just trying to do a piece of architecture. Even though I was an owner in this deal, I wanted to have a signature larger than mine and a product that was more historical-related than an I. M. Pei deal or something like that.
>
> Philip Johnson was real easy to get along with; a little uppity at first, but he calmed down pretty quick—a helluva nice guy. We got along fine 'cause if there

was a fuss over something or other, like one of these little drawings they would send down from New York, he'd say, "Who's running this deal?" and I'd say, "Hell, I am 'cause I'm the general partner!" and that stopped all the bullshit between the architects and we'd go on from there. We tried to pick up some historical pieces of Texas like with the ironwork, which we found in Galveston in some of those old houses with mansard roofs. It took seven foundries to produce all the grillwork in time, six million dollars of it. The style of the buildings came partly from Galveston and partly from Bath, England, and I liked the way the Beverly Wilshire Hotel is divided by a street and the "synergism" of the Peninsula Hotel in Hong Kong, where there's a lot of interaction. Let me say this: I *enjoyed* Philip Johnson, he's quite a character, personality-wise and everything. And he ran his show. Burgee didn't enter in much; he was always trying to *be* Philip Johnson.[38]

John Manley ruefully recalls working on the Crescent design for Johnson:

Shepherd had the upper hand because of his arrangement with the owners—he was sort of the client—but we provided all the basic design of the buildings along with their details, though I wish I could say that Phillip Shepherd furnished some of it. At the time, we were in an ardent phase of studying the past with Pittsburgh Glass, AT&T, the College of Architecture in Houston, and other historicized projects, so it wasn't a great jump for Mr. Johnson to employ French mansard roofs and grillwork. It seemed right for Dallas, I guess; apparently there was great money being spent there by the new rich on chateau-esque mansions.[39]

Steve Sands recalls:

I interviewed a lot of the name architects with Phil that he came up with but liked Philip Johnson the best. We signed him up, and I went to New York a number of times with Phil during the design phase and sat in on the meetings in the Johnson/Burgee offices in the Seagram Building, which were sometimes interrupted with Johnson losing his temper with Shepherd over something or other and threatening to take his name off the job. The meetings went like this: we would meet at 9:30 with him and Burgee and others in their office; I never knew where Burgee fit in, but he was always there with Johnson, who was really into classical architecture at the time and old things that worked in Europe and how they could be applied, that kind of thing. The meeting would last for three hours, with Johnson sometimes worrying and worrying over some little detail, and then we would go downstairs to the Four Seasons Restaurant and sit at his regular table. Johnson always ordered one Punt e Mes drink for himself, and then we would have lunch. It was always exactly the same.[40]

When the Crescent complex development was announced with a full-page story in the *Dallas Morning News,* Johnson was pictured, along with drawings of the multibuilding mixed-use project. In the news story he expounded at length on the "regional" design character of the buildings, endeavoring to tie them to something Texan, invoking the decorated nineteenth-century buildings of Galveston. Howard Barnstone had earlier taken Johnson to Galveston to see the island's Victorian houses, and Johnson was quite taken with Ashton Villa, the 1858 landmark residence in the then-popular Italianate style, with a double gallery framed in New Orleans Creole-style cast iron.

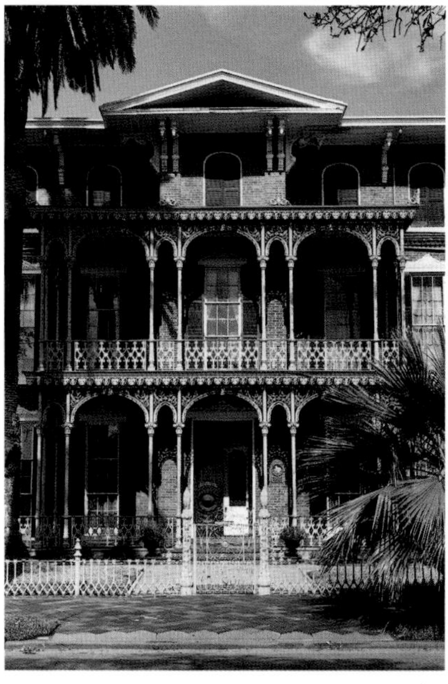

Detail, Ashton Villa, 1859. Photo by Ellen Beasley from Ellen Beasley and Stephen Fox, *Galveston Architecture Guidebook*, Rice University Press, Houston, 1996.

Peter Brink, then head of the Galveston Historical Foundation, joined Barnstone and Johnson at Ashton Villa and recalls the meeting: "We were of course impressed that Philip Johnson came down to Galveston to see our buildings. He was absolutely straightforward, smart and intent on his mission, very professional. He thought the iron grillwork was marvelous and sketched or took photographs of it. Later, after The Crescent was built, I went to Dallas, and there was the same Ashton Villa grillwork running up the sides of this skyscraper."[41]

There was other decorative ironwork used in the island city, but very little of this Creole influence took hold in Texas after the Civil War; the most prominent examples were the 1909 addition to San Antonio's historic Menger Hotel by Alfred Giles, and the Creole-influenced brick architecture of the twin Rio Grande cities of Brownsville and Matamoros, Mexico, in the second half of the nineteenth century.

For the regionalist architects of Texas, it was a nervy assertion of Johnson's in the Dallas paper; indigenous architectural traditions in the state were associated with simplicity of line and directness of structural expression, exemplified by settler buildings of the Central Texas Hill Country around Fredericksburg. Regionalist architects were dead serious about their philosophical province. The newspaper pictures of the elaborately lacy buildings of The Crescent seemed to have more to do with Frederick's of Hollywood than Fredericksburg.

Johnson's site plan for the project was direct and logical. The triangular site was divided into retail, hotel, and office high rise. The triangular four-story retail part of the complex was located at the narrow end of the site, pointed up Turtle Creek toward affluent Highland Park and University Park, whose ladies Rosewood hoped to lure to its luxury shops. Beneath this triangular structure, which had cast-iron balconies wrapped around an interior courtyard and fountain, was an eight-story parking garage, the largest such underground facility in Dallas at the time. On a north-south axis with the

Caroline Hunt Schoelkopf and model of The Crescent, Dallas, 1985. *Texas Monthly Magazine*, December 1985. Photo by Helmut Newton. Courtesy of Tutti i Diritti Riservati.

retail wing was located a curving four-story hotel which stretched across the block and was separated from the retail by a lush garden. A landscaped interior street, centered with a fountain surrounded by stylized columns and capitals, crossed the site between the hotel and the curving sixteen-story tripartite office building facing the downtown skyline. This 1,000,000 sq. ft. building was to be three buildings originally, but for rental flexibility was webbed together.

As built, the convex slab of offices facing downtown is topped with dormered mansards, which as "roofs" are visually puny in relation to the building's sheer mass of window-punched stone walls. The office building's three-part facades are joined with full-height concave bays marked with balconies festooned with metal grillwork and terminated at the top with half-dome "bra-cups" of the same grillwork. These soaring, upward-thrusting adornments also occur at the long building's outside corners. Remarkably, within this plethora of old-world filigree and the largest single use of Indiana

The Crescent

Dallas, 1985

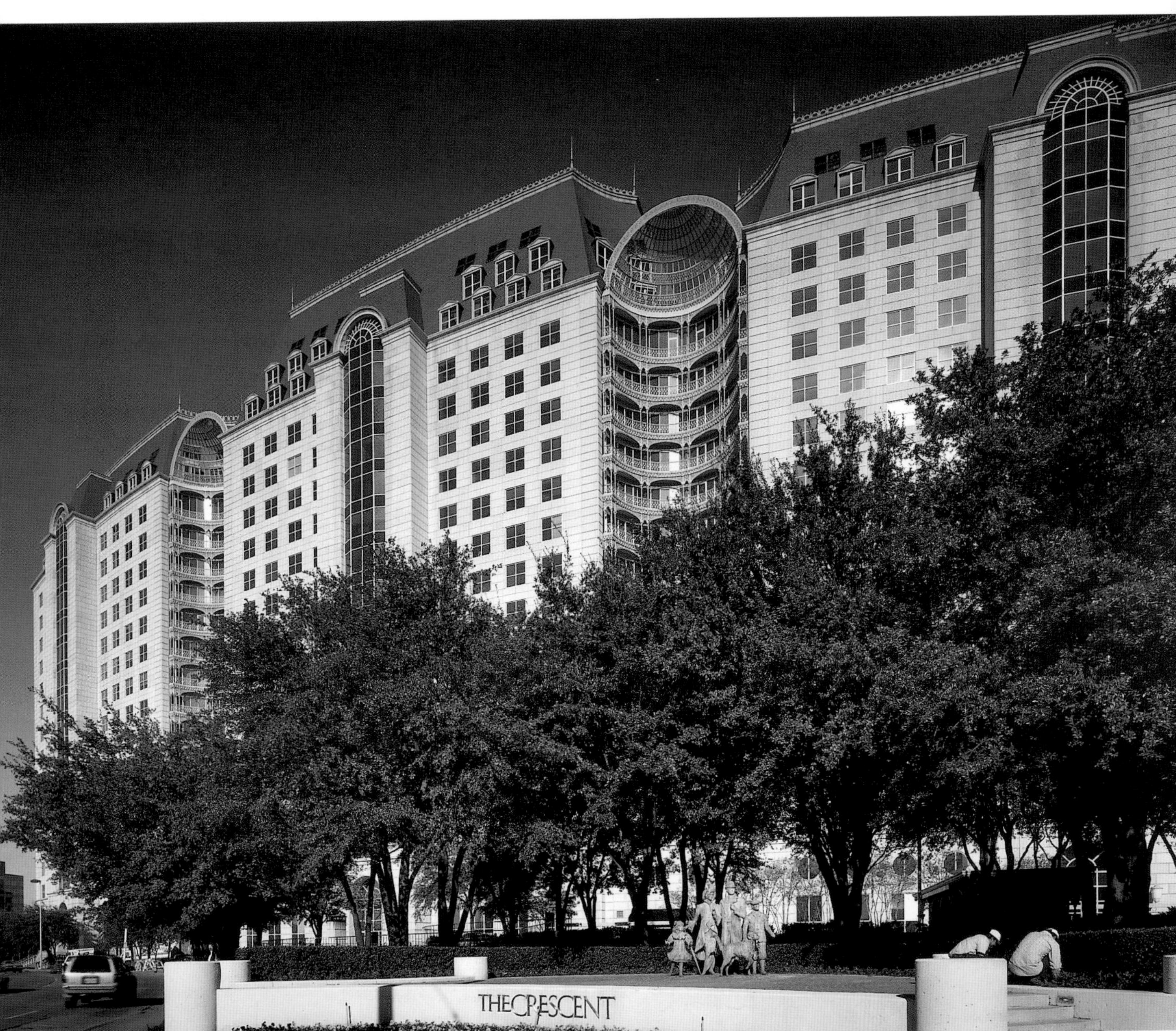

South facade of the office block.

JOHN BURGEE WITH PHILIP JOHNSON, ARCHITECTS; SHEPHERD & BOYD, ASSOCIATE ARCHITECTS.
PHOTOS BY PAUL HESTER, 1998–1999.

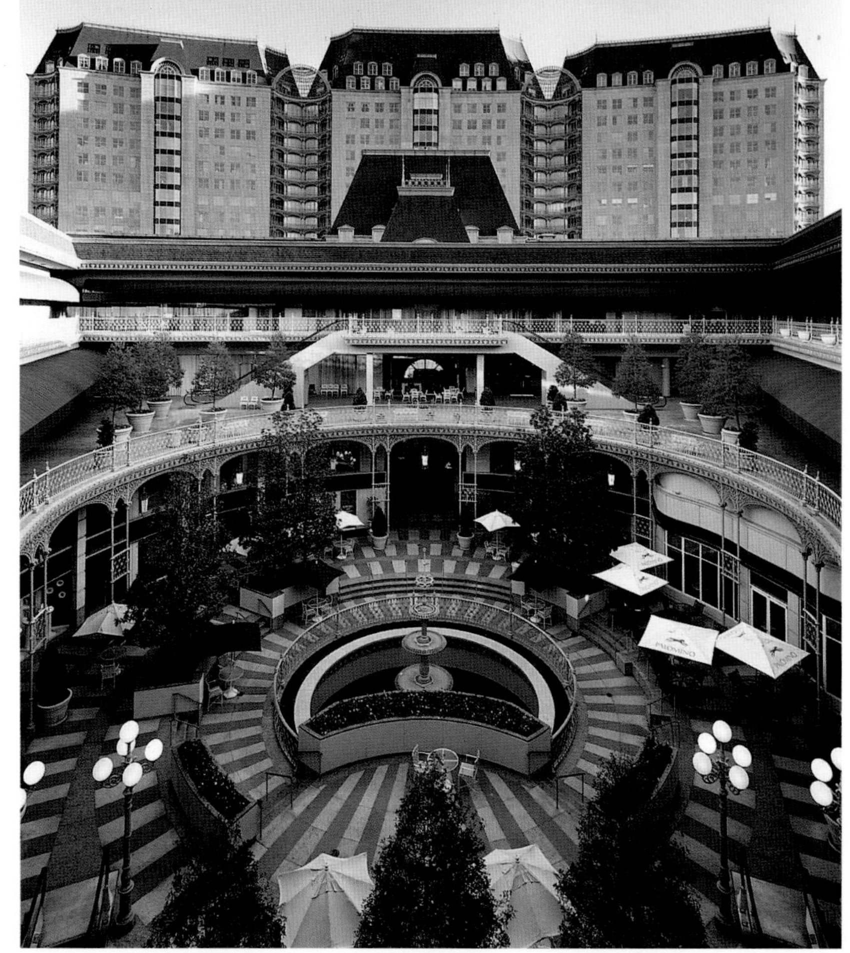

Above: courtyard of the retail block with three-part office block in background;
below: detail, south facade of the Crescent Court Hotel.

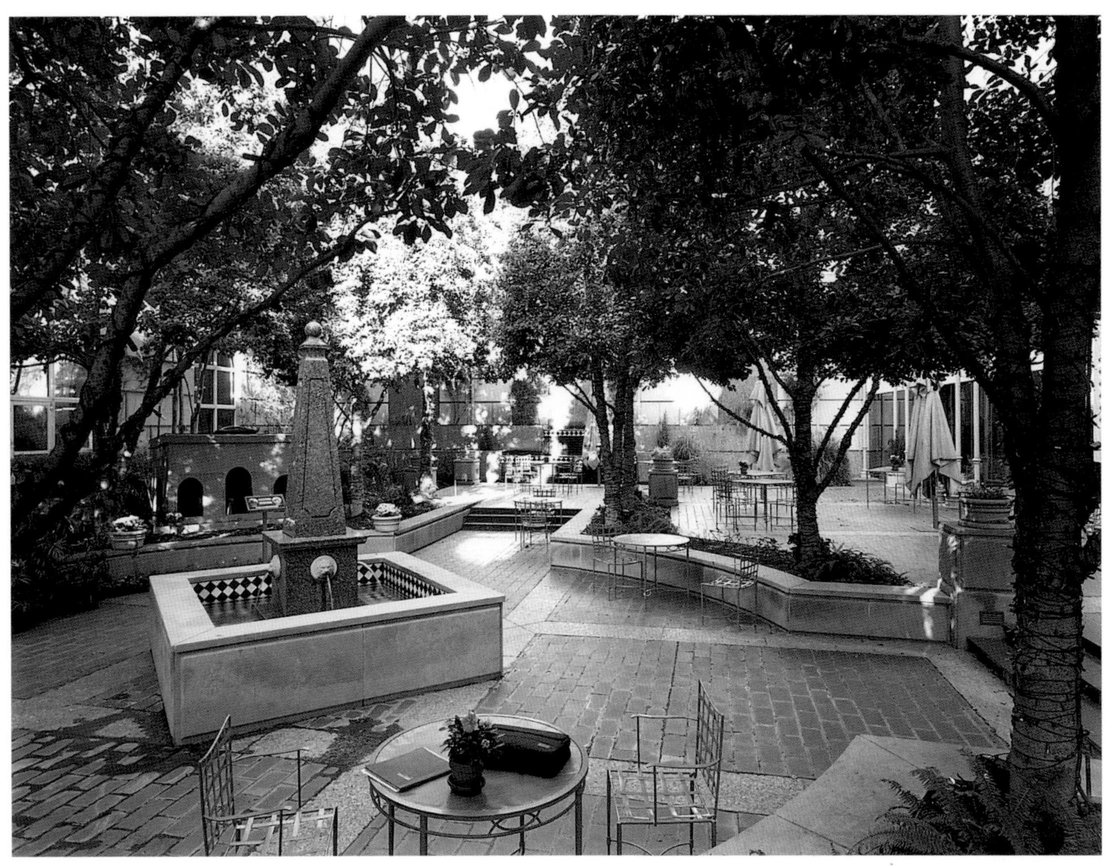

Above: courtyard of hotel; *below:* covered walkway through courtyard.

Parking garage level below retail block courtyard.

Hotel lobby.

Hotel restaurant.

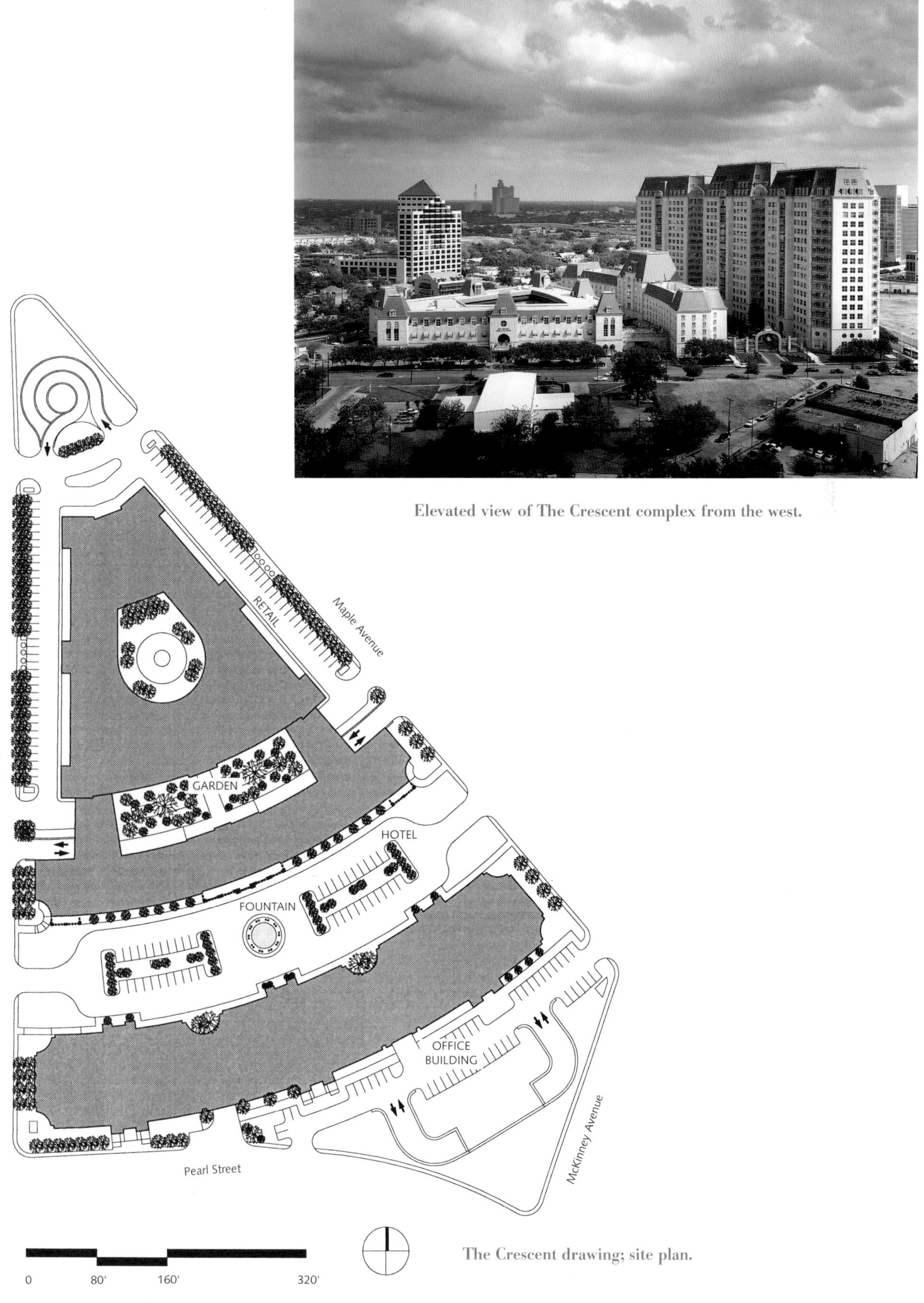

Elevated view of The Crescent complex from the west.

The Crescent drawing; site plan.

limestone since the Empire State Building—the same quarry was used—the architects inserted tall, arch-topped "bibs" of commercial grade window-wall, awkward convex bays centered in each of the building's three parts.

The scale of the other buildings of the complex drops across the interior street from the office block. The six stories of the hotel and the four stories of the retail building, at the narrow tip, bring those mansard-roofed parts into more agreeable line with the scale and idiom of seventeenth-century Paris that informs, in broad strokes, the general character of The Crescent. One is reminded, fleetingly, of the Place Dauphine and Place des Victoires in the French capital. Rusticated, six-storied stone walls beneath decorated, slate-covered roofs punctuated with dormers are terms of language everyone associates with old world Paris, not Texas. As a back lot stage set themed to an upscale market, The Crescent succeeds. Paul Goldberger, the usually astute critic, was swayed: " . . . a marvelous confection of French Second Empire construction that is so strongly composed, and so pleasantly detailed, that one easily forgives its basic silliness."[42] As urban design on the edge of a downtown district The Crescent is successful: it has strongly visual landmark identity; it is easy to access from its underground garage and pleasant to use for dining, shopping, or doing business in a variety of well-planned spaces; and finally, it possesses a clear, integrated sense of *place.* The architecture is anemic but as a civic locus, The Crescent is grandly robust.

In fact, the hotel, with its opulent but restrained interiors designed by the late Kalef Alaton, is very successful and has, as the slightly less swanky sibling of Rosewood's Mansion on Turtle Creek, become a major fixture in Dallas's social and entertainment culture. There is a lavish and exclusive rooftop club in the office building and a luxurious marble-clad spa in the hotel. When architects from Norman Foster's London office stayed at the Crescent Court Hotel in 1996, they could not believe that Philip Johnson was involved with its design.

As The Crescent opened with Texas-size fanfare in 1985, amidst the crumbling and then crashing Texas real estate and oil economy, Johnson and Burgee were completing work on their last job as collaborators: the Momentum Place bank tower, now Bank One, in Dallas. In retrospect, its huge budget and reach for attention with celebrity architects are sadly symbolic of the entire 1980s hubris of greedy excess that infected Texas to a greater degree than it did the rest of the nation.

The executives of MBank, the new name of Mercantile National Bank, one of Dallas's oldest financial institutions, wanted a prominent public statement of success and permanence in the form of a downtown landmark. Dallas was a banking city with large, competing players; Texas was booming, and it was important to think *big:* Momentum Place would be the building's name. Gene Bishop, president of MBank at the time, recalls that Cadillac-Fairview, the Canadian development company with big stakes throughout the nation and Texas, had the block, diagonally across from Neiman-Marcus's flagship store, for developing the building; a large list of architects for the bank project was considered but boiled down to "about five or so," according to Bishop.

"There was Skidmore Owings & Merrill and I. M. Pei and Johnson and Burgee in the final short list," recalls Bishop.

> They all made big, impressive presentations, with sketches and ideas, but the thing that got the job for Johnson was his personality as much as his presentation. I don't believe he and Burgee had much in the way of sketches; it was mainly Johnson's enthusiasm and ability to put in words what we vaguely envisioned for the building. We wanted it to be important on the skyline, be something lasting and permanent for fifty years or more. Burgee didn't say much during the presentation, but I later became very impressed with him and Raj Ahuja, who did a lot of work on the building.
>
> Incidentally, I had a great relationship with Philip Johnson; he was easy to work with. One of the things we wanted was something unique in terms of the *top* of the building. You know back then everything was just a square top—it looked terrible—and the first thing he brought in was *really* unusual; he really came up with something. It looked like a castle in medieval Europe with towers on the top at the four corners. I hesitated to speak up and be critical of his design, but I finally had to tell him, "I just don't like it." And he said, "Hell, we will change it!"[43]

He and Burgee were soon back in Dallas with a model so tiny that Johnson held it in one hand as he presented the revised scheme that formed the basis of the final design. Work on drawings for the project began in 1983, and the 1.5 million sq. ft. building was completed in 1987, surrounded by a wrecked Texas economy.

The pink granite tower has a language drawn not only from classical historical sources but from Johnson and Burgee's repertoire of large corporate structures. The six-story banking room base is set back on a shallow, landscaped forecourt and is centered with a large, inset barrel-vault entry reminiscent of both AT&T and Transco, with an upper window divided strongly with dark mullions as at AT&T and, earlier, in the large arched windows of New York's Grand Central Terminal. This sixty-foot-high base abuts the building's tower, which is marked on all sides with sheer, full-height window-wall sections. These taut vertical panels of glass soar upward between granite walls punched with windows, to barrel-vaulted roofs that intersect on the building's cruciform upper floors. The polished rusticated base has tall arched windows with spandrels ornamented with the rondels found in the Sugar Land Office Park building.

As intended, the bank lobby is a blockbuster. From the arched entry (Rojo Alicante marble from Spain), one crosses over and through the lobby beneath a sixty-foot-high glass barrel-vault, on a marble-floored bridge above the "trading floor," sixteen feet below. The lavish use of polished marble and exotic woods ("300,000 square feet of burnished cherry"), and the Greco-Roman X-railings throughout, similar to those at the University of Houston, bespeak financial power of an imperial magnitude. The bank's image of moneyed muscle turned hollow amid the Texas economy's crash; it changed hands and names several times after its opening, finally becoming Bank One. Momentum Place was fussed up with clashing, overwrought details like the Crescent complex and at odds with the pared-down singular vision of Johnson's best skyscrapers, Pennzoil, RepublicBank, and Transco in Houston. Even AT&T in New York holds together as a fit addition to that city's skyscraper tradition. Like an insecure arriviste with too much of the wrong kind of jewelry, the two Dallas projects reflected accurately the kind of fancy lifestyle being lived everywhere by the rich and newly rich, particularly in Dallas. To some, The Crescent and Momentum Place seemed to confirm Houston critic Stephen Fox's humorous observation that "Philip Johnson saved his worst Texas buildings for Dallas." Johnson later told Burdette Keeland, "They wanted something 'fancy-smancy' up there and I gave it to them."[44] When the bank opened and published a brochure, the architect firm's title appeared as John Burgee Architects beneath a photograph of a pleased Burgee, seated above and behind a grim-faced Johnson and an equally grim minority partner, Raj Ahuja.

Paralleling the economy's nosedive, Philip Johnson and John Burgee split up at Burgee's initiative. Aware that his partner was the one whom all of their clients wanted in charge of the design of *their* building, Burgee, a businessman-architect who wanted to be considered a creative designer, began, in the late 1970s, disengaging from Johnson and making his own name more prominent in the partnership. In the beginning, in the mid-1960s, it was Johnson and Burgee, then Johnson/Burgee. John Burgee Architects with Philip Johnson was followed by John Burgee Architects, Philip Johnson Consultant, and finally, in 1992, just John Burgee Architects when Burgee completed buying Johnson out with a hefty settlement. Burgee reasoned wrongly that by establishing more identity for himself before Johnson died, his design services would remain in demand. Not only was the economy in shreds, but, on his own, Burgee had

Momentum Place

(now BankOne), Dallas, 1987

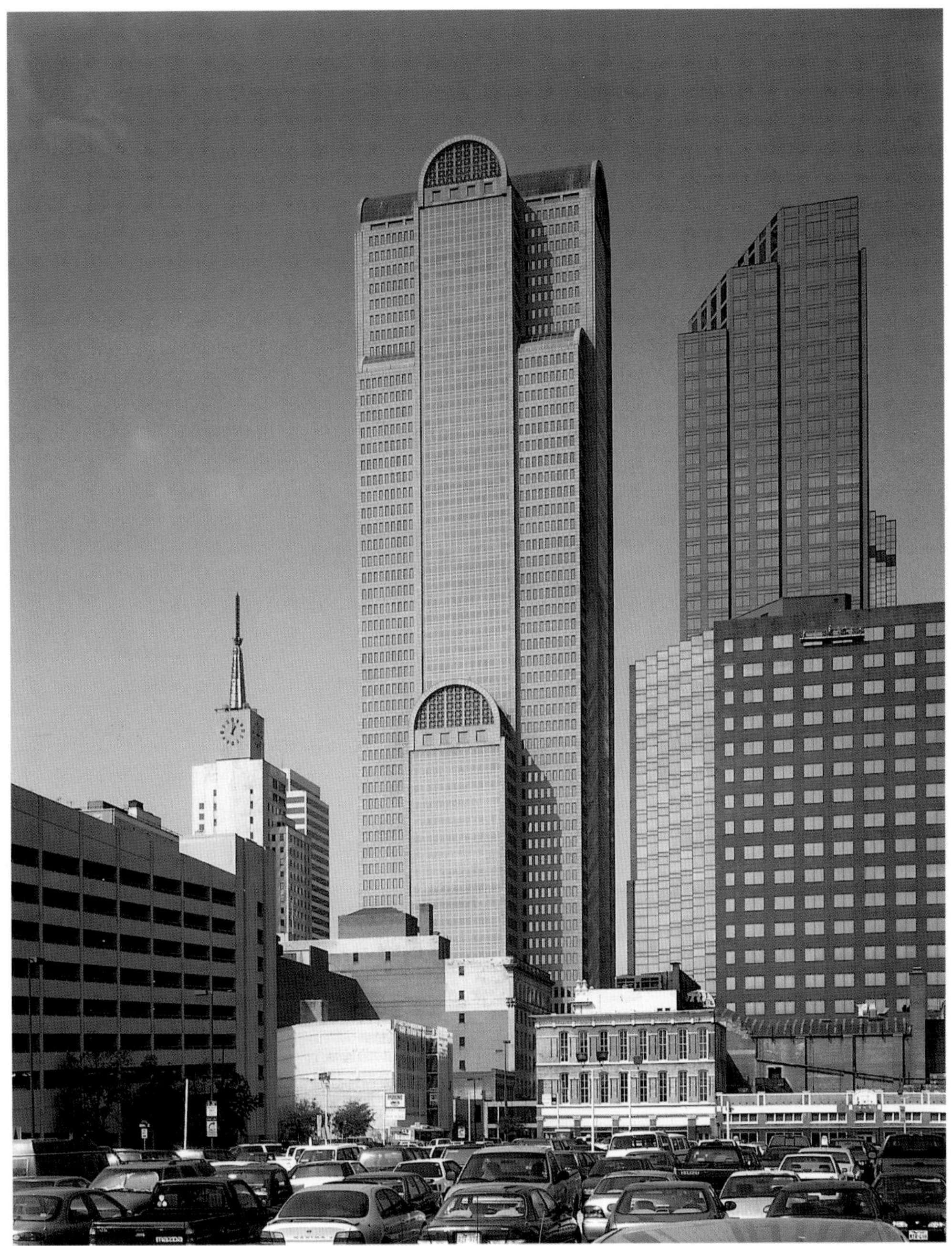

View from the east; building with clock and spire in left background is former bank building.

JOHN BURGEE WITH PHILIP JOHNSON, ARCHITECTS; HKS & PARTNERS, INC., ASSOCIATE ARCHITECTS. PHOTOS BY PAUL HESTER, 1998–1999.

Main entrance on Ervay Street.

Bridge to banking room inside main entrance.

Detail, skylighted vault above entrance.

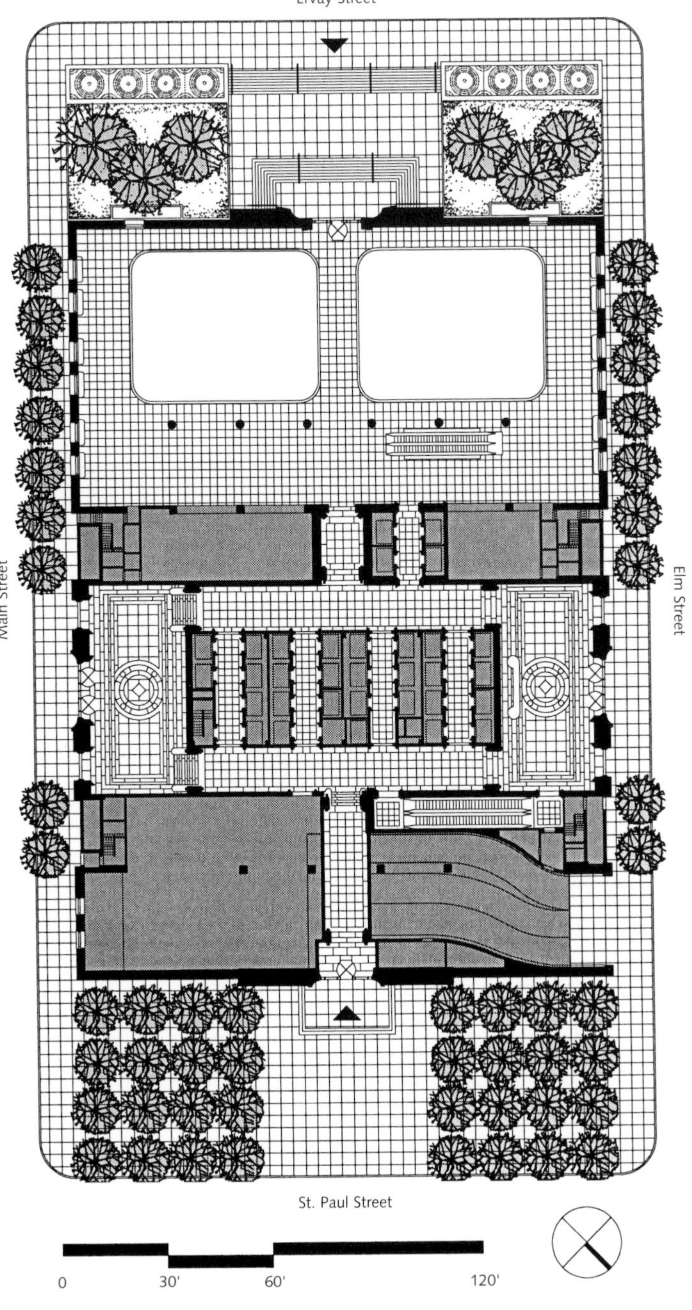

Momentum Place drawing; ground-floor plan.

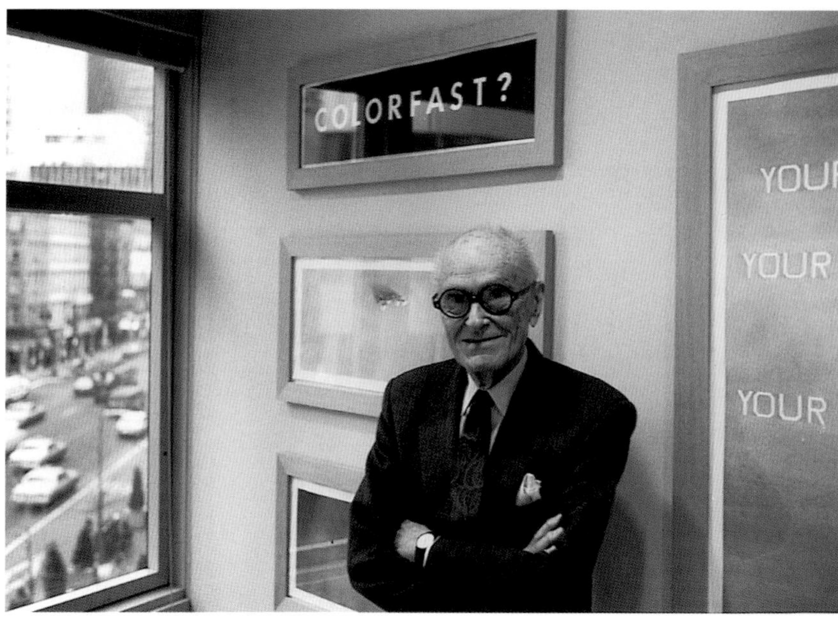

Philip Johnson in his old office overlooking Third Avenue at the time of the complete breakup of Johnson and John Burgee, 1992. Photo by the author.

trouble getting what jobs there were. The clients wanted Johnson. The final blow came when his minor-interest partner, Raj Ahuja, sued Burgee for fee shares owed him after Burgee fired Ahuja abruptly. Burgee's loss of a big court settlement to Ahuja bankrupted him in the mid-1990s.

Still in the center of New York's youthfully hip architectural culture, Johnson still met regularly with a coterie of younger architects at the exclusive Century Club for black-tie evenings of banter, discourse, and gossip. These protégés of Johnson's were a group of avant-gardists that developed from a small fraternity of architectural theorists formed as the Case Group at Princeton University under teachers Michael Graves, Timothy Vreeland, and Peter Eisenman in the late 1950s. In New York, the group eventually drew in Johnson and other older architects like Paul Rudolph, Kevin Roche, Cesar Pelli, and Harry Cobb and included up-and-coming architects Charles Gwathmey, Jacquelin Robertson, Richard Meier, and Robert A. M. Stern. They coalesced around Johnson, who became their mentor and muse when he took an interest in Eisenman's Institute of Architecture and Urban Studies (IAUS), a think tank of architectural theory established in the late 1960s. When the IAUS was particularly strapped for money, Eisenman, with Johnson cheering him on, went to Houston and, asking for $3,000,000, got $1,500,000 from board member Gerald Hines.

Johnson ran the clique not unlike the way of his Ash Street parties at Harvard and the Glass House salons for students and young faculty in the 1940s, 1950s, and 1960s. He approved the speakers and agendas for the Century Club dinners and maintained benign, patriarchal control of his "kids." Harvard design classmates and competitors of Johnson's like I. M. Pei and Edward Larrabee Barnes were never a part of the group; the personable Barnes, with his conservative modernism, was described as "a sheep in sheep's clothing." Johnson thought I. M. Pei was very likable but hermetic.

Lars Lerup, the Swedish-American architect and dean of the Rice University School of Architecture, was a young émigré at the IAUS in the late 1970s and is of several minds about Johnson:

> Sweden, where I grew up, has a tradition in its society of what I would call a nonhierarchical democracy among its architects where quality, not celebrity, is paramount. So seeing the way the New York designers prostrated themselves before Johnson was very strange to me. This hero worship, or rather the worship of someone with tremendous power, in a democratic society was distasteful.
>
> Looking at Johnson's work, I have a very different view now and can speak much more easily. I fault my moralistic past and regret that I didn't get to know him at that time at the IAUS. He's clearly an extremely brilliant man and has had an amazing effect on the architecture in this country. He has operated as a Brahmin who has promoted a small society of architects with huge egos and large names. The stargazing that goes on in this country brought on by Hollywood and so on is unique, and the celebrity Johnson, it seems to me, has always been as much of a "gazer" as a "gazed-upon."[45]

Eisenman the lecturer and architectural theorist has, since the demise of IAUS, created buildings as a practicing architect from his New York base since the early 1970s, and, as the century closes, he and Frank Gehry are Johnson's designated leaders of advanced design in the United States. Eisenman's puzzling public discourses about design theory (Johnson, inherently impatient with high-flown theory, called it "bullshit") have been replaced with popular lectures that are witty, open expositions of his life as a designer of cutting-edge buildings. In 1998, Eisenman, sixty-five, was full of praise and feeling for Johnson as *the* influential architect of his age.

"Philip is a universal man," Eisenman says.

> I recently gave him a book on the philosopher Heidegger, and he devoured it, faster than I did, and couldn't wait to discuss it. He can talk at length about lit-

erature and art in addition to architecture—past, present, and future—with the zest of a brilliant undergraduate. Look at him, ninety-two years old!

He was drawn to our group back in the sixties because we were young and were not, as he said, *boring*, like his generation of architects. We were sort of feisty, questioning the conventional wisdom, with ideas for new directions. It stimulated his curiosity, of which he has such abundance, and he proceeded to take us under his wing. Our generation in turn sort of energized and reinvented him when he was in his sixties, making us a part of Philip Johnson history. His inquisitiveness matched our need for the validation of architecture as art, which he gave us enthusiastically. We sought approval and he sought fellowship. Many nights he would come downtown to our studio here to look at what we were doing and offer support and suggestions. And literally nothing in our group of Century Club regulars got past him: when Jacque Robertson and I decided to form a partnership, we went up to New Canaan for Philip to bless the union, so to speak. The whole bunch of us were Philip's Boys.[46]

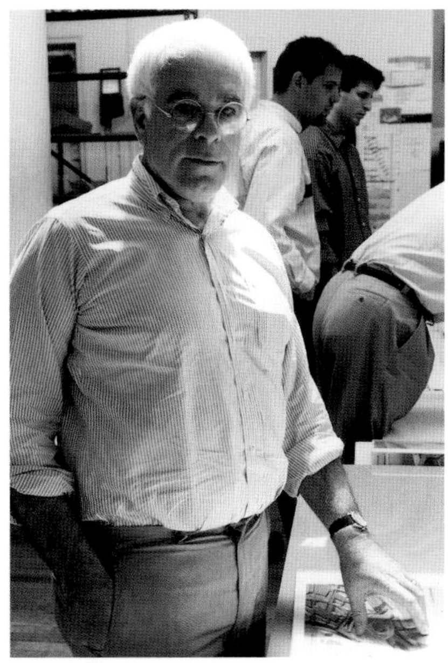

Peter Eisenman in his studio, New York City, 1997. Photo by the author.

Another one of Johnson's "boys," who had come on the national scene in the late 1970s, became, by 1995, his "favorite," most touted architect (along with the intellectual New Yorker Eisenman). Architect Frank Gehry of Los Angeles and Santa Monica was, from his beginnings in Los Angeles in the 1950s, a very good modernist architect designing residential and commercial buildings of great variety and scope. His heritage was Californians Richard Neutra, Rudolph Schindler, and Harwell Hamilton Harris, and his contemporary colleagues were not architects, but West Coast artists like Ed Ruscha and Billy Al Bengston. Art and artists form the foundation of Gehry's special sensibility.

He began making a name for himself in the early 1970s with small-scale expressionist jobs, more sculptural than conventionally architectural. One was a studio/residence for a friend, the painter Ron Davis, in Malibu. None of the building planes of the big shed, the walls and roof, was parallel to its opposite plane. In 1973, architect Tim Vreeland took Philip Johnson to see the rhomboidal structure and to meet Gehry. The California architect had wanted to meet Johnson for a long time because he cared about art as much as Gehry did. A friendship began, and one can speculate on how this building of warped volumes affected Johnson's subsequent work, particularly Pennzoil Place. Gehry can recall going to see Pennzoil in the late 1970s and thinking to himself, "I'm glad to see that Philip and I are playing with the same things."

In the early 1980s, Gehry along with many other architects entered the competition for the design of the Beverly Hills Civic Center, but lost the contest to Charles Moore's office. Charles Gwathmey and Peter Eisenman also entered and lost the competition and one evening joined Johnson and Gehry in Eisenman's office for a postmortem of their submissions. Gehry, who was teaching at Yale at the time, recalls that

> Johnson, drinking a big glass of gin, literally decimated all three of our competition designs. It was brilliantly vicious, brilliant, brilliant. We were all spanked. It was one of the most painful things in my life for me, one of the worst I've ever experienced. Later, I had to get on the train to go back to New Haven. I was pretty depressed and didn't see Philip for a while.
>
> It was later that I was invited to join the Century Club group's black-tie dinners. I like the people but not the event. David Childs even talked me into joining the Century but I never, ever go! How do I get out?
>
> Philip is the embodiment of support for architecture. He is the only living architect that has consistently supported the next generation. He may not even like the work, but he goes out of his way to support it because it is exciting and new. I believe that the *Time* cover with him holding the AT&T model was the turning point in the public's acceptance of architecture; it was the catalyst for the emergence of our generation. And his using the acceptance of the Gold Medal in 1978 to put the spotlight on the work of seven or eight younger architects was remarkable. Maybe it was the curator in him, selecting this one and that one for recognition. But nobody, I mean nobody period, gave that much time to young students and architects as Philip did, when he could have been doing much more important things.[47]

Frank Gehry following a Dallas Museum of Art symposium, January 1999. Photo by Nan Coulter.

In the middle 1990s Johnson himself was approaching ninety years of age. He remained as intellectually spry and ardent about new buildings as he was when he began. Gehry, thirty years his junior, was his architectural "hero," and Johnson extolled Gehry's sculpturally expressionist buildings at every opportunity. Meanwhile, he opened a small office on another floor of Fifty-third at Third, the Lipstick Building, where Johnson and Burgee had been located in a sumptuous space since 1984, and asked two former Johnson/Burgee employees, Alan Ritchie and David Fiore, to come back with him as partners. Ritchie and Fiore had left Burgee earlier when Johnson was shunted aside for the last time; they eagerly joined their former boss.

Outwardly, the near nonagenarian was beginning again with renewed optimism but undoubtedly reduced expectations. He was older than any other practicing architect of rank—could he live long enough to finish a job?—and after years of association with Burgee and the production of marketplace high-rises, his professional reputation was at its lowest point. Most of the time you could not see past the familiar bravado when he felt low. His life, for all its overt ebullience, was marked with major traumas, some private, some public: the breakdown at Harvard in the 1920s, the regrettable dance with fascism in the 1930s, two coronary operations (in 1986, on his eightieth birthday, and in 1996, shortly after his ninetieth), followed by severe depression or illness, and finally, being adrift in his eighties after the unpleasant split with Burgee. But he always came back.

One afternoon, in 1993, as he scuttled smoothly into his small office with its round marble table, Robert Venturi chairs, and Edward Ruscha paintings, he apologized for being late. And with a brighter expression than the one he had worn for several days, he bubbled, "Been on the phone planning a trip to Berlin, my first in sixty years. I have a new client and a new building! There's nothing more exciting than that for an architect, *is there?*"[48]

Philip Johnson, Menil Collection Founding Director Walter Hopps, and David Whitney at the Whitney-curated Franz Kline exhibition for the Menil Collection, Houston, 1994.
Photo by the author.

Chapter 6

Philip Johnson never wavered after the separation from John Burgee, his partner of thirty years. Staunch as ever, Johnson seemed unflappable. He stayed busy on the phone with his circle of protégés and still rapidly scooted around the city's streets like he was on wheels. Elderly, but celebrated, he had been phased out by Burgee, reportedly insecure about his position as a designer after Johnson's demise. The separation instigated by Burgee was gradual. Initially the firm was titled Philip Johnson & John Burgee, next Johnson/Burgee, then John Burgee Architects with Philip Johnson, and finally, John Burgee Architects, Philip Johnson Consultant. Johnson was well compensated in the "divorce" settlement; he continued to use the sumptuous office and personnel in the Lipstick Building to develop his own projects.

The consistency of the design of buildings by Johnson and Burgee was, to say the least, uneven, but there were triumphs during the partnership which charged the nation's cityscapes with show-biz buildings and made lots of money for the principals. On his own and with a lot of cash in his pocket, Johnson seemed to "come back" with verve intact and some of the astute, elemental feeling for architectural form that marked his best work through the years. His ninetieth year was coming up.

Franz Schulze's *Philip Johnson: Life and Work* was published in 1994. The 465-page biography was the architect's first. Johnson had admired Schulze's *Mies van der Rohe* of 1985. "It reads like a novel," he said. Schulze, a professor of art history at Lake Forest College in Illinois, spent many hours interviewing Johnson for the book that was planned for publication after Johnson's death, but which was speeded up as Johnson's ninetieth birthday approached. Johnson the historian, in addition to being fully cooperative about his buildings and philosophy, went all out in telling everything about his off-camera life. Described as an unauthorized biography, it was not seen by Johnson until its publication. The scholarly book seemed overweighted with details about the private world of this most public architect, while too often treating the buildings with offhand description and analysis. The paradox was that Schulze could take the dour, dense German master, Ludwig

Mies van der Rohe, and create a rich biographical narrative, but with Johnson and his novelistic life, the result was, by comparison, a rather pedestrian stroll—with sensationalist highlights—through the major triumphs and minor tragedies of a scintillating figure in the twentieth century's world of art. Johnson did not like the result.

When Schulze paid a courtesy visit to Johnson at The Glass House after the book's publication—and after the Johnson belittlers had had their say in print, more about the man than the book—his reception by Johnson and David Whitney was strained and chilly. When asked by a reporter in Cleveland several years later why he had told Franz Schulze so much about his personal and political life, Johnson replied, "Because I was a *fool!*"

In his *New Yorker* review of the biography *Philip Johnson: Life and Work,* Brendan Gill, Johnson's friendly foe, concluded:

> If I suggested that we see Johnson as an eccentric, it was partly because, given Johnson's penchant for alienating friends and creating enemies, I felt it would be prudent to install him in a kind of safe house until the person behind the mask of Peck's Bad Boy could step forth and be appraised. I may have exaggerated the scale of the problem. Johnson is an oddity, but he isn't really in need of protective shelter. He is a grander figure than the words *need* and *protective* imply and a far more formidable one. For me he has become the embodiment of heroic victory over advantages and disadvantages alike. Against high odds and at whatever cost in private anguish, he has wrested a good time from the world—no mean prize. He has also succeeded in passing the only test that matters: he has given back to the world more than he has taken from it.[1]

The first important commission designed in his new, small suite in the Lipstick Building with "Philip Johnson Architect" on the door was the revived plan for the long-delayed chapel for the University of St. Thomas. The Chapel of St. Basil would be in the location that Johnson had designated forty years before with his last master plan of 1957: at the north end of the campus's academic mall (the chapel's location shifted from south to north during master planning). Four decades had passed since his strict, Miesian design for the original campus buildings, and his subsequent approach to design had gone through many cycles, for which his critics were loath to forgive him: Classical-Modernism (Amon Carter Museum, Beck house), Postmodern-Eclecticism (Transco Tower, University of Houston College of Architecture, RepublicBank Center, the Crescent complex), Kineticism (Fort Worth Water Garden, Thanks-Giving Square), and Minimalism (Kennedy Memorial, Pennzoil Place).

By the time construction on the chapel had begun in 1995, Johnson had completed yet another experimental structure in his New Canaan compound. With plans afoot to open the Glass House estate to the public after Johnson's death as a property of the National Trust for Historic Preservation, he decided that a visitors' center in the form of a "gate house" was needed near the entrance to serve as an orientation base. His first, published design was radically different from what was finally built. The initial scheme was a clunky modernistic tower of several unconnected, irregular wall and roof planes in a faintly Deconstructivist style, the mode of the late 1980s, for which Johnson organized an exhibition at the Museum of Modern Art. He told University of Houston professor Peter Zweig, who assisted with that exhibition, that a Deconstructivist show would be an appropriate last architecture exhibition for him at the museum. Johnson, however, was never personally able to handle the Deconstructivist esthetic of "violated perfection"; his Puritan restraint prevented it. His aim—and it's not certain if he realized it—had always been *unviolated* perfection. He says that he and Alfred Barr were close because of their "Presbyterianism."

What he did complete in early 1996 was a small, voluptuously sculptural structure inspired both by a friend, artist Frank Stella, and the German Expressionist Herman Finsterlin, a designer of fantasy buildings in the 1920s. (Stella's proposal for a museum complex in Germany included a large-scale version of Johnson's exercise.) Frank Gehry's computer technology for producing curvacious, nonorthogonal structures—the "wibbly-wobbly" designs that Johnson was praising repeatedly and extravagantly as the "architecture of the future"—provided the means to produce the working drawings for the small, million-dollar structure of softly writhing forms just inside the entry to the forty-acre estate. Johnson's proud to say that there are no right angles in the building (he discovered one during construction and had it changed).

The sensuous shapes—described as "wanton" by Johnson—are constructed with a light armature of trussed steel members, cut and formed to shape the shell, before concrete is sprayed into this "cage" and troweled smooth inside and out. The two swooping, biomorphic shapes of the building were given exterior coatings of red and black which boldly delineate their primary forms. Johnson was gleeful during its construction, calling it his "baby hippo" as he planted a moist, smacking kiss on an out-leaning wall. The white interior reflects the exterior shape of the building that Johnson eventually dubbed the Monster, pronouncing the last syllable with a broad *a*, the "Monsta," as in "gangsta." It is lighted by a glass entry and one window placed like a large, torn rent in one wall; recessed floor lights shine up to illuminate the

Gate House (Visitors' Pavilion) at The Glass House, New Canaan, Connecticut, 1995; Philip Johnson, architect. Photos by Richard Payne, 1996.

disorienting free-form volumes. In *The New York Times,* critic Herbert Muschamp praised the gutsy little structure in his article "A 'Monster' of a Masterpiece in Connecticut."

He had to be enjoying approval in *The New York Times* after years of producing big, bottom-line commercial structures with John Burgee; these big buildings were ignored or got a drubbing from the critics. He was back in business, with young partners and new jobs coming in. He flew to Los Angeles and arrived at Gehry's office with pieces of pears in his hand, which he had carved en route, for Gehry's staff to translate into computer-generated drawings. (In 1983, when Burgee and Johnson were designing the Lipstick Building on Lexington Avenue, they paid the Dallas architects Dahl Braden & Chapman $150 for software that the Dallas architects had used to design a similar elliptically shaped high-rise hotel.)

Johnson was called back to Germany—the country whose history and culture had caused him such great pleasure and pain—and was honored and feted in the newly unified city of Berlin. As the German capital's reconstruction boom began, Johnson and his new young partners Alan Ritchie and David Fiore got a commission for a new seven-story office building, Philip Johnson Haus, to be located near Checkpoint Charlie.

In Dallas, Johnson was redesigning parts of Thanks-Giving Square for Peter Stewart, who wanted to embellish the triangular park with spiritual art and artifacts. In Manhattan, Donald Trump, mindful of celebrity value, called, and soon there was high-rise work for Trump's huge project along the Hudson River. "I'm amazed! His people are nice as they can be and do everything that we ask for," Johnson said. "And best of all: they pay their bills *fast.*"[2]

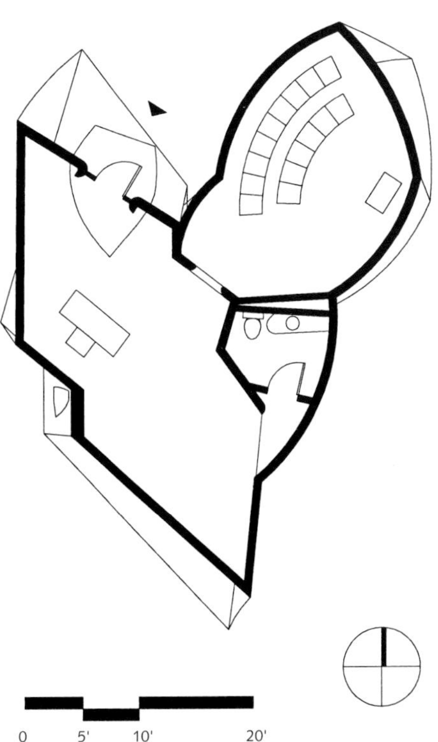

Gate House drawing; floor plan.

The Berlin and Trump designs evolved into banal commercial fare, but the effort for the chapel at the University of St. Thomas was proof that the Johnson sensibility could still focus and produce serious architecture. Like his personal experiments at The Glass House, the chapel project was relatively small, free of an amortization agenda, and forgiving of creative expression. He finally got the cube-shaped chapel that he first proposed for the campus in 1957, but with a dramatic difference. A lot of stylistic fluctuations appeared in Johnson's portfolio in the forty years since his Miesian "pupil architecture." As a champion of the ever-new in architecture—particularly if it was a new interpretation of the old—and with antennae supersensitive to the zeitgeist, he remained the despair of those who prize consistency and originality as design doctrine. His enemies, and he had not a few, remained steadfastly critical both in the press and in private. Robert Campbell, architecture critic for *The Boston Globe*, while praising some of his earlier work, once characterized Johnson as not believing in himself as an architect, treating his buildings in the 1980s as jokes. Michael Sorkin, critic and writer for New York's *Village Voice,* rarely missed an opportunity to berate Johnson. (Johnson remarked that Franz Schulze's book "Sorkinized" him.)

For forty years, buildings for the University of St. Thomas campus had accrued slowly, piece by piece, hewing to Johnson's 1957 master plan of a Miesian architectural language in a Jeffersonian University of Virginia concept. The subsequent buildings were often produced by Houston architects, Johnson friends like Howard Barnstone, who never strayed far from the grammar of Johnson's original three buildings. A library by Eugene Aubry and Wilson Morris Crain & Anderson closed the south end of the academic mall in 1971. For years the north end of the mall remained open and exposed to the rear of Gourmet Hamburgers, facing West Alabama Avenue. Finally, in 1990, the school authorities moved, and plans for a Chapel of St. Basil began to materialize. Johnson, eighty-four, was called back.

Among the several schemes for a chapel in 1957, Johnson proposed a stark brick-and-steel near-cube. He abandoned this for a more expressive form in 1965, the controversial scheme whose monumentality the de Menils objected to, but whose building footprint later evolved into the Rothko Chapel a few blocks away.

"From the beginning, in 1990, Johnson had in mind what he wanted to do with the chapel," John Manley recalls. "Deconstructivism was in its heyday then, he had just finished curating the Deconstructivist show at MoMA, and, in its way I suppose, the design reflects that approach. The basic design elements of the building remained intact from the beginning of our work in the office to the end. The cube, the dome, the diagonal wall, and the 'tent flap.'"[3]

Photographic reproduction, *Suprematist Painting*, Kazimir Malevich, 1927. Courtesy of Stedelijk Museum Amsterdam.

The architectural canon had experienced a number of vicissitudes since the International Style of the postwar 1940s and 1950s. Ever sensitive to "what was going on," Johnson produced a building that was both original and congruent with the times. Deconstructivist architecture had its roots in the art of prerevolution avant-garde Russia; it was a movement that was too radical for the Bolsheviks and went dormant for half a century. The Suprematist painter Kasimir Malevich (1878–1935), whose work, along with that of other Russians, was rediscovered and became exemplars for the Deconstructivist architects in the 1980s and 1990s, was one of the sources that Johnson referenced in describing the genesis of his 1949 Glass House design. The Russian abstractionist's use of the uncentered circle in a square shape—with scattered diagonals—seems to have inspired Johnson again in the chapel's extremely austere plan design. In the building there is the faintest aura of Deconstructivist theories, which dealt with taking apart and reassembling parts of a building in a personal, expressionist approach. Some prime examples looked "exploded," the parts scattered like jackstraws. The radical architecture of SITE surely played a part in the chapel's design, as did the midcentury religious structures of Le Corbusier, particularly the Ronchamp Chapel, which Johnson called "the most beautifully lighted chapel in the world."[4]

"The masonry wall slashing through the cube and dome was always there in Johnson's mind, as was the 'tent flap,'" recalls Manley, "but the wall was eventually lowered *into* the dome, which allowed for clerestories up there, and the entry went from being a glazed opening to a simple rent opening, allowing for an open-air narthex inside the cube but outside the chapel interior."[5]

After many years of fund-raising, the university officials were ready to begin construction when the Bishop saw the design and objected strongly to the location of the reconciliation chapel—the confessional—at the front of the sanctuary. A meeting was called between the church officials and Johnson and his Houston associates, Merriman Holt Architects. Johnson heard the Bishop's objections and said, "Well, I certainly agree with you; there's no reason that we can't change that," and quickly shifted the tiny enclosure's location to everyone's satisfaction.

Philip Johnson finally got his cube-shaped chapel, and the University of St. Thomas campus got a fitting climax to its long table of lawn. The chalk-white chapel measures 64' x 64' x 50', altered from a pure cube during design development, is surmounted by a gleaming, twenty-foot gold-leafed dome, and is embraced on one side with an arm of the university's double-gallery of steel. A freestanding, polished black granite wall, taller than the chapel roof but lower than the dome, cleaves completely through the building and the dome on the diagonal, opening the dome for natural light and directing attention to the building's entrance in the white plaster facade, which is seemingly cut and blown open by an inner force. (One is reminded of the draft of chilled air that emanates outward from the open doors of a medieval cathedral.) Yet this is a facade in the classical sense: a principal building face fronting on a "plaza," commanding it, informing it, but in a manner here and now in the 1990s; in Johnson's hands a facade rendered in a minimalist manner, yet no less potent in context than Jefferson's Rotunda in Charlottesville.

Johnson's vaunted sense of procession is much in evidence here. Looking down the mall of the school through the steel-framed arcade, one perceives and is drawn to the arresting form of the gleaming chapel with its polished gilt dome topped with a cross and is directed to the entrance by the thick black wall which passes through the white block at a thirty-degree angle. Inside the thirty-six-foot-tall rip in the wall—the chapel's entry portal is called the "flap"—the polished and pierced granite screen-wall forms an angled foyer—the narthex—a transition space to the chapel proper. Vertical and lofty, this open-air space faces the granite wall, pierced with glass windows and doors which partially reveal the chapel interior.

Passing through the granite wall, one is struck by the pristine white inte-

Chapel of St. Basil's

University of St. Thomas, Houston, 1995

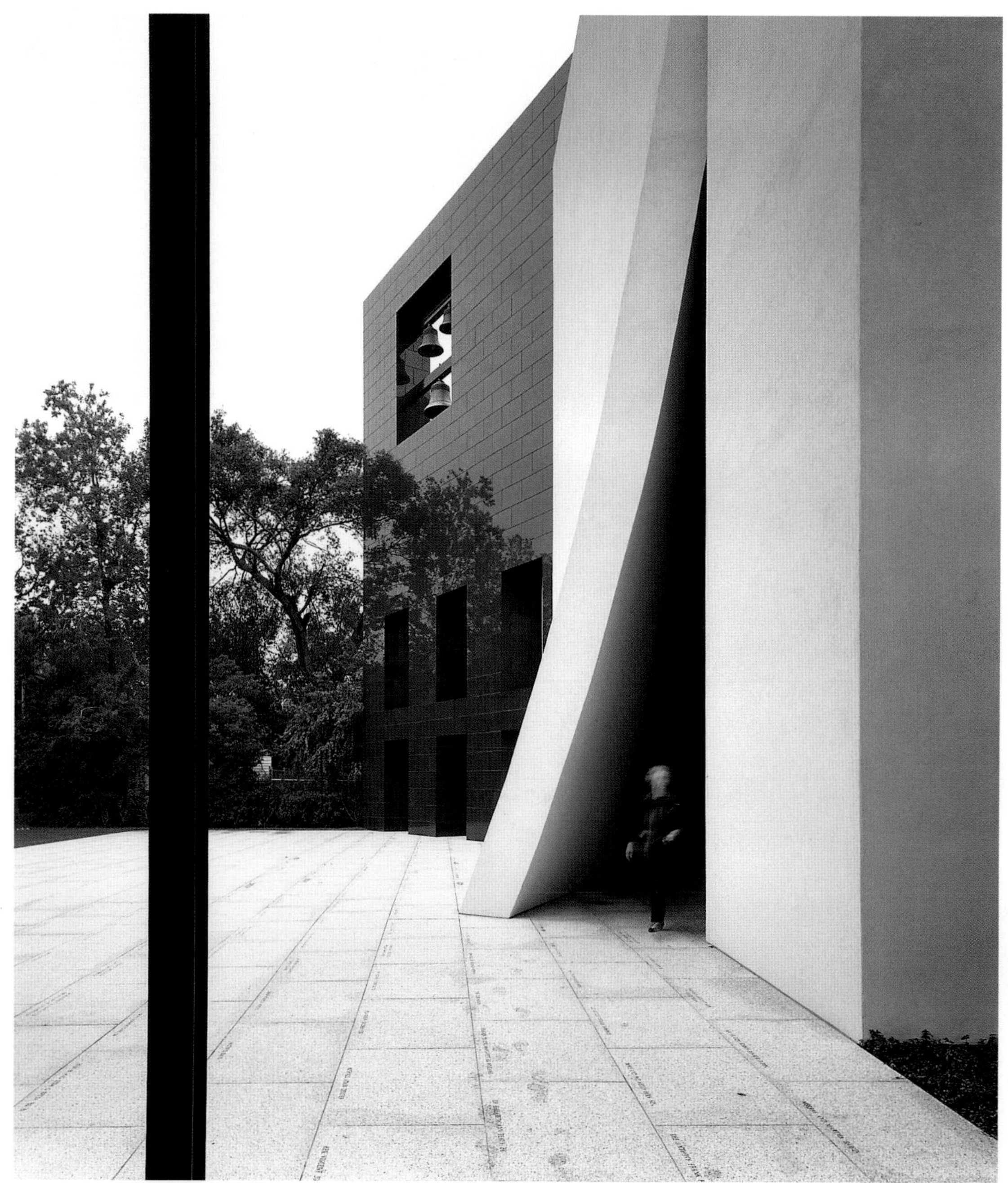

The "tent-flap" entrance.

PHILIP JOHNSON/ALAN RITCHIE, ARCHITECTS; MERRIMAN HOLT, ASSOCIATE ARCHITECTS. PHOTOS BY PAUL HESTER, 1998.

View from mall of the University of St. Thomas.

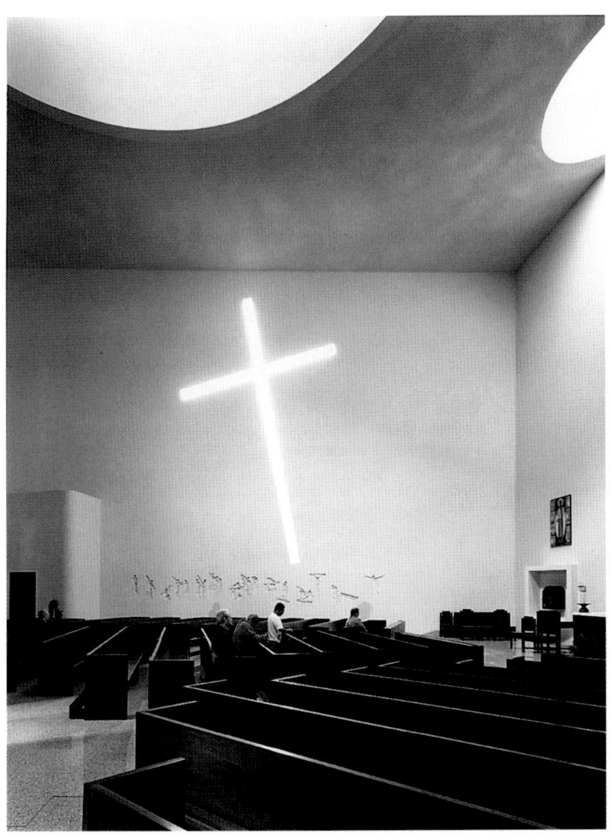

Interior, the west wall, stations of the cross below glazed cross.

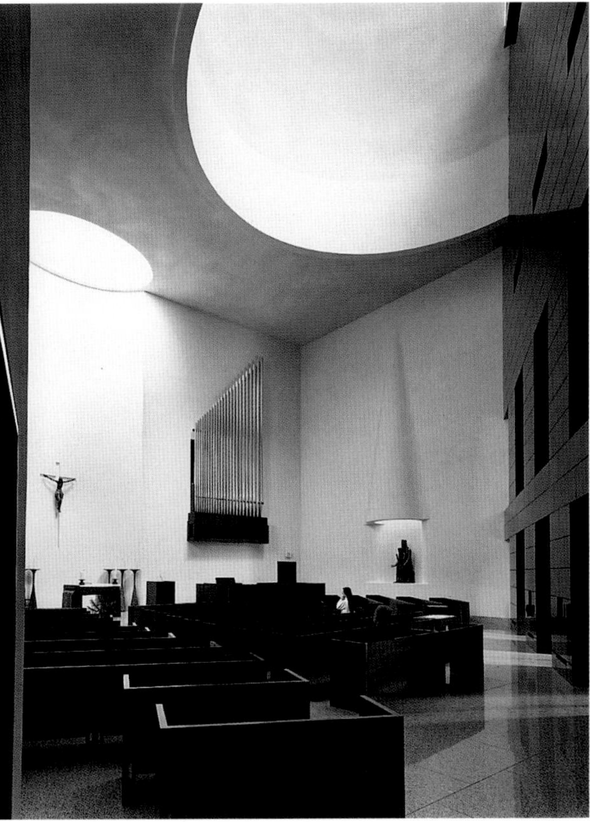

Interior below the dome; altar on the left, narthex wall on right.

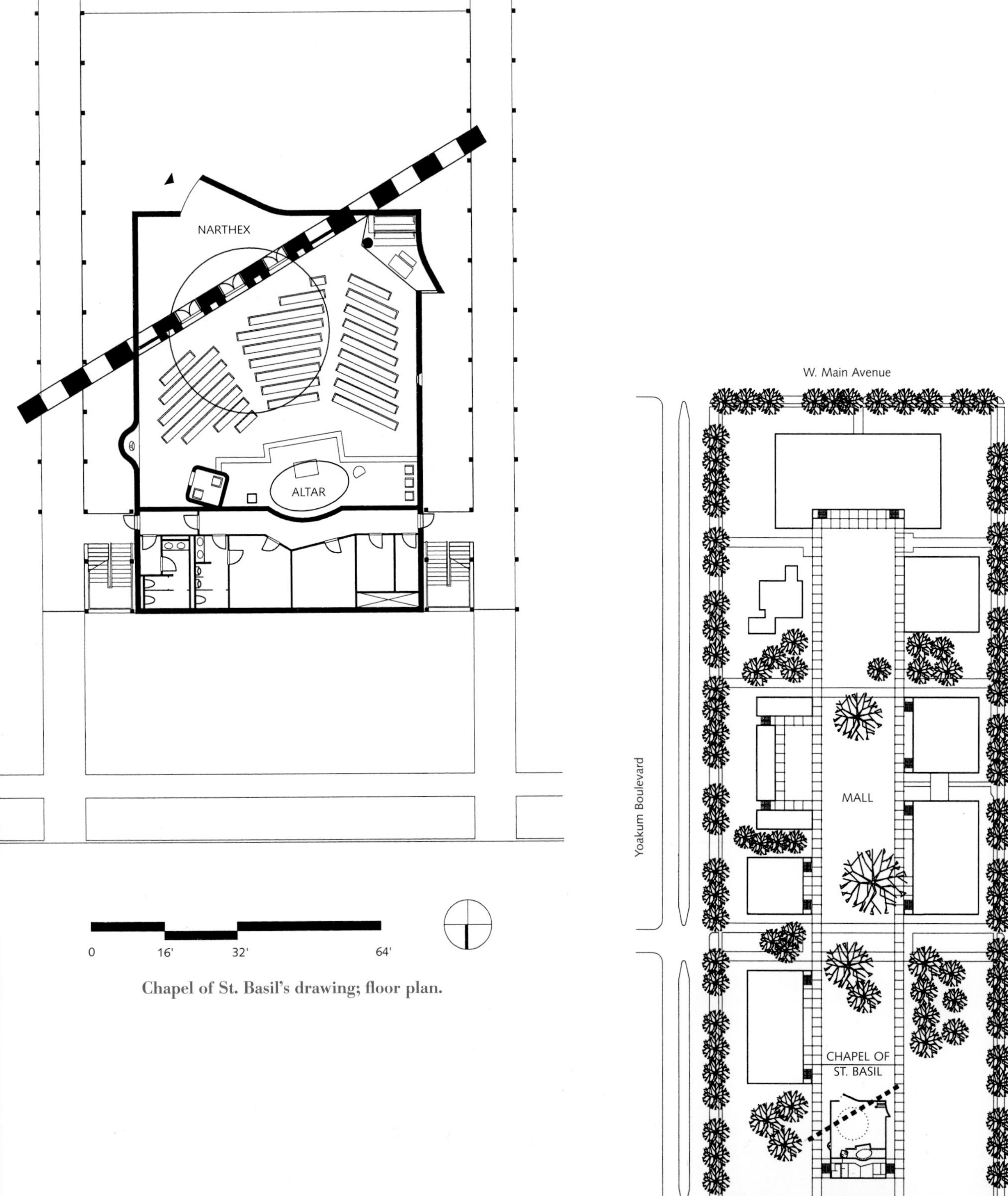

Chapel of St. Basil's drawing; floor plan.

Chapel of St. Basil's drawing; site plan.

rior richly bathed in ambient light from several sources: the clerestories from the split dome, a "faired-incursion" light-well above a niche on the right side holding a bronze, seated Madonna, an elliptical light-well defining the altar wall with an exquisite medieval *corpus*—a gift of Dominique de Menil—and the large asymmetrical cross cut into the west wall and glazed with translucent glass. This cross—a bold move of Johnson's—evokes, in strong, modern terms, Christ's carrying the cross before his crucifixion. Its genesis is a scumbled pencil drawing by Malevich.

All artificial lighting, designed by Claude Engle, is on the *outside* of the building, with concealed fixtures in the light-wells and recessed ground-lights for nighttime perimeter "wall washing." The artworks in the chapel, including the altar table, are by David Cargill and are generally successful, particularly the flesh-toned intaglio stations of the cross in the west wall under the great cross. The altar furnishings, however, are overscaled, especially the large floor candelabra; they visually crowd that limited area, distracting from the serenity of the whole. A stunning set of polished-chrome organ pipes in the upper wall to the right of the altar balances the composition.

Johnson was ill and missed the dedication of the chapel in 1997, but was told that the building was a great success with the public and critics, that music in the space was splendid, and that the university officials were thrilled with the building; he was warmed with that sharp, brief pleasure an architect feels when hearing praise. He had waited a long time for this building, but when it was suggested that *this* chapel is much better than the one he might have designed forty years ago, he retorted, "I'm a better *architect* than I was then!"

When Johnson reached ninety in July of 1996, the New York social, professional, and artistic circles of which he had long been a leading part made quite a to-do over the event, threw parties, large and small, and got out their dictionaries and looked up *nonagenarian.* The Museum of Modern Art honored him with a large party for the membership in late May, and on his birthday, trustee president Agnes Gund and her husband Daniel Shapiro joined David Whitney to give a sit-down dinner party for over two hundred at the museum. (Though Johnson usually ignored birthdays, this would be one he couldn't miss; in July 1986, as hundreds of guests gathered in the rain at The Glass House in honor of his eightieth, Johnson was rushed to a New York hospital to undergo emergency open-heart surgery.)

In the early evening of July 8 the streets of Manhattan's West Fifties near Fifth Avenue were dim and oppressive with heat and humidity; the thick twilight air was umber-colored. On West Fifty-third Street the lighted entrance to the Museum of Modern Art was receiving casually dressed people invited to attend the party for Johnson. As the crowd, dressed comfortably and stylishly in black, grey, and brown, increased in the coldly brilliant lobby, the rain started coming down in sheets, preventing a planned serving of cocktails in Johnson's Sculpture Garden.

The crowd circulated back and forth to the bar past the wall of glass which was a show window for the brightly lighted courtyard, with its trees and bronzes a monumental, glistening, empty object d'art. Its grey-and-white marble floor, lacquered with rain, resembled Holstein hide. Johnson, exhausted from days and nights of being entertained, arrived late in a dark suit and tie, and moved among the guests slowly, murmuring pleasantries.

With the exception of new client Donald Trump, the group was a major serving of the crème de la crème of New York's cultural cognoscenti, the insiders of its creative world, along with out-of-towners like Phyllis Bronfman Lambert from Montreal, Frank Gehry from Los Angeles, and from Europe, Deconstructivists Rem Koolhaas, in black open-collared shirt, and Zaha Hadid, in plum-colored sari. Johnson had been in the center of New York's art and architecture world since before most of the group were born or grown, but the transplanted Midwesterner's enthusiasm for his adopted city and devotion to its seventy-year-old Museum of Modern Art had never lagged. No one scanned the crowd under the glacial light to see who was missing; the sense was that *everyone* was there. The mood was celebratory, but of a restrained, cool kind enjoyed by the culturally hip.

Gucci-shod architect Robert Stern and friendly rival Charles Gwathmey, their eyes alert, circulated smoothly among the guests, and MoMA's most recent architect, rangy Cesar Pelli, accompanied by his handsome clone of a son, leaned over in polite chat. Richard Meier spent his time answering questions about the big Getty project in California. Diminutive Arthur Schlesinger, composed and ramrod straight, stood beside Alexandra, his very tall, pretty wife, dressed in a bright pink outfit which was the evening's startling grace note of color. Writer Cathleen McGuigan remembers the party as "all black and white."

Jasper Johns, joking in a rumpled blue suit, looked more like a small-town druggist than the country's leading artist. Roy Lichtenstein, youthful, with his sleek grey ponytail, joined artists Ellsworth Kelly, Frank Stella, Julian Schnabel, and David Salle, who stood around near the National Gallery's Carter Brown, who conversed with media tycoon Si Newhouse. David Rockefeller was his granddaughter's escort.

Boyish-looking Henry Cobb of Pei Cobb Freed was there, but I. M. Pei was not, nor was Edward Larrabee Barnes. Also missing was Brendan Gill, *New Yorker* critic, town crier for architectural conservation and longtime jousting adversary of Philip's ("We're public enemies and private friends," says Johnson). Peter Eisenman lounged alone against the garden's glass wall as frail Paul Rudolph moved carefully through the crowd. Writers Renata Adler, Susan Sontag, and Calvin Tomkins, along with critics Paul Goldberger and Peter Blake, milled around while *New York Times* architecture critic Herbert Muschamp stood alone on the lobby's mezzanine and studied the increasingly voluble crowd below. Houston's Dominique de Menil, Johnson's first and most influential Texas client, was represented by two of her children, Christophe and Francois, and Cathleen Gallander of Corpus Christi was there with graphic designer Milton Bishop. David Whitney, in a beige double-breasted suit and Western boots, hurried through the crowd looking ill at ease, while Johnson rested on a tall stool, receiving his court of admirers.

The guests wandered back and forth into a gallery where, marking his birthday, there was a large exhibition of works, *From Bauhaus to Pop: Masterworks Given by Philip Johnson,* drawn from the over twelve hundred pieces that Johnson had donated through the years. The multimillion dollar selection filled all the spaces of the temporary exhibition gallery. At eight P.M., the group of 220 guests moved slowly up the escalator in the Pelli-designed glassed-in atrium space to the second floor and into the members' dining room, large and dark and also Pelli-designed; it had been outfitted especially for the evening. Inside the door, guests were greeted with a life-size cutout of the honoree beside a big, flat cake adorned with sugared renderings of The Glass House and Johnson's trademark eyeglasses. As everyone found their seats, the rain stopped and the museum garden sparkled below the room's north wall of glass.

The dining room was a stunning piece of modernist theater: the large grey space shimmered with hundreds of votive candles on the custom-made steel and glass tables which filled the space; table centerpieces were cut-steel, stylized silhouettes of Johnson's major buildings. The seated guests were greeted by MoMA president Glenn Lowry and the Director of Architecture Terence Riley with words of praise and humorous affection for Johnson. During a pause in the encomiums, David Whitney rose to declare, "There is something I want to say about Philip's and my relationship. Even though he is ninety years old, is deaf and has false teeth, he is still *great* in the sack!" The roomful of seasoned sophisticates exploded with shouts and laughter, Johnson enjoying it the most.

A 1961 CBS television interview with Johnson and Louis Kahn was shown—Kahn's seriousness contrasting with Johnson's impertinence. Answering questions about his high-rise laboratories at the University of Pennsylvania, Kahn rationalized at length on the functional roles of the building's prominent and numerous masonry shafts which exhaust dangerous gases, causing Johnson to break in, "I think he put the 'chimneys' on the building because he likes the way they *look;* San Gimignano was rattling around in the back of his mind somewhere!"[6]

Writer-about-town Christopher Mason accompanied himself on a piano and sang a lengthy, rollicking ditty composed for the occasion to the tunes of Beatles' songs. It began,

> Nifty at 90, sharp as a tack,
> No fumbling retiree,
> The whippersnapper Alfred Barr was smart to seize
> Now is M.O.M.A.'s *éminence grise* . . .

and ended,

> He's an energetic and enthusiastic pup,
> A wondrous boy who never grew up;
> The man who brought the Bauhaus
> Right to our house
> Can build a curvy Monsta
> Any time he wants ta'
> HAPPY BIRTHDAY TO YOU![7]

The crowd rose as one and sang a lusty "Happy Birthday"; Johnson kissed the woman next to him and, to the surprise of many, proceeded slowly to the front of the room. The veteran campaigner for The New had not, for a second, lost his belief in the future of art and architecture and couldn't resist the opportunity to exhort once more.

"Hooray for Herodotus!"[8] Johnson declared in a tired, soft rasp.

> At my age the faster you change, the healthier you are. You see how healthy *I* am—all because I work too hard—it's the only way to have *fun!*
>
> The secret of life as an architect is to find a new way of doing architecture—and to do it at my age! We have architecture now that pulls and bends around you—like your body—no right angles, no straight lines.
>
> What is wrong with this room? It doesn't bend around you! Since I've lately discovered the secret of architecture, I can criticize all my friends, but I can't criticize the best architect in the country, who is here tonight! *Never mind!!* Comparisons are odious but they are a lot of fun—I would compare him to Brunelleschi or Wright but I won't mention his name.
>
> We are coming to an age when architecture will fold around you. Where *did* right angles come from? Corbu? I don't know. When I'm 106 I'll retire and

I will let you all come see me. We'll remember what 1996 looked like when we started folding buildings around us instead of vice versa. Thank you very much for your patience! I could talk all night but I think I won't.[9]

Johnson's rambling remarks synthesized his half-century life as critic, architect, and proselytizer for the avant-garde; the Herodotus name-drop recalled his devotion to history, in the scholarly and the architecturally active sense; his lobbying for a new trend in architectural design could be likened to his advocacy of the International Style in the early 1930s; his advancing the career of a current architectural "hero"—in this case, Frank Gehry—was not unlike his sponsorship of Mies in an earlier day; and finally, most importantly, his

Philip Johnson and birthday coterie, the Four Seasons Restaurant, New York City, July 9, 1996. Seated on the floor: Peter Eisenman and Jacquelin Robertson; first row: Michael Graves, Arata Isozaki, Johnson, Phyllis Bronfman Lambert, and Richard Meier; second row: Zaha Hadid, Robert A. M. Stern, Hans Hollein, Stanley Tigerman, Henry Cobb, and Kevin Roche; third row: Charles Gwathmey, Terence Riley, David Childs, Frank Gehry, and Rem Koolhass. Photo by Timothy Greenfield-Sanders.

remarks represented his longtime role as a stand-up friend and devotee of the art of architecture. (On the following evening there was a superselect black-tie gathering of architects, his closest clique of younger, award-winning avant-garde comrades—plus Phyllis Lambert and Terence Riley—at the Four Seasons Restaurant.)[10]

Not long afterward, he was in the hospital for open-heart surgery (his second, after an operation in 1986 on his eightieth birthday) to replace a faulty valve. It would be over a year before he recovered from ensuing complications, nearly dying, then remaining at The Glass House in a semicoma, which he later referred to as his "vacation." New York friends were thinking about eulogies, as it seemed his situation was hopeless, with recurring bouts of pneumonia and no signs of recovery. But when Eli Attia visited the bedridden Johnson, he remembered the steely strength of Johnson's handclasp. The Village Voice reported that he had "retired." David Whitney had the original art removed from the Johnson, Ritchie and Fiore office. Whitney, however, was responsible for saving his life, getting a physical therapist who got Johnson out of bed and put him on a regular regimen of exercise, walking around his estate every day. By the fall of 1997, he had recovered enough to get out of his wheelchair and start making regular visits to New York with the therapist, Maureen Knorr, whose role later evolved into that of personal assistant.

There were those who correctly thought that the boredom of inactivity would have killed him before anything else he could suffer. By year's end, the ninety-one-year-old luminary, who had been given up as lost, was starved to be *involved* again, and to get back in gear in new offices in his old building, the Seagram. (Partner Alan Ritchie was offered the Seagram space when negotiations for lease renewal in the Lipstick Building broke down with the Hines Interests.)

The New Yorker's "Talk of the Town" reported in the fall of 1997 that Philip Johnson was *back,* in new offices in the Seagram Building, and had resumed greeting friends and lunching at his regular banquette, No. 32, in the Four Seasons Restaurant. It was a remarkable piece of public relations, a city icon skewering the premature reports of his imminent demise. He completed work on The Turning Point, a large, five-piece sculpture group—of the carved pear slices genre—for the Case Western Reserve University campus in Cleveland. (Jeannette Dempsey can look down and see her brother's twenty-foot-high Stonehenge group from her apartment window nearby.)

He was soon back at work on the largest project since leaving Burgee, and his sixth religious structure. "I've got a big new church and you won't believe which congregation!" Johnson declared over the phone in 1995.

"Seventh Day Adventists??" ventured his caller.

"No! Worse than that: the largest gay and lesbian church in the world, and it's right there in Dallas. They want 2,500 seats, which is a little smaller than Schuller's Crystal Cathedral. *What will Peter Stewart think?*"[11]

The Reverend Michael Piazza of Dallas has red hair as bright as his face and is a persuasive, articulate speaker. Diminutive in stature but with a forceful, winning self-confidence, he was raised in a small South Georgia town near Savannah in a strict Methodist family and attended seminary at Emory University. He came to Dallas in 1987 from a gay congregation in Florida, not expecting to stay more than five years. His gay and lesbian congregation in Dallas, a member of the nationwide Metropolitan Community Churches, expanded rapidly under him, outgrowing its building in the Cedar Springs part of Oak Lawn, an older residential neighborhood between the downtown district and the affluent Park Cities farther north.

Piazza was frustrated when, needing more space, he tried to buy older church buildings becoming vacant. The owners of desirable buildings were conservative or fundamentalist and wouldn't sell to a gay church. He says that he was further thwarted when he wanted to build a building; most building contractors had ties to the Baptist church and wouldn't negotiate with Piazza. He finally purchased land in foreclosure bounded by commercial property near Love Field, Dallas's busy inner-city air terminal. A contractor from Tyler in East Texas agreed to build a new church, to be called the Cathedral of Hope, and Piazza and others in the congregation designed the eight-hundred-seat church with the help of the contractor and dedicated it in early 1993.

Piazza says:

> By Christmas of 1994, the congregation had increased to such a point and had become so large—with people coming from all over North Texas, requiring three full services every Sunday—that it was clear that we couldn't *grow* in that church and had to do something!
>
> Shortly afterwards, I attended a conference on problems of congregation growth at Dr. Robert Schuller's church in Garden Grove, California, the Crystal Cathedral. There are not many places where I am welcome, but Schuller is open and doesn't care, and I believe my going there for this meeting was a sort of epiphany. Schuller spoke of his architect and his great building as something that embodied Schuller's vision and "captured the imagination," and I began to wonder if this architect who had built a house of glass in earthquake country could do something special for us that would "capture the imagination." Schuller is probably the best-known man in the Western world due to his daily TV in every country; the network plus the building *made* Schuller.
>
> After I walked out of a service where Schuller had been talking about

> Philip Johnson, with things spinning in my head about what we could do with the Cathedral of Hope, a colleague came up to me—he was actually my predecessor in Dallas—and he said, "You know that Philip Johnson is a gay man, don't you?" I didn't know that, I knew he was an architect, but I didn't know he was gay; but that was the final piece to make it all come together, and I returned to Dallas knowing what I had to do.[12]

Johnson's sexuality had been speculated about for years by the public, particularly the architecture profession, and though his close circle knew he was homosexual, he maintained a show of conventional behavior until the reported scolding by Barbara Walters, who told him one night that he should stop the deception and start bringing David Whitney with him to dinner parties, which he did forthwith and never retreated. (As Johnson once said, "*Never look back* is the first principle!")

Kurt Anderson in a 1993 *Vanity Fair* remarked on Johnson's ability to "come back" from adversity, even death's door, describing his busy new *après Burgee* office with his solitary name on the door. But it was also the first story that mentioned his sexual orientation, as well as the political skeletons of the 1930s, which many critics would not let Johnson forget. At the time, David Whitney, a highly regarded curator of contemporary art, had been with him for over thirty years and was in charge of Johnson's art collection, most of which was staying in the underground gallery at The Glass House, under Whitney's supervision, until Johnson's death and the reversion of the entire property to the National Trust.

Michael Piazza returned to Dallas and suggested to his board that they think about a much larger building, even though their new church was only a few years old and still being paid out. They authorized him to write Johnson, but Johnson answered, saying he couldn't do the job, "You might not know it but I'm eighty-nine years old." Piazza felt he hadn't explained enough, so he went to New York to see him in person.

Johnson interrupted a conference and met Piazza for what was to be a ten-minute meeting. "He sat down and said, 'I'm awfully sorry that I wasn't able to do your project but I'm old and church projects tend to take a long time, but tell me about your church,'" Piazza recalled.

> I started telling him, almost nonstop, about the Cathedral of Hope, about why I wanted it to be more than a church and about its importance to history and the difference it will ultimately make in the world. It's so important for it to be a symbol of inclusion and that our intent was nothing less than changing the way the world feels about lesbian and gay people and the way that lesbian and gay people feel about each other and to begin to reclaim Christianity from

> some of the fundamentalists. Thirty minutes later he said, "How can I *not* do this?" and surprised, I said, "Are you saying *yes?* Are you telling me you will do this project?" and he said, "Oh yes, we will do it. How do we get started?" I told him I would like to announce his selection as architect at the church's twenty-fifth anniversary service in July and would like for him to be there. He stepped outside the room and canceled a conflicting July trip to Alaska.[13]

The anniversary service, which attracted the entire Cathedral of Hope membership, was held in Dallas's preeminent building for large gatherings, the Meyerson Symphony Center, by I. M. Pei, recently completed in 1989. (Johnson had been interviewed for the building but was passed over.) Piazza kept secret from everyone his plan to introduce Johnson, recounting the way the church's new architect was selected; first his refusal to do the job, then, after hearing Piazza out, his enthusiastic agreement. Then Piazza said, "And now I would like to introduce our new architect, Philip Johnson, and his partner of thirty-five years, David Whitney."[14] The huge, richly detailed hall erupted with a roaring, standing ovation as Johnson stood in the loge level beside Whitney and waved to the cheering crowd in the orchestra below and the balconies above. It was a stunning, formal "outing" for the world-famous architect, approaching his ninetieth birthday and publicly at peace with his nature.

Back in New York, the designing of a church to seat 2,500 began, went through several phases, and lasted for three years. Johnson made many sketches for John Manley to implement with scaled drawings. The first design, while free in form and similar in spirit to Johnson's Visitors Center, but vastly scaled up, featured a fan-shaped seating plan and, sprawling in the "wanton mode," was dubbed "the frog." No one liked it, including Piazza. The second one was a rectilinear shape, resembling Washington's Kennedy Center, with a colonnade-supported roof and an interior of closely spaced "columns" suspended from the ceiling above eye level. It was striking in concept but also rejected. The third scheme was another free-form concrete structure, divided by an entry, and was also abandoned; the final scheme was a simplification, but also a sculpturally intensified version, of the third and the one everyone settled on. It was compared to an ark, an iceberg, and the Rock of Gibraltar.

The Cathedral of Hope is a massively modeled form of shelter and grandeur rising from a low point at the entry to 117 feet at the prowlike upper part of the sanctuary above the altar. The shape follows roughly the restricting descending flight path to the airport to the west. The concrete walls are folded and heavily pleated in a highly abstract way, the pleats forming "buttresses" reminiscent of the supporting walls of early New Mexico adobe churches. A tall, broad bell-tower screen, attached to a rambling covered cloister joined to the church, abuts and mitigates somewhat the remodeled existing church. A small biomorphic chapel attaches to one side of the sanctuary's lobby like an aneurysm. The weaving and waving interior walls, without right angles or parallel lines, ascend to the 100-foot-high altar wall below the great space's skylight, concealed behind a floating ceiling. As monumental worship spaces go, it is the formal converse to the transparent Crystal Cathedral: one billowing and opaque, the other tautly transparent. Dr. Schuller's church possesses rigorous geometry; the Dallas building is an expressionist sculpture, simultaneously exuberant and somber. The nearly windowless space envelops and protects as it liberates and soars.

At a ground-breaking in 1998 for the bell-tower wall, when the congre-

Model, the Cathedral of Hope, Dallas, 1998; Philip Johnson/Alan Ritchie, architects.
(*top*) Photo by Michael Rogol. (*bottom*) Photo by Carol Bates.

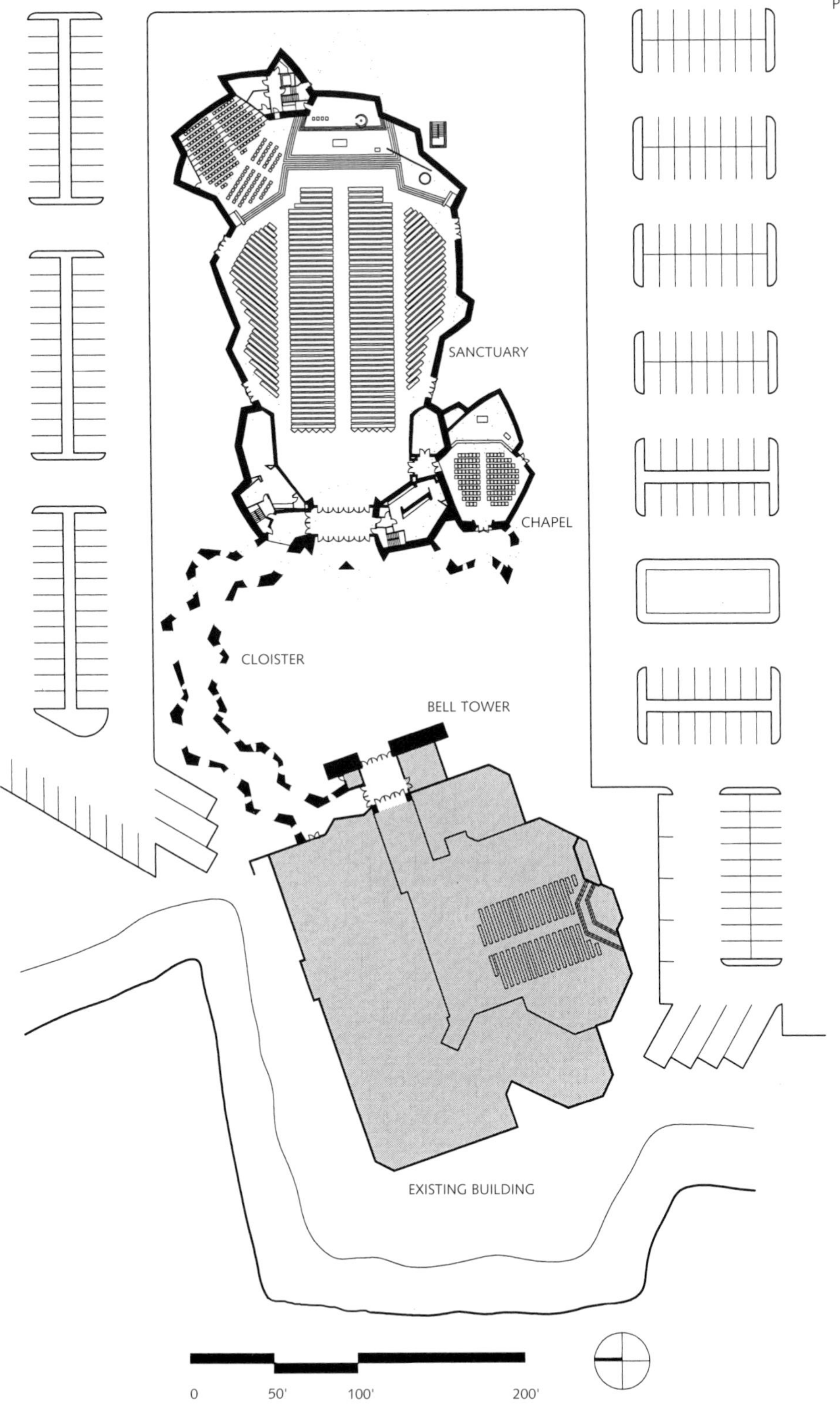

The Cathedral of Hope drawing; floor plan.

gation had $6 million pledged of the $22 million required for construction, Johnson, ninety-two, was quoted, "I keep telling them to hurry up! Twenty million dollars for a building like this is not expensive. Once people see it going up they'll rush in to help complete it. But they want a few more dimes in the box first.

"I'm doing real architecture again," he goes on. "No more kicking around bits of history. No more skyscrapers. Churches and synagogues are the only buildings worth doing, unless of course I'm doing something for myself."[15]

Many of Johnson's patrons, colleagues, friends, and friendly foes died during the 1990s. Lincoln Kirstein, his longtime friend and patron since Harvard, died in 1994; Paul Rudolph and Brendan Gill and Isaiah Berlin died in 1997. Berlin, a celebrated philosopher and lecturer at Oxford University, spent a lot of time in the United States (he was Churchill's liaison with Roosevelt during World War II) and enjoyed a social friendship with Johnson, who says, "We would see each other at a dinner party and spend the entire evening with our heads together, to the despair of the hostess. We didn't agree on politics, but that didn't matter; we just ignored that part, there was too much else to talk about."[16] Berlin's theories of the value of pluralism in our society were the philosophical equivalent of Johnson's longtime advocacy of the value of history and of multiple sources for postmodern, contemporary architecture. Berlin divided people into Foxes and Hedgehogs—the former holding many ideas, the latter having only one big idea—and said a healthy society was multifaceted in character.

Jeffrey Kipnis, a young teacher of design theory at Ohio State University, coedited *The Glass House* with David Whitney and describes his relationship with Johnson as more personal than intellectual. He says, "I originally thought that Philip Johnson was the incarnation of evil in architecture, taking ideas of great works by great architects—which were achieved at great struggle—and packaging and selling them to corporate clients. He did that, of course, but there is a lot more to him than that!" Kipnis chuckles when he muses:

> He has always known exactly what he was doing and wasn't doing; I ultimately came to understand and greatly appreciate the *depth* of his "superficiality."
>
> In my early thirties, Peter Eisenman brought me into Johnson's circle somewhat against my will, I guess, and when I met him the first time I tried to show him how smart I was and started talking about Nietzsche, which was a mistake; he just blew me out of the water! I was definitely off on the wrong foot. I didn't help matters when I later offered the opinion that he was actually not an architect, but an intellectual who uses his intellectual power to master the problem of architecture; it hurt his feelings. But we eventually became close

> friends and together gave a number of lectures together with slides, both here and abroad, a sort of Martin & Lewis thing, that dealt with historic influences in his buildings, how he *lifts* other people's work. It was all full of good humor.
>
> There is one thing, however, about Philip that is consistent and *his*. That is his generosity. Once—it was his ninetieth birthday—we were walking back from the office to his apartment and I was racing to keep up with him—he walks so fast—and I heard "Mr. Johnson, Mr. Johnson!" behind us and I looked back and it was Tommy Lee Jones about a block away, trying to catch up. Philip said, "Oh God! Who's he?" and I said it was Tommy Lee Jones, the Texas movie star, Academy Award winner, and I listed some of his credits; here's a guy I'm dying to meet, right? When Jones caught up, he says, "Are you Mr. Johnson?" and Philip says, "Yes, I'm Philip Johnson" and Jones says, "Hi, I'm Tommy Lee Jones" and Philip says, "Oh, don't introduce yourself, of course I know you and know your work perfectly *well!*" It was quintessential Johnson.[17]

In January 1998, Johnson and David Whitney flew to Houston for Dominique de Menil's funeral. She died on New Year's Eve at eighty-nine and left a great void in the cultural and human rights life of the city she and her husband John had served so brilliantly for half a century. (Shortly before, Dominique de Menil had attended the dedication of her last addition to the Menil Collection neighborhood, the Byzantine Fresco Museum. Francois de Menil, son and architect, designed a cubistic concrete and stone and steel repository for some twelfth-century frescoes that his mother had ransomed and restored.)

Her longtime friend, the writer Marguerite Barnes, wrote, "They [Dominique and John] were an incredible team. Over the years they had a profound influence on Houston in the arts, in education, in race relations and in international status. They demanded of Houston new and higher expectations of itself—and they got them."[18] At the Menil house, before the funeral, Johnson uneasily visited the bedroom where Dominique de Menil lay beneath a cashmere spread. "I usually don't like those sorts of things but I owe my career to her," he said afterward, and, referring to the Max Ernst painting hanging above the bed, he added, "She was under a moon." Nearby was a burning candle and a single rose. "Very Dominique," mused Johnson.

"She knew how to live in a house, and what to put with those amazing Charles James sofas," Johnson continued, with a mellowness acquired over the years. "She didn't change a thing for fifty years. It's like Balenciaga in there. She knew she had something perfect."[19]

The crowded funeral service at St. Anne's Catholic Church was attended by a cross section of mourners, from Houston's first black mayor to the wealthy art patrons and the artists and friends and museum staff members that had supported Dominique and John de Menil since the late 1940s. Music for the service included a Sufi sitar instrumental, Bach preludes, Gregorian chants, and Fauré and Mozart arias sung by a granddaughter, Victoria de Menil. The fragrant, newly milled plain pine coffin was borne by six Menil grandsons. A quotation from Dominique de Menil headed the Order of Service for the mass: "Everything I've learned, I've learned from love."

After Dominique de Menil's death, Louisa Stude Sarofim, a longtime benefactor of the arts in Houston, was elected president of the Menil Foundation board. A debate among the board members ensued on what to do with the fifty-year-old Menil house, the commission that brought Philip Johnson to Texas. There were those on the Menil board that wanted to raze the house and sell the property. Most, however, wanted to restore and keep the house, with its art, books, and furnishings, to form a prize possession of the Menil Collection.

Philip Johnson at the Menil house for a fund-raiser in February 1999. Photo by Paul Hester.

The arts community of Houston and Texas became involved, imploring the Menil board members to keep the house for what it represented in the cultural history of Houston. The board decided to keep the house, and in early 1999, Johnson returned to Houston for a small fund-raising party at the house on San Felipe and spoke on behalf of keeping Dominique and John de Menil's home as a museum and center for art study. Later, an initiative to restore the house, with its possessions intact, was established and led by Raymond Brochstein and William Stern, who signed on to coordinate the effort.

Stern said, at the fund-raising event, "It was a really bold move of Mr. and Mrs. de Menil to hire Philip Johnson, a well-known historian and critic, but just starting his architectural career, to design this house for their family. And I think it set a tone for a whole generation of young architects including Howard Barnstone, Burdette Keeland, Hugo Neuhaus, and Andy Todd, who built wonderful structures and influenced others and set the spirit of architecture in Houston in the 1950s and '60s."[20]

Johnson, "reborn" once again, amazed his friends. One of them compared him to the Frankenstein monster who "kept getting *up.*" He traveled, he lectured, he designed buildings with much of the same zip he had before his near death in 1997. In the spring of 1999, his old friend and protégé Robert Stern, a highly successful architect of large, eclectically styled houses (several in Texas), was dean of Yale's College of Architecture and invited him up to be a visiting critic. (Peter Eisenman served as Johnson's teaching assistant!)

Stern first met Johnson at Yale in the early 1960s when he was a graduate

The Glass House drawing; site plan, 1995.

student and Johnson was a regular visitor. Stern and other students, along with artists from New York, were often invited to New Canaan for informal Sunday afternoon get-togethers at The Glass House. Stern recalls:

> For a wet-behind-the-ears student, it was pretty heady stuff. To me, the thing that was amazing was the relationship of The Glass House, the pool, the Guest House, with its transformed interior, and the lawn sculpture, which he always had in those days. It was all very glamorous and in the modern vocabulary, but Philip was already beginning to rail against modernism, something that had such an influence on me. Soon he built the little half-scale pavilion on the pond, which was the real break with Miesian modernism.
>
> Philip is criticized for being inconsistent, but you have to take all that with a grain of salt. He's always been this wandering, wavering eclectic with an eye for the unusual. While he was at Yale recently, he had this unnerving way of always going for the student scheme that was intriguing, even if it wasn't worked out very well. Philip praised one in particular, though it would never be a building, not in a million years would it be a building! But Philip said it was "art" and tucked the model under his arm and made his exit.[21]

David Fiore left the partnership to go into real estate, and Johnson's only partner in the mid-1990s was Alan Ritchie. Johnson's deep-dyed genetic energy kicked in after the long illness, and the will to live and work returned. The church in Dallas had a summertime 1998 ground-breaking for its bell tower; there was a brief collaboration with Frank Gehry on a "billion dollar" casino for developer Steve Wynn; and a proposal for yet another Johnson design for New York's Times Square appeared in *The New York Times* under the headline "Philip Johnson Geometry in an Advertising Wrapper." The proposed buildings would not simply hold billboards, their facades would *be* billboards. The owners of the Chrysler Building planned an addition to the landmark building to the east across Third Avenue and hired Johnson and Ritchie for the job.

In 1997 the Museum of Modern Art held an invited competition[22] for its newest expansion program—enlarging gallery space from 86,000 sq. ft. to 133,000 sq. ft.—and selected the Japanese modernist Yoshio Taniguchi's design, whose crisply refined scheme includes rebuilding and restoring Johnson's Sculpture Garden to its original proportions and making it central to the museum's reconfigured ground floor spaces. "What's great about this expansion plan, nobody can explain," Johnson declared approvingly. "You will walk in and be smitten by art."[23]

The Glass House compound in its rolling park in New Canaan, Connecticut, remains his most revealing testament and enduring legacy, the quiet

Philip Johnson approaching The Glass House. Photo by Paul Hester, 1994.

place away from the city where, since 1949, his protean memory and imagination were channeled into ideas for building designs on thin pieces of paper. The place has changed in its composition from the time when it was just five acres and only held the two original residence buildings. It is now forty acres, with eight varied structures, the result of his constant reshaping of the natural and man-made landscape structure to suit his eye. In the late fall of 1998, he pridefully calls attention to the far hillside on the west, where he recently cleared acres of underbrush to reveal the march of trees down the slope, their trunks and fallen amber leaves backlighted in the winterish afternoon. Outside the opposite glass wall, against the old stone wall nearby, sits a striking little doghouse with sweeping lines that Johnson designed for David's new dogs, James and Alice. It is also a maquette for a future family cenotaph that Gerald Hines's wife, Barbara, has requested.

Doghouse at The Glass House, 1998. Photo by the author.

Johnson's estate is located several miles from the village of New Canaan, reached by winding wooded roads where traditional houses stand on large plots of land, interspersed with the occasional modern house by Eliot Noyes. Ponus Ridge Road runs north-south at the top, easternmost edge of the sloping Glass House property, which is defined at the road with a colonial-era stacked stone wall indigenous to this part of New England. An Art Deco–style gate in the stone wall frames a stand of pines to the left, behind which stands the new, colorful Visitors Center.

The driveway curves diagonally down, past more pines, to a parking area

Philip Johnson at the dining table, The Glass House, 1994. Photo by Paul Hester.

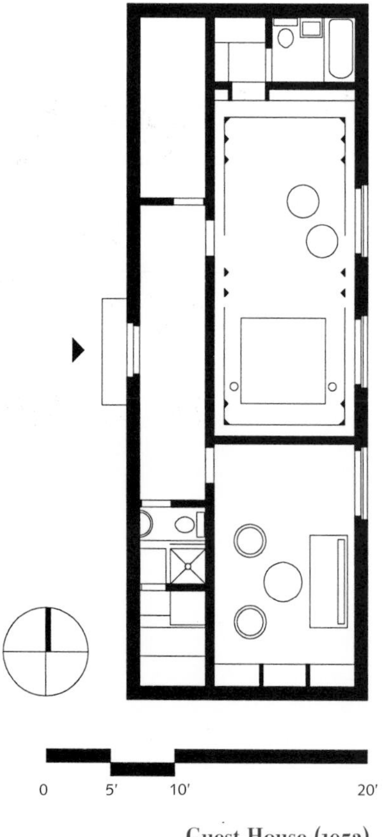

Guest House (1953)

next to a taller, freestanding stone wall, which partially conceals The Glass House. To the right is the rigorous, windowless block of reddish brick—shoebox in proportion—which is the Guest House. Its interiors are the only altered parts of any of Johnson's buildings; the bedroom was remodeled in 1953 with an added inner shell of a low-vaulted ceiling—inspired by the English Romantic Classicism of Charles Dance the Younger and Sir John Soane—on a peristyle of paired slender columns. The indirect lighting and pale Fortuny fabric covering the walls and the large round windows facing uphill create a sensuous ambience. A little farther north and to the left past the stone wall is The Glass House itself, reached from the parking area by a diagonal, crushed-granite path, a longer version of the shorter one which leads to the Guest House.

There is the shock of the familiar when one first comes upon the transparent residence. It's like seeing a celebrity in the flesh for the first time. There is an orientation problem: the image derived from two-dimensional media is wrenched in the exertion to take it in as a real thing. ("It's smaller than I thought"; or "She's taller than I thought.") The Glass House from a distance looks quite vulnerable, fragile, like it had been scooted in on skids, but as you approach it the gravity and formal strength of the building take over and dominate its setting. Anne Cleaver Grabowski was a Dallas teenager when she saw it in the 1970s, and describes the experience as stunningly serene and spiritual. It is so emphatically *there,* this icon, mutating inimitably as the reflections in its walls shift, overlap, and sparkle in the black steel framework. "I have the most wonderful wallpaper in the world!" its owner says.

There is a sweet irony to the fact that for an apostle of change, barely any change has been allowed in the interior layout. The cylindrical brick fireplace smoked at first, so Johnson added a piece of curved glass, and the original floor candelabra is gone, but the papier-mâché maquette of Elie Nadelman's coupled figures stands where it always stood on the dark, polished herringbone brick floor. All the Mies furniture and the rug are located as they were in the beginning, and the Poussin on the vertical steel easel is in its same place. "Alfred Barr was crazy about that picture and made me buy it for the house in Cambridge. Four thousand dollars, can you believe it?" Johnson reminisces.

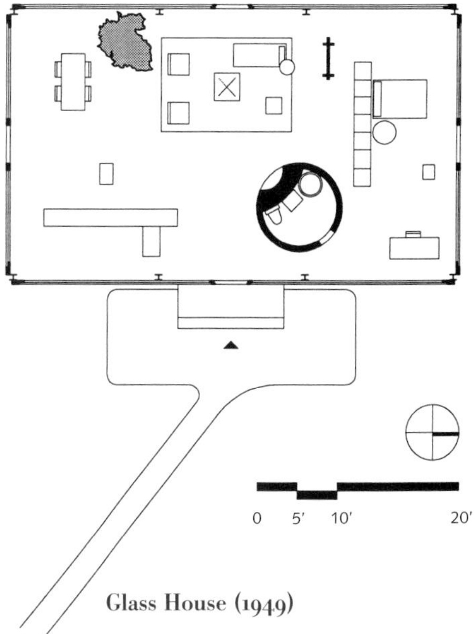

Glass House (1949)

> There are four of them, the same image, and some people say mine is not a Poussin, but at least one expert says mine is the best one; the Louvre of course thinks theirs is the authentic one. But I love it even though the sun has ruined it; I just have it repainted every ten years or so.
>
> Why do I have a painting like this in this modern house? Well, I've never gotten over my classicism. After all, look at the plan of this house. The house is absolutely symmetrical, with a door centered in each of the four sides; the interior cylinder of brick, holding the fireplace and a bath, and the storage casework for the bedroom and the kitchen are treated like pieces of furniture, and their composition is asymmetrical within the symmetrically scored vitrine on its brick base.[24]

From the low granite railing of the promontory that surrounds The Glass House one looks down to the left to a small man-made pond, on which there floats a pale decorative "barge," The Pavilion. It was Johnson's personal experiment with a modernism that was not the "new reality" of the master Mies, but a more fluid, decorative kind of modernism which Oscar Niemeyer was employing in his buildings in the fifties. The inside curve emphatically entered the modernist vocabulary in the sixties, Johnson having toyed with it in his Guest House alteration a decade earlier. The Pavilion has ranges of moulded, toed arches, three feet on center, in compound curves that evoke monumentality, but in reality are wittily downscaled. The plan of the structure is four rectangular peristyles fitted together in a pinwheel fashion, with integral fountains and ceilings of gold leaf. In the sixties, Johnson entertained there with luncheons served by staff; guests would sip and nibble while seated on large cushions, "trailing their fingers in the water and looking at the goldfish," according to Johnson. To the south, up the steep hill from the pond, is the thirty-foot-tall cubist totem of concrete blocks built as a tribute to Lincoln Kirstein in

Pavilion on Pond (1962), with Sculpture Gallery (1970) and Glass House (1949) in background, New Canaan, Connecticut; Philip Johnson, architect.
Photo by Paul Hester, 1994.

1985 and suggestive of a 1921 mahogany sculpture by Georges Vantongerloo in the collection of the Museum of Modern Art. From the Kirstein Tower, which Johnson loved climbing, one can see all the buildings on the forty acres.

At the far north is the white, glass-roofed 1970 Sculpture Gallery, rooted in the slope like a broken yacht washed ashore. One approaches the angular and rather puzzling building on a path lined with trees which traverses Johnson's "dangerous" footbridge, pliant and without railings. Outside the white painted brick gallery, at one side of the path, is a huge bronze log by Julian Schnabel, a giant's hitching rail, pointed to the door. On sunny days, the kinetic interior of the Sculpture Gallery is a visual jolt. It is stunning, with striated light patterns, cast through the roof's "rafters" of tubular steel, which crawl across the angled white walls and the turning, descending floor levels of brown brick in layers of shifting chevrons and fields of parallel lines. Walking up and down the steps, winding to five different levels of sculpture, reminds Peter Blake "of nothing so much as the experience of walking through those beautiful white-walled Mediterranean villages, on Greek islands or on the coasts of Italy and Spain."[25] The building's strict but twisted geometry reflects Johnson's search for forms; it also reflects certain art of the time, particularly the collages of Frank Stella, and predates an architecture of movement exemplified by Fort Worth's Water Garden of 1975. Nearer to The Glass House is an earlier, more internalized structure, Johnson's Painting Gallery.

Nicknamed the *Kunstbunker,* the Painting Gallery, completed in 1965, was the first enclosed structure built after The Glass House and maybe the most radical of all of Johnson's archive of personal structures. It is an underground building built by excavating the hill below the Ponus Ridge wall for the construction, then backfilling and covering the concrete building with earth except for three low, round vestigial roof parapets. One enters the pristine grotto of concentric volumes of differing diameters through a splayed red granite "culvert" and a low linear lobby. Johnson hinged great carpet-covered panels to columns centered in each of the circular, tangent volumes and let them rotate on casters and ceiling tracks, displaying and storing the paintings flexibly, like horizontal Rolodexes. Years before, he had seen Sir John Soane's fanciful house and museum in London where the great eighteenth-century architect had displayed his painting collection in a similar, smaller-scaled way, like leaves in an album.

Interior, Sculpture Gallery (upper level: *Prismatic Flake #4*, Michael Heizer, 1990; lower level: three untitled sculptures, Robert Morris, 1965–1970; lower level wall: *Neon Templates of the Left Half of My Body Taken at Ten-Inch Intervals*, Bruce Nauman, 1966; right foreground: *Raft of the Medusa*, Frank Stella, 1990), New Canaan, Connecticut, 1970; Philip Johnson, architect. Photo by Paul Hester, 1994.

Painting Gallery (1965)

Entrance and interior, Painting Gallery (two untitled paintings, Julian Schnabel, 1989 [left], 1992 [right]), New Canaan, Connecticut, 1965; Philip Johnson, architect.
Photos by Paul Hester, 1994.

Johnson likes to compare the Painting Gallery to the Tomb of Atreus in Mycenae, but the contrast and counterpoint to his transparent dwelling is more noteworthy. The gallery is an escape from nature in the way that The Glass House is an embrace of it and illustrates Johnson's inveterate way of questioning the conventional wisdom. Is natural light necessary to appreciate art? Must galleries be square? Does a building need to be visible? There is wit and some kinetic magic—and stagecraft—to seeing the great panels rotate to reveal Warhol, Rauschenberg, Johns, Salle, and Schnabel. *Let me entertain you.*

Walking back to The Glass House, passing over the springy low-vaulted bridge, past the round swimming pool, one sees in the distance the "white object in space" that is Johnson's refuge, his tiny Study, built in 1980. (Above it, on a hill, in the trees, one can barely make out the grey cubist Kirstein totem.) Located on a sloping, grassy meadow without benefit of a path, the Study is assertive as a formal hybrid of the square and the round. A square chimney plays off a tall conical form; it holds a skylight above the work table where Johnson does his weekend sketching, with a view of a corner fireplace and, through the window on the west, the gabled, bifurcated cage of chain-link mesh named the Gehry Ghost House—put up for the protected growing of lilies. The Study's walls are lined with well-thumbed books on architec-

Gehry Ghost House, New Canaan, Connecticut, 1984; Philip Johnson, architect. Photo by Paul Hester, 1994.

Exterior, Study, New Canaan, Connecticut, 1980; Gehry Ghost House, 1985, to the right. Philip Johnson, architect. Photo by Paul Hester, 1994.

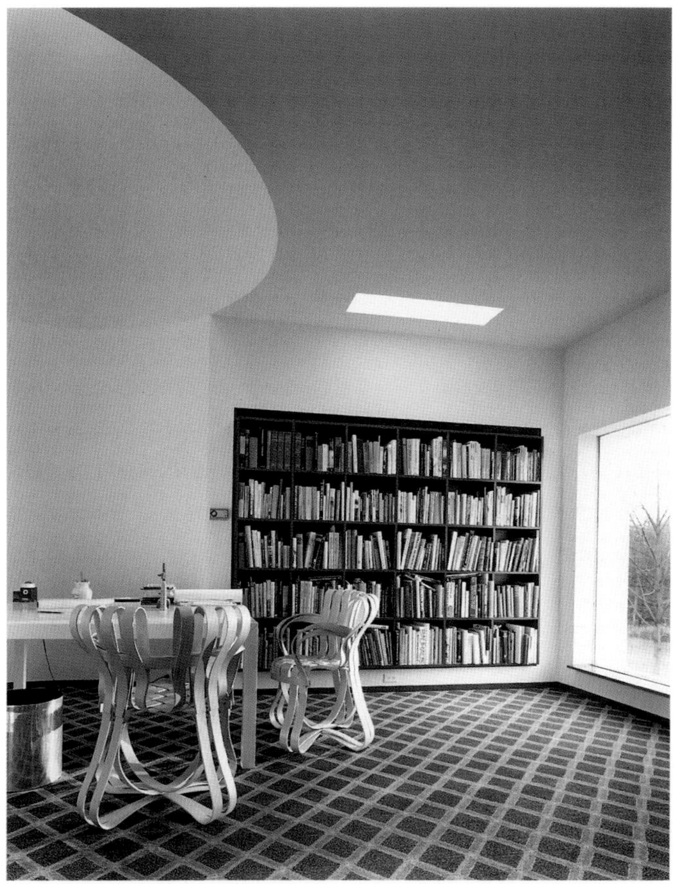

Interior, Study. Photo by Paul Hester, 1994.

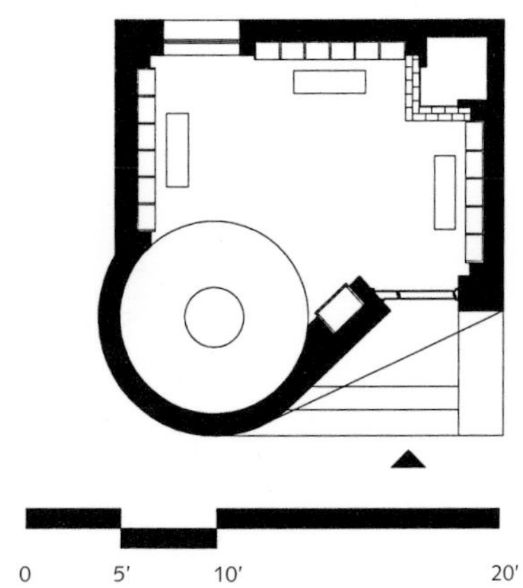

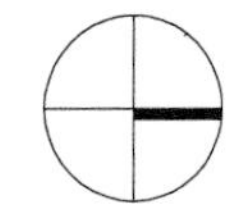

Library Study (1980)

ture—its histories and its artists—with the dust covers torn and peeling. The kitschy, patterned carpet is the same one once used in the Four Seasons Restaurant. There is no bathroom.

Johnson sits at the square white table beneath the skylit cone—a small version of what he wanted for the Rothko Chapel—with a neat arrangement of Black Warrior pencils, architect scales, and rolls of yellow tracing paper. He is designing one more structure for The Glass House: a grottolike chapel for a steep hill below his house. (It was not built.)

What makes a person, in his tenth decade, continue the pursuit of architecture with the verve and enthusiasm of a thirty-year-old? It *is* a pursuit, and with Johnson it is also as much a chase away from the boredom of the ordinary as it is a vindication of his existence. The intelligent energy and boyish enthusiasm, and yes, the charming, self-mocking manner, that the Texans saw and bought, beginning in the 1940s, is still with him, and it transcends his advanced age. He was responsible for over twenty projects for Texans, not including the ten big out-of-state office buildings Johnson/Burgee did for Gerald Hines.[26] Some of his most distinguished projects, certainly more large ones, emanated from relationships with Texas clients, but in assessing his Texas career, those have to be included with the forgettable efforts. Yet on how many occasions during his Texas career have Philip Johnson buildings "made" the institutions for which they were built?

The body has slowed but not the mind. "I will never retire," he says, "I would *die* without a project." Why does he continue? "Why make art?" asks the New York artist Chuck Close. "Because I think there's a child's voice in every artist: 'I am here. I am somebody. I made this. Won't you look?' The first painting ever was by some artist at Lascaux or Altamira or wherever, who put his hand on the wall and then blew soot through a straw around his hand. What is it about people that, since the dawn of time, we've wanted to mark our presence so that other people will see it?"[27]

Lincoln Kirstein Tower, New Canaan, Connecticut, 1985; Philip Johnson, architect. Photo by Paul Hester, 1994.

Mahogany sculpture, *Construction of Volume Relations*, Georges Vantongerloo, 1921. © 2000 the Museum of Modern Art, New York.

In the summer of 1998, the MoMA director received a call from Johnson during which the longtime MoMA trustee and benefactor casually mentioned that he wanted to give the museum nine paintings, but when Lowry asked which works Johnson was giving, Johnson said he preferred to keep that a surprise. When the paintings arrived there was general astonishment at the museum. Here were nine major works by five of America's ranking artists: Willem de Kooning, Philip Guston, Jasper Johns, James Rosenquist, and Andy Warhol. Their value: $19,000,000. Commenting on the gift, which perhaps represents a coda to the over twelve hundred works he has already given, Johnson said, "It isn't fair to the artists to keep these paintings at my home in the country. They are too important and should be at the Museum of Modern Art where the public can share them."[28]

Alan Ritchie, Philip Johnson, and Maureen Knorr following a lecture at the Dallas Museum of Art, November 1998. Photo by Nan Coulter.

Philip Johnson does not fit easily into a pantheon of twentieth-century master architects, and he repeatedly denies his inclusion. His rank is elusive, and he is enigmatic, not very helpful in serious self-analysis; architectural theorizing bores him and makes him uneasy. It is the *building,* its appearance and mise-en-scène, that interests him, not the analysis of its psyche. Johnson is, first and last, a visualist whose creative life has been marked repeatedly by what he has *seen.* His complete works of architecture constitute a narrative of the half-century's passing parade of design modes. In the age of pluralism Johnson is the champion architectural pluralist. One architectural writer, however, after interviewing him in 1993 about his career, came away expressing shock at his "non-ruminative lack of philosophic grounding." In 1991 he told critic Ann Holmes, "I'm a chameleon, so changeable. I see myself as a gadfly and a questioner. *And* I built some buildings. But I think I will be best known, finally, for my teaching, my influence."[29]

While he has seemingly been in repeated reinvention since he discovered modern architecture in his early twenties, his basic love of the Classical and monumental has never left him, though that love was expressed in the various ways of the moment. From the absolutism embodied by his art and politics in the 1930s, he matured into a more inclusive, liberal pluralist recognizing the many mansions in the realm of culture. He became a champion of variety and shifts in art. As he took up other forms of modernism and what followed it, his celebrity increased as his critics grew in number. Proclaiming, in the words of Heraclitus, that change is the only constant in life, he cleverly slipped and slid through the ebbing and flowing tides of the architectural thought of the last fifty years. As well known for exceptional buildings as for spontaneous, extravagant opinions, his structures and statements were given equal time; the press made him the number-one architectural celebrity of the media age.

Model, Texas A&M University College of Architecture Expansion, 1999; Philip Johnson/Alan Ritchie, architects. Photos by Paul Hester.

He was called back to Texas once again in 1998; he was ninety-two. John H. Lindsey, a successful Houston businessman and ardent alumnus of the 45,000-student Texas A&M University, was a longtime fan of Philip Johnson buildings and was determined to get one on his school's College Station campus. As a member of the Board of Regents Lindsey had influence and invited Johnson down to discuss several upcoming building projects. Johnson chose the plan for expanding the College of Architecture as the job that he wanted to do.

The 75,000-sq.-ft. expansion program was to house classrooms, offices, and a 400-seat auditorium on a tight site between existing buildings. In February Johnson and Alan Ritchie made a presentation to the president of the university and others at a much-anticipated meeting. Johnson thought he heard the president, Dr. Ray Bowen , mutter softly, "This is a boring campus." Johnson jumped at that: "Oh no, it is *not* boring! Sure, there is no consistent style to the buildings; they are all different, yet they are all the same. But that's not boring! That's wonderful! It forms the perfect setting for something fresh and new, heralding the future!"

The Johnson/Ritchie scheme was a stunner. A wedge-shaped tower with a sloped top, positioned like a piece of cheese resting on its widest end, slices the space between two existing buildings and is tethered to the main building by a swooping roof of metal and glass, creating a covered plaza below. The proposal would unite three disparate parts of the college and was received with enthusiasm by President Bowen. There were immediate concerns about the cost, however. In late 1999, the school had not moved ahead with Johnson/Ritchie to develop what would be a landmark building for the large collection of generic tan-brick structures that constitute the A&M campus.

Dilettante,[30] scholar, critic, curator, architect, landscape architect, and paterfamilias to the young, he is too many things on too many levels to too many people to be summed up succinctly, but one thing is certain: no architect of his period mounted the podium as eagerly or as often to extol architecture as art. History will determine Philip Johnson's place in the architecture of the twentieth century, but through the strength and color of his personality and the acuity of his mind, combined with the ambition and adventurous wealth of his Texas patrons, a prominent place of influence in the nation's architectural story, via his work in the big state, is assured. At ninety-three he is still making a good run and enjoying himself doing it.

Gerald Hines, Philip Johnson, and Burdette Keeland Jr. at the Blueprint Ball, Gerald D. Hines College of Architecture, University of Houston, 1998. Photo by Bruce Bennett.

In October 1998, a fund-raising black-tie fete, the Blueprint Ball, was organized by Burdette Keeland at the University of Houston to honor Johnson and Gerald Hines, who flew in from London and brought his two grandsons.

The party, which raised $100,000, was held in the architecture building's atrium, which had a podium at one end decorated in an abstract fashion with stretched, angular swatches of blue and white fabric. Johnson despised it and wouldn't pose for photographers in front of it. It really upset him, and when someone suggested that the students hadn't thought through the design enough, he retorted, "They could damn well *try!*"

However, before a full house of high-spirited guests filling the floor and the pink-lit galleries above, it became an evening of sweetness and light, with Hines and Johnson praising each other extravagantly. Hines started off by recalling that, when he first approached him, Johnson said, "I have never worked with a *developer!*" And, using a favorite word, he recounted development of their first collaborative effort, Post Oak Central—"it took four different *iterations*"—followed by a retelling of the problems of finding a *parti* for what became Pennzoil Place.

"We had just fired a particular architect for not coming up with a design for the Pennzoil block that I felt met the demands of Houston's midseventies declining market. I said, 'Philip, we've *really* got to have a building that I can gracefully get a second "major" included with the Pennzoil company,' and he said, 'Gerry, why not *two* buildings?' I said that no one has put *two* buildings on the same block in Houston! And that's how Pennzoil came to be, which proves that, in the hands of great architects, tough problems create great buildings."[31]

After an introduction by Keeland ("Philip, will you come up and sing us a song?"), Johnson made his way up to the lectern and, warmed by a cheering, standing ovation, began:

> This is one of the great moments of my life, in my favorite room, with my favorite people, with Gerry actually *here:* it's too much! I just want to say tonight that everything that I have done and everything I have been I owe to Gerry Hines; I don't think he knows this. So my idea is to tell him this tonight and not brag about my own work, which is negligible, though *some* of it is rather good!
>
> But what that man has done for the art of architecture is remarkable! I wonder what you children—and you're all children now—know about developers. Gerry's right when he said that in 1970 I was uncertain about working with a developer. The ones I knew were speculators and money-grabbers, but Gerry was not that at all. He is one of the princes of our time, and I am speaking as an architect. He gives us our jobs, he pays our bills, he lets us do what we want . . . *sometimes.*
>
> When he gave me the RepublicBank job—it's called BankAmerica now

and will be called something else tomorrow—I thought the building should *harmonize* with its neighbor Pennzoil; it seemed perfectly logical to me, but it didn't seem logical to *G-e-r-r-y!* He said, "No Philip, there has to be a point of *difference!*" That stuck with me, every building I have built since has been different from the one before, and that's what you all should do. That's what we are all here for, that's why *I* am here.

But the kids are going to be here after we're not. Life is short but art is long, very, very long. I can't say that we architects have done a very good job of the opportunities that we have had, but that doesn't mean we should stop trying! Remember what Martin Luther said: "If I knew the world was going to end tomorrow, I would still plant my apple tree today." There's no such thing as old age . . . the *end* of things . . . just go out and plant your apple tree! Thank you very much.[32]

Photos on pages 276 and 279 are by Paul Hester, 1994.

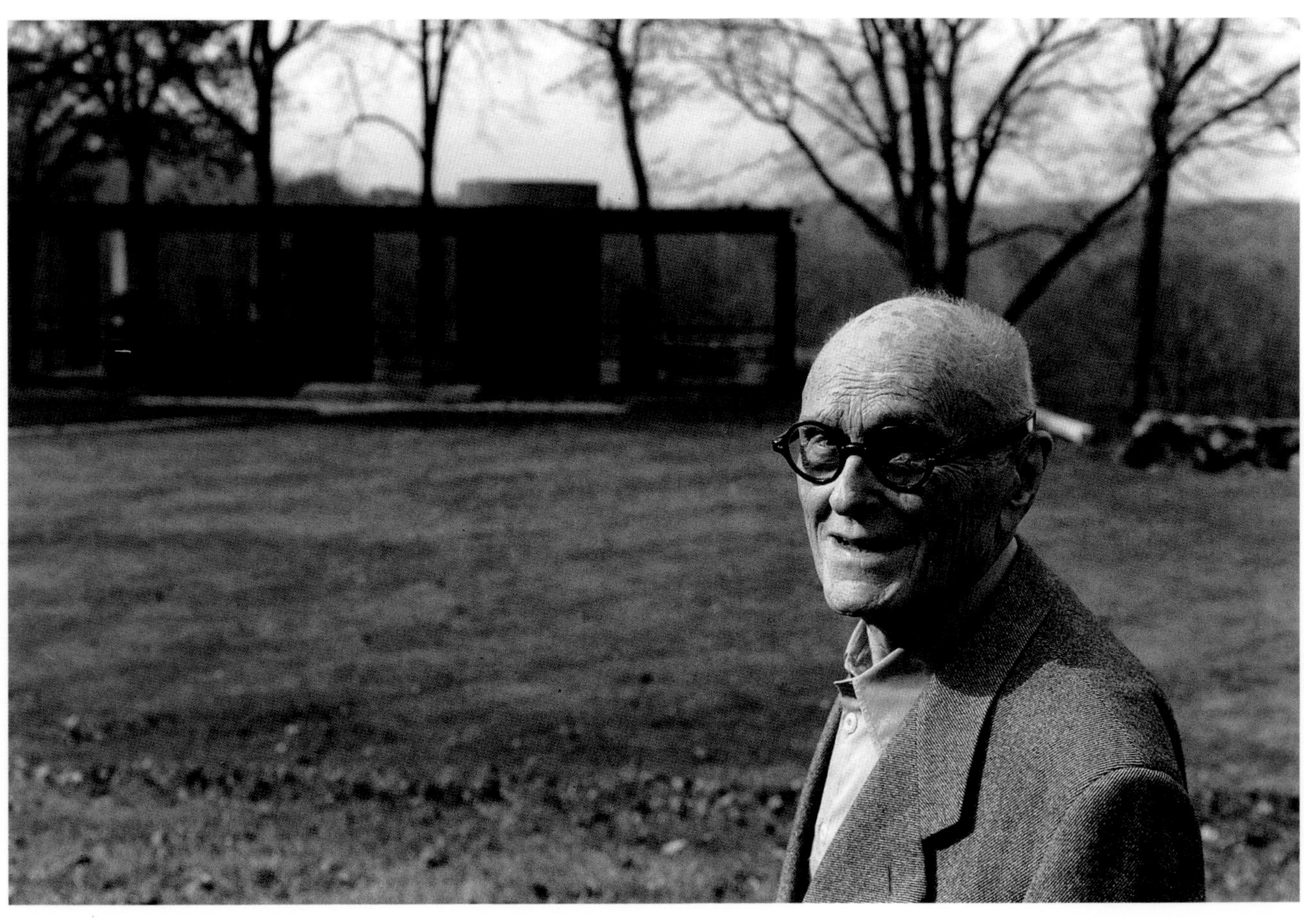

The tragedy of growing old is not being old but being young.

—Oscar Wilde

Notes

PREFACE

1. Duncan Boeckman, conversation, Dallas, September 1992.
2. Philip Johnson, conversation, New York City, October 1992.
3. Ibid.

PROLOGUE

1. Jeannette J. Dempsey, conversation, Cleveland, August 1993.
2. Philip Johnson, conversation, New York City, January 1993.
3. Ibid.
4. Dempsey, conversation.
5. Ibid.
6. Steven Watson, *Prepare for Saints* (New York: Random House, 1998), p. 83.
7. Franz Schulze, *Philip Johnson: Life and Work* (New York: Knopf, 1994), p. 52.
8. Johnson, conversation, January 1993.
9. Calvin Tomkins, "Forms under Light," *New Yorker,* May 23, 1977, p. 47.
10. Johnson, conversation, January 1993.
11. Joseph Giovannini, "Henry-Russell Hitchcock Dead at 83," *New York Times,* February 20, 1987.
12. Schulze, *Philip Johnson,* p. 30.
13. Ibid., p. 68.
14. Wright was miffed for years at Johnson by what he considered unrepresentation and Johnson's reference to him as the "greatest architect of the nineteenth century."
15. Nicholas Fox Weber, "Revolution on Beekman Place," *House and Garden,* August 1986, p. 57.
16. Frances X. Clines, "When Oratory Wasn't Mush," *New York Times,* October 16, 1996.
17. Johnson, conversation, January 1993.
18. Ibid.
19. Ibid.
20. Richard Ford, "The Master of Ambiguity," *New York Times,* October 17, 1996.
21. Johnson, conversation, January 1993.
22. Schulze, *Philip Johnson,* p. 149.
23. John Johansen, conversation, New York City, January 1992.
24. Anderson Todd, conversation, Houston, September 1995.
25. Tomkins, "Forms under Light," p. 51.
26. Johansen, conversation.
27. Johnson, conversation, January 1993.

28. Victoria Newhouse, *Wallace K. Harrison, Architect* (New York: Rizzoli, 1989), p. 29.
29. Johnson, conversation, January 1993.
30. *Sachlichkeit:* German, "objectivity" or "matter-of-factness."
31. Jean Ely, *New Canaan Historical Society Annual* 5 (5): 12.
32. Johnson, conversation, January 1993.
33. Ibid.
34. Landes Gores, FAIA, *N.C. Historical Society Annual* 10 (2): 4.
35. Eugene George, conversation, Austin, July 1998.
36. Johnson, conversation, January 1993.
37. Anthony Alosofin, *Frank Lloyd Wright: The Lost Years, 1910–1922* (Chicago: University of Chicago Press, 1993), p. 59.
38. "A Glass House in Connecticut," *House and Garden,* October 1949, pp. 168–173.
39. Nina Bremer, conversation, New Canaan, March 1993.
40. Nancy O'Boyle, conversation, Dallas, September 1995.
41. Bremer, conversation.
42. James Reece Pratt, letter to author, June 19, 1998.
43. Tomkins, "Forms under Light," p. 54.
44. Philip Johnson, conversation, January 1993.
45. Ibid.

CHAPTER 1

1. Marguerite Johnston Barnes, conversation, Houston, September 1993.
2. Ibid.
3. Dominique de Menil, conversation, Houston, March 1994.
4. Barnes, conversation.
5. Philip Johnson, conversation, New York City, May 1994.
6. Philip Johnson, conversation, New York City, November 1992.
7. Dominique de Menil, conversation, Houston, September 1993.
8. Barnes, conversation.
9. D. de Menil, conversation, September 1993.
10. Herbert Wells, conversation, Houston, January 1996.
11. Charles James's birth date was a few days after Johnson's, and according to Johnson, the two never met during James's New York years.
12. D. de Menil, conversation, September 1993.
13. See Elizabeth Ann Coleman, *The Genius of Charles James* (Brooklyn: Brooklyn Museum, 1982).
14. D. de Menil, conversation, September 1993.
15. Burdette Keeland Jr., conversation, Houston, October 1992.
16. See Howard Barnstone, *The Architecture of John Staub: Houston and the South* (Austin: University of Texas Press, 1979); Howard Barnstone, *The Galveston That Was* (New York: Macmillan, 1966), photographs by Henri Cartier-Bresson and Ezra Stoller.
17. Burdette Keeland Jr., conversation, Houston, January 1996.
18. Ibid.
19. D. de Menil, conversation, September 1993.
20. Johnson, conversation, November 1992.
21. Tape, Philip Johnson speaking at University of Houston School of Architecture, Fall 1952.
22. Anderson Todd, conversation, Houston, October 1994.

23. Karl Kilian, conversation, Houston, February 1996.
24. Jane B. Owen, conversation, New Harmony, Indiana, August 1994.
25. Ibid.
26. Ibid.
27. Ibid.
28. Ibid.
29. Johnson, conversation, May 1994.
30. Owen, conversation, August 1994.

CHAPTER 2

1. Jerry Flemmons, *Amon: The Texan Who Played Cowboy for America* (Lubbock: Texas Tech University Press, 1998), p. 188.
2. Josephine Hudson, conversation, Fort Worth, June 1997.
3. Cynthia Brants, conversation, Granbury, Texas, November 1994.
4. Jane Brown, conversation, San Francisco, February 1998.
5. Ruth Carter Stevenson, conversation, Fort Worth, February 1999.
6. Lisa Germany, *Harwell Hamilton Harris* (Austin: University of Texas Press, 1991), pp. 157–160.
7. Ruth Carter Stevenson, conversation, Fort Worth, May 1997.
8. Ibid.
9. Betty Blake, conversation, Dallas, August 1997.
10. Amon Carter Museum board members suggested by Philip Johnson: Richard Brown, Rene d'Harnoncourt, John de Menil, along with Johnson himself. C. R. Smith of American Airlines, Amon Carter Jr., Katrine Deakins, and Ruth Johnson were the others.
11. Frank Sherwood, conversation, Fort Worth, October 1997.
12. Gwen Weiner, conversation, Fort Worth, June 1997.
13. Stevenson, conversation, May 1997.
14. Ibid.
15. Ibid.
16. Ibid.
17. Henry-Russell Hitchcock, *Philip Johnson Architecture, 1949–1965* (New York: Holt Rinehart and Winston, 1966), p. 25.
18. Ibid.
19. Jay Presson Allen, conversation, New York City, February 1998.
20. *Philip Johnson Writings* (New York: Oxford University Press, 1979), pp. 76–77.
21. "Seagram's Bronze Tower," *Architectural Forum,* July 1958, p. 67.
22. John Manley, conversation, New York City, May 1997.
23. *Philip Johnson Writings,* pp. 227–231.
24. Stevenson, conversation, May 1997.
25. Tom Seymour, conversation, Fort Worth, July 1999.
26. Philip Johnson, conversation, New York City, January 1992.
27. Stevenson, conversation, May 1997.
28. Sharon Zane, *Monument for a City* (Fort Worth: Amon Carter Museum, 1997).
29. Ibid.
30. "Portico on a Plaza," *Architectural Forum,* March 1961, pp. 87–88.
31. Stevenson, conversation, May 1997.

32. Ronaldo Giurgola and Jaimini Mehta, *Louis I. Kahn* (Boulder, Colo.: Westview Press, 1975), p. 15.
33. Patricia Cummings Loud, *In Pursuit of Quality: The Kimbell Art Museum* (New York: Abrams, 1987), p. 9.
34. Ibid.
35. Stanley Marcus, conversation, Dallas, March 1998.
36. Don Kirk, conversation, Fort Worth, June 1997.
37. "A House for Two or Two Hundred," *House and Garden,* November 1970, pp. 14–23.
38. Architects in Modern Museum competition: Tadao Ando, Andrew Gluckman, Carlos Jimenez, Ricardo Legorreta, Arata Isozaki, David Schwarz.
39. David Dillon, "Classical Concoction," *Dallas Morning News,* May 8, 1998.

CHAPTER 3

1. Fort Worth buildings of the 1960s: Amon Carter Museum, Philip Johnson; First National Bank, Skidmore Owings & Merrill; Neiman-Marcus Ridglea Store, Edward Larrabee Barnes; the Sid W. Richardson Physical Sciences Building, Texas Christian University, Paul Rudolph; Tandy house, I. M. Pei; Kimbell Museum, Louis Kahn (commissioned in 1966).
2. Patty D. Beck, conversation, Dallas, April 1996.
3. Henry C. Beck, conversation, Dallas, May 1995.
4. P. Beck, conversation.
5. Lucille "Lupe" Murchison, conversation, Dallas, March 1999.
6. P. Beck, conversation.
7. H. Beck, conversation.
8. P. Beck, conversation.
9. Kalita Beck McCarthy, conversation, Dallas, April 1999.
10. Howard Rachofsky is a major Dallas collector and supporter of contemporary art; in 1997 he built a landmark Richard Meier house on Preston Road, which he opens regularly to the public.
11. Murchison, conversation.
12. Alan Peppard, "For NM, Credit's Not Just a Card," *Dallas Morning News,* July 4, 1997.
13. Stanley Marcus, conversation, Dallas, August 1996.
14. Philip Johnson, conversation, New York City, August 1997.
15. John Schoelkopf, conversation, Dallas, August 1997.
16. Johnson, conversation, August 1997.
17. Ibid.
18. Ibid.
19. David Dillon, "Making a Memorial: Seeking the Appropriate," *Dallas Morning News,* November 20, 1983.

CHAPTER 4

1. Jane Flato Smith, conversation, San Antonio, September 1997.
2. Philip Johnson, "We Shall Not Be Thanked by Posterity," *Fortune,* July 1966.
3. Cathleen Gallander, conversation, New York City, November 1997.
4. Blissie Blair, conversation, Corpus Christi, May 1999.
5. Edwin Singer, conversation, Corpus Christi, January 1998.
6. John Manley, conversation, New York City, May 1997.

7. Eugene Aubry, conversation, Orlando, August 1997.
8. Gallander, conversation.
9. Aubry, conversation.
10. The show was *Deconstructivist Architecture* at MoMA in 1988. Postmodernist Graves, a member of Johnson's coterie, was getting a lot of press at the time.
11. Aubry, conversation.
12. John Dykema Jr., "Corpus Christi's Ocean Drive," *Texas Architect,* September/October 1981, pp. 30–37.
13. Paul Goldberger, "Philip Johnson," *Architectural Forum,* January/February 1973, pp. 41–42.
14. Ellis Shamoon, conversation, Dallas, October 1997.
15. Gallander, conversation.
16. Terrell James, conversation, Houston, May 1997.
17. Singer, conversation.
18. Ibid.
19. Ibid.
20. Yolette Garcia, conversation, Dallas, February 1998.
21. Philip Johnson, "A There, There," *Architectural Forum,* November 1973, pp. 39–42.
22. Robert Cadwallader, conversation, San Antonio, August 1998.
23. Peter Papademetriou, "Big Splash in Fort Worth," *Progressive Architecture,* January 1975, pp. 22, 23.
24. Ibid.
25. Martin Price, conversation, Fort Worth, September 1997.
26. Nory Miller, *Johnson/Burgee: Architecture* (New York: Random House, 1979), p. 45.
27. Johnson, conversation, January 1992.

CHAPTER 5

1. Victor Neuhaus III, conversation, Hunt, Texas, October 1997.
2. Cynthia R. Taylor, conversation, Houston, October 1997.
3. Anderson Todd, conversation, Houston, January 1996.
4. Raymond Brochstein, conversation, Houston, December 1994.
5. Ibid.
6. Nory Miller, *Johnson/Burgee: Architecture* (New York: Random House, 1979), p. 65.
7. Gerald Hines, conversation, Houston, March 1993.
8. Miller, *Johnson/Burgee,* p. 55.
9. J. Hugh Liedtke, conversation, Houston, December 1997.
10. Grace Glueck, "Geometry, Man's and Nature's," *New York Times,* May 9, 1997.
11. Miller, *Johnson/Burgee,* p. 55.
12. Paul Goldberger, *The Skyscraper* (New York: Knopf, 1981), p. 124.
13. "Hines Changes Houston's Skyline—Profitably," *Business Week,* April 19, 1976, pp. 114, 115.
14. Ibid.
15. Ibid.
16. "Master Builder," *Forbes,* June 12, 1978, pp. 78, 83.
17. Paul Goldberger, "High Design at a Profit," *New York Times Magazine,* November 14, 1976.
18. Peter Stewart, conversation, Dallas, October 1997.

19. Ibid.
20. Reagan George, conversation, Dallas, September 1997.
21. "Philip Johnson's Gold Medal Acceptance Speech," Dallas, May 24, 1978, printout courtesy of the American Institute of Architects.
22. Hilary Lewis and John O'Connor, *Philip Johnson: The Architect in His Own Words* (New York: Rizzoli, 1994), p. 98.
23. Eli Attia, conversation, Tel Aviv, March 1998.
24. "Dossier, Philip Cortelyou Johnson," *Esquire,* December 1983, p. 282.
25. Ibid.
26. Tom Buckley, "Philip Johnson: The Man in the Glass House," *Esquire,* December 1983, p. 272.
27. Philip Johnson, conversation, New York City, January 1992. (The book by Hitchcock is *Netherlandish Scrolled Gables of the Sixteenth and Early Seventeenth Centuries* [New York: New York University Press, 1978].)
28. Ann Holmes, conversation, Houston, March 1999.
29. Burdette Keeland Jr., conversation, Houston, November 1997.
30. Ibid.
31. Ibid.
32. Martha Seng, conversation, Houston, October 1998.
33. Stephen Fox, *Houston Architectural Guide, AIA* (Houston: American Institute of Architects, Houston Chapter, 1990), p. 159.
34. William Stern, conversation, Houston, November 1998.
35. The original Century Club group included David Childs, Peter Eisenman, Michael Graves, Charles Gwathmey, Richard Meier, Jacquelin Robertson, and Robert A. M. Stern, plus visitors.
36. Danny Samuels, conversation, Houston, October 1997.
37. Ibid.
38. Phillip Shepherd, conversation, Dallas, November 1997.
39. John Manley, conversation, New York City, November 1997.
40. Steven Sands, conversation, Dallas, November 1997.
41. Peter Brink, conversation, Galveston, February 1998.
42. Paul Goldberger, "Philip Johnson, at 80, Is Dean and Gadfly of the Profession," *New York Times,* June 29, 1986.
43. Gene Bishop, conversation, Dallas, April 1999.
44. Keeland, conversation, November 1997.
45. Lars Lerup, conversation, Houston, December 1997.
46. Peter Eisenman, conversation, New York City, June 1998.
47. Frank Gehry, conversation, Dallas, May 1999.
48. Johnson, conversation, January 1993.

CHAPTER 6

1. Brendan Gill, "Philip the Bold," *New Yorker,* November 14, 1994, p. 141.
2. Philip Johnson, conversation, New York City, January 1995.
3. John Manley, conversation, New York City, February 1998.
4. Gerald Moorhead, "Scenes from a Mall: Philip Johnson's University of St. Thomas Chapel," *CITE,* Rice Design Alliance, Fall 1991, pp. 8–9.

5. Manley, conversation.
6. "The Architect," *Accent* series, James Fleming, host, CBS Television, May 11, 1961.
7. Courtesy of Christopher Mason, New York City, July 8, 1996.
8. Herodotus: fifth-century Greek historian, known as "the Father of History."
9. Philip Johnson, remarks, MoMA, New York City, July 8, 1996.
10. Four Seasons dinner party, July 9, 1996: Philip Johnson, Peter Eisenman, David Childs, Henry Cobb, Frank Gehry, Michael Graves, Charles Gwathmey, Zaha Hadid, Hans Hollein, Arata Isozaki, Rem Koolhaas, Phyllis Bronfman Lambert, Richard Meier, Terence Riley, Jacquelin T. Robertson, Kevin Roche, Robert A. M. Stern, and Stanley Tigerman.
11. Johnson, conversation, January 1995.
12. Michael Piazza, conversation, Dallas, February 1998.
13. Ibid.
14. David Dillon, "Gay Church's Cathedral Begins to Take Shape," *Dallas Morning News,* July 26, 1998.
15. Philip Johnson, conversation, December 1997.
16. Ibid.
17. Jeffrey Kipnis, conversation, Columbus, Ohio, April 1999.
18. Frank Welch, "A Passion for Art and Rights," *Texas Architect,* March–April 1998, pp. 11, 12.
19. "Philip Johnson and Other Friends Take Their Leave of a Singular Patroness," *New Yorker,* January 26, 1998, p. 29.
20. William Stern, remarks, Houston, February 1999.
21. Robert A. M. Stern, conversation, New York City, April 1999.
22. MoMA's architect list for expansion competition: Jacques Herzog & Pierre de Meuron (Switzerland), Steven Holl (U.S.A.), Toyo Ito (Japan), Rem Koolhaas & Wiel Arets (Holland), Dominique Perrault (France), Yoshio Taniguchi (Japan), Bernard Tschumi (U.S.A.), Rafael Vinoly (Argentina), and Tod Williams & Billy Tsien (U.S.A.). Short list: Herzog & Meuron, Taniguchi, Tschumi.
23. Walter Robinson, "MoMA's New Architect," *Artnet Magazine,* December 8, 1997.
24. Philip Johnson, conversation, November 1997.
25. *New York Times,* June 12, 1998.
26. Projects for Hines outside of Texas: 101 California, San Francisco, California, 1.2 million sq. ft., 48 stories, 1983; Associate Architects: Kendall/Heaton Associates. One Norwest Center, Denver, Colorado, 1.3 million sq. ft., 52 stories, 1983; Associate Architect: Morris*Aubry. 580 California, San Francisco, California, 340,000 sq. ft., 23 stories, 1984; Associate Architect: Kendall/Heaton Associates. Fifty-third at Third (Lipstick Building), New York City, New York, 587,000 sq. ft., 35 stories, 1986. Five Hundred Boylston, Boston, Massachusetts, 650,000 sq. ft., 25 stories, 1988; Associate Architect: Kendall/Heaton Associates. Franklin Square, Washington, D.C., 505,000 sq. ft., 12 stories, 1989; Associate Architect: Richard Fitzgerald & Partners. One Ninety One Peachtree Tower, Atlanta, Georgia, 1.2 million sq. ft., 50 stories, 1991; Associate Architect: Kendall/Heaton Associates. Comerica Tower at Detroit Center, Detroit, Michigan, 1 million sq. ft., 50 stories, 1991; Associate Architect: Kendall/Heaton Associates. AEGON Center, Louisville, Kentucky, 600,000 sq. ft., 35 stories, 1993; Associate Architect: Richard Fitzgerald & Partners.
27. M. Kimmelman, "Sought or Imposed, Limits Can Take Flight," *New York Times,* February 5, 1997.

28. "Philip Johnson Gifts," *MoMA,* February 1999.
29. Ann Holmes, "The Man in the Glass House," *Houston Chronicle Magazine,* October 6, 1991, p. 18.
30. Italian: "lover of the arts."
31. Gerald D. Hines, remarks at Blueprint Ball, University of Houston, October 17, 1998.
32. Philip Johnson, remarks at Blueprint Ball, University of Houston, October 17, 1998.

Index